T0306177

Renewable Energy and the Public

Renewable Energy and the Public
From NIMBY to Participation

Edited by Patrick Devine-Wright

from Routledge

First published by Earthscan in the UK and USA in 2011

For a full list of publications please contact:

2 Park Square, Milton Park, Abingdon, Oxfordshire OX14 4RN
711 Third Avenue, New York, NY 10017

First issued in paperback 2015

Earthscan is an imprint of the Taylor and Francis Group, an informa business

Copyright © Patrick Devine-Wright, 2011. Published by Taylor & Francis.

ISBN 13: 978-1-138-98513-1 (pbk)
ISBN 13: 978-1-84407-863-9 (hbk)

Typeset by MapSet Ltd, Gateshead, UK
Cover design by Yvonne Booth

A catalogue record for this book is available from the British Library

Library of Congress Cataloging-in-Publication Data

  Renewable energy and the public : from NIMBY to participation / edited by
  Patrick Devine-Wright.
       p. cm.
   Includes bibliographical references and index.
   ISBN 978-1-84407-863-9 (hbk.)
   1. Renewable energy resources—Social aspects. 2. Energy development—Citizen participation.
   3. Energy policy—Citizen participation. I. Devine-Wright, Patrick.
  TJ808.R4173 2010
  333.79'4—dc22

                                                                    2009052235

Contents

Section I
Conceptual approaches

Section II
Empirical studies of public engagement

Part 1: Stakeholder and media representations of public engagement

Part 2: Case studies of public beliefs and responses:

Figures, Tables and Boxes

Figures

Tables

Boxes

Contributors

Dana Abi-Ghanem is a Research Associate at the Tyndall Centre, University of Manchester, and holds a PhD from Newcastle University. Employing theories from science and technology studies, Dana researches the co-evolution of technology and society, especially the diffusion of renewable energy technologies and processes that shape their meaning and use.

Peta Ashworth is the Group Leader of CSIRO's Science into Society Group. The group investigates stakeholder attitudes to a range of complex issues that are of strategic importance to Australia. Peta has gained an international reputation as a leading researcher in understanding public perception to climate change and low emission technologies.

John Barry is Associate Director of the Institute for a Sustainable World and Reader in Politics at Queen's University Belfast. His areas of interest include green political theory, the political economy of sustainability and the political and policy dimensions of the transition to a renewable, low carbon economy.

Paul Bellaby is Professor of Sociology, University of Salford, and was at East Anglia (1989–2000) and Keele (1968–1989). He took his first degree and PhD from Cambridge. He has researched encounters with risk in both workplace and transport; risk communication in public health; and public engagement with new energy technology.

Catherine Butler is a postdoctoral researcher at Cardiff University. Her background is in sociology and her research interests include socio-environmental risk, governance, social and cultural aspects of climate change, and flood policy.

Sally Caird is a Research Fellow in the Sustainable Technologies Group, and has worked at the Open University in several research and teaching posts since 1991. She has published papers on user-centred ecodesign, innovation and entrepreneurship, and low carbon technology in the micro-power, environment and pollution control, and transport industries.

Noel Cass is a researcher based in the Lancaster Environment Centre, Lancaster University, focusing on the social aspects of environmental issues, in particular those related to low-impact living, energy systems and renewable energy technologies. Other research interests involve power and inequalities, participation and deliberation in decision-making, and mobilities.

Matthew Cotton is Associate Research Fellow in Exeter University's School of Geography. His PhD work encompassed environmental ethics and deliberative engagement with radioactive waste management policy. His recent and forthcoming publications on public engagement appear in the journals *Public Understanding of Science, EnvironmentalValues* and the *Journal of Risk Research*.

Hannah Devine-Wright holds an MSc in Environmental Psychology and a PhD in Social Psychology, both from the University of Surrey. She was a co-investigator in the Beyond Nimbyism research project, specializes in the use of visual methods to research energy issues and is a director of Placewise Ltd.

Patrick Devine-Wright is a Professor at the School of Geography, University of Exeter, and is an experienced leader of multidisciplinary research projects. He is interested in concepts of place attachment and place identity, and their relevance for environmental issues such as climate change and the social acceptance of energy technologies.

Geraint Ellis is Senior Lecturer and Director of Undergraduate Planning Studies in the School of Planning, Architecture and Civil Engineering at Queen's University, Belfast. His teaching and research interests include the relationships between sustainable development, energy, governance and equality in the spatial planning process.

Jeremy Firestone is Associate Professor, University of Delaware, USA, and Research Scientist at the Center for Carbon-free Power Integration. He has spoken widely and published in leading journals on wind power social acceptance.

Rob Flynn is Professor of Sociology at the University of Salford. He has published widely in urban sociology, health services research and medical sociology. Current interests are in public perceptions of risk, and public engagement in, hydrogen energy. He was co-editor of *Risk and the Public Acceptance of New Technologies* (2007).

Paul Graham manages CSIRO's Energy Futures research programme. In this role, Paul is responsible for developing innovative approaches to modelling the Australian energy sector, forming partnerships with external organizations and overall research programme design. He is an economist with expertise in energy market analysis, forecasting and economic modelling.

Claire Haggett is Lecturer in Human Geography in the Centre for the Study of Environmental Change and Sustainability (CECS) at the University of Edinburgh, and Programme Director of the MSc in Environmental Sustainability. Her work explores the social construction of environmental issues and policy, with a particular focus on renewable energy implementation.

Mike Hodson is Research Fellow at the SURF Centre, University of Salford. His research interests focus on city–regional transitions to low carbon economies, the ways in which this may or may not happen, and understandings of the lessons to be learned from such processes.

Rafaella Lenoir Improta is a psychologist who graduated from the University Federal of Santa Catarina, Brazil, where she began her research on issues related to environmental and human sciences. In 2008 she obtained a Master's in Psychology from the Federal University of Rio Grande do Norte, Brazil, where she studied the socio-environmental impact of wind farm implementation on the nearby community.

Anna Littleboy is the Deputy Director of CSIRO's Minerals Down Under Flagship and has championed research into the impacts of sustainable development on the resources industry. Anna has 20 years' research and management experience in the fields of environmental impact assessment and sustainability for minerals, water and energy resources.

Simon Marvin is Professor and Co-Director of SURF. He is an expert on the changing relations between neighbourhoods, cities, regions and infrastructure networks in a period of resource constraint, institutional restructuring and climate change.

Carly McLachlan is a lecturer in Climate Change, Sustainability and Project Management at the Tyndall Centre for Climate Change Research at the University of Manchester. Her research focuses on how people and organizations engage with energy. Particular areas of interest include the contestation of knowledge claims, interpretations of consultation activities, and symbolic meanings of energy and technology.

Simon Niemeyer is a research fellow with the Centre for Global Deliberative Governance, Research School of Social Sciences, The Australian National University. He has conducted and analysed a large number of public engagement processes concerning environmental and social issues.

Karen Parkhill is a researcher in the School of Psychology at Cardiff University. She has a human geography PhD from the School of City and Regional Planning at Cardiff University. Her research interests include: risk perceptions, constructions of place, people's perceptions of low carbon energies, and how energy is consumed.

Martin J. Pasqualetti is Professor in the School of Geographical Sciences and Urban Planning at Arizona State University. He was twice appointed by the Arizona Governor as Chair of the Arizona Solar Energy Advisory Council and is a member of the Board of Directors of the Arizona Solar Center.

Nick Pidgeon is Professor of Psychology at Cardiff University. His research looks at risk perception, risk communication and public engagement around environmental controversies such as nuclear power, climate change, GM agriculture and nanotechnologies. Co-editor (with Roger Kasperson and Paul Slovic) of *The Social Amplification of Risk* (2003).

José Q. Pinheiro is a psychologist with a Master's in Social Psychology from the University of São Paulo, Brazil, and a PhD in Environmental Psychology from the University of Arizona. He is Professor at UFRN, Natal, Brazil and Coordinator of the People–Environment Research Group (CNPq). Interests include time perspectives and sustainability, pro-ecological commitment, spatial behaviour, global-scale cognition and environmental evaluation.

Miriam Ricci is a Research Fellow at the Centre for Transport and Society, University of the West of England. Her research interests include social studies of science, technology and innovation, specifically around energy and climate change, and in the theory and practice of public engagement with energy and sustainability issues.

Robin Roy is Professor of Design and Environment at the Open University. He has contributed to many OU distance teaching courses on design, technology and the environment. In 1979 he founded the Design Innovation Group to conduct research on product development, innovation and sustainable design, and has many publications on design, innovation and environment.

Cynthia Schwartz is a doctoral student in the interdisciplinary Human and Social Dimensions of Science and Technology programme housed in the Consortium for Science, Policy and Outcomes (CSPO) at Arizona State University. She examines the capacity of public policy to link solar energy technologies to beneficial social outcomes.

Petra Schweizer-Ries is a social and behavioural scientist with 20 years' experience in renewable energies. After founding an interdisciplinary work group at the Fraunhofer Institute, she became a Junior Professor for Environmental Psychology at the University of Magdeburg and represents the Sustainable Development chair at the Universität des Saarlandes.

Fionnguala Sherry-Brennan received her PhD in social psychology from the University of Manchester and is currently research associate at the School of Geography at the University of Exeter. Her research interests include applying the theory of social representations to public understanding of hydrogen technologies and expert understanding of 'smart grids'.

Paul Upham is a Research Fellow at the Tyndall Centre, Manchester and the Manchester Institute for Innovation Research. He works on public and stakeholder perceptions of low carbon energy technologies from a variety of social science perspectives. Socio-technical systems that Paul has worked on include air transport, bioenergy and biofuels, hydrogen as a transport fuel, carbon capture and storage, and also carbon labelling.

Gordon Walker is Professor at the Lancaster Environment Centre, Lancaster University. He has a distinctive profile of research on the social and spatial dimensions of environment and sustainability issues, including work on environmental justice, socio-technical transitions, renewable energy and forms of 'natural' and technological risk.

Maarten Wolsink has an MA in methodology and political science and a PhD in social psychology. Associate Professor in Environmental Geography at the University of Amsterdam, he is a leading author on the topic of social acceptance of renewable energy innovations, and other environmental concerns.

Acronyms

ACC	Arizona Corporation Commission
ADEQ	Arizona Department of Environmental Quality
ADOC	Arizona Department of Commerce
APS	Arizona Public Service
ASERS	Arizona Solar Electric Roadmap Study
BBC	British Broadcasting Corporation
BERR	Department for Business, Enterprise and Regulatory Reform
BS	biomass stove
BWEA	British Wind Energy Association
CCAG	Climate Change Advisory Group
CCAP	Climate Change Action Plan
CCHP	combined cooling heat and power
CCS	carbon capture and storage
CEDC	Commerce and Economic Development Commission
CEPEL	Centro de Pesquisa em Energia Elétrica
CERT	Carbon Emissions Reduction Target
CHP	combined heat and power
CMRP	Clyde Muirshiel Regional Park
CSIRO	Commonwealth Scientific and Industrial Research Organization
CSP	concentrating solar power
DCC	Devon County Council
DECC	Department of Energy and Climate Change
DEFRA	Department for Environment, Food and Rural Affairs
DFT	Domestic Field Trial
DIS/BCN	Social Impact Detection/Barcelona
DNO	distribution network operator
DRET	Department of Resources, Energy and Tourism
DSM	demand-side management
EFF	Energy Futures Forum
EIA	Environmental Impact Assessment
EMEC	European Marine Energy Centre
EOW	European Offhore Wind
EPSRC	Engineering and Physical Sciences Research Council
ES	Environmental Statement

ESCO	energy services company
EST	Energy Saving Trust
ETF	Energy Transformed Flagship
GDP	gross domestic product
GHG	greenhouse gas
GLA	Greater London Authority
GM	genetically modified
GSHP	ground source heat pump
HEP	hydroelectric project
IAPS	International Association of People–Environment Surroundings
IEA	International Energy Agency
IPC	Infrastructure Planning Commission
IPCC	Intergovernmental Panel on Climate Change
IPPR	Institute of Public Policy Research
LCBP	Low Carbon Buildings Programme
LCCA	London Climate Change Agency
LDA	London Development Agency
NaREC	New and Renewable Energy Centre
NERC	Natural Environment Research Council
NFFO	Non-Fossil Fuel Obligation
NGC	National Grid Company
NGO	non-governmental organization
NIMBY	'Not in my back yard'
NPS	National Policy Statement
NRW	North Rhine–Westphalia
OFGEM	Office of the Gas and Electricity Markets
OU	Open University
PCED	people-centred ecodesign
PERF	Parque Eólico de Rio do Fogo
PIDD	Paloma Irrigation and Drainage District
PPA	power purchase agreement
PPS22	Planning Policy Statement 22
PSE	public and stakeholder engagement
PURE	Promoting Unst's Renewable Energy
PUS	public understanding of science
PV	photovoltaic
PV	public value
RDA	Regional Development Agency
RES	Renewable Energy Standard
RES	Renewable Energy Strategy
RET	renewable energy technology
RFP	
RN	Rio Grande do Norte
ROC	Renewables Obligation Certificate
SINS	Shetland in Statistics

SPA	special protection area
SRT	social representations theory
SSSI	site of special scientific interest
STHW	solar thermal hot water
STS	science and technology studies
SWRDA	South West Regional Development Agency
TNO	transmission network operator
UK	United Kingdom
UKSHEC	UK Sustainable Hydrogen Energy Consortium
UPE	upstream public engagement
US	United States (of America)
WFB	wood-fuelled boiler
WGA	Western Governors Association
WINBEG	Winkleigh biomass gasifier
YIMBY	'Yes in my back yard'

Public Engagement with Renewable Energy: Introduction

Patrick Devine-Wright

Changes to the earth's climate are the foundation for this book. According to an international panel of the world's leading climate scientists, the concentration of carbon dioxide (CO_2) and other greenhouse gases in the atmosphere has reached 435 parts per million (ppm) of carbon dioxide equivalent (CO_2e) (IPCC, 2007). This compares with about 280ppm before industrialization in the 19th century. The IPCC has predicted that, as a result of continuing increases in greenhouse gas emissions, the average global temperature will rise by 5° or more over the next 100 years in comparison with pre-industrial times. It has been more than 30 million years since temperature was that high (Stern, 2009), raising the spectre of a more hostile physical environment than the human species, which has been around for no more than 200,000 years, has experienced before.

In many countries, the energy required for transport, heat and power is derived predominantly from fossil fuels (e.g. natural gas, coal and oil). In response to the threat of climate change, governments around the world are making commitments to reduce their reliance upon these sources of energy and to increase the use of low carbon energy sources, specifically nuclear and renewable energy. Moves to reduce the use of fossil fuels are also motivated by concerns over energy security and, in particular, reliance upon what may in future be increasingly scarce and expensive supplies of natural gas and oil.

Renewable energy is an umbrella term describing a wide variety of energy sources that are non-depleting with use, including solar, wind, tidal, wave or bioenergy. Globally, the use of these sources of energy is rapidly increasing (see Figures I.1 and I.2). During 2008, at least 73 countries set policy targets for renewable energy, up from 66 in 2007, and many countries have opted for a path of low carbon growth in response to the international financial crisis, notably the US, where US$150 billion has been pledged over the next ten years (REN21, 2009). China, India and other developing countries are increasingly playing major

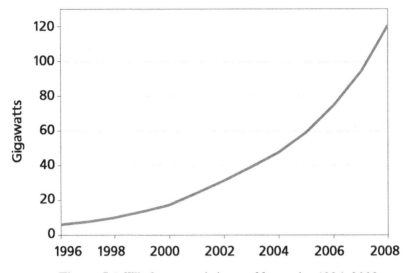

Figure I.1 *Wind power, existing world capacity, 1996–2008*

Source: REN21, 2009

roles in both the manufacture and installation of renewable energy: for example, China's total wind power capacity doubled in 2008 for the fourth year running.

However, the transition to low carbon energy systems has not proved straightforward. The growth in the use of renewable energy over the past 20 years has been extremely variable across different social, political and economic contexts, from a

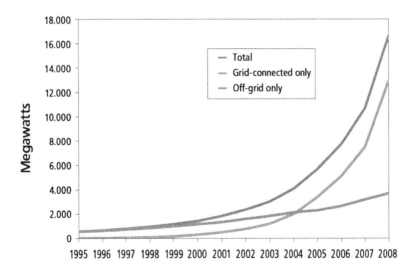

Source: REN21, Renewables Global Status Report: 2009 Update

Figure I.2 *Solar PV, existing world capacity, 1995–2008*

Source: REN21, 2009

rapid implementation in countries such as Germany and Denmark, to a more stagnant level of growth in the UK. Commentary in the media and advocacy by interest groups has often pitted different sources of low carbon energy against each other as mutually exclusive alternatives (e.g. nuclear vs. renewables; large scale vs. microgeneration). Social movements have arisen to challenge proposals to develop increasing numbers of onshore wind farms in rural areas (e.g. the Country Guardian organization in the UK), while concepts such as 'NIMBYism' ('Not in my back yard') have had a strong influence in shaping how industry, policy-makers and media commentators think about and respond to the sometimes sceptical responses of local residents to proposals for renewable energy in their locality.

The NIMBY concept is often used to address what at first seems to be a confusing 'social gap' (Bell et al, 2005) between high levels of public support for renewable energy and frequent local hostility towards specific project proposals. As Haggett documents in Chapter 2 of this volume, local hostility to renewable energy is a global issue, having been documented in the US, Australia and Asia, as well as in many European countries. But many social scientists have argued that the NIMBY concept is a misleading, inaccurate and pejorative way of under-standing local objections (Burningham et al, 2006; Wolsink, 2006; Devine-Wright, 2009). Instead, academics have revealed the complexity of public responses, and stressed the importance of public participation, arguing that a lack of meaningful and timely opportunity to have a say in decision-making can contribute to public scepticism, mistrust and opposition (Bell et al, 2005).

When done well, increased public input into diverse forms of environmental assessment and decision-making can improve both the quality and the legitimacy of such activities, enhancing trust and understanding (National Research Council, 2008). Such a call for increased citizen involvement is based upon criti-cism of the view that lay people are inadequately informed or irrational about science and therefore need to be 'educated' by experts (see Flynn et al, Chapter 17, this volume). The use of analytic-deliberative methods of public engagement, including mechanisms such as citizens' panels, at an early or 'upstream' stage of policy or technology development, can enable the integration of public values into policy formation and decision-making, leading to enhanced legitimacy and trust (Renn, 2008). This implies the abandonment of technocratic planning perspec-tives, since 'decide–announce–defend' approaches have been denounced as contributing to social conflict, and leading to delays or even cancelled project proposals (Wolsink, 2010).

Given the ambitious targets that many governments have now adopted for increasing the deployment of renewable energy, systematic and robust social science research into public engagement with renewable energy is urgently required. Research and development into renewable energy has been rather dominated by technological and economic approaches to date, to the detriment of social science input. This book, which brings together the latest international research findings in a single volume, reveals the capacity that social scientists have to inform industry practices and policy-making, and to serve as a more useful and reliable evidence base than commonsense beliefs such as NIMBYism. But the book can do more than this. It can demonstrate a broader scope to social science research beyond the issue of social acceptance. As Walker and Cass make clear in Chapter 4, there are multiple roles that publics can play when engaging with renewable energy technologies – NIMBY-type objection to large-scale energy projects is merely one of these. The book's contributors reveal a vibrant and burgeoning literature characterized by a diversity of conceptual and empirical approaches, encompassing a range of energy technologies at different scales of deployment and levels of maturity, and a range of contexts of engagement, from upstream deliberation on national energy futures to local responses to siting proposals. This range of social science input suggests a more expansive and varied future research agenda on public engagement, with the consequent ability to think more creatively about policy and practice implications.

The Structure of This Book

The book is divided into two sections. The first section comprises five chapters addressing theoretical aspects of public engagement with renewable energy.

Conceptual approaches to public engagement with renewable energy

Chapter 1 by Walker and colleagues proposes a comprehensive conceptual frame-work for understanding public engagement, which arose from a multidisciplinary research project conducted in the UK between 2005 and 2009. At the heart of the framework is the notion of symmetry – that public engagement encompasses not only public reactions to technology proposals, but also the actions of those actors who are involved in promoting technology development and engaging with publics in various ways. The framework also seeks to capture the *expectations* involved in shaping how people and organizations seek to engage or not engage with others, the *dynamic* nature of such expectations and responses over time, and the *contextuality* of engagement, shaped by both broad policy and economic landscapes and the characteristics of local places and communities.

Haggett, in Chapter 2, addresses the rationale and methods used for engaging the public in decision-making about the development of renewable energy, placing this discussion within the specific context of recent UK legislation on spatial planning and the transition to a low carbon economy. She advocates that developers build long-term relationships in communities, seem concerned and involved in them, and accountable for the strategies developed that will effect them, while remaining sceptical that recent UK policies, which suggest early, abstract agenda setting and limited consultation later, will provide a suitable context for addressing local scepticism and objection.

In Chapter 3, Barry and Ellis also build on recent changes to UK planning legislation to explore alternative ways of thinking about conflict around renewable energy. They argue that in order to make sense of the struggles over project proposals, we must step back and understand both protagonist and antagonist viewpoints, and by doing so may be able to use the conflictual engagement of such disputes to the broader advantage of delivering low carbon societies. Arising from this perspective upon conflict, they suggest that the hegemonic idea that planning practice should seek 'consensus' is not only counterproductive but also damaging to democratic ideals.

Walker and Cass adopt a socio-technical approach in Chapter 4 in seeking to broaden perspectives on how the public and renewable energy are related beyond the dominant focus on questions of acceptability, local responses to development projects, and how engagement operates between developers and local communities. They argue that there are many other important points of encounter and connection and many other roles into which publics can be cast, yet these have typically been overlooked to date. They identify ten discrete roles and argue that these roles and their interrelation is a necessary first step towards pursuing a more expansive and varied future research agenda and thinking more creatively about policy and practice implications.

In Chapter 5, Patrick Devine-Wright critically reflects on the ways that the locations of renewable energy projects are commonly thought of. Two predominant ways of thinking about locations by policy-makers, industry and academics are identified – as 'sites' for development and as 'backyards' defended by NIMBYs. Each of these is argued to provide an inadequate means of conceptualizing objective and subjective aspects of project locations. Instead, the perspective of emplacement is proposed, drawing on social science literature on the concept of place, and particularly notions of place attachment and place identity. The practical implications of the emplacement perspective for public engagement activities are discussed.

Empirical Research on Public Engagement with Renewable Energy

Section II of the book comprises empirical research on public engagement, and is subdivided into two parts. Part 1 takes a look at stakeholder and media representations of public engagement with renewable energy.

Stakeholder and media representations of public engagement

In Chapter 6, Wolsink uses Q-methodology to investigate stakeholder representations of public engagement with wind energy development in three European countries: Germany, The Netherlands and the UK. The analysis revealed four discourses with varying presumptions of community involvement, unconditional or conditional support for development, and concerns about landscape impacts. He concluded that discourses were most polarized in the UK, while representations in Germany reflect a position of conditional support that has arisen from learning, stemming from successful implementations.

Hodson and Marvin look at transformation in urban energy systems, using London as a case study, in Chapter 7. With a predominant interest in governance, they investigate the emergent roles of new intermediary organizations in system transformation. Specifically, the authors investigate the ways in which public engagement is conceived and practised by the London Climate Change Agency as part of its Green Homes programme to reduce carbon emissions. Using documentary analysis and in-depth interviews, they identify five types of public engagement in the Green Homes programme, and conclude that the programme views publics primarily as consumers characterized by deficits of knowledge rather than active citizens willing to participate in envisioning alternative visions of urban energy systems. They conclude by calling for intermediaries to engage with a wider variety of publics in the constitution of similar initiatives.

In Chapter 8, Hannah Devine-Wright investigates how public engagement with renewable energy technologies has been depicted in the media, specifically in visual images printed in UK newspapers in the years 2006 and 2007. Informed by social representations theory, this study indicates how wind turbines are used symbolically to refer to renewable energy generally; how images have increased in number over time and have evolved to contain members of the public alongside these technologies, replacing technical experts or politicians. She concludes that despite this increased prevalence of publics in media images, the narrow focus upon passive, individual supporters fails to capture the variety of roles that individuals can take in relation to the siting of renewable energy technologies.

Cotton and Patrick Devine-Wright in Chapter 9 investigate how transmission network operators in the UK conceive and practise public engagement in the context of siting new overhead power lines, for example, when connecting new wind farms to the national grid. Using interview and document review methods, they observe that, while rhetoric of thorough, transparent community engagement was evident, in practice this was narrowly limited to seeking feedback on pre-selected routing options, thus providing little effective decision-making power to communities. This narrow form of engagement was interpreted as being founded upon NIMBY presumptions of limited technical expertise and an inability to adopt strategic perspectives. The authors conclude that the approach taken in the UK may well prove counterproductive, reinforcing public opposition rather than ameliorating it.

Public beliefs and responses to diverse renewable energy projects or initiatives

The second part of Section II focuses upon public beliefs and responses to renewable energy projects or initiatives, via specific case studies.

In Chapter 10, Ashworth and colleagues evaluate the use of citizens' panels as part of a wider stakeholder engagement programme that aimed to devise scenarios for alternative energy futures for Australia, a country facing severe threats from climate change, as well as abundant fossil fuel reserves. The panels indicated broad overall concern with climate change, yet markedly different attitudes regarding technology futures. Analyses indicated that five broad groupings could be identified, differing primarily in their attitudes to risks associated with large-scale technologies, their concern for the future shape of society, and their willingness to accept risks as a trade-off for energy security. For many individuals, their initial views were susceptible to change when presented with new information and exposed to group discussion.

Chapter 11 is the first of four chapters on public engagement with microgeneration technologies. Abi-Ghanem and Haggett investigate residents' engagement with solar photovoltaics in homes; comparing social and private housing schemes within the UK Government's domestic field trial, drawing on literature from science and technology studies. Technology users are represented as four types: conscious, opportunistic, interested and non-users. The authors then discuss how the designers' and trial managers' perceptions of the users were built into the PV systems' design and directly influenced how people were able to engage with the technology. The success of the particular policy initiatives behind the trials is reflected upon, and the implications for the wider use of microgeneration technology discussed.

In contrast, Pasqualetti and Schwartz in Chapter 12 investigate public engagement with a 280MW solar power station in the US. They note how historically developers have tended to overlook social barriers to wind energy development, being predominantly concerned with technical aspects. They wonder whether this pattern is likely to continue in relation to solar energy, with an absence of early engagement and complete information provision leading to numerous instances in the project's development where there has been a failure to assess public values towards the project. They conclude that early and complete involvement should become an element of the planning and construction of every solar project.

In Chapter 13, Schweizer-Ries advocates inter- and transdisciplinary research, rather than the conventional technical approach, on the concept of energy sustainable communities. Through analysis of three contrasting case studies in Latin America, Europe and Africa, she characterizes alternative socio-technical approaches to solar energy development: a technically driven integration lacking participation of the communities; a socially driven one featuring technical deficiencies; and a participative integration that functioned properly and helped to further develop the community. She concludes that successful implementation of renewable energy must be based upon collaboration between social scientists, technical specialists and full participation by communities as equal partners.

'Yes in my back yard', the title of Chapter 14, is an analysis by Caird and Roy of consumer perceptions and experiences of several microgeneration technologies for generating heat or electricity at the household level. Drawing on interview and survey data, they conclude that current demand for microgeneration is largely confined to a niche market of environmentally concerned, older, middle-class householders, often those living in larger rural properties off the mains gas network. Their research reveals that, despite considerable public consideration in adopting microgeneration, the UK market is still at an early phase of the diffusion curve, mainly attracting 'pioneers' who are driven by conviction to reduce carbon emissions coupled with the hope of saving money and enjoying the pleasure of using low or zero carbon energy. Nevertheless, there is considerable potential to widen the appeal of microgeneration beyond the small niche of technology pioneers.

Wind energy development is the context for a study of public engagement in Chapter 15 by Improta and Pinheiro. Using a sophisticated multi-method approach, they profile Brazil's first large-scale wind farm, concluding that local residents were predominantly in favour of the wind farm, yet quite disengaged from it, being unaware of the names of the companies who proposed the project, and having no contact with the workers or managers involved. The authors reflect on the ethics of wind energy deployment in developing countries, noting the low levels of education and poor living conditions of the local community, many of whom have no access to electricity. They conclude that it is necessary to eliminate the differences between advanced energy technologies and the general living conditions of the people who live in proximity to the wind farm.

In Chapter 16, Firestone investigates offshore wind energy in the US, commenting that development of this sector has been slow, due in part to concerns over public opposition as epitomized by a long-standing dispute over the wind farm in Cape Wind, Nantucket Sound. Reviewing a range of findings from several empirical studies, he points out that, in contrast to NIMBY assumptions, respondents were more likely to accept development proposals if they perceived proposals to be embedded within a larger energy transition towards renewable energy; that topography plays an important role, with citizens less accepting of offshore proposals in semi-enclosed bays; and finally that developers need to be sensitive to communities' attachment to place.

Upstream deliberative engagement with a novel energy vector – hydrogen energy – is the subject of Chapter 17 by Flynn and colleagues, summarizing the findings from citizens' panels held in different regions of the UK. They note the challenges of involving members of the public in upstream engagement with a technology that is embryonic or nascent, requiring the description of alternative scenarios embodying choices and consequences. This, in turn, presents the necessity to relate hydrogen to whole-systems perspectives on the generation, supply and use of energy decades into the future. They conclude that upstream public engagement may be a democratically valuable endeavour, but its achievement is always likely to be limited and incomplete.

In Chapter 18, Sherry-Brennan and colleagues investigate public engagement with wind–hydrogen energy via two contrasting Scottish case studies. A social representations theoretical perspective was adopted to study public beliefs, drawing on data collected from interviews, focus groups and surveys with local residents. In common across the cases was how residents drew on representations of place, identifying why certain aspects of the locality were important to them and how this subsequently oriented their evaluation of the project. This was more important than levels of knowledge about hydrogen, including how each project might mitigate climate change. The authors conclude that developing technology which is seen to be congruous with a place can be seen as essential in the future development and deployment of wind–hydrogen energy.

Marine energy is the subject of Chapter 19, where McLachlan analyses public engagement with the Wave Hub infrastructure currently in construction off the southwest coast of the UK, which will connect with the electricity grid when operational in 2011. It has generated concerns about environmental and social impacts, and Lachlan's study focuses upon how the surfing community has interpreted the project, in a perspective informed by sense of place. She concludes that the notion that wave energy will be opposition-free in comparison with wind energy is misplaced, and advocates that developers and planners engage with the diversity of symbolic meanings with which both the technology and the place can be imbued.

In Chapter 20, Upham draws on insights from an interdisciplinary research programme that investigated public and stakeholder attitudes to the cultivation and use of biomass for energy in the UK. The chapter suggests that the politics and psychology of objection, particularly place attachment, are interconnected. Attitudes are in part contingent on their context: if national energy and climate targets are to be met, rural and coastal communities will need to be convinced that additional energy infrastructure is part of a serious national and international drive to mitigate climate change and that they are not being asked to unilaterally accept changes to their local environment without others also playing their part in emissions reduction.

Butler and colleagues, in Chapter 21, investigate public beliefs about renewable energy held by the members of a 'nuclear community' (i.e. residents living near the Hinkley Point nuclear power station in southwest England). Through in-depth interviews, they reveal the ways in which participants connected to low carbon technologies: through material experience with local nuclear energy or wider social discourses about wind and wave energy. The findings reveal disillusionment with formal processes of engagement and a sense of powerlessness arising from this. They conclude by noting the importance of engagement, not just with new energy developments, but with wider value-based concerns about the purposes of development and future societal directions.

Following these chapters, a Conclusion is provided, which identifies the different roles that social science research can play in investigating public engagement with renewable energy. It shows how this volume challenges pre-existing, narrow framings of social science input into renewable energy, requiring a far broader conceptualization spanning different technologies, public roles and contexts, taking place in both developed and developing countries. It concludes by advocating an increased use of participatory mechanisms to enable publics to input into assessment and decision-making on renewable energy, founded upon systematic, robust social science and critical commentary.

References

Bell, D., Gray, T. and Haggett, C. (2005) 'Policy, participation and the social gap in wind farm siting decisions', *Environmental Politics*, vol 14, no 4, pp460–477

Burningham, K., Barnett, J. and Thrush, D. (2006) *The Limitations of the NIMBY Concept for Understanding Public Engagement with Renewable Energy Technologies: A Literature Review*, Beyond Nimbyism research project Working Paper 1.3, http://geography.exeter.ac.uk/beyond_nimbyism/deliverables/outputs.shtml

Devine-Wright, P. (2009) 'Rethinking NIMBYism: The role of place attachment and place identity in explaining place-protective action', *Journal of Community and Applied Social Psychology*, vol 19, no 6, pp426–441

IPCC (Intergovernmental Panel on Climate Change) (2007) *Climate Change 2007: Synthesis Report: Summary for Policymakers*, Intergovernmental Panel on Climate Change, Geneva

National Research Council (2008) *Public Participation in Environmental Assessment and Decision-making*, The National Academies Press, Washington, DC

REN21 (2009) *Renewables Global Status Report: 2009 Update*, REN21 Secretariat, Paris

Renn, O. (2008) *Risk Governance: Coping with Uncertainty in a Complex World*, Earthscan, London

Stern, N. (2009) 'Going for low-carbon growth', in J. Clarke (ed) *Britain in 2010: Annual Magazine of the Economic and Social Research Council*, ESRC, Swindon, pp8–10

Wolsink, M. (2006) 'Invalid theory impedes our understanding: A critique on the persistence of the language of NIMBY', *Transactions of the Institute of British Geographers*, vol 31, no 1, pp85–91

Wolsink, M. (2010) 'Near-shore wind power: Protected seascapes, environmentalists' attitudes, and the technocratic planning perspective', *Land Use Policy*, vol 27, pp195–203

Section I

Conceptual Approaches

Chapter 1

Symmetries, Expectations, Dynamics and Contexts: A Framework for Understanding Public Engagement with Renewable Energy Projects

*Gordon Walker, Patrick Devine-Wright, Julie Barnett,
Kate Burningham, Noel Cass, Hannah Devine-Wright,
Gerda Speller, John Barton, Bob Evans, Yuko Heath,
David Infield, Judith Parks and Kate Theobald*

Introduction

As this book ably demonstrates, there is a growing body of research on public beliefs, reactions and responses to large-scale renewable energy projects of various forms, often focused on case studies of controversy and local conflict. The profile of available cases has expanded significantly, covering a diversity of locations and contexts around the world and a wide range of types of renewable energy technology and modes of project development. Alongside the reporting of empirical research, there have also been various attempts to describe and characterize public responses to renewable energy projects and develop explanatory frameworks or predictive models. These include the NIMBY ('Not in my back yard') explanations of public opposition that are often favoured in media reporting and political debate (Toynbee, 2007), broad frameworks for thinking about social acceptance (Wüstenhagen et al, 2007) and statistical models that characterize and measure variables that are believed to predict the nature of public opposition (Wolsink, 2000) or planning decision outcomes (Toke et al, 2008).

While these models and frameworks contribute to our understanding of the patterns of public responses to renewable energy projects, we argue in this chapter that they do not present a satisfactory representation of the processes, dynamics and interactions involved. To address some key limitations in existing conceptualizations, we put forward a framework which has a number of distinctive characteristics. First, it is *symmetrical*, giving equal attention to both the public and to the actors who are involved in promoting technology development and engaging with publics in various ways. Second, it seeks to capture the *anticipations and expectations* that are involved in shaping how people and organizations respond and strategically seek to engage or not engage with others. Third, it is *dynamic* in recognizing that, over time, anticipations and expectations evolve and that both the details of proposed projects and the currents of local debates can shift considerably. Fourth, it recognizes the *contextuality* involved, and the importance of situation in both broad policy and economic landscapes and in the characteristics of local places, communities, cultures and politics. In combination, we argue that this framework provides an effective and multifaceted representation of the processes involved in public engagement with large-scale renewable energy projects and how these can and do evolve over time.

Developing the Framework

This framework has emerged from a multidisciplinary project examining public engagement with renewable energy technologies (RETs) in the UK. The project has addressed many aspects of the engagement between the technologies, actors and publics involved with the deployment of RETs, and started from the position that engagement happens in two directions: publics engage with technologies in various ways and to varying degrees; and developers and technology promoters engage with publics in various ways and to varying degrees. The empirical research therefore involved both interviews with key industry, policy and political actors at national and regional levels and case studies of engagement processes and public responses to specific RET development proposals. Table 1.1 lists ten case studies that were undertaken, covering onshore and offshore wind developments, biomass and marine (wave and tidal stream) RET projects in different parts of the UK.

The methodology for each case study involved semi-structured interviews with developers and local stakeholders, focus groups and questionnaire surveys with local people. Although the design of the study was not longitudinal, by using these methods and tracking the project process in each case, we were able to reveal and observe at least some of the dynamics involved. Over the course of the 3.5-year research programme, we were also able to situate the case studies in relation to wider currents of change in UK policy and industry practice.

The framework discussed in this chapter emerged from looking repeatedly across this substantial body of comparative, multidimensional and multidisciplinary research. A first version of the framework was proposed early on in the

Table 1.1 *Summary information on case studies (as of early 2009)*

Project name	Sector	Scale	Location	Local opposition group	Planning status
Gwynt y Mor	Offshore wind	750MW	Wales	Yes	Consented
Lincs	Offshore wind	250MW	England	No	Consented
Baxterley	Bioenergy	2.1MW	England	Yes	Refused/appeal granted/revised application
Port Talbot	Bioenergy	350MW	Wales	Yes	Consented
Ladymoor	Onshore wind (plus hydrogen)	48MW	Scotland	Yes	Wind farm refused/ H2 consented
Falkirk	Onshore wind (urban)	Both 2MW	Scotland	No	Consented
Northants	Onshore wind (urban)	1MW	England	Yes	Refused
Sea Gen	Marine	2MW	Northern Ireland	No	Consented
Wave Dragon	Marine (wave)	7MW	Wales	No	Applied for
Lunar	Marine (tidal stream)	16–20MW	Wales	No	Not yet applied for

research process, drawing at that stage largely on a review of the literature. It was then repeatedly and iteratively revisited during the project, at meetings of the project team and in interactions with a project advisory group including academics and representatives from industry and policy organizations. The focus and form of the framework evolved considerably, with different versions being tried out, worked on and then reformulated to better capture the insights being developed through the different elements of empirical work.

Throughout this process we debated the purpose and function of the framework at some length. In seeking to go beyond the kinds of models, concepts or frameworks already mentioned (e.g. Wüstenhagen et al, 2007), many options were available, and achieving clarity and agreement was difficult. It is therefore important in presenting the framework in this chapter to be clear both about what the framework is intended to be and what it is not.

First, it is primarily a framework for conceptualizing the elements and processes involved in shaping the interactions that take place between technology promoters and local publics in relation to proposed RET developments. It is aiming to be descriptive and explanatory rather than prescriptive or normative – it is not intended to act as a toolkit or a guide to action. It does not suggest how interactions *should* take place or how engagement *should* be practised. It also does not attempt to be simplistically predictive, either about how responses will develop in any given situation or about how final decisions about project approval may turn out.

Second, it does not attempt to be fully inclusive, encompassing every element, process or causal interconnection that might be relevant to an RET project development. As a framework, it is inevitably abstracted to some degree, and selective in what it highlights and what it downplays. In this respect, its formulation and geometry reflects what has emerged from our programme of research and from the discussions we have engaged in as a multidisciplinary team.

Third, and given the preceding point, there is much detail that lies behind or within the framework that cannot be conveyed in the space of this chapter. In what follows, some glimpses of the cases and data that we have examined are provided, but readers are encouraged to follow references to related papers and outputs from the project to find out more.

Over the following sections of the chapter we gradually build the framework, part by part, organizing this construction through the four distinctive features highlighted in the title of this chapter. We begin with the core elements, before gradually drawing out their interconnection and relation to others.

Symmetry: Publics and RET Actors in Interaction

It has long been argued in the literature on 'locally unwanted land uses' (Armour, 1991) that there are (at least) two sides in every case of dispute or conflict, and multiple actors involved in every project development. Public responses are not developed in a vacuum or in the abstract, but rather in interaction with others who have an interest in a development – particularly those who are advocating and promoting it. Thus, rather than seeing people as being predisposed to oppose or support particular developments, we might view local responses as 'emergent, negotiated and shifting' (Futrell, 2003, p360) in relationship to a variety of contextual factors. NIMBY explanations for opposition to development proposals have, in this light, been criticized for focusing attention entirely on the public, often pejoratively (Burningham, 2000; Wolsink, 2000, 2006a). Opposition is accounted for by blaming people for being concerned only about their own self-interest and property values. No attention is given in such an account to what developers and technology promoters are doing and saying, and how decision processes are structured and enacted. We take this on board in Figure 1.1, in having at the core of our framework the interactions between 'public actors' and 'renewable energy actors'.

Public actors we see as situated in 'places', comprising particular locations and communities that are the focus of RET development proposals, making responses that are also situated in particular spatial and cultural contexts. The phrase 'public actors' is intended to encompass both individuals and the collectives that they may be, or become, part of. Renewable energy actors we see as a broad category of people in organizations with roles in supporting or implement-

Figure 1.1 *The main actors and their interactions*

ing RET developments – including developers, consultants, PR and marketing companies, trade associations, financiers and technology manufacturers. These actors we characterize as operating in networks, across which information, expertise and experience is exchanged; sometimes in competition, sometimes in collaboration and mutual interest.

This generalized distinction between 'public actors in places' and 'RET actors in networks', we would argue, is a valid one to make, although, as we recognize, not entirely watertight. Public actors can clearly have networks that extend beyond specific places and communities; for example, through the involvement of regional or national pressure groups in local disputes, or the making of strategic connections between local groups with a common interest but situated in different places. But such extended networks are still made sense of and utilized to achieve agency and impact in local place-based processes. RET actors may have connections or associations with particular places – such as some small-scale developers who have developed regional profiles, or where a series of proximate projects have been constructed (as was the case in one of our offshore wind case studies) – but they are undoubtedly more 'footloose'. Their inter-organizational networks and interests are not place-bound to the same degree. Rather they are structured functionally and professionally, with networks extending across regional and often national borders, within larger companies and globalized supply chains.

In between these two categories of actors, Figure 1.1 positions a slightly murky 'cloud' of interactions: a space within which RET actors and public actors communicate, exchange information and opinions, find out about and engage with each other. We have listed a series of examples of the types of interaction and communication that can be involved here: informal conversations, local media reporting, developers' brochures and exhibitions, public meetings, letters to the paper, protest activities and petitions. Others could be added and there is no one all-inclusive or expected 'menu'. Opportunities for interaction are structured to some degree through familiar routines and mechanisms for communication and engagement, but are also open to more organic 'making up' and evolution over time. From any one case to another, we would expect variation in how much such forms of interaction take place (if at all; some of our case studies had very little local engagement), who is involved in them, their interrelation and sequencing, and their significance and impact. However, as discussed below, we see these interactions as potentially significant in shaping how the dynamics of local responses evolve and how different actors learn, react and strategically behave in relation to each other over both the short and longer term.

Expectations: Anticipations of Projects, Developers, Publics and Processes

The next step in building the framework is to begin to unpack what is going on over time in how different actors think and behave. The key notion here, as shown in the new elements added in Figure 1.2, is that of expectation or anticipation. Actors always have, to some degree, expectations about what is likely to happen. For the local 'public in places', these expectations can take various forms:

• First, and centrally, *expectations about the form and impact of a proposed RET development*: what a proposed wind farm, biomass plant or tidal stream development would 'be like' if constructed in that locality. What good and bad local impacts it might have, how it might perform in generating energy or mitigating climate change, and so on. These expectations may be more or less developed depending on the status of the technology, its familiarity, and its currency and representation within the media.
• Second, there may be *expectations about the project developer*: what they will be like, how they are likely to behave and how they ought to behave. These expectations again might be more or less developed, and may be potentially connected to a specific company with a local, regional or national profile that is known positively or negatively, or to a broader category of 'industry', 'large utility', 'large multinational', 'local landowner' or 'local developer', with the associations that go with each of these.
• Third, they might have *expectations about the process* that is to be gone through to examine and then make decisions about a development proposal. They may have normative expectations of what is just, fair and right in decision-making (or forms of procedural justice (Wolsink, 2006b)); how they should be communicated with and involved; and also pragmatic or 'realistic' expectations of what the process will really be like, how they might expect to be excluded or included and how information flows may or may not transpire.
• Fourth, they might have *expectations about what a proper and appropriate distribution of benefits* from a development should be, and what a community potentially hosting a development should 'get out of it' (Wolsink, 2007; Cass et al, 2010) in comparison with the other actors.

Each of these forms of expectation figured in our survey analysis as shaping local acceptance of projects. Importantly, they move the focus beyond technology-specific expectations to those associated with organizations, modes of organization (Walker and Cass, 2007) and political processes.

For 'RET actors in networks' there are also expectations of various forms. Most important, given our focus, are the expectations of 'the public'. As laid out

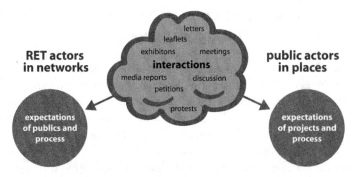

Figure 1.2 *Actors, interactions and expectations*

and argued more systematically in Walker et al (2010), our interviews with such actors showed that they do hold coherent expectations of publics and public responses to RET development – 'imagined publics' to use a phrase drawn from Maranta et al (2003). These expectations are shared across a diversity of industry and policy actors, having been developed in various ways, including through direct experience, the circulation of narrative accounts and media reporting and representations. Among these actors we found an almost universal expectation of the *possibility* of hostility to project implementation – as a real and present danger – latent; sometimes materializing among particular publics for particular reasons and in particular circumstances and places, and set alongside a positive general public orientation to the idea of generating energy in renewable ways. For some RET actors this went further, with an expectation of the public always behaving as NIMBYs or as being emotionally rather than rationally driven (see Cass and Walker 2009, for a detailed discussion). RET actors also have expectations of development and decision processes, of how they ought to operate, how they do operate, and how they can and should engage with the public. These expectations again are drawn from experience across multiple projects, and from hearing from others how they have 'got on' in different localities and with different planning authorities, where processes may be more sympathetic or more hostile to development applications.

For RET actors and publics, such expectations are likely to pre-date any initiation of a specific development proposal and may, to varying degrees, be entrenched and resistant to change. However, as shown in Figure 1.2, we would expect them to be, in part, shaped by the 'interactions' that take place – as publics learn about project proposals, see media reports, attend exhibitions, hear about developers and so on, so their expectations might be expected to evolve and change; as RET actors similarly see media reports, encounter local people, and hold exhibitions and meetings, their expectations of specific local publics and processes may be reinforced, or begin to shift or modulate. Interactions therefore have consequences for expectations – and vice versa.

Dynamics: Evolving Engagements and Expectations

This brings us directly to the dynamics of the framework and to the interrelation between its central elements. In Figure 1.3 two main additions are made: first, 'engagement strategies and actions' by both sets of actors; and, second, two circles of interconnection and influence. The engagement actions on both sides represent the decisions that are made by both public and RET actors about how they are to engage and become involved (or otherwise) in the central 'interactions' space. Engagement actions may be limited or non-existent – we found much evidence of disengagement by local people and also some developers who chose not to actively communicate and become engaged with local publics; while for others, engagement actions could be extensive, repeated and multifaceted.

We see (on both sides) these decisions about engagement as being shaped significantly by expectations, although not only by these (see below). The initial expectations that are held or developed by local people will shape the extent to which they seek more information, read or listen to media reports, become concerned in any way, talk to others, attend meetings or exhibitions, and so on. This process of interconnection can be unpacked into several stages that unfold over time: becoming aware of a project that is proposed in a locality, interpreting it (making sense of it and how it might impact upon the place or the community), evaluating the proposal (judging it to be a threat or opportunity), and responding to it in diverse ways (e.g. by ignoring it, supporting it or opposing it; see Devine-Wright, 2009).

Crucially, though, this linkage between expectations and engagement actions is not one-off but iterative and accumulative. Initial expectations shape engagement actions, which feed into interactions, which then shape expectations, and so on. Hence the circular flow between each of these elements.

Similarly, the shared expectations of the public held by RET actors shape the engagement actions, approaches and strategies pursued by developers and others on the front line of interactions with the public. For example, where public views

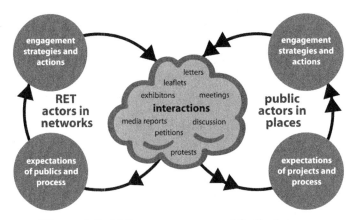

Figure 1.3 *Adding engagements and feedback processes*

opposing a development are conceived of as knowledge deficiency, the provision of information is likely to be a primary focus of engagement. This, in turn, may militate against early engagement with the community, as there may be little certain and clear information to provide at this stage (Barnett et al, in press). Hearing about the project late in the day is often a trigger to public disquiet, and thus these engagements and interactions will, in turn, further shape expectations of the public and decision processes, which feed back into engagement actions and so on. Here we can think about feedback processes operating within specific project processes, but also more broadly influencing the circulation of narrative and expectations within RET networks. When both of the circular flows in Figure 1.3 are conceived as operating simultaneously, a degree of 'gearing' between them can be imagined.

The scope for such dynamics to operate was clear within our case studies. None of the decision processes were entirely straightforward, most involving projects that evolved in their details, with changes being made either in response to local debates or to initial approval decisions. In the more controversial projects, where local opposition materialized, key events or interventions marked out the progression of local debate, with interviewees telling their own stories of develop-ing viewpoints and involvement in relation to 'what happened when' and 'what followed what'. Two of our case studies are illustrative. The first, for a major offshore wind farm in North Wales, took over three years, with an initial planning proposal revised following public and stakeholder engagement, and later a local benefits package was also introduced into the mix. The second, for a biomass plant in South Wales, took four years, and interview and focus group data revealed that it was the decision process as well as the nature of the decision made at a meeting of the local council that triggered a heightened wave of opposition activity. Participants in the very active opposition group saw this as being a key driver of their decision to apply for a judicial review in the High Court.

Over longer time scales, we also found changes in broader engagement strategies. For example, across the renewables industry, but particularly within the wind sector, we observed during the period of the project far more emphasis being given to the provision of community benefits. These took various forms, including 'packages' of regular income to a local community organization, benefits in kind, or specific employment-related measures (Cass et al, 2010). Early on in the research, such practices were rare, but by the end they had become commonplace, featuring in case study engagement strategies, in local debates and, to some degree, in the expectations and anticipations of various actors. Such a shift was rooted in part in how industry actors were viewing publics as amenable to the provision of community benefits and able to be influenced in their responses to the project by whether or not a benefits package was attached.

An additional exchange between the two sides of the framework is added in Figure 1.4. We found that RET actors' expectations of the public fed into other dimensions of their work, rather than only into shaping engagement actions and approaches (Walker et al, 2010). In interviewee accounts, some degree of influ-ence was recognized on the engineering and design of technologies – with

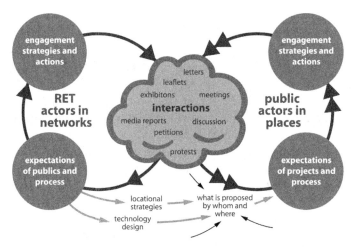

Figure 1.4 *Adding connections between expectations of publics, technology design and locational strategies*

attempts in particular to make their physical appearance less intrusive – although many other more important factors shape engineering and design decisions. Some degree of influence was also found on the locational strategies and decisions of developers, with the choice of development sites, the shift towards offshore and, in some cases, the shift to working in other countries – all, in part, attributed to expectations of public responses and reactions. In these ways, as shown in Figure 1.4, the expectations of the public have a role (although not necessarily a primary one) in shaping what projects are proposed by developers, where they are proposed, and the form of the engineered technology. These project characteristics then feed into the expectations developed by specific publics of what is proposed, and we can trace feedback processes that are part of these flows of influence. Over a long time scale of 20 or so years of wind power development in the UK, we could arguably trace such dynamics, with the repeated experiences of opposition to onshore wind farms and expectations of public resistance encouraging the move to offshore wind farms. This shift, in turn, feeds into the expectations and engagement decisions of coastal communities presented with a new generation of offshore wind farm development proposals contextualized by preceding debates and experiences of onshore wind.

Contextualities: Policy, Regulation, Places, Histories

Contextuality is the last characteristic of the framework which, along with how interactions feed into formal development decision processes and outcomes, achieves its final form in Figure 1.5.

There are many ways in which the processes we have discussed up to this point are situated in context, and several dimensions are highlighted in Figure

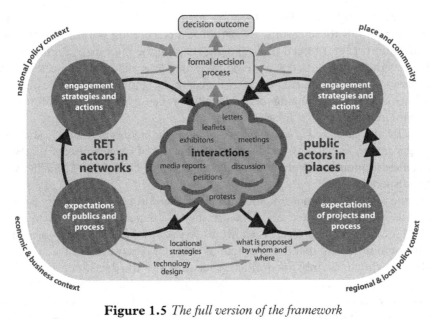

Figure 1.5 *The full version of the framework*

1.5. On the right-hand side, characteristics of *place and community* are seen as shaping how public actors develop expectations and engagement strategies. Senses of place, attachments to place, and specifically attachments to landscapes, have been found to be important where RETs are proposed (Devine-Wright and Howes, 2010), and this was evident across our case studies. For example, regarding the Gwynt y Mor offshore wind farm, analysis indicated that the more that residents felt attached to the town of Llandudno, the more they opposed the wind farm. Tapping into place meanings provided contextual information as to why this was the case – Llandudno was represented as a distinctive place that was attractive to tourists, characterized by its scenic, natural beauty (including the views out to sea) and Victorian heritage. These place meanings were widely perceived to be threatened by a wind farm that would 'industrialize' the area and 'fence in the bay' (Devine-Wright and Howes, 2010). In contrast, in the case of the biomass plant in Port Talbot, the local historical context manifested itself in a kind of ambivalence. On the one hand, the long association of the town with heavy industry was linked to recognition of the reliance of the community on the jobs that this provided. On the other hand, residents also showed little confidence that local decision-makers would be willing or able to exercise their duty of care towards local residents around the health concerns that they linked to emissions from the proposed plant; emissions that would only worsen the existing poor air quality in the area.

The nature of the communities involved in terms of their socio-demographics, levels of prosperity, mix of long-established and more recent incoming residents, and levels of social capital can also be significant in explaining patterns of expectation and engagement.

Policy contexts are highlighted – both 'regional and local' and 'national and international' – as these can be important in determining the drivers of, and funding support for, project development; shaping the discourses, legitimation and engagement strategies that are employed and determining the processes and boundaries of decision-making through, for example, land use policy. The distinction between decisions being made locally or being made in London was important in a number of our case studies.

Finally, the *business and economic context* is highlighted as particularly shaping the engagement, technology and locational strategies of renewable energy developers, their relationships with other RET actors, and their degree of sensitivity to public responses.

At the top of the framework, the formal decision process for granting project approval (which can take several forms in the UK, depending upon the nature, size and location of the project) is shown as feeding into decision outcomes. It is important to note here that the interactions that go on between RET actors and publics are shown as only one influence feeding into the decision process and outcome. Experience, and indeed our case studies, have shown that high apparent degrees of local activity, anticipation of negative impacts, and multidimensional interaction do not necessarily lead to RET projects being turned down – and that, similarly, patterns of disengagement, lack of interaction, or anticipation of positive local outcomes do not always lead to project approval. The factors that influence local planning authority or government department decisions are far more involved than this, and are not so directly linked to local public consent – however that may be claimed or judged.

Conclusions

The framework we have outlined is an attempt to represent the complex sets of processes, dynamics and interactions that are involved in understanding public responses to large-scale, developer-led RET developments. As we have begun to show, behind the relatively simple diagrammatic form of the framework are further layers of detail that can be brought into view both in the abstract and in the particular cases of real proposed developments in real places. Overall, the framework encourages a recognition of these complexities and, in particular, of the dynamics that operate over both short and longer time scales. In doing so, the framework challenges simplistic accounts of public engagement, particularly the NIMBY concept, which ignores the way in which the responses of public actors are inevitably embedded in real places and communities, and intertwined with the expectations and actions of RET actors.

Producing the framework was a multidisciplinary endeavour, involving members of a research team with geography, psychology, sociology, planning and engineering backgrounds. This is reflected in its attempt to incorporate aspects of individual expectation and belief, social processes of interaction and exchange, concerns about decision-making processes and fairness, dimensions of technology design and project formulation, and aspects of place, community and history. Whether the framework can effectively incorporate such diversity is an open question, but the ambition to present a rounded and more – rather than less – faceted picture is, we think, an important one.

In terms of future work and how the framework might be applied and developed, we can see a number of different directions and avenues. We have not, in this chapter, attempted to systematically demonstrate the framework's empirical validity or how it provides a better way of representing real cases of patterns and processes than other approaches. To spell this out, for example, through applying the framework to case study analysis, would be a logical next step. This could include generating research questions and hypotheses about the interactions between publics and other actors and the ways in which these might lead to particular sets of outcomes. The emphasis on dynamics that has emerged from our deliberations also suggests that there is a need for longitudinal research designs that can track processes and changes over time, following the feedback loops that we have argued are in operation. This can be a difficult task, with implications for scales and lengths of funding as well as the use of methodologies that can track change, but nonetheless one that we think should be pursued. Finally, another way of making use of the framework, particularly for those involved in policy and practice, is to think about the points of influence and intervention that it reveals. Where can intervention towards achieving the desired outcomes (such as meeting targets for renewable energy generation or carbon reduction) be exerted and with what potentially systemic short- and longer-term outcomes? It is through such deliberations that a framework presented in this chapter as descriptive and explanatory could begin to take on a more normative and prescriptive function.

Acknowledgements

We wish to thank all the interviewees, focus group participants and survey respondents who contributed to the research. Funding was made available by the UK Research Councils' Energy Programme under award number RES-152-25-1008.

References

Armour, A. (1991) 'The siting of locally unwanted land uses: Towards a cooperative approach', *Progress in Planning*, vol 35, no 1, pp1–74

Barnett, J., Burningham, K., Walker, G. and Cass, N. (in press) 'Imagined publics and engagement around renewable energy technologies in the UK', *Public Understanding of Science*.

Burningham, K. (2000) 'Using the Language of NIMBY: A topic for research not an activity for researchers', *Local Environment*, vol 5, no 1, pp55–67

Cass, N. and Walker, G. P. (2009) 'Emotion and rationality: The characterisation and evaluation of opposition to renewable energy projects', *Emotion, Space and Society*, vol 2, pp 62–69

Cass, N., Walker, G. and Devine-Wright, P. (2010) 'Good neighbours, public relations and bribes: The politics and perceptions of community benefit provision in renewable energy development in the UK', *Journal of Environmental Policy and Planning*, vol 12, no 3, pp255–275

Devine-Wright, P. (2009) 'Rethinking NIMBYism: The role of place attachment and place identity in explaining place-protective action', *Journal of Community and Applied Social Psychology*, vol 19, no 6, pp426–441

Devine-Wright, P. and Howes, Y. (2010) 'Disruption to place attachment and the protection of restorative environments: A wind energy case study', *Journal of Environmental Psychology*, vol 30, no 3, pp271–280

Futrell, R. (2003) 'Framing processes, cognitive liberation and NIMBY protest in the US chemical-weapons disposals conflict', *Sociological Inquiry*, vol 73, no 3, pp359–386

Maranta, A., Guggenhgeim, M., Gisler, P. and Pohl, C. (2003) 'The reality of experts and the imagined lay person', *Acta Sociologica*, vol 46, no 2, pp150–165

Toke, D., Breukers, S. and Wolsink, M. (2008) 'Wind power deployment outcomes: How can we account for the differences?' *Renewable and Sustainable Energy Reviews*, vol 12, no 4, pp1129–1147

Toynbee, P. (2007) 'Nimbys can't be allowed to put a block on wind farms: Plans to meet renewable energy targets are being stymied by local councils – mostly run by the Tories and the SNP', *Guardian*, 5 January, www.guardian.co.uk/commentisfree/2007/jan/05/comment.politics

Walker, G. and Cass, N. (2007) 'Carbon reduction, "the public" and renewable energy: engaging with sociotechnical configurations', *Area*, vol 39, no 4, pp458–469.

Walker, G., Cass N., Burningham, K. and Barnett, J. (2010) 'Renewable energy and sociotechnical change: Imagined subjectivities of "the public" and their implications', *Environment and Planning A*, vol 42, pp931–947.

Wolsink, M. (2000) 'Wind power and the NIMBY-myth: Institutional capacity and the limited significance of public support', *Renewable Energy*, vol 21, no 1, pp49–64

Wolsink, M. (2006a) 'Invalid theory impedes our understanding: A critique on the persistence of the language of NIMBY', *Transactions of the Institute of British Geographers*, vol 31, no 1, pp85–91

Wolsink, M. (2006b) 'Planning of renewables schemes: Deliberative and fair decision-making on landscape issues instead of reproachful accusations of non-cooperation', Paper presented at the International Research Conference on Social Acceptance of Renewable Energy Innovation, Tramelan, Switzerland

Wolsink, M. (2007) 'Wind power implementation: The nature of public attitudes: Equity and fairness instead of "backyard motives"', *Renewable and Sustainable Energy Reviews*, vol 11, no 6, pp1188–1207

Wüstenhagen, R., Wolsink, M. and Burer, M. J. (2007) 'Social acceptance of renewable energy innovation: An introduction to the concept', *Energy Policy*, vol 35, no 5, pp2683–2691

Chapter 2

'Planning and Persuasion': Public Engagement in Renewable Energy Decision-making

Claire Haggett

Introduction

Renewable energy is on the political and policy agenda as never before. On 15 July 2009, when the UK Labour Government published its much anticipated 'Low Carbon Transition Plan', it included wide-ranging strategies to cut carbon emissions. It also included ambitious plans to generate 30 per cent of electricity from renewable sources by 2020, up from the current figure of 5 per cent. The then UK Secretary of State for Energy and Climate Change, Ed Miliband, stated repeatedly and unequivocally that 'planning and persuasion' are the way to realize these ambitious targets.

The emphasis on 'planning' refers to the new Planning Act (2008); a radical overhaul of the UK planning system. The emphasis on 'persuasion' means convincing people that climate change is a more pressing environmental concern than the localized impact of a renewable energy development. The aims are to dramatically increase the proportion of energy generated from renewable sources, to encourage people to support renewable energy, and to remove the 'problem' of public opposition. The intention was to achieve this through education, and through changing the timing and number of engagement opportunities available. This chapter considers the effects of these proposals, and how they fit with wider philosophies on the role and value of engagement in the UK context and beyond. In doing so, it discusses how the terms 'public' and 'engagement' are themselves complex and contested and, indeed, at the heart of this contentious debate. It will therefore be useful to start by briefly outlining some of the reasons for engaging the public in decision-making, and how this engagement is carried out.

Planning: The Principles of Public Engagement

The ethos of engaging the public in decision-making is a key part of the UK planning system. There is a requirement in government policy that decisions are discussed with local communities (Rydin and Pennington, 2000), and that the planning system should work to protect and serve 'the public interest' (Campbell and Marshall, 2002). Indeed, the encouragement of public engagement in planning procedures and decision-making about renewable energy has been well documented (Alexander, 2002) for three key reasons, which are useful to consider here (following Yearley et al, 2003).

Firstly, pragmatically, public engagement can be used to increase the likelihood of a successful siting. When people are consulted, they are less likely to oppose (and may even support) decisions, and at the very least there is perhaps the hope that engagement of the public may lead to 'better' or more competent decisions.

Secondly, ethically, the public may be engaged because they are deemed to have a right to participate in decisions that affect them, and this engagement may be seen as an end in itself. Establishing 'fair' processes of public engagement may be one way to restore diminished trust in authorities and institutions (Healey, 1996, p213); and in their report on behaviour and attitudes to climate change, the Institute of Public Policy Research (IPPR) state that public engagement with energy issues is beneficial because 'empowering people to exert control and resolve problems is a good thing in its own right: improving governance, deepening democracy and rebuilding trust' (IPPR, 2007, p4). Jobert et al's (2007) study of renewable energy implementation in France and Germany concluded that trust in decision-making processes about renewables is crucial; and Gross (2007) discusses the issues of trust and fairness in participation in decision-making for wind farms in Australia. She argues that perceptions of both fairness of *outcomes* and fairness of *process* are vital for encouraging engagement and acceptance. Indeed, for some, a fair process is just as important as the decision that is finally made, if people feel that they 'have the opportunity to speak and be heard' (Gross, 2007, p2734).

Thirdly, local people may be 'local experts', and fully engaging them in decision-making means that a rich and contextualized knowledge of the local area, local dynamics and local contingencies can be drawn on – superior to relying on outside expertise alone (Irwin, 1995; Wynne, 1996). Decisions that do not take into account local factors, issues and values may be seen as questionable (Cass, 2006; Haggett, 2009), and 'objective' and 'value-free' judgements may be impossible or unacceptable (Owen et al, 2004).

These reasons resonate with the broader culture of 'collaborative' forms of planning, influenced by Habermasian ideas, which opposes 'rationalist' models of land use planning. Pennington (2002, p187) describes the latter as 'based on a technocratic conception of decision-making, whereby public managers in possession of objective knowledge make decisions on the basis of maximizing social welfare'. In contrast, collaborative planning considers knowledge to be socially situated, not somehow objective or solely the preserve of the scientific or technical domain. Such a focus values rather than ignores tacit understandings and everyday knowledge. Planning methods that de-emphasize on this form of knowledge may lead to poorly developed policies and also to disempowerment from, and distrust of, decision-makers. This reflects what Habermas (1976) identified as a 'legitimation crisis' for those in power who are distant from their electorate and make decisions without involving them on the basis of knowledge that has little relevance to people's lives. This discussion of the rationale for engaging people and communities also resonates with Arnstein's classic conceptualization of the 'ladder of citizen participation' (1969), in which she outlines a scale of engaging and empowering communities, from 'empty ritual' to 'real power'. Arnstein outlines some of the processes through which this engagement is enacted, which will be drawn on in the following sections.

The Procedures of Public Engagement

So there are principles and benefits to engaging the public; and there are various different means to attempt to do so. One method is to provide information about a particular development or the need for renewables in general. The objectives of this form of 'engagement' seem most focused on pragmatic attempts to win support for an application, and to avoid the 'problems' of opposition (Cowell, 2007). It is in keeping with the 'decide–announce–defend' tradition in planning and development, informing people of plans that have been made, and involves such methods as distributing leaflets, advertising, and providing exhibitions and displays. This is engagement as '*information provision*', the 'bottom-line' approach to engagement and 'the minimum level allowed by law' (Chilvers et al, 2005, p28). This engagement as information provision is unlikely to be effective in terms of encouraging public support and trust; both for the particular proposals and for the planning process as a whole. Indeed, Arnstein (1969) describes how these attempts to 'educate' a public or even engineer their support through very minimal involvement are merely 'illusory' forms of (non)participation. Giving information can be an important first step but, with an emphasis on a one-way flow of information only, people have little influence or opportunity even to express themselves. It is, however, the form most frequently used by both government and industry when attempting to engage the public about renewable energy.

An alternative to the provision of information to a public assumed to be passive is to actively elicit responses: engagement as '*consultation*'. This then becomes a dialogue between the people and the developer, instead of a one-way flow of information. If this happens, it may help to address the reasons behind what Bell et al (2005) have described as 'qualified support' for renewables: if people support renewables in general but oppose particular schemes, their support may depend on certain conditions being met. Engagement as consultation provides the opportunity to discuss with people what their reasons for 'qualified support' are – such as the size and scale of a development or the impact on local wildlife. A dialogue can allow questions to be asked, and directed responses to be given. Arnstein (1969) again says that this can be a useful step towards full participation, but the auspices under which the consultation are carried out, the questions that are permitted and the options presented, and the action taken on the basis of the results, are all key in determining its effectiveness.

A third way of envisaging engagement, therefore, is as '*deliberation*', where the public are not just permitted to discuss any plans, but are more thoroughly involved in developing them, along with wider policy, in the first place. The approach is based on public participation rather than public consultation, recognizing and including all interests, and necessitates a shift in emphasis from competitive interest-bargaining to collaborative consensus-building (Harris, 2002). It may be more akin to what Arnstein (1969) describes as 'partnership', where participation is taken much more seriously and decision-making reflects the views of people and communities. This may overcome what Bell et al (2005) have described as a 'democratic deficit' in renewable energy decisions, where the apparent minority who do not support developments (the 25 per cent who are commonly in opposition, according to opinion polls) is able to impose its will on decision-making processes, leading to the low success rate for applications (Toke, 2005). As Bell et al (2005) discuss, it is important to assess what the majority thinks, and more deliberative processes about renewable energy may achieve this.

Examples of this kind of approach include citizens' juries, interactive panels, workshops and conferences, where issues are broadly considered and recommendations for decision-makers discussed. However, this approach is rare; with only two notable instances recorded. Such a process was conducted for the development of the UK Government's Energy White Paper in 2003, involving 'all levels of engagement strategy, from simple information provision to complex deliberative processes' (Chilvers et al, 2005, p24), and was widely welcomed by those involved. Such a process was also enacted in the spring of 2009, where residents in nine communities across England, Wales and Northern Ireland were invited to be part of citizens' forums, considering a range of options for insulating, heating and powering homes and communities (Ipsos MORI, 2009). The input from these forums is intended to inform the UK Government's final plans, and more details of these will be available shortly.

Planning, Persuasion, and Government Policies

The apparent success of the above examples suggests that deliberative forms of engagement should be considered as widely and frequently as possible. The planning processes would be less about deciding, announcing and defending, and more about local people and decision-makers working together. Views would be sought, and listened to, and outcomes that were satisfactory to all could be negotiated.

Indeed, this would appear at first to be the emphasis of the new Planning Act in the UK. The changes made represent a radical overhaul of the planning system, intended to speed up decisions, and deemed necessary as part of the measures to increase renewable energy development. The act brought about a new system for the approval of major infrastructure projects, encompassing water, waste, transport and energy. This included the introduction of 'national policy statements' (NPSs): documents which set out a framework for this infrastructure development and establish the need for such projects. It was intended that individual proposals would then be decided on by an independent body, the Infrastructure Planning Commission (IPC), within the context of these policy statements.

The intention is to streamline decisions and avoid long public inquiries. The planning system is commonly criticized for being cumbersome, bureaucratic and inefficient, and is blamed for delaying apparently valuable projects at huge expense. The intention with the new Act is to cut dramatically the time taken. The existence of a policy framework (contained within the NPSs) means that applicants will not have to establish the broader need for a proposed development. The permitting process, therefore, will only be concerned with the specifics of an application; thus theoretically speeding up the time taken to reach a decision.

What is important to note, in terms of this chapter, are the three opportunities that people will have to express their views under the Act. First, this will be during the public consultations on the draft NPSs (the NPS for energy was launched at the start of 2010); second, during the preparation of applications for submission to the IPC, where developers are required to consult with local communities about what they plan to do; and finally, during the IPC's examination of applications, individuals and groups can submit evidence in writing as well as attending in person at 'open floor' hearings held by the IPC.

The emphasis on early consultation – during the development of NPSs – would seem to resonate with Arnstein's recommendations about more thorough participation, and Habermasian ideals about formative discussions which then lead to policy, rather than consultations on plans already developed. Indeed, the government stated that one of the aims of the new Act is to 'facilitate participation in decision-making, strengthening the voice of communities', to ensure a 'fairer' system, and to improve the old regime, where 'many individuals, communities, and other stakeholders [found] the system archaic and opaque and had difficulty making their voices heard' (Department for Communities and Local Government, 2009a, pp3–4).

Planning in Practice

While this seems admirable, there are a number of important issues to take into account about power, representation and procedure. These relate to the power differentials that may emerge between local people, officials and vested interests; whether all relevant interests can (and should) be fairly represented; and the particular methods of outreach and engagement adopted.

For example, while the NPSs are about generating strategy; conflicts and power relations may not be fully recognized within communicative planning ideals. Any deliberatively developed policies may be disrupted by manipulation, control and exclusions (Richardson, 1996): a 'sobering' realization (Flyvbjerg, 1996, p389). It is debatable whether local people and decision-makers can ever be in a situation where power relations do not shape both process and outcome. Even if collaborative planning methods are being attempted, people will have differential access and influence, through factors such as language, education, social position, ethnicity and gender, despite any compensatory measures (Tewdwr-Jones and Thomas, 1998). Powerful interests may, for instance, go 'over the heads' of those in the collaborative process, to directly influence the decision-maker. In the case of the new Act, there is no guarantee that people will be able to have their say fairly without the interference of these power relations in the development of the NPSs, and there are concerns about the influence and unaccountability of the unelected officials on the IPC. Indeed, a coalition of many of the major UK environmental and conservation groups has been formed to campaign against the Bill on these grounds, uniting under the banner 'Planning Disaster', based on these (and other) concerns.

There are also questions to be asked about representation: who should or can be involved, and what influence they should have. The 'public' is hardly a homogeneous entity, and includes many different (and competing) interests. Gross (2007) has shown that, although decisions that involve people are laudable, decisions perceived to benefit some sections of a community over others will cause protests and disputes (a point reiterated by Walker and Devine-Wright, 2008). The NPSs are about setting national strategy – which, when put into practice, may affect certain places and people differently – people who have not had an input into this process.

Not only are there different publics to involve, but they may prefer or need different forms of involvement: procedure and method are crucial. In a study of the engagement between offshore wind power developers and fishing communities, Gray et al (2005) discuss how both of these groups had a very different view of the process. The developers had held a series of public meetings and felt they had made every feasible effort to consult with the fragmented fishing industry. However, large open meetings were not an appropriate form of communication for the informal, non-hierarchical culture of the fishing communities, and were consequently not attended by the fishers. These issues compounded the distance between the two groups, and led to scepticism, distrust and a seemingly entrenched divide. This example demonstrates the difficulties of achieving appropriate forms of engagement which mean that all of those with an interest in the outcomes are able to participate.

While engaging all those who could or should be involved in drawing up the NPSs may be problematic, the second stage of consultation in the Planning Act may also be difficult. The onus in the Planning Act is very clearly on developers to make efforts to engage with those interested or affected: when a development is proposed within a particular location, developers will have a 'duty to consult the local community' (Planning Act, 2008: Section 46, p1). While the government gives detailed guidance about this pre-application consultation (Department for Communities and Local Government, 2009b), the responsibility rests with the applicant to ensure that they have publicized their proposals and consulted the relevant stakeholders and local people. The IPC will have the power to refuse the application if they deem that the applicant has not complied with these procedural requirements; but how a developer identifies these people, how they chose to engage them, and whether they do so in ways that are meaningful, is key. The Planning Act states that after publicizing their proposals and consulting with the local community, applicants must 'have regard to any relevant responses' (Planning Act, 2008: Section 48, p2); but it is not clear which responses these might be, or how responses will or must be incorporated into plans. As mentioned above, engagement may be mere information provision, rather than a meaningful attempt to consult and listen; and while some renewable energy developers do make efforts in this regard, many others do not have such a good track record (Haggett, 2008).

Finally, the third stage – where people can respond to plans – also suggests difficulties. At inquiries into specific developments, the public will not be able to call into question the principles of the NPSs; and one of the groups campaigning against these changes, Friends of the Earth, believes that this is intrinsically problematic:

> *'attempts to limit people from questioning national statements at public inquiries will be controversial and bring the process into disrepute, further distancing people from government decisions and increasing the risk of conflict'* (Friends of the Earth, 2007, p3).

Indeed, the only chance that local people will get to speak at an inquiry into a proposal will be at the end, in what is being termed an 'open floor' session. This will take place after the members of the IPC have examined the evidence, leading to suspicions that decisions will already have been made.

This is important, because people may well want to try and express their views at this stage. Wolsink (1994), Bell et al (2005) and Haggett and Vigar (2004) have shown that people's attitudes change between what they are when thinking about an idea in the abstract and what they become when faced with an imminent development in reality. So, while a person may agree in principle with something in the NPSs, it may be a different matter when the particular contingencies of any application are announced. In sum, therefore, it seems likely that the new Act – and the opportunities for involvement that it allows – will only distance people from the planning process. Fair and open engagement processes, in principle, are very difficult to implement in practice. Furthermore, by the time that many people are effectively engaged with the decision-making processes –

and have a proposal intended for their locality – the judgements about its necessity will already have been made.

Public Involvement through Education and Persuasion

So far, this chapter has reviewed the reasons and methods of public consultation, and discussed the effect of changes in the planning system. The second tenet of the plan to increase energy from renewables is through 'persuasion' – convincing people about the benefits of renewables and the risks of climate change. Engaging the public in decisions about renewable energy by attempting to educate them is not new. Indeed, this emphasis is directly in line with 'Planning Policy Statement 22' (PPS22), the UK Government's planning policy document for renewable energy. PPS22 exhorts local authorities to 'promote knowledge of and greater acceptance by the public of prospective renewable energy developments' (Office of the Deputy Prime Minister, 2004: Section 1, pviii).

However, the public may well not need 'education' or even 'information' about a proposal. It may well be that some concerns, such as the effect on local bird populations of a wind turbine, or the fire risks from a hydrogen filling station, can be addressed by independent research from sources that people will trust. But the assumption in PPS22 and the corresponding emphasis accompanying the new Planning Act implies that opposition can be addressed by closing an information gap through 'education'. This cites the 'public deficit' model: the idea that 'if only people knew better' they would support renewable energy and/or the particular development. But there is not necessarily a direct correlation between information and attitudes, nor is it sufficient or accurate to say that the people who oppose a development are uneducated or misinformed. More often, protesters are very familiar with the details of a particular proposal (Wolsink, 1994). An example of this is the public 'engagement' that took place about the offshore wind farm planned off the coast of North Wales (Haggett, 2008). Local people were very familiar with and very knowledgeable about the local area, local issues, local landscape and seascape – whereas the representatives of the developer (from London) were not.

Indeed, attempts to educate people about the necessity for renewable energy because of climate change may not work because, while people may be concerned about global issues, local, tangible and immediate problems command more attention. Indeed, the contrast between the invisible global benefits and direct disbenefits is one of the key aspects of the opposition to renewable energy. Developers often frame the need for wind power in terms of the global imperative – but this is often rejected by local people (Haggett and Smith, 2004). This does not mean they are 'NIMBYs' – people who are only concerned with their own 'backyards' – but that they are genuinely concerned about daily detrimental impact. It is precisely these sorts of concerns that are likely to be sidelined by the new Planning Act. There is guidance from the Department of Trade and Industry, and new policies being developed at the Department of Energy and Climate Change on the role of community benefits: developers making payments to communities or providing facilities to compensate for the disadvantages which a development may bring. A recognition of the lack of tangible benefits may be useful; however, as Wolsink (1994, p864) states, 'this strategy of compensation is becoming popular, but it is also very dangerous'. Payment can be seen as a bribe, especially when it is not proposed at an early stage but is offered after a division between developers and opponents emerges. Attempts to try and 'buy support' may confuse the interests and motives of affected communities, and do nothing to address their concerns by listening to them.

Discussion

This chapter has discussed some of the reasons and means of engaging the public in decisions about renewable energy, and placed these in the context of forthcoming changes to the UK planning system. The impetus behind these changes is the opposition that exists to renewable energy in many cases, its effectiveness, and the current low siting rate for renewables (compared with other forms of development: see Bell et al, 2005; Haggett and Toke, 2006).

However, these are considerations which have much wider resonance far beyond the UK context. Conflict over renewable energy siting has arisen across Europe (see, for example, Pedersen and Persson Waye, 2004; Breukers and Wolsink, 2007; Jobert et al, 2007; Nadai, 2007; Wolsink, 2007; Wüstenhagen et al, 2007; Agterbosch et al, 2009), America (see, for example, Thayer and Hansen, 1988; Pasqualetti, 2001; Firestone et al, 2004), Australasia (Gross, 2007; Phipps, 2007) and Asia (Kogaki et al, 2007) – in fact, almost everywhere that a development is planned. While the reasons for protest against renewables are not straightforward (and are considered in depth elsewhere in this volume) what underlies many of them – across these different case studies and continents – are the opportunities people have for meaningful engagement in the decision-making process. This relates not just to renewable energy, but to development and project management much more broadly. Crucially, in her Australian case study, Gross (2007) has shown that, if people feel that fair and just processes have led to an outcome, they are more likely to support that outcome, whatever it may be. In cases where engagement was felt to be lacking or ineffective and the process unfair, this can directly lead to opposition. In the example from North Wales above, local people criticized the process for the development of the offshore wind farm, feeling that the decisions had already been made and that there was a lack of 'real' consultation – which hardened their opposition against both the development and the developer (Haggett, 2008).

The different means of engagement and the ethos under which it is carried out will affect the trust that people have in both the process and the outcomes. Information provision alone may not address any concerns or needs, and may even incite protest if these are ignored. Consulting people can be workable and effective and can, in some cases, lead to more mutually beneficial outcomes. 'Ideal' deliberative processes, where people are involved with the generation of policy, rather than commenting on plans after they have been made, can mean that issues and values are incorporated into strategic and detailed decisions. However, such examples are rare and are certainly not simple or straightforward to deliver.

What does this mean for planning and public engagement? If renewable energy is a core part of tackling carbon emissions and climate change, issues of public support and opposition have to be addressed – and diverse publics have to be meaningfully engaged. Seeing the public as a 'barrier' or as ignorant about renewables (or any other issue) is unlikely to be helpful. Instead, a more thorough approach to understand the concerns that people have, and how these might be mediated, is required.

This would mean acknowledging and valuing local expertise and tacit knowledges, and recognizing the important contribution that different groups can bring. It would mean framing discussions not in terms of theoretical ideals but in ways that are meaningful to local people, taking account of local contingencies and people's conceptions of place and the importance of their local surroundings. For officials and developers, it means building up long-term relationships in communities, seeming concerned and interested and being involved in them, and being accountable for the strategies developed that will affect them. Finally, it means employing methods that are not exclusive, but actively seeking to engage divergent communities.

The difficulties of this – from having a conceptual framework within which engagement processes are adopted, to the practical difficulties of gathering diverse interests together, encouraging them to express their views and genuinely incorporating their concerns and interests into policy – are clear. A planning and development system of 'deciding–announcing–defending' did not achieve this. It remains to be seen whether a new system of early and abstract agenda-setting and limited consultation later will fare any better – and the effect this will have both on public support for renewables and the decision-makers.

References

Agterbosch, S., Meertens, R. M. and Vermeulen, W. J. A. (2009) 'The relative importance of social and institutional conditions in the planning of wind power projects', *Renewable and Sustainable Energy Reviews*, vol 13, no 2, pp393–405

Alexander, E. R. (2002) 'The public interest in planning: From legitimation to substantive plan evaluation', *Planning Theory*, vol 1, no 3, pp226–249

Arnstein, S. R. (1969) 'A ladder of citizen participation', *Journal of the American Institute of Planners*, vol 35, no 4, pp216–224

Bell, D., Gray, T. and Haggett, C. (2005) 'Policy, participation and the social gap in wind farm siting decisions', *Environmental Politics*, vol 14, no 4, pp460–477

Breukers, S. and Wolsink, M. (2007) 'Wind power implementation in changing institutional landscapes: An international comparison', *Energy Policy*, vol 35, no 5, pp2737–2750

Campbell, H. and Marshall, R. (2002) 'Utilitarianism's bad breath? A re-evaluation of the public interest justification for planning', *Planning Theory*, vol 1, no 2, pp163–187

Cass, N. (2006) 'Participatory-deliberative engagement: A literature review', published by the School of Environment and Development, Manchester University

Chilvers, J., Damery, S., Evans, J., van der Horst, D. and Petts, J. (2005) *Public Engagement in Energy: Mapping Exercise*, Report for the Research Councils UK Energy Research Public Dialogue Project, University of Birmingham, Birmingham, UK

Cowell, R. (2007) 'Wind power and "the planning problem": The experience of Wales', *European Environment*, vol 17, no 5, pp291–306

Department for Communities and Local Government (2009a) *Infrastructure Planning Commission: Implementation Route Map December 2009*, Communities and Local Government Publications, London, www.communities.gov.uk/documents/planningandbuilding/pdf/routemap.pdf

Department for Communities and Local Government (2009b) *Planning Act 2008: Guidance on Pre-application Consultation*, Communities and Local Government Publications, London, www.communities.gov.uk/publications/planningandbuilding/guidancepreapplication

Firestone, J., Kempton, W., Krueger, A. and Loper, C. E. (2004) 'Regulating offshore wind power and aquaculture: Messages from land and sea', *Cornell Journal of Law and Public Policy*, vol 14, no 1, pp71–111

Flyvbjerg, B. (1996) 'The dark side of planning: Rationality and *Realrationalitat*', in S. Mandelbaum, L. Mazza and R. Burchell (eds) *Explorations in Planning Theory*, Center for Urban Policy Research, New Brunswick, NJ, pp383–394

Friends of the Earth (2007) *A Better Plan: An Alternative View of the Land Use Planning System*, Friends of the Earth, London, www.foe.co.uk/campaigns/fair_future/resource/campaigners.html

Gray, T., Haggett, C. and Bell, D. (2005) 'Wind farm siting: The case of offshore wind farms', *Ethics, Place and Environment*, vol 8, no 2, pp127–140

Gross, C. (2007) 'Community perspectives of wind energy in Australia: The application of a justice and fairness framework to increase social acceptance', *Energy Policy*, vol 35, no 5, pp2727–2736

Habermas, J. (1976) *Legitimation Crisis*, translated by T. McCarthy, Beacon Press, Boston, MA

Haggett, C. (2008) 'Over the sea and far away? A consideration of the planning, politics and public perception of offshore wind farms', *Journal of Environmental Policy and Planning*, vol 10, no 3, pp289–306

Haggett, C. (2009) 'Public engagement in planning for renewable energy', in S. Davoudi and J. Crawford (eds) *Planning for Climate Change: Strategies for Mitigation and Adaptation for Spatial Planners*, Earthscan, London, pp297–307

Haggett, C. and Smith, J. (2004) 'Tilting at windmills? Understanding the attitude–behaviour gap in renewable energy conflicts', Paper presented at the British Sociological Association Conference, York, 22–25 March

Haggett, C. and Toke, D. (2005) 'Crossing the great divide: Using multi-method analysis to understand opposition to wind farms', *Public Administration*, vol 84, no 1, pp103–120

Haggett, C. and Vigar, G. (2004) 'Tilting at windmills? Understanding opposition to wind farm applications', *Town and Country Planning*, vol 73, no 10, pp288–291

Harris, N. (2002) 'Collaborative planning: From theoretical foundations to practice forms', in P. Allemendinger and M. Tewdr-Jones (eds) *Planning Futures: New Directions for Planning Theory*, Routledge, London, pp21–43

Healey, P. (1996) 'Consensus-building across difficult divisions: New approaches to collaborative strategy making', *Planning Practice and Research*, vol 11, no 2, pp207–216

IPPR (2007) *Positive Energy: Harnessing People Power to Prevent Climate Change*, Institute for Public Policy Research, London

Ipsos MORI (2009) 'The Big Energy Shift: Report from Citizens' Forums', www.big-briefs.com/big_energy_shift/Big_Energy_Shift_Final_Report_300609.pdf

Irwin, A. (1995) *Citizen Science: A Study of People, Expertise, and Sustainable Development*, Routledge, London

Jobert, A., Laborgne, P. and Mimler, S. (2007) 'Local acceptance of wind energy: Factors of success identified in French and German case studies', *Energy Policy*, vol 35, no 5, pp2751–2760

Kogaki, T., Matsumiya, H., Ushiyama, I., Nagai, H., Higashino, M., Iwasaki, N., Nakao, T. and Ogawa, S. (2007) 'Prospect of offshore wind energy development in Japan', *International Journal of Environment and Sustainable Development*, vol 1, no 4, pp304–311

Nadai, A. (2007) '"Planning", "siting" and the local acceptance of wind power: Some lessons from the French case', *Energy Policy*, vol 35, no 5, pp2715–2726

Office of the Deputy Prime Minister (2004) *Planning Policy Statement 22: Renewable Energy*, The Stationery Office, London

Owen, S., Rayner, T. and Bina, O. (2004) 'New agendas for appraisal: Reflections on theory, practice and research', *Environment and Planning A*, vol 36, no 11, pp1943–1959

Pasqualetti, M. J. (2001) 'Wind energy landscapes: Society and technology in the California desert', *Society and Natural Resources*, vol 14, pp689–699

Pedersen, E., and Persson Waye, K. (2004) 'Perception and annoyance due to wind turbine noise: A dose–response relationship', *Journal of the Acoustical Society of America*, vol 116, no 6, pp3460–3470

Pennington, M. (2002) 'A Hayekian liberal critique of collaborative planning', in P. Allemendinger and M. Tewdr-Jones (eds) *Planning Futures: New Directions for Planning Theory*, Routledge, London, pp187–205

Phipps, R. (2007) 'In the matter of Moturimu wind farm application: Evidence to the Joint Commissioners', Palmerston North, New Zealand, 8–26 March, www.ohariupreservationsociety.org.nz/phipps-moturimutestimony.pdf

Planning Act (2008) Available from the Office of Public Sector Information, www.opsi.gov.uk/acts/acts2008/ukpga_20080029_en_1

Richardson, T. (1996) 'Foucauldian discourse: Power and truth in urban and regional policy making', *European Planning Studies*, vol 4, no 3, pp279–292

Rydin, Y., and Pennington, M. (2000) Public participation and the local environmental planning: The collective action problem and the potential of social capital, *Local Environment*, vol 5, no 2, pp153–169

Tewdwr-Jones, M. and Thomas, H. (1998) 'Collaborative action in local plan-making: Planners' perceptions of "planning through debate"', *Environment and Planning B: Planning and Design*, vol 25, no 1, pp127–144

Thayer, R. L. and Hansen, H. (1988) 'Wind on the land: Renewable energy and pastoral scenery vie for dominance in the siting of wind-energy developments', *Landscape Architecture*, vol 78, no 2, pp69–73

Toke, D. (2005) 'Explaining wind power planning outcomes: Some findings from a study in England and Wales', *Energy Policy*, vol 33, no 12, pp1527–1539

Walker, G. and Devine-Wright, P. (2008) 'Community renewable energy: What should it mean?', *Energy Policy*, vol 36, no 2, pp497–500

Wolsink, M. (1994) 'Entanglement of interests and motives: Assumptions behind the NIMBY-theory on facility siting', *Urban Studies*, vol 31, no 6, pp851–866

Wolsink, M. (2007) 'Planning of renewable schemes: Deliberate and fair decision-making on landscape issues instead of reproachful accusations of non-cooperation', *Energy Policy*, vol 35, no 5, pp2692–2704

Wüstenhagen, R., Wolsink, M. and Burer, M. J. (2007) 'Social acceptance of renewable energy innovation: An introduction to the concept', *Energy Policy*, vol 35, no 5, pp2683–2691

Wynne, B. (1996) 'May the sheep safely graze? A reflexive view of the expert–lay knowledge divide', in S. Lash, B. Szerszynski and B. Wynne (eds) *Risk, Environment and Modernity: Towards a New Ecology*, Sage, London, pp44–83

Yearley, S., Cinderby, S., Forrester, J., Bailey, P. and Rosen, P. (2003) 'Participatory modelling and the local governance of the politics of UK air pollution: A three-city case study', *Environmental Values*, vol 12, no 2, pp247–262

Chapter 3

Beyond Consensus?
Agonism, Republicanism and
a Low Carbon Future

John Barry and Geraint Ellis

Introduction

The underperformance of the wind energy sector against the expectations and available wind resources in the UK has been a source of frustration to government and those wishing to see a transition to a low carbon economy. Although there has been much debate over diagnosing why there has been such a relatively slow deployment of wind power, it is the spatial planning system that is often reported as being a key cause (e.g. British Wind Energy Association, 2008). Indeed, there is a common policy discourse that portrays planning not as a system of necessary environmental regulation, but as a burdensome bureaucratic process (Department of Trade and Industry, 2007), subject to interest capture by those objecting to wind farm proposals (Hadwin, 2009; Local Government Chronicle, 2009). This discourse has been powerful enough to underpin government proposals to remove planning decisions on energy projects from arenas that may be subject to democratic control or opposition-induced delay (such as the local planning committee) and place them where they become subject to 'safer' technocratic policy processes (Healey, 1990). Initiatives range from the lifting of planning controls over micro-renewables to the Infrastructure Planning Commission (IPC) for authorizing major energy projects. The effect of this has been that the planning system has been used to assert the national interest over unwilling local host communities rather than attempts being made to use it to build local activism in support of wind power (Toke and Strachan, 2006).

We can understand this in terms of a broader approach to governance followed by New Labour in that it has:

> '*sought to depoliticize: to introduce a series of unquestionable assumptions, derive from them a necessary framework of action and then create the kind of governance structure that will help people act autonomously but always within it*' (Finlayson, 2009, p20).

Indeed, in his analysis, Finlayson suggests that this reflects an open hostility to adversarial processes, leading to key decisions bypassing the rigours of contestation and democratic debate; the very processes that have been so vital to the evolution of policy regimes in the past (e.g. Cowell and Owens, 2006). This also reflects New Labour's underlying account of the political economy of globalization and its formulation of 'ecological modernization' (Barry and Paterson, 2004), which sees State-supported technological (and labour market) innovation as essential to attracting foreign investment to drive economic growth and enhance Britain's competitiveness.

However, while these policy initiatives may induce a short-term increase in the deployment of renewable energy, it is unlikely that they will contribute to a more lasting response to the challenges of climate change and peak oil. For this there is a need for a more fundamental transformation in society's relationship with energy, including a reduction in demand. The dominant policy discourse seeks therefore to increase energy security and respond to climate change while maintaining an ultimately unsustainable increase in energy consumption (from whatever source). This is understandable when linked to the State imperative for orthodox economic growth and the growth in consumption of carbon energy (Dryzek et al, 2003). As with all Western governments, New Labour's 'ecological modernization' perspective of our energy supply effectively implies 'business as usual' in that economic growth is driven by increasing consumption of low carbon technologies and renewables[1] rather than carbon energy.

In this chapter we reflect on this wider context in order to explore alternative ways of thinking about conflict around renewable energy infrastructure, by drawing on a number of theoretical insights. In particular, we wish to elaborate on the previously made point (Smith and Marquez, 2000; Ellis et al, 2007) that in order to make sense of the struggles over wind farm proposals, we must not focus solely on those objecting to such developments, but must step back and understand both protagonists' and antagonists' viewpoints. We take this argument further here by suggesting that it may be possible to use the conflictual engagement of such disputes to the broader advantage of delivering low carbon societies. To do this, we first briefly review existing research on the disputes around wind farms and then consider some of the potential policy responses to such conflicts. We then go on to suggest that the hegemonic idea that planning practice should seek 'consensus' is not only counterproductive but also damaging to democratic ideals. In arguing this, we suggest that, by adopting agonistic practices coupled with a 'republican' political framing of objector mobilizations, it may be possible to develop more meaningful social engagement around the energy challenges we face.

Wind Farms and Discourses of Objection

There is now an extensive body of research on the social (un)acceptance of wind farms, recently summarized by Ellis et al (2009, pp10–12), who suggest that this research tells us the following:

- Local opposition is not as influential on the ultimate outcome of the planning process as often presumed, with the vast majority of wind developments successfully gaining planning consent, and with proposals very rarely being refused on the grounds of opposition alone.
- Local opposition can be fuelled by insensitive handling of proposals by local planning authorities rather than the innate views of the objectors alone.
- Although visual impact is the most common cause of opposition, it is given a low priority in the planning process.
- Regulatory and developer discourses portray opposition as somehow 'deviant', thus heightening local antagonism.
- Regulators are often seen as implicit supporters, rather than arbiters, of wind farm proposals, further encouraging oppositional activity.
- Objectors rarely oppose wind farms from a position of ignorance on climate change or energy futures.
- Local opposition to wind farms is dynamic, peaking when projects are proposed and declining once they have been implemented.

Thus, it has become clear that not only is opposition to wind farms a more complex phenomenon than dominant discourses suggest, but that in focusing on such disputes as a prime causal factor in the slow rate of wind deployment, we have overlooked a range of other opportunities to hasten the transition to a low carbon economy. Before considering how this may be so, we first want to typify the existing theoretical and policy responses to this, and other, planning conflicts.

Responding to the 'Objection' Problem

The responses to such issues of contestation in the planning system can be typified into two polarized approaches.

Deliberation and consensus-seeking

The first approach has been a suggestion that more, or better, participation around local developments such as wind farms could help in achieving consensus over siting decisions. Although often oversimplified as a theoretical perspective, such views draw heavily on the 'deliberative turn' (Healey, 1997) in planning and environmental politics (Barry, 1999) and, while dominant amongst academic commentators, it also has a strong presence within the discourse of planning policy and practice (Tewdwr-Jones and Thomas, 1998). Drawing on Habermas' concept of communicative rationality, this approach, epitomized in Healey's concept of 'collaborative planning' (Healey, 1997) has been claimed to represent a 'new paradigm' for planning (Innes, 1995) and has given much impetus to developing more effective and extensive participative processes. Although Healey's theory of collaborative planning has a number of core elements (see, e.g., Harris, 2002; Healey, 2003), it is the call for a shift from competitive interest-bargaining to consensus-building that has been identified as its dominant feature. While highly influential in shaping how we think of participation and, indeed, the purposes of the planning process itself, this approach has attracted a range of criticisms based on the *realpolitik* of planning practice (e.g. Flyvbjerg, 1998; Tewdwr-Jones and Allmendinger, 1998; Huxley, 2000). A common criticism has been that the consensus-seeking process is naive to the way in which power is exerted, with the powerful able to emasculate, coopt and 'control' the less powerful, under a veil of democratic inclusivity and popular participation (O'Neill, 2002). This is particularly acute in the case of complex planning decisions made under tight time constraints and deadlines, where 'experts' have an inbuilt position of power. While deliberative mechanisms may take the blunter edges off these asymmetries of power, they cannot render the debate truly egalitarian in the Habermasian sense required. This is particularly so when one thinks about the wider unequal and unjust social and economic contexts within which any deliberative process takes place.

Thus we accept that not only are there well-founded critiques of the collaborative paradigm, but also highlight that the types and levels of conflict in relation to wind farms make the pursuit of consensus unrealistic. Indeed, wind farm proposals induce such levels of opposition that the hope of a consensual outcome becomes idealistic – and, given that the regulatory process acts as an adjudicator rather than an arbitrator, the outcome is generally that the wind farm is permitted or it is not, with perhaps some scope for negotiating fewer or smaller turbines and, more rarely, alternative locations or compensatory measures. Yet, as we have seen, opposition is often very deep-seated and usually based on strong place-specific or cultural arguments, informed by notions of vulnerability, powerlessness, justice and sacrifice (Barry et al, 2008). Furthermore, Barry et al point out that the oppositional framing of proposals for wind energy projects can distort nuances within objector positions, thus effectively creating two artificially hegemonic oppositional blocs, rather than a more pluralistic array of positions ranked on a continuum from outright rejection to uncritical acceptance. Such debates are thus constructed around an 'either/or' logic that not only makes the pursuit of 'consensus' idealistic, but which is also positively *counterproductive* in securing more renewable energy projects. Adopting a more agonistic framing – as outlined below – can potentially provide a more fruitful way of securing a more acceptable settlement, support and governance arrangements for such projects.

Streamlining and planning reform

In contrast to the deliberative approach, what has been witnessed in the UK through the Planning Act 2008, and in a number of other jurisdictions,[2] is an actual reduction in participative opportunities to 'streamline' planning with the aim of enhancing 'investor confidence' by speeding up the regulatory process and reducing the impact of dissent. Thus, major infrastructure projects, such as wind farms, are subject to a swifter regulatory process that relies on technocratic assessments rather than politico-rational or consultative deliberation (Healey, 1991). As noted by Cowell and Owens (2006), a consequence of this planning reform has been a rescaling of the political arenas for planning decisions so that they become not only more remote from individual communities but also, critically, exert a strong influence on which conceptions of sustainable development become dominant in planning decisions. One consequence of such planning reform is that there is a closing down of 'crucial institutional spaces for challenges to the status quo' (Cowell and Owens, 2006, p405). These spaces include public inquiries, which have allowed a questioning of core policy assumptions (such as those for transport or aggregates) and, in so doing, have made a vital contribution to shaping a more sustainable (or less unsustainable) development trajectory.

The justification for this planning reform is heavily based on notions of competitiveness (Barker, 2006) and discourses that portray potential objectors as deviant and unworthy, based around the persistence of the concept of NIMBYism.[3] However, in our previous work, we have shown how those objecting to local developments (Ellis, 2004) and wind farms in particular (Ellis et al, 2007) should not be seen as dogmatic or irrational. Indeed, objectors often share many of the same citizenship concerns, in terms of tackling climate change or supporting the creation of a low carbon economy, as those supporting these developments. Not acknowledging this can lead to the idea that objectors to wind farms are something of a marginalized group, motivated by self-serving rather than public-minded goals – thus further stoking up resentment and distancing sections of the community from supporting the transition to a low carbon economy.

If we take a wider view and consider democratic decision-making as a form of collective 'problem-solving' (Barry, 1999) or 'social learning' (Habermas, 1984), we begin to see how planning reform may actually run counter to the long-term interests of wind power deployment. Szarka (2006) suggests that social learning can be applied to at least three key areas of policy; measures to increase production capacity (the Renewables Obligation); measures that affect institutional capacity (ownership, technological evolution or regulation); and those measures that foster the social capacity to accept wind power as a new form of energy production. The rationality of New Labour, as described above, has meant that government has sought to address the two former areas, but neglected the latter. Yet without more engagement on issues of social (un)acceptance, the sector will continue to struggle to develop its 'implementation capacity' (Agterbosch et al, 2009). Thus the reduction and erosion of this democratic space may serve to undermine, rather than enhance, longer-term social innovation and adaptation for our energy future. We would go beyond Szarka and argue that any debate around the transition to a low carbon future must also allow for the questioning of the implicit assumption of increased energy production and consumption. That is, the issue is not simply the 'social acceptance' of renewable energy, but also the 'social acceptance' of the need to more fundamentally challenge the way we use energy, regardless of its source (whether carbon-based or renewable).

We would therefore argue that neither of these approaches is well suited to the broader challenges of shifting to a low carbon economy and, more specifically, to the wider deployment of wind power. Based on our previous work (Ellis et al, 2007; Barry et al, 2008), combined with further reflection on political and planning theory, we suggest alternative ways of looking at how conflicts over wind farms should be conceptualized and related to the broader objectives of securing more sustainable energy systems. This involves more active engagement between those representing the spectrum of views on specific wind farm proposals, not based on the principle of 'consensus-seeking' but on other forms of settlement. This does not necessarily mean that we agree with the anti-wind lobby, but we do respect their civic entitlement to use formal and informal political processes to argue their case. Following Hillier, we therefore explore the potential of agonism in planning as a way of 'domesticating' antagonism to provide a more constructive contribution to democratic decision-making (Hillier, 2002, p122). We seek to integrate this agonistic perspective with a broader 'republican' approach to decision-making around energy in order to offer an alternative way of conceptualizing conflict over wind farm proposals.

Republicanism, Agonism and Energy Planning

Chantal Mouffe, one of the most prominent theorists of political agonism, has defined it thus:

> '*I use the concept of agonistic pluralism to present a new way to think about democracy which is different from the traditional liberal conception of democracy as a negotiation among interests and is also different from the model which is currently being developed by people like Jürgen Habermas and John Rawls ... while we desire an end to conflict, if we want people to be free we must always allow for the possibility that conflict may appear and to provide an arena where differences can be confronted. The democratic process should supply that arena*' (Mouffe, 1998).

In this way, agonism can be sharply distinguished from both consensus and antagonism. The latter denotes a situation of conflict with little prospect of any agreement, in which the only two outcomes for the protagonists are either 'winning' or 'losing'. An antagonistic encounter is founded on a simplistic and radical 'self–other' relation, which focuses on the differences rather than commonalities between agents. In contrast, 'agonism is a we/they relation where the conflicting parties, *although acknowledging that there is no rational solution to their conflict, nevertheless recognize the legitimacy of their opponents. They are "adversaries" not "enemies"* (Mouffe, 2005, p20, emphasis added).

In this way, agonism lies between 'consensus' and 'antagonism', and one could define it as being concerned (like 'consensus' approaches) with seeking agreement (or at least settlement), but doing this by using rather than suppressing antagonism. An agonistic theory insists upon preserving democratic struggle as something both *inevitable* and indeed *intrinsically good* for the health of democracy and democratic citizenship. Of the two broad approaches outlined above – consensus-seeking and streamlining/planning reform – it is clear that an agonistic approach, while disapproving of both approaches, is more critical of the latter in its attempt to depoliticize and undermine democratic decision-making processes. Equally important to emphasize is the *provisionality* inherent in agonistic politics, which is in stark contrast to the current dominant discourse of renewable energy, which is portrayed as a 'once and for all' solution, as if the widespread deployment of renewable energy or increase in nuclear power settles and definitively 'solves' the energy crisis. An agonistic perspective does not take such a definitive attitude: all settlements can be re-examined afresh, re-argued and renegotiated in the light of new circumstances, scientific evidence or normative claims.

An agonistic approach can be further developed in the case of local energy governance by a distinctively *republican* conception of democratic politics, which potentially makes it a better political frame for planning for renewable energy. Republicanism accepts pluralism (in values, lifestyles, perspectives) as a positive feature of a democratic polity, and emphasizes the importance of active citizens participating and defending the collective way of life of their free community. It is important to note that a republican politics *does not* require that there be one commonly held view of the good life, as long as the differences in viewpoint do not threaten or undermine the freedoms of the community. Furthermore, republicanism regards contestation as more important to democratic politics than consensus and agreement (Pettit, 1997), thus sharing much with the outline of agonism above. Part of the reason for this is that robust debate can help social learning and can provide imaginative solutions to problems. That is, in keeping with the deliberative approach, a republican view accepts the potential of debate and argument to result in unexpected and unforeseen collectively created solutions, which administrative, non-democratic decision-making cannot. It is also important to note that republicanism has a different conception of liberty than liberalism. For mainstream liberalism, freedom is understood as 'non-interference'; while for republicanism, liberty is seen as 'non-domination', which enables people to 'live in the presence of people but at the mercy of none' (Pettit, 1997, p80). It also opens up the possibility of the State 'interfering' in the business of individuals or private actors (such as corporations) in the name of minimizing the exercise of arbitrary power and domination of some citizens.

Here there is a need to distinguish a republican from a deliberative-democratic approach, although there is some overlap. A republican approach is not seeking consensus but rather the non-violent and solidarity-enhancing solution of encouraging people to honestly air their differences and seek settlement (even if this is an agreement to disagree), and is also pragmatic in being willing to use majoritarian decision-making rules. It may also be that a republican approach taps into some of the findings from research into wind farm disputes, in that what people want is for their concerns to be respected and not dismissed disrespectfully. This encourages the identification of common ground, but the process is not contingent on it. Therefore, even if people remain in disagreement as to the particular decision made about the siting (or not) of a renewable energy proposal, both sides are aware of the background context of their respective positions, some of which may be shared by protagonists with very different views. That is, a republican approach is marked by seeking to create a deliberative mechanism in which 'citizens of good faith can disagree, and disagree robustly and honestly'. Such processes may at least affirm/reaffirm the fact that all involved are citizens (which unites them), and this should not be lost in the public articulation of their different views on the renewable energy decision (which divides them).

A civic republican approach to energy planning would involve the open and meaningful engagement of concerned citizens (through public inquiries, citizen juries, planning appeals) with the relevant public bodies to seek what is the best for the public interest. Thus, rather than fearing open debate on wind energy proposals, it should be welcomed as an opportunity for negotiated agreement to elicit public-spiritedness and engaged citizenship. Enhancing meaningful engagement would, of course, represent a radical departure from current planning practice[4] and means that, of the two positions outlined above – deliberation and streamlining – our position is closer to the former than to the latter.

Our argument is that the impending 'energy crisis' (i.e. the 'troika' of climate change, peak oil and energy security) provides the motivation for a range of interests to engage with discussions over local energy governance. The energy crisis acts as a tableau to local disputes on wind farm proposals, yet our experience (Ellis et al, 2007; Barry et al, 2008) is that an individual's position on, for example, climate change denial does not necessarily have a strong negative impact on whether they object to a local wind farm or not. Indeed, some prominent climate change deniers, such as Sammy Wilson, former Environment Minister for Northern Ireland, had no difficulty in accommodating support for renewable energy with an alarmingly ignorant position on the anthropogenic causes of climate change (*Belfast Telegraph*, 2009). Similarly, many of those who do object to wind farms often accept the seriousness of our energy futures and may, in fact, have alternative suggestions as to how the local community can meet such challenges. Thus it is completely counterproductive – even from a strategic/instrumental point of view of wanting to 'win' – for supporters of wind energy to even insinuate that those who object are necessarily ignorant about environmental or energy issues. Hence, the call by John Prescott, for 'Age of Stupid' awards to be given to those who object to wind farms (Charlesworth, 2009) is precisely the wrong approach to take if one is seeking negotiated agreement.

Figure 3.1 is an attempt at providing a simplified conception of how we see this relating to achieving the transition to a low carbon economy. The horizontal axis shows a notional continuum running between consensus and dissensus – i.e. the degree to which communities are likely to agree on whether action is needed to meet the challenge of their energy future. On the vertical axis is the notional continuum between action and inaction on local energy. Using this, we can portray four scenarios. In the bottom-left sector, there is the situation where there is a consensus that nothing can or should be done; hence a denial of the energy crisis. The bottom-right sector is where some parties recognize that action should be taken, but disputes over the appropriate action leave the status quo intact. In this case, the political or planning institutions are unable to effectively 'domesticate' disagreements; hence stalemate, as no party is willing to negotiate. The top-left sector represents a situation where there is total consensus on the need for action; hence the ability to develop a low carbon economy. The top-right sector represents the transition option, where the need for action is recognized but the potential options (i.e. to host a wind farm or not) are contested. The situation in the UK today probably lies between the two right-hand sectors. The arrows therefore represent the potential for agonistic practice – to help shift stalemate to local bargaining,[5] with an aspiration that increased negotiation will gradually and ultimately lead to a low carbon economy.

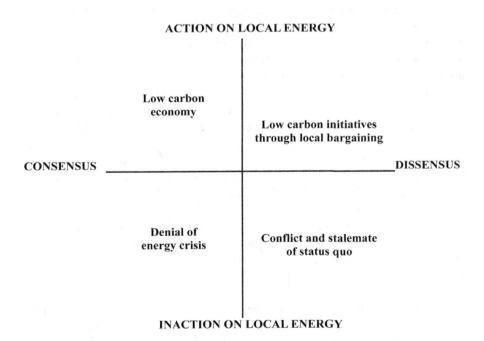

Figure 3.1 *Scenarios of local energy governance (after Hillier, 2002)*

Republicanism, Pluralism and Local Energy Governance

From a republican point of view, the key is to place local wind proposals within the wider non-local context of the 'energy crisis' and to use this to frame the bargaining of local commitments to a sustainable energy solution. This will therefore prompt debates not so much on the need to replace current forms of energy with more renewable ones, or whether we should sacrifice important landscapes to wind farms, but how the local community envisages its energy future.

From a republican point of view, the ability of communities to bargain an appropriate energy future 'package' from as wide a choice of policy options as possible is of crucial importance. One could imagine, for example, that, if a community accepted an obligation to reduce greenhouse gas emissions, it may either choose to host a local wind farm and bear any perceived deterioration in landscape quality, or alternatively commit to energy conservation equal to the emission saving offered by the wind farm. This may also mean that the community debate and agree (through a democratic process, not necessarily a consensus) that it commits to reducing car dependency, sourcing more food locally, recycling more, or reducing the carbon intensity of its waste. It could enter partnership with other institutions, such as the local authority, to become a 'low carbon zone' or 'energy action area', with the local community becoming a Transition Town (Hopkins, 2008); the installation of smart meters; or committing the local community to embark on other behavioural changes in its use of energy.

The measures through which individuals or communities express their 'opt in' to tackle the 'energy crisis', could thus take a variety of forms other than dutifully (or resentfully) acquiescing to the mass deployment of renewable energy proposals. *In short, positively contributing to the transition to a low carbon energy future cannot be reduced to renewable energy production: a much longer list of possible actions that authorities, businesses and civil society organizations, as well as citizens, can take is urgently required.* It is therefore problematic that the policy discourse around the 'energy crisis' is dominated by the 'predict and provide' model. Clearly, energy efficiency and energy conservation are part of the policy discourse, but they do not receive a fraction of the government support and commercial interest that the 'rush for wind' or 'dash for nuclear' models receive. A key reason for this is that, while efficiency and conservation can contribute to economic growth, by focusing on reducing energy *use and consumption*, they do not have the same returns on economic growth as low carbon energy *production*. Thus any local bargaining around the deployment of wind farms would be hampered by a failure to allow non-production decarbonizing options to be included in the discussion and a lack of focus on the 'big picture' of the energy question.

This could be further facilitated through a national low carbon energy plan that can be disaggregated to the devolved regions, and from there down to local authority level, to ensure proportionate and fair emissions reductions by everyone. One local authority region may opt for wind farms, another may opt to reduce its energy consumption rather than increasing its renewable energy production, or may take into account building construction and maintenance, land use, food production and consumption and spatial planning.

Such approaches are being pioneered by the Transition Movement and they could, in partnership with local and national governments, help to facilitate and broker local carbon reduction targets. As a grassroots organization, the Transition Movement can operate to achieve solutions to the energy crisis at the local level which would be impossible to articulate or achieve through State-led initiatives. The Transition Movement's focus on localized 'energy descent planning' (Hopkins, 2008) serves as a useful counterpoint to the dominant official energy narrative of the State in the UK and provides a valuable pluralistic element to this debate. Here we come full circle in reference to the argument made above about the underlying expansionist, pro-growth imperative at the heart of the energy policy, which has crowded out non-expansionist policy options, effectively substituting 'carbon lock-in' with 'low carbon energy expansion lock-in'. Until the latter is removed as the non-negotiable imperative framing the debate around energy futures, it is difficult to see how the 'either/or' logic of local renewable energy proposals can be decisively broken so as to facilitate a greater plurality of options being available to local communities.

Conclusions: Beyond Consensus and 'beyond Energy' to Get beyond Carbon?

The argument we have outlined is that, by allowing a greater range of options for communities to choose *how* (but not *whether*) they 'do their bit', changes their incentive structure to allow a greater range of low carbon options to be negotiated in each locality. This requires moving beyond a focus on energy production to include reducing energy consumption, increasing, efficiency and adopting non-energy carbon options such as 'green' waste management, food, transport, housing etc. This would require a major reformulation of the institutions in which energy and development are regulated; for example, changing *land use planning* to *energy descent planning*. Indeed, a rethink of the regulatory system is necessary in order to provide the appropriate context for the bargaining we have outlined here, with a need for a nationwide low carbon energy strategy in which communities (spatial or aspatial) know that they *must* achieve carbon reduction targets, but with a degree of flexibility about how they do this. This may (paradoxically) deliver more renewable energy deployment than one which narrowly focuses on the installation of renewable energy technologies. However, the greater penetration of renewable energy is not the only, or indeed the most, important consideration – it is but one among a variety of means by which the transition to a low carbon economy can be achieved. We need to take a 'bigger view' than renewable energy production as the only way in which we can create a sustainable energy future: allowing communities the option, for example, that a sustainable energy future may be one that uses less energy.

Given the scale of the task to transform our energy economy and the relatively short time frame – a decade or so to meet government carbon reduction targets – this transition to a low carbon economy will be difficult. The key is to engage those who object to wind and other renewable energy projects, while at the same time abandoning the counterproductive search for 'consensus' and instead adopting a more robust republican and agonistic-pluralist approach. Such open and honest (if also robust and administratively 'messy') republican decision-making procedures could, if also backed by public enforceable targets for each locality, produce not only compromise agreements but also innovative and creative responses to our energy challenge. If 'necessity is the mother of invention', then we currently do not have the 'incentive structure' and creative space within which communities are given targets but then left to decide themselves how they should be achieved.

We are beginning to understand how the inevitable transformation of our energy economy will impact on virtually every aspect of our carbon-based society, yet we have not worked out how to include people whose lives will be affected in the decisions which will lead to those changes. This is not just the confirmation of an important political principle (i.e. those who suffer laws and policies should have some part in their making) but also for eminently practical reasons. We believe that we are *more*, not *less*, likely to get people supporting the types of changes needed if we include them in the decision-making process.

Notes

1. We do not see these terms ('low carbon' and 'renewable') as interchangeable, since low carbon includes nuclear energy, which is non-renewable.
2. The Planning Act 2008 in England and Wales proposes a number of streamlining proposals very similar to those already adopted in the Republic of Ireland (The Planning and Development [Strategic Infrastructure] Act, 2006), The Netherlands (2004 Spatial Planning Bill) and in Norway (see Cowell and Owens, 2006).
3. For example, NIMBYs are blamed for delays in the planning process by Scottish Power in their response to the Barker Review (www.hm-treasury.gov.uk/d/scottish_power.pdf), while the final report of the Review (Table 3 in Barker 2006) reproduces evidence from the annual 'NIMBY survey' carried out by the Saint Consulting Group (see http://tscg.co.uk/survey/summary.html).
4. We do recognize that this poses significant institutional and policy challenges and, while we do not make any detailed procedural proposals that accompany our more normative argument here, we acknowledge that this is an area that needs further exploration.
5. As noted in Hillier (2002), while consensus may be sought through deliberative processes, compromise is achieved through bargaining and voting.

References

Agterbosch, S., Meertens, R. M. and Vermeulen, W. J. V. (2009) 'The relative importance of social and institutional conditions in the planning of wind power projects', *Renewable and Sustainable Energy Reviews*, vol 13, no 2, pp393–405

Barker, K. (2006) *Barker Review of Land Use Planning*, HM Treasury, London

Barry, J. (1999) *Rethinking Green Politics: Nature, Virtue and Progress*, Sage, London

Barry, J. and Paterson, M. (2004) 'Globalisation, ecological modernisation and New Labour', *Political Studies*, vol 52, no 4, pp767–784

Barry, J., Ellis, G. and Robinson, C. (2008) 'Cool rationalities and hot air: A rhetorical approach to understanding debates on renewable energy', *Global Environmental Politics*, vol 8, no 2, pp67–98

Belfast Telegraph (2009) 'DUP call for green investment "not at odds with Sammy Wilson"', 17 February, www.belfasttelegraph.co.uk/news/politics/dup-call-for-green-investment-not-at-odds-with-sammy-wilson-14191572.html

British Wind Energy Association (2008) *Wind Energy in the UK: A BWEA State of the Industry Report*, BWEA, London

Charlesworth, A. (2009) 'Prescott proposes stupidity awards for wind farm "nimbys"', *BusinessGreen*, www.businessgreen.com/business-green/news/2248512/prescott-proposes-stupidity

Cowell, R. and Owens, S. (2006) 'Governing space: Planning reform and the politics of sustainability', *Environment and Planning C: Government and Policy*, vol 24, no 3, pp403–421

Department of Trade and Industry (2007) *Meeting the Energy Challenge: A White Paper on Energy*, The Stationery Office, London

Dryzek, J., Downs, D., Hernes, H. K. and Schlosberg, D. (2003) *Green States and Social Movements*, Oxford University Press, Oxford

Ellis, G. (2004) 'Discourses of objection: Towards an understanding of third-party rights in planning', *Environment and Planning A*, vol 36, no 9, pp1549–1570

Ellis, G., Barry, J. and Robinson, C. (2007) 'Many ways to say "no", different ways to say "yes": Applying Q-methodology to understand public acceptance of windfarm proposals', *Journal of Environmental Planning and Management*, vol 50, no 4, pp517–551

Ellis, G., Cowell, R., Warren, C., Strachan, P. and Szarka, J. (2009) 'Wind power: Is there a "planning problem"?' and 'Expanding Wind Power: a problem of planning, or of perception?', *Journal of Planning Theory and Practice*, vol 10, no 4, pp521–547

Finlayson, A. (2009) 'Planning people: The ideology and rationality of New Labour', *Planning Practice and Research*, vol 24, no 1, pp11–22

Flyvbjerg, B. (1998) *Rationality and Power*, Chicago University Press, Chicago

Habermas, J. (1984) *The Theory of Communicative Action*, Vols 1 and 2, translated by T. McCarthy, Beacon Press, Boston, MA

Hadwin, R. (2009) 'The problems of planning: A developer's perspective', *Journal of Planning Theory and Practice*, vol 10, no 4, pp521–547

Harris, N. (2002) 'Collaborative planning: from theoretical foundations to practice forms', in P. Allmendinger and M. Tewdwr-Jones (eds) *Planning Futures: New Directions for Planning Theory*, Routledge, London, pp21–43

Healey, P. (1990) 'Policy processes in planning', *Policy and Politics*, vol 18, no 1, pp91–103

Healey, P. (1997) *Collaborative Planning: Shaping Places in Fragmented Societies*, Macmillan, Basingstoke, UK

Healey, P. (2003) 'Collaborative planning in perspective', *Planning Theory*, vol 2, no 2, pp101–123

Hillier, J. (2002) 'Direct action and agonism in democratic planning practice', in P. Allmendinger and M. Tewdwr-Jones (eds) *Planning Futures: New Directions for Planning Theory*, Routledge, London, pp110–135

Hopkins, R. (2008) *The Transition Handbook: From Oil Dependency to Local Resilience*, Green Books, Totnes, Devon, UK

Huxley, M. (2000) 'The limits to communicative planning', *Journal of Planning Education and Research*, vol 19, no 4, pp369–377

Innes, J. (1995) 'Planning theory's emerging paradigm: Communicative practice and interactive practice', *Journal of Planning Education and Research*, vol 14, no 3, pp183–190

Local Government Chronicle (2009) 'Prescott blasts wind farm "nimbys"', 26 August, www.lgcplus.com/news/environment/prescott-blasts-wind-farm-nimbys/5005648.article

Mouffe, C. (1998) 'Hearts, minds and radical democracy', *Red Pepper*, www.redpepper.org.uk/Hearts-Minds-and-Radical-Democracy

Mouffe, C. (2005) *On the Political: Thinking in Action*, Routledge, London

O'Neill, J. (2002) 'The rhetoric of deliberation: Some problems in Kantian theories of deliberative democracy', *Res Publica*, vol 8, no 3, pp249–268

Pettit, P. (1997) *Republicanism: A Theory of Freedom and Government*, Oxford University Press, Oxford

Szarka, J. (2006) 'Wind power, policy learning and paradigm change', *Energy Policy*, vol 34, no 17, pp3041–3048

Smith, E. and Marquez, M. (2000) 'The other side of the NIMBY syndrome', *Society and Natural Resources*, vol 13, no 3, pp273–280

Tewdwr-Jones, M. and Allmendinger, P. (1998) 'Deconstructing communicative rationality: A critique of Habermasian collaborative planning', *Environment and Planning A*, vol 30, no 11, pp1975–1989

Tewdwr-Jones M. and Thomas, H. (1998) 'Collaborative action in local plan-making: Planners' perceptions of "planning through debate"', *Environment and Planning B: Planning and Design*, vol 25, no 1, pp127–144

Toke, D. and Strachan, P. A. (2006) 'Ecological modernisation and wind power in the UK', *European Environment*, vol 16, no 3, pp155–166

Chapter 4

Public Roles and Socio-technical Configurations: Diversity in Renewable Energy Deployment in the UK and Its Implications

Gordon Walker and Noel Cass

Introduction

There is no doubt that renewable energy, as a category, is becoming increasingly heterogeneous in technological forms, scales and applications. In our previous work we have argued that this heterogeneity has implications for the forms of social relation between 'publics' and technologies that are being brought forward in shifts towards a low carbon transformation of the energy system (Walker and Cass, 2007). Drawing on perspectives and analytical tools from science and technology studies, we argued that a far more embedded and multidimensional conceptualization of the roles, engagements and potentiality of 'the public' within the energy system is, as a consequence, now required. In this chapter we revisit and rework the analysis and arguments made in our earlier study, contextualize these in the ongoing evolution of renewable energy technologies, infrastructures and applications in the UK, and draw out wider set of implications concerned with the dynamics involved, processes of activation and interconnection and the characteristics of spatial and social profiles.

Our objectives in the context of this book are twofold:

1. To bring some distinctive conceptual ideas and language into the discussion about renewable energy technologies and how the public engages with these.

2. To broaden perspectives on how the public and renewable energy are related beyond the dominant focus on questions of acceptability, local responses to development projects and how engagement operates between developers and local communities.

While these questions are important, and we have ourselves focused on them at some length (see Chapter 1 in this volume), there are many other important points of encounter and connection and many other roles into which publics can be cast. Identifying these roles and their interrelation is a necessary first step towards pursuing a more expansive and varied future research agenda, and thinking more creatively about policy and practice implications. We begin by briefly outlining the conceptual foundations of our analysis, then discussing its component parts in the context of recent and ongoing developments in the UK energy scene.

Configurations of the Social and Technical

At the core of our analysis, as shown in Figure 4.1 is the integrated configuration of relations between technologies, modes of social organization and public roles. This geometry has its underpinning in the literature, in science and technology studies which conceive technologies not simply as designed and engineered material objects, but as embedded components of socio-technical systems – in which producers, infrastructures, users, consumers, regulators and other intermediaries are all embroiled (Bijker et al, 1987; Coutard, 1999; Elzen et al, 2004). Under such a conceptualization, it is argued that the technical and the social are co-constitutive, continually interacting and shaping each other, with exchanges in both directions (Bijker and Law, 1992). Accordingly, we can conceive renewable energy technologies not simply as a series of engineered artefacts performing energy conversions, but as configurations of the social and technical which have emerged contingently in particular contexts.

A key focus here needs to be on the relationships between an object and the surrounding actors, including, importantly for our analysis, 'the public' as users, consumers, customers and so on (Akrich, 1992). Technology and system develop-

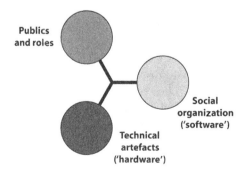

Figure 4.1 *The configuration of technology, social organization and publics*

ers ascribe imagined roles for actors, which they may or may not take up, and spaces in which they may or may not operate (Bijker, 1995). These actors, in turn, can devise their own roles and alternative meanings for objects that have interpretive flexibility in how they are understood and represented. Understanding how changes in socio-technical systems take place therefore requires an analysis that recognizes the interactive roles of multiple actors at different scales of activity (Elzen and Wieczorek, 2005), the structural factors and distributions of power and agency that promote and constrain potential trajectories (Klein and Kleinmann, 2002), and the patterns of everyday practice (Shove, 2003) in which technologies are implicated.

In applying these ideas to renewable energy as a category of energy generation technology (broadly defined), we can progress through examining the three parts of Figure 4.1. First the technological artefacts involved (or, in shorthand, the 'hardware'); second, the modes of social organization involved (or, in shorthand, the 'software'); and third, the roles of 'publics'.

Technical Artefacts: Diversity in Hardware

In our earlier paper (Walker and Cass, 2007) we emphasized the increasing diversity of the artefacts and engineered objects that are contained within renewable energy as a socially constructed category. Only one common characteristic is shared – that, through generating useable energy in the form of electricity or heat, the resource base is not depleted or significantly diminished – and little else besides. An offshore wind farm has little in common, physically or technically, with a woodchip-burning boiler or a photovoltaic (PV) cell. We also emphasized 'hyper-sizeability', in that renewable energy technologies can be implemented at markedly different material sizes ranging from macro, down to meso, micro and pico sizes of implementation.

In both these respects, recent developments in the UK are continuing to increase the diversity of hardwares. For example, a plethora of new forms of marine technology devices are currently being developed, trialled and deployed around the coast of the UK. Each of these has distinctive physical and technical characteristics with little commonality beyond their reliance on the movement of sea water to generate electricity. Some of these new hardwares are intended as fairly discrete and limited implementations to capture particular strong water flows (e.g. tidal stream technologies); while some of the new wave devices may have the potential (if proven) for scaling up to become installations of many hundreds of devices flexibly deployed in offshore arrays.

In the wind sector, both sizing up and sizing down can be observed. Ever larger commercial turbines are being deployed, in ever larger-scale wind farms, with the imminent third round of offshore development identifying even larger areas of the seabed extending much further offshore than in the past. Simultaneously the range of applications of micro-wind is increasing, including those for domestic roofs, and the powering of rural road signs, canal barges and the like. There is some continuity in physical appearance between the pico size and the macro size turbine (they have blades, hubs and columns), but also much that is different.

Biomass generation is in the process of dramatically sizing up. Contrast the established small-scale domestic wood burner, providing heat for household use, with the series of radically larger-sized, industrial-scale biomass facilities currently being planned for the generation of electricity around the UK. Just one of these, planned for Port Talbot in South Wales and importing woodchip from overseas, is intended to generate 350MW of electricity, approximately 70 per cent of the Welsh renewables target for 2010.

This increasing diversity in form and size of hardware has various implications for relations to publics. First it is becoming increasingly difficult to talk about renewable energy as a coherent technical category, about which attitudes or opinions are voiced (a point to be returned to later). We should expect, and maybe hope for, more differentiation and sophistication than such general categories can allow – even categories of marine, wind, biomass and solar are becoming increasingly problematic. Second, the geography of renewable energy generation is becoming increasingly stretched and complex: the immediate urban rooftop, the hills and valleys of rural spaces, the water-filled landscapes of marine environments – and more besides – are each now acting as the sites of energy generation. It then becomes increasingly difficult to generalize about the interaction of technologies with types of places/spaces, as their relational qualities can be quite distinct. The interaction between a largely underwater tidal stream device and its socio-environment is quite different from the urban-industrial multi-megawatt biomass plant and its socio-environment. Third, matters of proximity and familiarity are becoming highly differentiated. Renewable energy hardwares are, on the one hand, becoming incredibly familiar, taken for granted and proximate to bodies and everyday practices (at one extreme the solar-powered calculator or watch, for example); while at the same time becoming increasingly remote and hidden away in offshore spaces, with a spectrum of other proximal orientations in between. These competing movements again question the integrity of the renewable energy category, stretching the social positioning and everyday meaning of relevant technical artefacts to an extreme degree.

Modes of Social Organization: Diversity in Software

The second element of the configuration shown in Figure 4.1 is the 'software' of social and infrastructural organization through which alternative 'hardwares' are utilized and given purpose and meaning: see Van Vliet (2002), Chappells (2003) and Southerton et al (2004) for discussions related to various sustainable technologies. Drawing from such literature, we have argued that what makes up the software of social organization for renewable energy implementation is a combination of different interacting arrangements and relations between actors and institutions that can be extrapolated from the four sets of questions in Table 4.1.

Table 4.1 *The key elements of social organization*

Elements of social organization	Key questions
Function and service	What is the generated energy being used for in terms of the services (comfort, warmth, visibility, mobility etc.) that it is providing? Who utilizes these potential services and what physical and institutional distance is there between the point of energy production and the point of service 'consumption'?
Ownership and return	Who owns the technology and how is this ownership organized (privately, publicly, collectively) and at what scale (locally, nationally, internationally)? What benefits, monetary or otherwise, are returned as a consequence of ownership?
Management and operation	Who manages, controls and maintains the hardware and how is this organized (privately, publicly, collectively; locally, remotely)? To what extent is management regulated and through what principles and mechanisms?
Infrastructure and networking	Is the energy that is generated fed into an electricity or heat network (is it on or off grid?) and if so what scale of network (local, regional or national)? What/who does this network supply and how is it managed (locally, distantly, publicly or by regulated market)?

The key point here is that there are a large number of permutations to how these four sets of questions can be answered individually and in combination. Any one combination of hardware form and size does not *necessarily* imply any one particular configuration of social organization; alternatives are always theoretically available. It is then a question of which hardware and software combinations become configurations that 'work' at a particular place and time, and which remain unrealized or marginalized.

To demonstrate this point in our previous paper (Walker and Cass, 2007), we identified five different modes of implementation that have been utilized for organizing renewable energy generation in the UK – public utility, private supplier, community, household and business – each of which represents different combinations of the elements of social organization in Table 4.1.

Looking across the current and ongoing development of this profile of modes of implementation in the UK, we can comment in various ways. The 'public utility' mode in which publicly owned organizations act as monopolistic generators and suppliers of energy to consumers has now entirely disappeared from the UK scene (although leaving behind a legacy of now privatized large-scale reservoir hydroelectric project (HEP) installations). The 'private sector' mode is now very much dominant. The entrepreneurship and capital investment of the private sector, combined with the use of a series of market incentives, has grown the total contribution of renewables to electricity supply from 1.8 per cent in 1990 to 5.5 per cent in, 2008. There is now a diversity of energy generators involved: major utilities such as npower, E.ON and Scottish Power, as well as more specialist companies. Under this mode, 'green' electricity has become a distinct commodity, with a diversity of tariffs available.

The third mode, 'community', was brought into the mainstream of UK energy policy in the early 2000s (Walker et al, 2007). In our previous work we noted that, by late 2004, an estimated 500 'community' projects (variously defined: Walker and Devine-Wright, 2008), predominantly in rural areas, were under development. Many more have since been added, particularly in Scotland (Adams, 2008; van der Horst, 2008), and a recent report has identified a signifi-cant potential for further economically efficient expansion at a community scale (Energy Saving Trust, 2009). Community projects have implemented various technologies at meso and micro sizes, and utilized a multiplicity of configurations of the different elements of social organization. A recent review has, for example, identified multiple ways in which complete or partial community ownership of renewable energy generation is being achieved (Walker, 2008).

The fourth mode, 'household', has been the focus of much rhetorical and some material attention. Recent policy initiatives have promoted the diffusion of a wide range of technologies; infrastructures of technology supply, marketing and support have begun to emerge; and a shift to feed-in tariff incentive arrangements in 2010 is expected to significantly boost the economic viability of home genera-tion. In the household mode, the deployment of technology is necessarily localized; however, different models of ownership, operation, management and networking can still be utilized.

The fifth mode we have renamed here as 'organizational' (rather than business), to encompass both private and public sector organizations. This mode shares much in common with the 'household' mode except that it is organizations of diverse sizes and sectors – retail, leisure, manufacturing, farming, educational, health, local government – that are the locus of implementation, producing electricity at their own property for their own use and/or grid supply. A range of technologies are being used, at meso as well as micro sizes, under a diversity of models of ownership, management and return.

Excluding 'public utility', each of these modes of implementation all now coexist in the UK in an evolving 'constellation' of co-provisioning (Van Vliet et al, 2005, p71). Each of them is also internally diverse, containing different possible combinations of technology and social organization. Socio-technical heterogene-ity and innovation in hardware and software therefore continues to characterize the evolving pattern of renewable energy implementation in the UK, and since our earlier paper there is ever more evidence of this trend.

Forms of Social Relation:
Diversity in Public Roles

Having laid out the heterogeneity of 'renewable energy' as a socio-technical category, we now come to the third element of our framework – 'the public'. Our core argument is that ongoing diversification of hardwares and softwares is matched by diversification in their social relations with publics. We characterize this diversity in terms of 'public roles'. Our argument is that the different modes of renewable energy implementation we have discussed have a spectrum of ways in which people, or 'the public' in a more general sense, are or may be implicated. We have separated out ten such roles, as in Table 4.2.

There are several initial points to be made about these ten roles. First, the roles are not independent from the modes of social organization previously discussed, but are to varying degrees embedded within them and structured by them. It has been argued in various literatures that there are many different 'publics', that 'the

Table 4.2 *Public roles and renewable energy*

Captive consumers	Pay bills to established energy supplier
Active customers	Actively choose between suppliers, including green tariffs which partially or entirely involve renewable generation.
Service users	Use the services (light, heat, motion etc.) provided by energy generated using renewable technologies, potentially in many different everyday settings and forms and function of building.
Financial investors	Invest in shareholding or interest-earning arrangements relating to specific projects, to the broad financing of renewable energy projects, or to the investment choices of particular companies.
Local beneficiaries	Receive benefits in addition to energy services; financial, infrastructural, educational, technological or intangible. Such benefits are increasingly negotiated in formal (planning) engagement.
Project protestors	Actively object to projects through, for example, organization of a local protest group, attending meetings, writing to the press, lobbying, signing petitions etc.
Project supporters	Actively engage in similar actions to protestors, although support is typically less visibly organized and vocal.
Project participants	Get involved in community mode of implementation, including membership of organizing groups, attending meetings, or hands-on installation or maintenance.
Technology hosts	Owners of buildings or land used for hosting technology, but not the renewable energy technology itself.
Energy producers	Directly own and operate generation technologies of different forms.

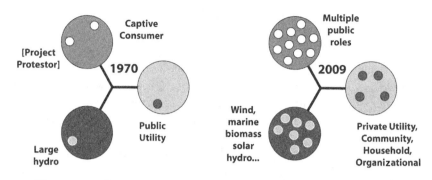

Figure 4.2 *Comparing diversity in hardwares, softwares and public roles between 1970 and 2009*

public' is not one thing, but is plural and is differentiated and demarcated in many different ways. It is also argued that 'publics' do not exist as such, but are imagined, inscripted and produced through various practices, such as when designing, deploying and debating about technologies (Maranta et al, 2003; Marres, 2005). In this light, as configurations of renewable energy technology and social organization have evolved over recent decades, we can see that new and distinct social roles have not simply emerged, but have been actively produced.

Figure 4.2 makes the point by characterizing the situation in 1970 and at the present day. If we look back to the universal 'public utility' mode of 1970, the configuration of renewable energy technology, social organization and public roles could be simply characterized. There were large-scale HEP stations, operated by public utilities, and the primary public role was that of 'captive consumers' paying electricity bills to their one and only possible supplier. No other renewable energy technologies or modes of social organization existed, and public roles only extended sporadically to 'project protestors' opposing new HEP installation development. The public was viewed *en masse* as citizens with rights to universal provision of electricity, however that might be generated.

Roll forward nearly 40 years and there are many available patterns of configuration, and many more simultaneous public roles being enacted. As different modes of social organization have emerged, they have structured particular public roles. The 'private supplier' mode redefines customers as active consumers able to choose between tariffs and actively select a green electricity supply, and also to act as investors in green funds. It reflects a neoliberal ideology that individualizes, segments and privileges private choice above community. The 'community' mode, in contrast, imagines people very much as collectives rather than individuals – as participants in community processes or local beneficiaries from community projects, collectively contributing and collectively receiving in various forms of local solidarity. The 'household' mode transgresses the producer-consumer to now define publics not only as consumers but also as energy producers, appealing to the logics of responsibility and efficiency as well as independence and self-reliance.

Second, while some roles might be embedded and produced in these ways by system or mode advocates, there are others that are defined externally to them. Here the role of project protestors is particularly significant as a self-activated engagement that resists the implementation of particular socio-technical configurations. The relation between degrees of protest or support and forms of configuration is interesting to explore. As it has already been pointed out, technology hardwares of different forms and sizes occupy very different spaces and have very different degrees of physical presence and impact. This alone might point us towards expecting some form–size hardware combinations to be seen as quite unproblematic by local publics, while others are reacted against in strongly emotional and emphatic ways – and both size and form might act independently in such distinctions.

However, as the literature on public attitudes to technology developments in general, and renewable energy technologies specifically, has emphasized, it is not only the material impact of technologies that matters. Issues of the distribution of benefits, trust in those responsible for project development and operation, the process of decision-making, and other social and political dimensions can also be paramount. In this light, the parameters of social organization or software can also be very much part of the subjectivities and associated political activity which develop around particular renewable energy developments. A project that is identical in physical terms (form and size) may accordingly be viewed differently if it is owned and managed under private utility mode, community mode or organizational mode, depending upon how people view the different actors involved, the use of the energy that is generated, the income that is produced, the process of development that has been applied, and so on. In this light, we can speculate that people may make increasingly fine distinctions between the particular configurations of hardware and software that they encounter.

Third, and a related point, the existence of these multiple roles provides the potential for a diversity of everyday encounters and interactions with energy technology, both in an abstract and in a material sense – stretching the renewable energy category yet further. People signing up for a green tariff or investing in green funds engage with renewable energy as an abstracted and spatially distanced category. They may well have imagined of what they are supporting or paying for, but this lacks a direct knowable and perceivable material form. In stark contrast, when acting as participants in community projects or as household microgenerators, people interact with the material implementation of specific forms and sizes of technology in a place – the landscape, the village, the household, the seascape – and with the specific social arrangements that are applied. In mobilizing as protestors against prospective developments, people may engage both with the generality of renewable energy as a means of energy production or carbon reduction, and the specifics of an unwanted project in a particular location. Furthermore, in each of these encounters and across the various roles, technology may readily take on different meanings and identities – an anonymous engineered artefact, an expression of ethical principle, a means of community empowerment, a commercial opportunity or a symbol of cultural defilement.

Implications for Low Carbon Transition

Having now discussed the three related elements of our analysis, for the remainder of the chapter we consider some of the implications for low carbon transitions. There is an enormous impetus around carbon mitigation and materializing a low carbon transition in the energy system over tightening time scales. UK energy policy is now directly orientated to this task, and the growth of renewable energy generation is a key part of objectives and targets: the current UK objective is to generate 15 per cent of all UK energy by 2020, from 2.25 per cent in 2008 (HM Government, 2009). Embedded within the current profile of relevant policy is much of the technical, and to some degree the social, diversity that we have discussed. While, as noted earlier, some technology categories (wind and biomass) and one mode of organization (private utility) are currently dominant over others, there is recognition, at least, of the need to support greater socio-technical heterogeneity. The need to engage and mobilize publics in various ways behind the growth of renewable energy generation is also recognized, but exactly how this is might be enacted and how it intersects with the set of roles we have identified is worthy of closer examination. Here we do so in three respects: considering the significance of different roles; matters of interconnection; and questions of social and spatial differentiation.

The significance of different roles

While multiple roles can be identified, they are not all equal. We first note that only one is overtly negative or problematic for technology advocacy and development – the project protestor who, in the media and in political debate, is often accorded great significance and obstructive power (Walker et al, 2010). No other roles have this character, but instead fall somewhere along a spectrum from being overtly supportive to more ambivalently positioned. Service users, for example, may be experiencing the energy services produced from renewable energy technologies in a building – light or heat, for example – without having any explicit knowledge that it is from a renewable energy source. They have no inherent direct engagement, but may potentially make judgements about the quality of the energy service that is being provided. However, if such users are actively made aware that they are in a building with renewable energy technologies through means of displays or publicity, maybe (although it is a significant maybe) this will have significance for how they orientate themselves subjectively towards either the specific technology configurations involved or renewable energy more generally. Other roles are more obviously essential – community projects cannot emerge without willing participants, and microgeneration will not grow without householders who are prepared to become energy producers. These roles thus become central to the socio-technical configurations that policy measures may seek to support.

Interconnection and clustering

Related to these points are questions about how different roles cluster, interrelate and interconnect. As the ten roles are not mutually exclusive, but rather can be simultaneously embodied and enacted, they may in principle interact through learning mechanisms. Certainly there are assumptions embedded in policy which do envisage such learning taking place. For example, one of the motives for government support for community renewables was that work could be done on 'hearts and minds' (Walker et al, 2007), improving understanding of unfamiliar technologies and making people feel more positive about renewable energy in general – thereby reducing public opposition to wind farms. In terms of the roles we have identified, a learning mechanism was presumed between the roles of participant/beneficiary and protestor; the former serving to erode the latter. However, this mechanism may well not exist if the distinctions between different modes of social organization and between the general and specific meanings of renewable energy discussed above are paramount. The same person might quite reasonably be a protestor against a large-scale wind farm proposed by an internationally owned utility and at the same time an active participant in a community hydroelectric project (HEP) in the same locality, and a producer in their own home.

Spatial and social profiles

A related and final question is the extent to which different socio-technical configurations and public roles are likely to have particular spatial and social profiles. If we focus on urban spaces as an example, we can ask what configurations work better in urban spaces, what attracts certain configurations and certain roles and resists or limits others? In physical and material terms, there is much in urban spaces that limits the availability of renewable energy resource flows and the technological possibilities for capturing these. Where urban resource flows are available to be tapped – such as in urban wind – the accepted standards of separation from people limit the scale of deployment typically to single turbines, and at smaller sizes than in rural and marine spaces. In this sense, the urban population *'en masse'* is cast in the role of a negatively impacted population and thereby potential protestors, limiting the scope for capturing a technically available resource. Where the material form of cities does, however, enable sustainable technologies is through the multiplicity of built structures which can physically accommodate and host modular technologies such as solar hot water and photovoltaic (PV) panels; and for locally networked heating systems fuelled by biomass, heat pump, waste to energy, or geothermal power. Here the density of buildings, people and energy demand become not constraints but positive, if not essential, dimensions of what makes particular configurations of hardware and software possible.

In considering social profiles and differentiations, we can focus on urban inhabitants, their everyday lives and the possibilities for taking up certain of the ten roles in relation to some renewable energy technologies and not others. For the urban middle classes, there are possibilities for embodying multiple roles despite the material limits to technology implementation within the physical spaces of cities. The 'reasonably well off' urban dweller can still form spatially extended relationships with a diversity of renewable energy technologies through becoming an active consumer choosing a (normally more expensive) green tariff; an investor in share issues for near or, more likely, distant cooperative community projects; and very directly through becoming a producer, installing and operating microgeneration technology on their own property. In each of these roles, the availability of finance and the ability to commit 'spare' resources is necessary and enabling.

For low-income urban populations, the roles of active consumer, investor and producer are more problematic, with various kinds of structural barriers in place. Beyond the problem of having limited financial resources, low-income households who rent rather than own their property (and its associated electricity and heating infrastructure) are unable to instigate their own installation of microgeneration technology. Households on pre-payment metered tariffs (a particular characteristic of payment arrangements in the UK, sometimes imposed by energy suppliers as well as being 'chosen' by customers) are unable to engage in green tariffs, and often – in fact – pay the highest rates of all.

Such observations suggest that the trends and potential futures for relations between publics and renewable energy technology (RET) may not be accessible to all, but are likely to produce inequalities in the profiles of the roles that can be taken up – with disadvantaged urban residents possibly unable to move much beyond the 'captive consumer' category. However, the extent to which this is the case is dependent both upon which modes of socio-technical configuration are pursued and exactly how these are implemented. For example, 'community' modes, which embody social goals and outcomes with an egalitarian rather than market-driven logic, can intentionally direct actions towards disadvantaged and energy-poor households (Walker, 2008). There is some debate about the extent to which urban communities exhibit the characteristics of high social capital and networking which may be required for effective community action, but this does not preclude the possibility of community projects that are more driven by urban local authorities, housing associations and third-sector organizations (Walker and Devine-Wright, 2008).

Conclusions

Our objective in our original paper (Walker and Cass, 2007) and in this chapter has been to open up the study of renewable energy and the public to a different conceptual perspective and also to a recognition of the profound changes – or indeed innovations – that have taken place in the social as well as the technical landscape of renewable energy implementation. We have accordingly performed much 'opening up' but relatively little 'closing down', beyond some rather speculative comments on different dimensions of the more complex picture we have presented and a partial exploration of some evident policy implications in a UK context. Looking forward, we would hope that others will find value in following some of the ideas and lines of enquiry that we have laid out. Those that we see as most intriguing and significant include how renewable energy technologies take on different meanings and associations, how publics differentiate between socio-technical configurations, how multiple public roles are interconnected, and the forms of social and spatial differentiation that are likely to emerge. We would also hope that researchers in other countries might investigate whether the analysis we have laid out is specific to the UK context or whether we have isolated broader patterns and trends of change that are mirrored elsewhere.

Acknowledgements

We are grateful to academic colleagues, and those in policy, non-governmental and business communities who have discussed the ideas in this chapter with us and contributed to its refinement. Funding was made available by the UK Research Councils' Energy Programme under award number RES-152-25-1008.

References

Adams, S. (2008) *Local Carbon Communities: A Study of Community Energy Projects in the UK*, Rural Community Carbon Network, www.ruralnet.com

Akrich, M. (1992) 'The de-scription of technical objects', in W. E. Bijker and J. Law (eds) *Shaping Technology/Building Society: Studies in Sociotechnical Change*, MIT Press, London

Bijker, W. E. (1995) *Of Bicycles, Bakelites and Bulbs: Toward a Theory of Sociotechnical Change*, MIT Press, Cambridge, MA

Bijker, W. E. and Law, J. (eds) (1992) *Shaping Technology/Building Society: Studies in Sociotechnical Change*, MIT Press, London

Bijker, W. E., Hughes, T. P. and Pinch, T. (eds) (1987) *The Social Construction of Technological Systems*, MIT Press, Cambridge, MA

Chappells, H. (2003) 'Reconceptualising electricity and water: Institutions, infrastructures and the construction of demand', PhD Thesis, Lancaster University, Lancaster, UK

Coutard, O. (ed) (1999) *The Governance of Large Technical Systems*, Routledge, London

Elzen, B. and Wieczorek, A. (2005) 'Transitions towards sustainability through systems innovation', *Technological Forecasting and Social Change*, vol 72, no 6, pp651–661

Elzen, B., Geels, F. G. and Green, K. (eds) (2004) *System Innovation and the Transition to Sustainability: Theory, Evidence and Policy*, Edward Elgar, Cheltenham, UK

Energy Saving Trust (2009) *Power in Numbers: The Benefits and Potential of Distributed Energy Generation at the Small Community Scale*, EST, London

HM Government (2009) *The UK Renewable Energy Strategy*, Cm 7686, The Stationery Office, London

Klein, H. K. and Kleinmann, D. L. (2002) 'The social construction of technology: Structural considerations', *Science, Technology and Human Values*, vol 27, no 1, pp28–52

Maranta, A., Guggenheim, M., Gisler, P. and Pohl, C. (2003) 'The reality of experts and the imagined lay person', *Acta Sociologica*, vol 46, no 2, pp150–165

Marres, N. (2005) 'Issues spark a public into being: A key but often forgotten point of the Lippman–Dewey debate', in B. Latour and B. Weibel (eds) *Making Things Public: Atmospheres of Democracy*, MIT Press, Cambridge, MA, pp208–217

Shove, E. (2003) *Comfort, Cleanliness and Convenience: The Social Organization of Normality*, Berg, Oxford and London

Southerton, D., Chappells, H. and Van Vliet, B. (2004) *Sustainable Consumption: The Implications of Changing Infrastructures of Provision*, Edward Elgar, Cheltenham, UK

van der Horst, D. (2008) 'Social enterprise initiatives in renewable energy: Communities of practice and learning by doing in the Scottish Highlands', *Social Enterprise Journal*, vol 4, no 3, pp171–185

Van Vliet, B. J. M. (2002) 'Greening the grid: The ecological modernisation of network-bound systems', PhD Thesis, Wageningen University, Wageningen, The Netherlands

Van Vliet, B. J. M., Chappells, H. and Shove, E. (2005) *Infrastructures of Consumption: Environmental Restructuring of the Utility Industries*, Earthscan, London

Walker, G. P. (2008) 'What are the barriers and incentives for community-owned means of energy production and use', *Energy Policy*, vol 36, no 12, pp4401–4405

Walker, G. and Cass, N. (2007) 'Carbon reduction, "the public" and renewable energy: Engaging with sociotechnical configurations', *Area*, vol 39, no 4, pp458–469

Walker, G. and Devine-Wright, P. (2008) 'Community renewable energy: What should it mean?', *Energy Policy*, vol 36, no 2, pp497–500

Walker, G., Hunter, S., Devine-Wright, P., Evans, B. and Fay, H. (2007) 'Harnessing community energies: Explaining and evaluating community-based localism in renewable energy policy in the UK', *Global Environmental Politics*, vol 7, no 2, pp64–82

Walker, G., Cass, N., Burningham, K. and Barnett, J. (2010) 'Renewable energy and sociotechnical change: imagined subjectivities of "the public" and their implications', *Environment and Planning A*, vol 42, no 4, pp931–947

Chapter 5

From Backyards to Places: Public Engagement and the Emplacement of Renewable Energy Technologies

Patrick Devine-Wright

Introduction

Social science research on renewable energy technologies began in the late 1980s and has burgeoned in recent years. This body of literature has typically been problem-focused, seeking to explain the reasons for public antipathy or even hostility towards project proposals. Two basic orientations to research can be discerned. Initially, research looked to the various properties of the technologies involved (typically wind turbines), attempting to identify which real or symbolic characteristics of the technology underlay local opposition. This describes many applied research studies conducted during the 1990s, commissioned by industry or media organizations, which targeted 'public perceptions' of wind energy and which tended to focus upon visual and acoustic impacts (Simon, 1996), and which led to attempts to render turbines as silent and invisible as possible, presuming that this would increase their social acceptability.

More recently, research has shifted the focus of enquiry towards the process of technology deployment, presuming that local opposition is not so much caused by characteristics of the technology itself, as by predominantly top-down decision-making procedures sometimes referred to as the 'decide–announce–defend' model (Wolsink, 2007). From this perspective, public opposition arises due to a lack of meaningful opportunities for local residents to participate in, or benefit from, renewable energy projects (for example, by becoming financial stakeholders in cooperative ventures, by contributing to decision-making in land use planning, or by receiving tangible rewards from community benefit packages) (Bell et al, 2005; Gross, 2007; Hindmarsh and Matthews, 2007). In parallel with this research, there has been a flow of policy guidance and best practice documents encouraging project developers to engage with the public and other stakeholders in more meaningful and timely ways, and to consider distributing financial benefits to local residents (e.g. British Wind Energy Association, 2007; Department of Trade and Industry, 2007a,b; Renewables Advisory Board, 2009).

In this chapter, I wish to open up a third focus of enquiry in social research on renewable energy technologies, and to explore the implications of this for public engagement. I would argue that both of the stages of research that I have identified, with their predominant emphases upon *what* is developed and *how* it is deployed, have tended to play down a third crucial aspect – an emphasis upon the *where*. My argument is not that the *where* has been entirely absent from past research – after all, studies have consistently mentioned 'the landscape' in relation to visual impacts, and useful points have been made about the implications of spatial distance between energy generation and use (Pasqualetti, 2000). My point is that, to date, there have been two predominant ways of thinking about the *where* of renewable energy projects – as 'sites' to be developed, or as 'backyards' replete with NIMBY ('Not in my back yard') opponents – and that both are problematic. Consequently, in this chapter, I aim to reveal some of the implications of these two common representations of the *where* for the ways in which public engagement with renewable energy is conceived and practised; and then to argue that a more preferable means of representing the context of technology deployment is via the concept of *emplacement* (literally of putting something into place; Cresswell, 2004), drawing upon social science literature on the concept of place from environmental psychology, geography and other academic disciplines. I conclude by identifying the practical implications of an emplacement perspective for processes of public engagement by referring to an empirical case study of an offshore wind farm in the UK, drawing on data from interviews, focus groups and questionnaires.

The Siting Perspective upon Energy Technology Implementation

Perhaps the predominant expert perspective on the context of renewable energy projects is to regard it as a 'site' to be developed, and it is not difficult to identify the language of technology siting in UK policy guidance and planning documents as well as industry reports. For example, developers describe their projects in terms of 'site statistics' (e.g. npower renewables, 2009) and recent Government guidance on the development of wind energy projects refers to different phases of development, commencing with 'site identification' (see Box 5.1; Department of Trade and Industry, 2007a, p29).

The key point to make about the siting perspective is that, while it is extremely effective at drawing attention to salient *objective* features of potential locations for

---

Box 5.1

Phase 1: Site Identification

In order to identify sites that may be suitable for wind development, developers will carry out a 'constraints mapping' exercise. This process will identify potential sites that might be suitable for wind turbines and would, typically, take into account some or all of the following constraints:

- annual average wind speed (usually obtained from on-site measurements from a previously permitted wind monitoring mast);
- proximity/ suitability of electricity grid;
- aspect of the site, e.g. direction that any slope faces;
- construction access – suitability of local roads;
- landowner agreement;
- Ministry of Defence/Civil Aviation Authority constraints;
- telecommunications – e.g. microwave links, TV, radar, radio;
- proximity of residential dwellings;
- visual impact from key points in area;
- proximity of other wind farms
- landscape designations – e.g. presence of Area of Outstanding Natural Beauty, Heritage Coast, National Parks);
- ecology – e.g. local flora and fauna, bird migration paths, protected species; nature conservation designations such as Sites of Special Scientific Interest (SSSI);
- archaeological/historical heritage – e.g. presence of listed buildings, conservation areas, archaeological sites.

Extract from text on the site identification phase of wind energy projects.

---

renewable energy projects, it plays down more *subjective* features; specifically the symbolic or emotional associations that local residents or visitors may have with that place. Locations of renewable energy projects are not merely sites with topographical, ecological or archaeological features; they are also places replete with memories, experiences, stories and myths that are as much a feature of any locality as the soil type, height above sea level or average wind speed. It is as if the siting perspective enables a blinkered gaze, stripping out certain aspects and concentrating solely upon others.

Another difficulty with the 'siting' perspective is the way that it prioritizes certain social and environmental values over others. Over the past few decades, research has shown that support for the environmental movement has grown in tandem with an increasing proportion of society adopting a biocentric view of nature/human relations called the 'new ecological paradigm' (Dunlap et al, 2000). This paradigm shapes people's attitudes towards development and presumes that nature is fragile and easily unbalanced, that resources are limited or finite, and that humans are part of, rather than dominant over, nature (Dunlap et al, 2000). Conceiving localities of energy projects as 'sites' suggests what Dunlap and colleagues have called the 'dominant social paradigm': that the earth has plentiful natural resources, and that it is appropriate for humans to interfere with nature to suit social needs. Adopting the siting perspective can therefore lead to conflict between developers holding more anthropocentric values and stakeholders or residents holding more biocentric values, who may look with dismay at presumptions that the exploitation of local resources through technological means is self-evidently justified and appropriate, since it will benefit social needs for electricity supply. This potential conflict between industry and public values encapsulated in the siting perspective echoes more recent studies that have identified higher-order dimensions of utilization and preservation that underlay environmental attitudes (Bogner and Wiseman, 2006), with 'siting' clearly suggesting environmental utilization rather than preservation.

The siting perspective has several adverse consequences for public engagement. Firstly, it provides a rather limited perspective from which to capture the full range of locational issues that may come to the fore during consultations on a specific development proposal, since residents and visitors do not engage with a site, they engage with a place that is simultaneously material and psychological, objective and subjective. Public engagement strategies informed by the siting perspective are in danger of playing down or completely overlooking the symbolic and emotional associations that people may have with the locality faced with development. Engagement informed by siting may never reveal important place-related issues that inform local responses to development proposals. Overlooking such associations may only serve to exacerbate pre-existing sceptical beliefs and a lack of trust between residents and development companies. It may contribute to an inability of residents and development companies to find a common language to talk about proposals for change; thus magnifying the likelihood of social conflict.

Secondly, the siting perspective promotes a rather hierarchical, manipulative and managerial approach towards public engagement (O'Riordan, 2000). Since technological development, from this perspective, is primarily about modifying material locations to ensure that a given technology fully exploits available local resources; as a consequence, it is difficult to discern what meaningful contribution lay publics could make at the early stages of project development. As such, siting fosters an 'information deficit' view of public knowledge in environmental planning and development (Owens, 2000), presuming local residents to have little or no substantive knowledge regarding ecological or archaeological processes. As a consequence, the aim of public engagement in technology siting is likely to be information provision rather than deliberative engagement, only serving to notify residents and communities about the changes that are planned. As has already been mentioned, this overlooks more subjective aspects of the locations of energy projects, effectively putting them out of reach in planning or engagement processes.

The 'Backyard' as a Context for Energy Technology Implementation

A second common representation of the location of energy projects is the 'backyard', bound up with 'NIMBYism', a term that has frequently been used to refer to local opposition to a diverse array of technologies or facilities, including waste dumps, gas pipelines and, more recently, renewable energy technologies such as wind farms (Burningham et al, 2007). The NIMBY concept has multiple meanings. Descriptively, NIMBY is used as a pejorative label to describe the kinds of individuals or communities who oppose development. It is also used to describe the kinds of attitudes held by project opponents, chiefly the viewpoint that, while the proposal is a good idea in principle, it should not be sited in close proximity to their particular homes or 'backyards'. In a more explanatory way, the NIMBY concept presumes some of the reasons why opposition occurs. Firstly, that opposition is determined by spatial proximity – the closer people live to the site, the more they will oppose development, since it will negatively affect the economic value of their homes and their quality of life. Secondly, that opposition stems from the personal characteristics of the individuals involved: being too emotional to deal with development proposals in a sufficiently rational manner; being ignorant of the facts; and being overtly selfish in focusing upon private disbenefits, while overlooking important public or collective benefits arising from development.

The concept has become a common shorthand, used by journalists, policy-makers and industrialists not only to describe opposition to renewable energy projects but to undermine it. However popular, it has received harsh criticism. The validity of 'deficit' views of knowledge have been challenged by illustrating contexts where members of the public have been highly informed (Petts, 1997). The very notion that opposition is necessarily bad has been challenged, with the argument that controversies have a social value in signalling political or technical problems that may have been overlooked at earlier stages of technology development (Bauer, 1995). The 'rational actor' model of the person, which assumes that human behaviour is fundamentally motivated by self-interest, has been challenged; instead pointing to the importance of beliefs about fairness and justice (Gross, 2007). It has been pointed out that the provision of incentives can increase rather than decrease local opposition, if symbolically regarded as a bribe (Bell et al, 2005). The stereotypical NIMBY attitude has been critiqued as simplistic, instead of emphasizing the interplay of contextual, social and psychological factors that shape public responses (Devine-Wright, 2008). Finally, empirical studies have not supported the spatial proximity assumptions embedded in NIMBYism (Jones and Eiser, 2009).

Representing locations of energy projects as 'backyards' is as problematic as the NIMBY concept it relates to. While the backyard more explicitly recognizes social and subjective aspects in comparison with the siting perspective, it does so merely to problematize them. It overemphasizes the impact of spatial proximity upon subjective responses; it oversimplifies the attitudes that people hold about the suitability of specific technologies to particular locations; and it presumes that local concerns only arise from selfishness, ignorance or irrationality. It can lead to development strategies that distance renewable energy technologies from people's homes (e.g. by deploying wind farms offshore), yet it overlooks how seascapes may be as valued as onshore locations, regardless of their objective distance from where people live. It results in advocacy for separating fact from myth in siting disputes (Devine-Wright and Devine-Wright, 2006) and of excluding emotional responses from energy planning (Cass and Walker, 2009). The outcome is to support the emphasis already manifest by the 'siting' perspective upon preserving a purely rational and objective approach to the locations of technology deployment. In short, conceiving project locations as 'backyards' actually serves to bolster the legitimacy of the siting perspective, illustrating the complementary and interdependent nature of each concept.

Fundamentally, the backyard concept is built upon an impoverished view of the 'home'. A backyard would typically refer to land that is privately owned by an individual or household, yet local concerns about the impacts of renewable energy projects clearly transcend the boundaries of specific properties, often implicating wider spatial domains such as publicly owned landscapes or seascapes. These locations are spaces of collective as much as individual concern, and the backyard concept fails to recognize that the sense of home can refer to places beyond the narrow boundaries of gardens or yards, to broader locations which are not legally owned, yet people feel a sense of ownership over; a sense of care and a feeling of attachment. As a result, industry efforts to counter 'myths' about the potentially negative impacts of renewable energy projects upon property values (see, e.g., British Wind Energy Association, 2009) offer a highly selective and impoverished perspective upon the different ways in which locations matter to individuals and communities.

'Place' as a Way of Thinking about the Context for Energy Technology Deployment

Place is a concept that spans several academic disciplines, of interest to architects, geographers, sociologists, planners and psychologists. A common principle is that place is distinct from more general concepts, such as space, in reflecting a physical location of varying size or scale that is imbued with socially constructed meanings and emotions by individuals or groups of people (Tuan, 1977; Farnum et al, 2005). In this sense, it is preferable to the concepts of 'site' and 'backyard' already mentioned, by simultaneously capturing both objective and subjective aspects of a particular location (Easthorpe, 2004).

Academic research on place has developed into a number of strands. Environmental psychologists have focused upon subjective aspects of place by devising concepts such as *place attachment* (emotional bonds between person and environment; Manzo, 2005) and *place identity* (connections between the self and particular environments; Carrus et al, 2005). In human and cultural geography, there has been interest in *sense of place* (a conscious awareness of locatedness and distinctions between places; Tuan, 1980) and in place as a socially constructed nodal point within a complex web of social interactions which may stretch over local, regional and national boundaries (Massey, 1995). Interweaving these strands is a persistent interest in a particular kind of place – the home – emphasizing its subjective and emotional aspects (thus differentiating it from the notion of a 'site'), its spatially diffuse nature (thus differentiating it from the notion of a 'backyard'), and how it is bound up in a sense of control over what happens there (Moore, 2000; Easthorpe, 2004).

Some energy research studies have already used the concept of place. Vorkinn and Riese (2001) showed that place attachment was important in explaining public beliefs about a proposed hydropower project in Norway. They found that the more attached that local residents felt towards the affected areas, the more the residents opposed the proposal. Kempton et al (2005) found that local opposition to offshore wind energy in the US was rooted in particular beliefs about the ocean as a 'special place that should be kept natural and free from human intrusion' (p119). Van der Horst (2007) claimed that people who 'derive a more positive sense of identity from particular rural landscapes are likely to resist such potential developments, especially if they live there' (p2705), while Brittan (2001) stressed how wind energy developments disrupt the sense of place by undermining local distinctiveness.

This literature suggests that concepts such as place attachment and place identity can be useful in order to capture subjective, contextual aspects of energy projects. I have recently proposed that public opposition may arise in physical and social contexts where pre-existing place attachments and place identifications become 'disrupted' (Devine-Wright, 2009). Research on place attachment has identified diverse causes of disruption, including forced relocation (Fried, 2000); changes to the fabric of places arising from environmental disasters (e.g. Brown and Perkins, 1992); or changes in the legal character of places, when localities become labelled as polluted (Bonaiuto et al, 1996) or are re-designated as protected areas (Carrus et al, 2005). Of particular relevance is research on responses to housing proposals in a lakeland region of Wisconsin (Stedman, 2002), which found that intentions to oppose development were explained by two key factors: (1) the person's strength of attachment to the place, and (2) the kinds of symbolic beliefs held about the place. He found that, when individuals represented the lakeland area as 'up north' (i.e. a place 'to escape from civilization', p571), they were more likely to express intentions to oppose development; however, this was not the case if they represented the place as a 'community of neighbours' (p570), regardless of strength of attachment.

Drawing upon social psychological theories of identity (Breakwell's theory of identity processes, 1986; see Devine-Wright and Lyons, 1997) and social knowledge (Moscovici's theory of social representations, 2000), I have argued that the reason why individuals feel emotional attachments to specific places, which in turn form an important element of their sense of self or identity, stems from the ways in which places are represented – that is, how they are redolent with symbolic meanings, memories and personal experiences that contribute to and constitute a positive sense of self. Specifically, it is due to the fact that the meanings associated with specific places can enable a person to feel a sense of continuity over time (perhaps from living in or visiting a place on numerous occasions over years or decades), a sense of positive distinctiveness (stemming from the unique characteristics of the locality and its inhabitants), and a sense of self or collective efficacy (the ability to capably manage living in, or visiting a place). To the extent that proposals to deploy renewable energy technologies may be represented by local residents to negatively impact upon place-related continuity, distinctiveness or efficacy, these can disrupt place attachments and place identities, potentially leading to 'place-protective' action (Devine-Wright, 2009).

To provide an example of how such processes can play out in a renewable energy development context, I will briefly refer to a case study of offshore wind energy in North Wales (see Devine-Wright and Howes, 2010). In this case, a 750MW wind farm was proposed by a multinational company to be built about 15km from the coast, opposite coastal towns that have sought to attract tourist visitors since the 19th century. Once the project proposal was announced in 2005, residents in the town of Llandudno set up an action group (Save our Scenery) to oppose the wind farm. As the group's name suggests, they interpreted the project proposal as a threat to the character of the place and have campaigned since then for the wind farm to be refused planning consent. By contrast, the developer has emphasized the importance of the project for tackling global warming, and policy-makers have referred to its importance in helping to meet national policy targets for renewable energy.

As part of the 'Beyond Nimbyism' research project, interviews were conducted with the opposition group and the developer, and data were collected from local residents in Llandudno and in neighbouring towns by means of group discussions and questionnaires. The data revealed that local residents represented the wind farm as a large-scale, industrial development, yet the degree to which the project was evaluated as a threat differed across locations, depending upon the nature of the symbolic meanings people drew upon to represent each place and the perceived 'fit' with that place of an 'industrial' form of development. The predominant way of representing the town of Colwyn Bay was a place that was run-down and in decline. In this context, the wind farm's impact was perceived as uncertain, and analysis of questionnaire data yielded a lack of relation between strength of attachment to the place and acceptance of the project. In the focus groups, one person suggested rather uncertainly that the project had the potential to be place-enhancing in terms of offering a local means of employment. By contrast, the predominant representation of Llandudno was a place of natural beauty, a unique location framed by a coastal topography of the bay and adjoining headlands, and a historic haven for tourists. Evaluations of the impact of the wind farm were more certain, and analysis of questionnaire data indicated a significant negative relation between strength of attachment and project acceptance – the more that people felt attached to the place, the less they supported the wind farm.

Attachment was also linked to emotional responses – the more that Llandudno residents felt attached, the more they felt angry and threatened by the wind farm. That such views were influenced by the local action group was suggested by the fact that place attachment was also significantly positively related to levels of trust in the local action group and negatively related to levels of trust in the project developer.

But such responses were by no means inevitable. What was fascinating about the Llandudno focus groups was how they offered a glimpse of what might have been – of alternative ways of constructing a narrative about the 'fit' between place and project that might maintain, or even enhance, the historic character of the place. For example, the way that such a large-scale technology project could symbolize the historic continuity of the area, and particularly its Victorian heritage:

> *'Llandudno, as we all know, was built and set out by the Victorians, and it's my opinion that had they had the technology at that time [i.e. wind turbines], they would have proceeded with this scheme, along with the pier and the electric trams and we'd have all been very pleased with the achievement, to be quite honest, and we would have accepted it'* (Jim (pseudonym), Llandudno focus group 1).

Another example related to the distinctiveness of Llandudno as a tourist resort – another key aspect supposedly under threat from the wind farm according to the local action group. In the group discussion, residents reflected on the potential of the wind farm to enable a new form of 'ecotourism' to develop in the area:

> *Jane: 'You could argue, I mean, if it is going to be the largest wind farm in Europe, I mean, potentially it could even draw people in, and you know, they might be interested in seeing, we don't know.'*
>
> *Sue: 'Ecotourism.'*
>
> *Jane: 'I bet that would happen.'*
>
> *Emily: 'They could do it, spin a new thing, spin it up as ecotourism.'*

Of course, the reference to 'spin' makes clear how mindful the participants were about the prevalence of propaganda in conflicts around energy projects. Yet, even so, the quotation suggests that the narrative of place-threat propagated by the local opposition group could have been challenged, and certainly was not the only way that the project could have been interpreted in relation to the place's history and unique character.

Implications of Emplacement for Public Engagement with Renewable Energy Projects

Adopting 'place' as a perspective on technology implementation differs from siting and backyard perspectives by encouraging developers to re-conceive in a more positive manner the social aspects of a locality when proposing renewable energy technologies. 'Site identification' would become 'place identification', involving assessment not only of objective issues (e.g. resource availability, grid connection), but also the various ways in which local people associate the place with particular symbolic meanings and emotions. These could be identified through early public engagement activities that sought to listen to local residents talking about what the place means to them, instead of informing them of the technology planned for local deployment. Representations of the place could be captured using a variety of techniques and engagement mechanisms, including those used in the case study described here involving group discussions, question-naires and specific techniques such as free association tasks.

Once such meanings and emotions had been identified, the goal would be to attempt to construct an overarching narrative for the project (perhaps co-created by a developer working inclusively in collaboration with members of the community and other local stakeholders) that attempts to emplace the project in the area in such a way as to demonstrably maintain or enhance place-related continuity with the past, distinctiveness, and self or collective efficacy. The main challenge of the emplacement perspective for developers would be to avoid the status quo of talking to residents about their technology project, and instead opt to listen to stories and memories held by residents about the place, its history and character. Instead of aiming to secure technology acceptance from residents, developers would adopt a place-based perspective, looking outwards from a given place with its inhabitants in order to find ways of ensuring a good 'fit' between place and technology. A measure of 'goodness of fit' would be the degree to which local residents considered the project to maintain a place's continuity with the past and local distinctiveness. The fact that such narrative possibilities were overlooked by the developer, in the example provided, is testimony to the influence of the 'site' and 'backyard' representations, which leads to symbolic and emotional aspects of places being overlooked, and lost opportunities to embed the project in the symbolic meanings of the place.

Conclusions

Large-scale renewable energy projects have diverse human and environmental impacts and, as a consequence, have frequently encountered opposition in the past. This chapter proposes that social science research has tended to overlook the *where* of energy projects in comparison to *what* or *how* dimensions, focusing upon characteristics of the technology or decision-making process in contrast with characteristics of the context or locality. There are encouraging signs that this is beginning to change, and several of the chapters in this book refer to the importance of place in explaining local responses (for example, the chapters by Walker, McLachlan, Upham and Firestone). All of these contributions point in a similar direction – that the *where* of renewable energy development is an important issue to consider alongside *what* and *how* dimensions when researching public engagement.

Two common ways of representing the context were identified: as 'site' and as 'backyard'. Each was found to be problematic, providing a limited means of representing subjective and objective aspects of localities, and an inadequate basis for public engagement with technology proposals that does not presume pejorative views about human–environment relations. Emplacement was conceived as a process of putting technologies into place, with places defined as at once both physical-material and social-psychological, with pre-existing patterns of topography and geology as well as memories, beliefs, emotions and myths. While this offers a more comprehensive conceptual basis for the *where* of renewable energy projects, it has the disadvantage of adding a further layer of complexity to technology deployment. Indeed, 'place' has been referred to as 'one of the trickiest words in the English language; a suitcase so overfilled that one can never shut the lid' (Hayden, 1995, p112). However, I would argue that such complexity is nevertheless more useful than deficient, pejorative accounts of context such as 'sites' and 'backyards' that have, in the past, merely contributed to uncertainty, risk and local antipathy towards development proposals. The challenge for industry and policy-makers is to design procedures for public engagement with place attachments and place identities in mind. This implies using innovative mechanisms of engagement to identify symbolic and emotional aspects of energy project locations, and to construct credible and coherent narratives of place enhancement.

Acknowledgements

The 'Beyond Nimbyism' research project was funded by the Economic and Social Research Council (Grant ref. RES-152-25-1008). The author would like to acknowledge the helpful contributions of the project team and all participants.

References

Bauer, M. (1995) Towards a functional analysis of resistance, in M. Bauer (ed) *Resistance to New Technology: Nuclear Power, Information Technology and Biotechnology*, Cambridge University Press, Cambridge

Bell, D., Gray, T., Haggett, C. (2005) 'The "social gap" in wind farm policy siting decisions: Explanations and policy responses', *Environmental Politics*, vol 14, no 4, pp460–477

Bogner, F. X. and Wiseman, M. (2006) 'Adolescents' attitudes towards nature and environment: Quantifying the 2-MEV model', *Environmentalist*, vol 26, no 4, pp247–254

Bonaiuto, M., Breakwell, G. M. and Cano, I. (1996) 'Identity processes and environmental threat: The effects of nationalism and local identity upon perception of beach pollution', *Journal of Community and Applied Social Psychology*, vol 6, no 3, pp157–175

Breakwell, G. M. (1986) *Coping with Threatened Identities*, Methuen, London

British Wind Energy Association (2007) *Best Practice Guidelines: Consultation for Offshore Wind Energy Developments*, www.bwea.com/pdf/bwea-bpg-offshore.pdf

British Wind Energy Association (2009) *Factsheet: Onshore Wind Farms: Facts on Wind: Top 7 Wind Farm Myths Dispelled*, www.bwea.com/pdf/Briefing_Sheet_Artwork_Screen.pdf

Brittan, G. G. (2001) 'Wind, energy, landscape: Reconciling nature and technology', *Philosophy and Geography*, vol 4, no 2, pp171–178

Brown, B. and Perkins, D. D. (1992) 'Disruptions to place attachment', in I. Altman and S. Low (eds) *Place Attachment*, Plenum, New York, pp279–304

Burningham, K., Barnett, J. and Thrush, D. (2007) 'The limitations of the NIMBY concept for understanding public engagement with renewable energy technologies: A literature review', University of Exeter, www.geography.exeter.ac.uk/beyondnimbyism/

Carrus, G., Bonaiuto, M. and Bonnes, M. (2005) 'Environmental concern, regional identity and support for protected areas in Italy', *Environment and Behavior*, vol 37, no 2, pp237–257

Cass, N. and Walker, G. (2009) 'Emotion and rationality: The characterisation and evaluation of opposition to renewable energy projects', *Emotion, Space and Society*, vol 2, no 1, pp62–69

Cresswell, T. (2004) *Place: A Short Introduction*, Blackwell, Oxford

Department of Trade and Industry (2007a) *The Protocol for Public Engagement with Proposed Wind Energy Developments in England: A Report for the Renewables Advisory Board and DTI*, Centre for Sustainable Energy, Garrad Hassan and Partners Ltd, Peter Capener and Bond Pearce LLP, www.berr.gov.uk/files/file38708.pdf

Department of Trade and Industry (2007b) *Delivering Community Benefits from Wind Energy Development – A Toolkit: A Report for the Renewables Advisory Board and DTI*, Centre for Sustainable Energy, Garrad Hassan and Partners Ltd, Peter Capener and Bond Pearce LLP, www.berr.gov.uk/files/file38710.pdf

Devine-Wright, P. (2008) 'Reconsidering public acceptance of renewable energy technologies: A critical review', in M. Grubb, T. Jamasb and M. Pollitt (eds) *Delivering a Low Carbon Electricity System: Technologies, Economics and Policy*, Cambridge University Press, Cambridge, pp443–461

Devine-Wright, P. (2009) 'Rethinking Nimbyism: The role of place attachment and place identity in explaining place protective action', *Journal of Community and Applied Social Psychology*, vol 19, no 6, pp426–441

Devine-Wright, P. and Devine-Wright, H. (2006) 'Social representations of intermittency and the shaping of public support for wind energy in the UK', *International Journal of Global Energy Issues: Special Issue on Intermittency*, vol 25, no 3/4, pp243–256

Devine-Wright, P. and Howes, Y. (2010) 'Disruption to place attachment and the protection of restorative environments: A wind energy case study', *Journal of Environmental Psychology*, doi:10.1016/j.jenvp.2010.01.008

Devine-Wright, P. and Lyons, E. (1997) 'Remembering pasts and representing places: The construction of national identities in Ireland', *Journal of Environmental Psychology*, vol 17, no 1, pp33–45

Dunlap, R. E., Van Liere, K. D., Mertig, A. G. and Emmet Jones, R. (2000) 'Measuring endorsement of the new ecological paradigm: A revised NEP scale', *Journal of Social Issues*, vol 56, no 3, pp425–442

Easthorpe, H. (2004) 'A place called home', *Housing, Theory and Society*, vol 21, no 3, pp128–138

Farnum, J., Hall, T. and Kruger, L. E. (2005) *Sense of Place in Natural Resource Recreation and Tourism: An Evaluation and Assessment of Research Findings*, Gen. Tech. Rep. PNW-GTR-660, USDA, Portland, OR

Fried, M. (2000) 'Continuities and discontinuities of place', *Journal of Environmental Psychology*, vol 20, no 3, pp193–205

Gross, C. (2007) 'Community perspectives of wind energy in Australia: The application of a justice and community fairness framework to increase social acceptance', *Energy Policy*, vol 35, no 5, pp2727–2736

Hayden, D. (1995) *The Power of Place: Urban Landscapes as Public History*, MIT Press, Cambridge, MA

Hindmarsh, R. and Matthews, C. (2008) 'Deliberative speak at the turbine face: Community engagement, wind farms, and renewable energy transitions, in Australia', *Environmental Policy and Planning*, vol 10, no 3, pp217–32.

Jones, C. R and Eiser, J. R. (2009) 'Identifying predictors of attitudes towards local onshore wind development with reference to an English case study', *Energy Policy*, vol 37, no 11, pp 4604–4614

Kempton, W., Firestone, J., Lilley, J., Rouleau, T. and Whitaker, P. (2005) 'The offshore wind power debate: Views from Cape Cod', *Coastal Management*, vol 33, no 2, pp119–149

Manzo, L. (2005) 'For better or for worse: Exploring multiple dimensions of place meaning', *Journal of Environmental Psychology*, vol 25, pp67–86

Massey, D. (1995) 'The conceptualisation of place', in D. Massey and P. Jess (eds) *A Place in the World? Places, Cultures and Globalisation*, Open University Press: Oxford, pp87–132

Moore, J. (2000) 'Placing home in context', *Journal of Environmental Psychology*, vol 20, no 3, pp207–218

Moscovici, S. (2000) *Social Representations: Explorations in Social Psychology*, Polity Press, London

npower renewables (2009) 'Site statistics for the Rhyl Flats offshore wind farm', www.npowerrenewables.com/rhylflats/stats.asp

O'Riordan, T. (ed) (2000) *Environmental Science for Environmental Management*, Prentice Hall, London

Owens, S. (2000) 'Engaging the public: Information and deliberation in environmental policy', *Environment and Planning A*, vol 32, no 7, pp1141–1148

Pasqualetti, M. (2000) 'Morality, space and the power of wind-energy landscapes', *Geographical Review*, vol 90, no 3, p381–394

Petts, J. (1997) 'The public-expert interface in local waste management decisions: Expertise, credibility and process', *Public Understanding of Science*, vol 6, no 4, pp359–381

Renewables Advisory Board (2009) 'Delivering community benefits from wind energy development: A toolkit', www.renewables-advisory-board.org.uk/vBulletin/showthread.php?p=221 (accessed 3 May 2010).

Simon, A. M. (1996) 'A summary of research conducted into attitudes to wind power from 1990–1996', British Wind Energy Association, www.bwea.com/ref/surveys-90-96.html

Stedman, R. C. (2002) 'Toward a social psychology of place: Predicting behaviour from place-based cognitions, attitude, and identity', *Environment and Behaviour*, vol 34, no 5, pp561–581

Tuan, Y. F. (1977) *Space and Place: The Perspective of Experience*, University of Minnesota Press: Minneapolis, MN

Tuan, Y. F. (1980) 'Rootedness versus sense of place', *Landscape*, vol 24, no 1, pp3–8

van der Horst, D. (2007) 'NIMBY or not? Exploring the relevance of location and the politics of voiced opinions in renewable energy siting controversies', *Energy Policy*, vol 35, no 5, pp2705–2714

Vorkinn, M. and Riese, H. (2001) 'Environmental concern in a local context: The significance of place attachment', *Environment and Behavior*, vol 33, no 2, pp249–263

Wolsink, M. (2007) 'Planning of renewables schemes: Deliberative and fair decision-making on landscape issues instead of reproachful accusations of non-cooperation', *Energy Policy*, vol 35, no 5, pp2692–2704

Section II

Empirical Studies of Public Engagement

Part 1

STAKEHOLDER AND MEDIA REPRESENTATIONS OF PUBLIC ENGAGEMENT

Chapter 6

Discourses on the Implementation of Wind Power: Stakeholder Views on Public Engagement

Maarten Wolsink

Introduction

A crucial dimension of the context of institutional key variables that can be held responsible for the variation in implemented wind power capacity is how actors with different stakes perceive the deployment of wind power. Among key stakeholders, very strong conflicts between views exist. These conflicts are linked with the positions that actors hold within the domain of wind power development, and they concern all aspects of implementation. Among these are the financial procurement system and government policies, but they also concern the engagement of civil society in wind power schemes.

In an international comparative study in three countries on the institutional setting of wind power implementation (Breukers, 2007) the current discourses among all key actors involved in the implementation process were investigated, as these perspectives can be related to the historical-institutional legacy of the geographical cases. For that purpose the Q method was used; this is a formal reconstructive methodology which measures quantified unique responses to stimuli, allowing for a qualitative evaluation and comparison of human subjectivity. The complete patterns of stakeholder views, as reported in Wolsink and Breukers (2010) include all aspects that were marked as significant by the stakeholders themselves.

Involvement in Wind Power Schemes

In the case of wind power, the domains of significant stakeholders are energy policy, spatial planning and environmental policy. Here we focus on the views of stakeholders from these domains concerning the engagement of civil society in wind power schemes, which mainly concerns planning regimes and decision-making about projects. Planning systems in most countries, although very different, apparently all seem to have difficulty with decisions over wind power; they almost seem 'designed to fail' (Wolsink, 2009). The starting point is often that developers, authorities or hired experts need to do nothing more than present information to the still ignorant local civilians. Most studies on decision-making show, in fact, that developers and their associates urgently need to be informed, for example, about the crucial role of factors of community and landscape identity, and how to deal with the culturally rooted and fundamental subjectivity of these. Usually their knowledge about this is limited, and understanding of how to include the community values in decision-making on wind farms is mostly not supported by existing planning procedures. Planning systems and planning agencies have difficulty in incorporating landscape valuation because of its subjectivity and the variation of this subjectivity. As 'knowledge' about landscape valuation is in 'the eye of the beholder' (Lothian, 1999), ultimately the people who identify themselves with the landscape ('place identity') are the 'experts'. At the same time, landscape is the most important attribute in shaping attitudes towards wind energy projects (Wolsink, 2007) and therefore community involvement in the development of wind power schemes is crucial.

Unfortunately, planning systems are seldom designed to handle the required involvement of civil society; in fact they are often designed to avoid this kind of involvement. The reaction of governments to adapting planning systems to deal with the 'obstacle course' caused by developers seems to be merely a reinforcement of that design (for example, in the UK; Ellis et al, 2009; Haggett, 2009, p304). Do these efforts reflect the views of all key stakeholders? In particular, do they reflect the views of those who have experience of successful implementation, and if not, what are their perspectives? This analysis of patterns in stakeholder views reveals that strong dissimilarities exist in perspectives on planning and on the need for involvement and participation.

Research Approach

In a geographical study of onshore wind power developments in The Netherlands, North Rhine–Westphalia (NRW) and England, the institutional conditions and changes in the domains of energy policy, spatial planning and environmental policy were compared with respect to how they influenced the clear differences in the implementation rates of wind power in those countries (Breukers and Wolsink, 2007). A crucial dimension of the institutional context is how key actors with different interests perceive the realization of wind power

Table 6.1 *Samples of respondents representing stakeholders (2003–2005)*

Stakeholder category	North Rhine–Westphalia	England	The Netherlands
Local, regional, national governments and agencies	7	6	5
Citizen projects, cooperations	1	1	1
Private wind project developers	2	1	1
Anti-wind power groups	1	2	1
Environment/nature protection/ landscape preservation organizations	3	5	2
Wind power/renewables branches	4	2	4
Conventional energy sector	1	2	2
Researchers	1	1	1
N (total N=56)	20	19	17

projects. These perspectives on implementation processes and considerations about economics, spatial planning and the environment are defined as the current stakeholder positions in ongoing environmental discourses (Dryzek, 2005). To reveal the common narratives, representatives of all key stakeholder groups in the relevant policy domains were identified and interviewed. In this 'P sample' (in the method applied to be distinguished from the 'Q sample of statements; see below), all levels of governance from local to national were included (Table 6.1).

These interviews started with collecting the data for the Q study. Q methodology provides a structural model that measures quantified unique responses to stimuli (a set of statements) that allow for a qualitative evaluation and comparison of human subjectivity. The method has been applied in a study of decision-making on wind power (Ellis et al, 2007), but it can also be applied as a tool to support public participation itself (Doody et al, 2009). Similarities between individual views make it possible to articulate a condensed number of social narratives on a topic (Webler et al, 2001). Unlike surveys and interviews, it bypasses the researcher, because the patterns that are revealed by the analysis are produced by the respondents and not by the analysing researcher (Eden et al. 2005). It allows 'the categories of the analysis to be manipulated by respondents' (Robbins and Krueger, 2000, p645). Explications of the technique can be found in Stenner et al (2008) and McKeown and Thomas (1988). The entire procedure and full results on all aspects of wind energy implementation are described in Wolsink and Breukers (2010), but here we emphasize the essential contrasts in the views on community involvement and focus on how the presented data can be interpreted.

The first step was to formulate and select a set of 60 statements (the 'Q sample') that would represent the entire opinion domain. The statements included all the possible diverse viewpoints on all sub-themes present within the realm of the topic. They were spread over the following categories:

- arrangements within the policy domains of energy and environment;
- the role, position and objectives of the incumbents in the energy sector, in particular existing energy companies; and
- financial support regimes and their stability.

These categories are not directly associated with the involvement of the public. The following categories, however, are all directly linked with issues of public involvement:

- *The impact of spatial planning and of location decision-making.* Political institutions that do not support local collaborative approaches and that do not allow the community to negotiate on the impact on the landscape reduce the success of national wind power programmes. These negotiations concern the choice of the site for achieving a good fit between the wind power project and the landscape identity, as perceived by the community that holds a commitment to the landscape of the site.
- *Community acceptance of wind power projects.* This element has received most of the attention in social acceptance studies (Wüstenhagen et al, 2007). Developers tend to misunderstand their planning problem as an attitude–behaviour 'gap' among local residents. However, the attitude concerns the object of wind as an energy source, whereas the behaviour is directed at the object of a wind power project, including a certain site and a particular investor. These objects are very different and, furthermore, an attitude is a bi-polar evaluation (negative or positive) whereas in behaviour the focus is on resistance, which implies that the position in favour of a proposed scheme is not questioned in the first place. As wind power is a contested realm, the legitimacy of national policy is problematic as well, in particular when hierarchical power is overtly used to site turbines. In addition to landscape concerns, community acceptance may also suffer in response to dissatisfaction with the planning and decision-making processes (Wolsink, 2007), in particular, on how public consultation is organized (Aitken et al, 2008). All studies of the underlying reasons for opposition show that the objections are very heterogeneous (Ellis et al, 2007; Jones and Eiser, 2009).
- *Participation in investments or ownership.* Related to the community acceptance of wind power projects is the question of whether institutional settings allow direct involvement in locally organized or publicly owned wind power. In fact, wind power might become an essential part of community energy provision (Walker and Devine-Wright, 2008). This is important, as it is the level where decisions about investments and siting of concrete wind power schemes are taken, and the community may be involved as shareholder and as stakeholder. 'Ownership' should not even necessarily be legal ownership, as the way in which the community is involved in the project might create identification with the wind farm ('sense of ownership'; Warren and McFadyen, 2010).

Table 6.2 *Number of statements in each rank of the Q sort*

Column number		1	2	3	4	5	6	7	8	9	10	11	12
Number of statements		1	2	4	6	7	10	10	7	6	4	2	1
Score		−6	−5	−4	−3	−2	−1	+1	+2	+3	+4	+5	+6

In the second step, the 56 representatives (see Table 6.1) sorted the Q sample statements on a board with 60 boxes. The number of columns from left to right was 12, and the numbers per column allowed them to sort the statements in a forced 'normal' distribution only (Table 6.2).

The statements in Table 6.3 have letters in the column alongside them, so that they can be referred to easily in the text. This table also presents the results as scores from −6 (far left, 'Least in accordance with my opinion') to +6 (far right: 'Most in accordance with my opinion'). Although the respondents gave their personal opinion, they were fully aware of the fact that they were involved in interviews representing their category of actor.

The Four Discourses on Public Involvement

In the analysis the similarities in the patterns of sorting the statements were analysed, revealing four fundamentally distinct patterns that can be interpreted as sets of coherent views on all the aspects of wind power implementation. The figures presented in the next sections give the ranks of the 'ideal respondent' in each of the four separate discourses.

In the analysis, some statements appear to reflect a certain consensus. An example of that is 'If good arguments exist for constructing a wind farm in one local community instead of another, then the local authorities will agree to this'. The statement ranked mainly neutral and there was no significant variance between the four perspectives. In the analysis of the results, we focus only on 'distinguishing statements' – those that revealed significant differences between perspectives. As we zoom in on the perspectives on public involvement we only present data concerning statements that are associated with the categories of involvement of civil society in wind schemes, as described above. However, the reader should bear in mind that all figures are related to the complete set of statements and therefore the ranking figures on each statement are not independent from the ranks for all other statements.

Community involvement and room for independent developers

The first three discourses represent support for wind power implementation, but from different perspectives. The first is a discourse of mainly independent developers. In North Rhine–Westphalia (NRW), representatives of several of these, who cannot be considered to be developers themselves, shared the views of these

Table 6.3 *Distinguishing statements on public engagement in wind energy developments (factor arrays; 'ideal rankings of statements')*

	Statements	Factor arrays 'discourses'			
		1	*2*	*3*	*4*
A	Opponents of wind farms are not willing to compromise, so it is pointless to involve them in decision-making.	−2	−4	0	−2
B	The problem with public input is that it is primarily based on emotions.	2	1	4	0
C	The government is not capable of adequately directing the decision-making process around wind energy.	−1	−3	−2	1
D	Power companies will always try to keep third parties from entering the wind energy market.	4	−1	0	1
E	Power companies have no understanding of planning and are unaccustomed to dealing with local actors.	0	−2	−2	0
F	Initiators take too little time and effort to fit a wind farm into the existing environment.	1	2	−1	3
G	Local initiatives are decisive for the successful implementation of wind energy.	3	3	1	1
H	It is wrong to take decisions without giving neighbouring residents a decisive influence.	3	4	0	4
I	Local opposition to wind turbines is caused by the way in which decision-making processes take place.	−1	0	−1	2
J	Professional know-how and scientific expertise ought to play a decisive role in decision-making on infrastructure.	1	1	3	1
K	It is imperative to involve all concerned parties locally before the first design for a wind farm ever sees the light of day.	3	3	0	5
L	Disappointing implementation of wind energy is usually a result of unnecessarily slow and arduous rounds of decision-making.	0	−1	3	−1
M	More citizen participation leads to even more opposition and even fewer windmills.	−3	−2	−1	0
N	Public consultation procedures make the decision-making process more complicated and lengthy than necessary.	1	2	1	−3
O	The local community should be able to exert its influence in every phase and on all aspects of the decision-making process.	0	3	0	3
P	Involving potential opponents to a wind farm in a timely manner will increase its chances of getting built.	3	5	1	0
Q	The input from the public in a decision-making process often shows a lack of expertise.	−1	−1	2	−2
R	Local interests are not taken into account enough at the national and regional level, so that every time a wind farm is planned it is understandable that there is local resistance to it.	−1	0	−1	4
S	Most of the time, important parties are insufficiently consulted during the design phase of wind turbine projects.	1	3	−3	3
T	Initiators of wind farm projects underestimate the value of the landscape when developing locations.	−1	2	−2	5
U	National and regional governments should be able to issue directives when local authorities fail to cooperate with the construction of a wind farm.	0	2	4	−4
V	Local opposition to a wind farm is nothing more than defending one's self-interest.	3	1	5	−3
W	Offering financial participation in wind turbine projects to nearby residents is a good way to defuse opposition.	4	4	2	−1

independent developers: the NRW Environmental Ministry, the Federal Ministry for the Environment, Nature Conservation and Nuclear Safety. In contrast, in England, only one actor represented this perspective, a civilians' cooperative (Baywind). This discourse is particularly strong in the successful case of NRW, and its main characteristic is that it entails the view that support programmes should not focus on industry but on those who develop and invest in the projects. It is a discourse that emphasizes the need for certainty for potential investors and therefore the importance of clarity and the reliability of renewable energy policies. In this discourse, guaranteed prices for wind power and guaranteed access to the grid are strongly preferred above financial support incentives for investments in wind power capacity. This view is strongly connected to the idea that power companies will try to prevent the entrance of third parties into the wind energy market. This statement is ranked very positively (statement D, Table 6.3); a score that differs significantly from the ranking in the other three discourses.

The discourse clearly recognizes the importance of the involvement of civil society, new private developers and local communities in wind power schemes. Financial participation of nearby residents in wind power projects is welcomed (W), as it would also help to defuse opposition. Similarly public involvement in decision-making on views on planning and public involvement in decision-making and planning is appreciated relatively positively and the responsibility of the developers themselves is recognized. In the interviews, respondents stressed the importance of informing the local community early in the process, and requiring that information should not primarily be seen as the task of the authorities but also of the project developers themselves. The idea that increasing the amount of citizen participation will eventually lead to more opposition is more strongly rejected than in the other discourse (M). Early involvement of potential opponents will even increase the chances of success (P).

Early community involvement required

In the second discourse, the views are also generally in favour of implementing wind power, but the actors represent various commitments. These are actors linked with the turbine industry and also government agencies, such as the NRW State Initiative for Future Energies, the UK Ministry of Trade and Industry, and the Dutch Ministry of Economic Affairs. Furthermore, some local governments and nature protection organizations supported these views. There is support for wind energy, but most of these actors have, in certain circumstances, also opposed wind projects that they considered harmful. Conditional support is advocated. In many aspects, the views in this discourse are congruent with those in the first discourse, but there are some major differences. Only one of all the seven independent developers in the P sample, the citizen's project Baumberge in NRW, moderately supported the views in this discourse. For all other respondents in this cluster, wind power is not their core activity.

Compared with the previously discussed discourse, there is a stronger commitment to the involvement of local communities in all phases of the process (O). The rejection of the statement that opponents are not willing to compromise and that it is useless to involve them is also stronger than in the first discourse (A). Fully in line with the independent developers' views is also the recognition that if local residents can share in the profits success becomes more likely (W).

The emphasis on the conditions for support to wind schemes becomes apparent with the recognition of the undesirability of rigid planning from above, as this generates resistance.

> *'If you oppose, you don't necessarily oppose the whole idea of a wind farm. Usually some sort of development can still take place ... but in a different way. For instance, in a project with ten turbines, it might be that only three cause a problem, so we can negotiate that they are moved to another place'* (Interview).

Concerning the conditions, it is clear that more attention should be given to the spatial and societal feasibility of wind projects. A clear difference from the first discourse is the notion that initiators of wind farms tend to underestimate the value of the landscape (T).

The views about public and local involvement in the project, as well as decision-making, do not show clear differences compared with the discourse of the independent developers. The strongest contrasts between these two conditionally supportive perspectives can be found in the ideas about how to deal with the existing powers. Within this second discourse, the idea that the government is not capable of adequately directing the decision processes around wind energy is more clearly rejected than in the other discourses in favour of wind power (C). The strongest difference clearly concerns the impact of the incumbent power companies. Whereas power companies are expected to create barriers for other parties to enter the wind energy market, the second discourse does not recognize that problem (D), and the view that power companies do not understand planning and do not know how to deal with local actors is moderately rejected (E).

Unconditional support with no eye for community involvement

The perspective of unconditional support is apparently the strongest perspective in England. Most of the actors supporting views that are prominent in this discourse are part of the wind industry. An obvious representative in England is (among others) the British Wind Energy Association (BWEA). In The Netherlands it is endorsed most clearly by Nuon (an energy company) and by Greenpeace, whereas in NRW this discourse is rather weak, with the only strong representative being a medium-sized project developer (ABO Wind). Moderate support for this perspective also comes from some governmental actors in The Netherlands and England, and a few environmental organizations, such as Greenpeace UK.

The most prominent characteristic of this unconditional support is its rather distinct hierarchical view with regard to project planning and decision-making.

Wind power deployment is strongly defined as a public interest, whereas local opposition is much more strongly appreciated as being merely about defending one's own self-interest (V). There is clearly a technocratic view on planning decisions (U), and participation beyond formal consultation is rejected, because such public input would be primarily based on emotions (B) and because the input from the public often shows a lack of expertise (Q). Unlike the other three perspectives, the discourse of unconditional support does not agree that important parties are often insufficiently consulted during the design phase of wind turbine projects (S). Involvement of potential opponents in an early phase is not considered an approach that might increase the chances of success, as it is in both conditional support discourses, and there is a strong reliance on the value of professional know-how and scientific expertise that should play a decisive role in decision-making (J). A clear hierarchical approach is preferred; professionals and experts work out a project plan, while other (local) stakeholders can only respond afterwards. Slow and complex decision-making is held responsible for delayed implementation (L). Furthermore, the ideas about the limited involvement of the local community in decision-making runs parallel with the most clear-cut rejection of the notion that initiators of wind farm projects tend to underestimate the value of the landscape when developing locations (T). Involving local residents in participation in the project is only slightly appreciated as positive; far less than by the other two favourable discourses.

The discourse of contested wind power

The fourth perspective differs from the first three in that it is critical of wind power developments and also to the manner in which wind projects are implemented. This is the discourse of criticism of wind energy deployment and it combines fierce opponents and conditional supporters who share concerns about landscape impact, local interests, and frustration about project planning and decision-making. This perspective is most apparent in England, and includes mainly national and local civil society organizations for environmental and rural countryside protection. Moderate support comes from some regional authorities. In fact, this discourse reflects the English tradition of strong interest in landscape protection. From the Dutch case, only two respondents were very supportive: an anti-wind power organization and the WaddenVereniging, the organization for the protection of the Wadden Sea that effectively opposed the large near-shore wind farm in the Wadden Sea (Wolsink, 2010). Support for the contested wind discourse in NRW came from a landscape protection anti-wind group but also from the German branch organization for the conventional energy sector and the Federal Ministry of Economy and Technology, while neither landscape nor local interests were their primary concerns. The support of the latter actors can be explained as a reflection of the success of the German wind power deployment, as this has been achieved against the will of the incumbents in the power sector (Stenzel and Frenzel, 2008).

The perspectives that dominate this discourse are strong doubts about the public benefit in wind energy, or even outright denial, combined with the idea that the small amount of clean energy generated by wind cannot adequately compensate for the negative impact on the landscape. Whereas the denial of the public benefit of wind energy is primarily related to an emphasis on landscape values, this is also translated in the strong belief that decision-making on wind power implementation does not adequately take into account local interests and that the value of the landscape is underestimated by the initiators of wind farm projects (T).

The dominant issue of landscape valuation follows the research evidence that the most salient concerns in considering the costs and benefits of wind power schemes are related to landscape values (Johansson and Laike, 2007; Wolsink, 2007). Placing emphasis on the significance of early local involvement in projects to safeguard these values is a key characteristic in the discourse of contested wind power (K). The involvement of the local community in all phases of planning is advocated at a similar level as in the second discourse (O), but the expectations of the early involvement of potential opponents are very different. For the 'early involvement required' perspective, such involvement will increase the chances of successful implementation, whereas the contested wind power discourse has no such expectations (P).

In all three wind energy-supporting discourses, there is a slight notion of public consultation procedures complicating and slowing down the decision-making processes. The opponents' perspective, however, clearly rejects this statement (N). Furthermore, it emphasizes the limited value of consultation, as these actors recognize the difference between engagement and consultation.

> 'We want to be engaged in decision-making processes at an early stage, rather than being consulted at the last minute, when decisions have already been taken and agendas have already been set' (Interview).

Table 6.4 *Discourses compared with implementation achievements in three countries*

	Discourse	Independent developers	Involvement necessary	Unconditional support	Contested wind
Characteristics		Involvement helps	Landscape is an issue	Technocratic	Landscape issue under-estimated
		Participation investment/ ownership	Early involvement necessary	Local Involvement impediment	Denial public good
		Incumbents impediment	No doubts about incumbents	Hierarchic planning	Local interest undervalued
	Implementation				
England	Unsuccessful	Low	Low	Strong	Strong
Netherlands	Very toilsome	Medium	Low	Medium	Medium
NRW	Successful	Strong	Strong	Low	Medium

The actors holding this perspective consider that the way in which decision-making processes usually take place is a reason for the emergence of local opposition.

Concluding Remarks

The geographical comparison between the three countries was carried out to investigate how the institutional capacity for implementation affected the relative success or failure of wind power deployment. In Table 6.4 the discourses are briefly characterized and the strength of each one is compared with the rates of success in the countries concerned. It would be satisfying to conclude that the existence of certain discourses is a determinant for success, but in fact an opposite causal relation seems more likely. The development of views on what is needed for successful implementation will largely be the result of learning from experience. The enormous growth in wind power capacity in Germany, including the state of North Rhine–Westphalia, was based on the success of initiatives of civilians and private investments in wind power schemes, and a lot of experience had been gained about how to site wind turbines and about which factors are important for positive decisions. Hence, the dominance of the two nuanced conditional support discourses could be the result of learning. In the other two countries, the amount of learning was significantly lower.

In England, in particular, the debate is more polarized, as is clearly indicated by the statement that most clearly distinguished the four discourses in the study (U). The extreme positions (see Table 6.3) on the statement 'National and regional governments should be able to issue directives when local authorities fail to cooperate with the construction of a wind farm' are held by the two discourses that are both particularly strong in England (Table 6.4). The unconditional support perspective is dominant, on the one hand, and on the other hand the wind contested discourse, with its emphasis on landscape values, is stronger than in both the other countries. The unconditional support discourse clearly deviates from the other three, as it is the only perspective to deny the significance of elements in renewables planning which are increasingly recognized as crucial for successful local decision-making and renewables deployment.

If the dominance of the two discourses in England reflects an already polarized situation based on culturally rooted values, the technocratic perspective is certainly strongly reinforced by the policy choices of the UK government. The fact that these two are the dominant discourses does not seem very promising for wind energy development. This may be part of a vicious circle, because it also prevents the kind of experience and learning in North Rhine–Westphalia which is based on successful projects with high involvement of civil society. Involvement of civil society initiatives is hardly encouraged in the UK, as it has been in NRW since 1989, with the establishment of grid access for any wind power generator by means of the feed-in tariff system. The financial procurement system in the UK is based on the NFFO and ROCs (the Non-Fossil Fuel Obligation and Renewables

Obligation Certificates), with a competitive tender system that strongly favours large players, and these are mainly incumbents in the energy sector. Because of this policy bias, there are not so many independent developers and, hence, their perspective is not prominent in England.

In Table 6.4, the characteristics of the discourses are presented only with regard to public engagement, but in the discourses the perspectives on the role of energy companies and the design and background of the policy support regimes are associated with the ideas on participation and involvement (Wolsink and Breukers, 2010). The independent developers' discourse adheres to the view that support programmes should not focus on industry (as the ROC and tender system does) but on anyone who develops and invests in projects, and the experience in the successful countries is that these are not primarily the incumbents in the existing energy sector. This perspective also emphasizes the importance of guaranteed prices for wind power fed into the grid (a feed-in system) rather than financial support incentives for investments in wind power capacity (like the certificates). There is no doubt that feed-in systems generally perform better than certificate markets (Verbruggen and Lauber, 2009), but this is clearly not recognized in current UK policy. However, the independent developers' discourse also exists in England and, even in the technocratic unconditional support discourse, the effectiveness of full access to the grid and guaranteed prices is recognized. Therefore, a policy shift may be possible because the ideas underpinning such a shift exist in the relevant domains. This shift does not seem very likely for the time being, as the policy preferences for tradable certificates seem to be strongly determined by ideological preferences.

References

Aitken, M., McDonald, S. and Strachan, P. (2008) 'Locating "power" in wind power planning processes: The (not so) influential role of local objectors', *Journal of Environmental Planning and Management*, vol 51, no 6 pp777–799

Breukers, S. (2007) 'Changing institutional landscapes for implementing wind power: A geographical comparison of institutional capacity building: The Netherlands, England and North Rhine–Westphalia', PhD Thesis, Amsterdam University Press, http://dare.uva.nl/record/209600

Breukers, S. and Wolsink, M. (2007) 'Wind power in changing institutional landscapes: An international comparison', *Energy Policy* 35, no 5, 2737–2750

Doody, D. G., Kearney, P., Barry, J., Moles, R. and O'Regan, B. (2009) 'Evaluation of the Q-method as a method of public participation in the selection of sustainable development indicators', *Ecological Indicators*, vol 9, no 6, pp1129–1137

Dryzek, J. (2005) *The Politics of the Earth: Environmental Discourses*, 2nd edn, Oxford University Press, Oxford

Eden, S., Donaldson, A. and Walker, G. (2005) 'Structuring subjectivities? Using Q methodology in human geography', *Area* vol 37, pp413–422

Ellis, G., Barry, J. and Robinson, C. (2007) 'Many ways to say "no", different ways to say "yes": Applying Q-methodology to understand public acceptance of wind farm proposals', *Journal of Environmental Planning and Management*, vol 50, no 4, pp517–551

Ellis, G., Cowell, R., Warren, C., Strachan, P. and Szarka, J. (2009) 'Expanding wind power: A problem of planning, or of perception?', *Planning Theory and Practice*, vol 10, no 4, pp521–547

Haggett, C. (2009) 'Public engagement in planning for renewable energy', in S. Davoudi, J. Crawford and A. Mehmood (eds) *Planning for Climate Change: Strategies for Mitigation and Adaptation for Spatial Planners*, Earthscan, London, pp297–307

Johansson, M. and Laike, T. (2007) 'Intention to respond to local wind turbines: The role of attitudes and visual perception', *Wind Energy*, vol 10, no 5, pp435–451

Jones, C. R. and Eiser, J. R. (2009) 'Identifying predictors of attitudes towards local onshore wind development with reference to an English case study', *Energy Policy*, vol 37, no 11, pp4604–4614

Lothian, A. (1999). 'Landscape and the philosophy of aesthetics: Is landscape quality inherent in the landscape or in the eye of the beholder?', *Landscape and Urban Planning*, vol 44, no 4, pp177–198

McKeown, B. and Thomas, D. (1988) *Q Methodology*, Sage, Thousand Oaks, CA

Robbins, P. and Krueger, R. (2000) 'Beyond bias? The promise and limits of Q method in human geography', *Professional Geographer*, vol 52, no 4, pp636–648

Stenner, P., Watts, S. and Morell, M. (2008) 'Q methodology', in C. Willig and W. Stainton-Rogers (eds) *The Sage Handbook of Qualitative Research in Psychology*, Sage, Los Angeles, pp215–235

Stenzel, T. and Frenzel, A. (2008) 'Regulating technological change: The strategic reactions of utility companies towards subsidy policies in the German, Spanish and UK electricity markets', *Energy Policy*, vol 36, no 5, pp2645–2657

Verbruggen, A. and Lauber, V. (2009) 'Basic concepts for designing renewable electricity support aiming at a full-scale transition by 2050', *Energy Policy*, vol 37, no 12, pp5732–5743

Walker, G. and Devine-Wright, P. (2008) 'Community renewable energy: What should it mean?' *Energy Policy*, vol 36, no 2, pp497–500

Warren, C. R. and McFadyen, M. (2010) 'Does community ownership affect public attitudes to wind energy? A case study from south-west Scotland', *Land Use Policy*, vol 27, no.2, pp204–213

Webler, T., Tuler, S. and Krueger, R. (2001) 'What is a good public participation process? Five perspectives from the public', *Environmental Management*, vol 27, no 3, pp435–450

Wolsink, M. (2007) 'Planning of renewables schemes: Deliberative and fair decision-making on landscape issues instead of reproachful accusations of non-cooperation', *Energy Policy*, vol 35, no 5, pp2692–2704

Wolsink, M. (2009) 'Wind power: Is there a planning problem?' and 'Planning: problem "carrier" or problem "source"?', *Planning Theory and Practice*, vol 10, no 4, pp521–547

Wolsink, M. (2010) 'Near-shore wind power: Protected seascapes, environmentalists' attitudes and the technocratic planning perspective', *Land Use Policy*, vol 27, no 2, pp195–203

Wolsink, M. and Breukers, S. (2010) 'Contrasting the core beliefs regarding the effective implementation of wind power: An international study of stakeholder perspectives', *Journal of Environmental Planning and Management*, vol 53, no 4, DOI: 10.1080/09640561003633581

Wüstenhagen, R., Wolsink, M. and Bürer, M. J. (2007) 'Social acceptance of renewable energy innovation: An introduction to the concept', *Energy Policy*, vol 35, no 5, pp2683–2691

Chapter 7

Governing the Reconfiguration of Energy in Greater London: Practical Public Engagement as 'Delivery'

Mike Hodson and Simon Marvin

Introduction

This chapter takes the example of the London Climate Change Agency (LCCA) to examine 'public engagement' in relation to systemic energy efficiency, behavioural change and new energy technologies at the city–regional scale. Large world cities are at the forefront of producing 'emblematic' and 'exemplary' responses to the challenges of climate change and resource constraint. A critical part of these responses involves attempts to shape systemic change in the socio-technical organization of energy systems at the city–region scale and to seek to increase 'security' of resource flows (Hodson and Marvin, 2009a,b).

Yet in many Western cities, attempts to reconfigure energy systems are confronted by the paradox of the relative inability of public authorities and agencies to control these systems, particularly in an era of (variable levels of) liberalization and privatization. The multiplicities of social interests implicated in energy systems (policymakers, utilities, regulators, consumers etc.) span across many levels of governance and encompass a wide range of motivations for involvement in reconfiguring energy systems at an urban scale.

Such a range of social interests often includes well-established institutions and organizations, both in the context of urban decision-making and also in the functioning of socio-technical energy systems. Pressures to reconfigure energy systems at an urban scale create an impetus for bringing together – but do not determine – both existing urban interests and those involved in energy systems.

Additionally, 'entrepreneurial' interests are attracted to the 'new' urban energy context.

In this respect there is often significant capacity to act in reconfiguring urban energy systems that remains latent due to a missing organizational context for its coordination according to a mutually agreeable rationale or vision (Hodson and Marvin, 2009b). Increasingly this is being addressed in relation to different cities, where new 'intermediary' organizational contexts are being developed to create the capacity and capability to reconfigure urban energy systems (Hodson and Marvin, 2009c).

In this chapter we address one example of this attempt to create a new 'intermediary' organizational context through the development of a climate change agency in London (LCCA, 2006a). In doing this, we focus on the climate change agency, the types of social interests involved in it and the social interests it proposes to engage with, the practices through which 'the public' is engaged and what the significance of this is.

We use a case study of the LCCA's Green Homes programme to ask: 'How do intermediaries (such as the LCCA) "localize" energy demand management initiatives and with what consequences for styles of public engagement?' In addressing this question we:

- critically analyse Green Homes' proposed engagement with 'publics' through the development of a package of energy services and programmes;
- examine Green Homes' practices of enacting engagement with 'publics' through a concierge service, a social housing and fuel-poor programme, an advice service, and so on;
- develop a typology of interactions with publics through the Green Homes programme.

The chapter then considers the implications of the ways in which engagement with publics is envisaged and practised. This, we suggest, is the dominance of a 'practical public engagement' as 'delivery', which prioritizes technical and policy knowledges – in the transfer of information, 'education' and the creation of 'market opportunities' – to the relative neglect of lay knowledges.

Locating the Changing Relationships between Cities and Energy

Systemic transition in energy systems is increasingly a key strategic priority for the world's largest cities. This is primarily the case as cities seek to maintain or enhance their position as 'motors' of economic growth in a context where resource scarcity is an increasingly salient concern and where cities are being confronted with the emissions and carbon-related consequences of increasing economic growth.

Cities can be characterized as significant contributors to the production of climate change while also being large resource consumers. Furthermore, cities – with their concentrations of populations and often coastal and riverside locations – are likely to be vulnerable to, and significant 'victims' of, climate change-related extreme weather events. Yet, given their concentrations of population, potential economies of scale and concentrations of expertise, cities are also frequently viewed as potential contexts of innovative response, experimentation and novel approaches through which the challenges of securing access to resources and responding effectively to climate change can be addressed (see Clinton Climate Initiative, 2010).

In response, new visions of urban energy infrastructure provision are emerging. London, for example, is engaged in a strategy of vigorously attempting to reconfigure its energy infrastructures to address and gain 'control' over its carbon dioxide emissions, to secure the availability of resources necessary to underpin its growth and expansion, and to position London as the context within which responses to resource change and climate change are formulated and which are being claimed as 'transferable' and replicable. Through the previous Mayor of London, Ken Livingstone, the current incumbent, Boris Johnson, and the Greater London Authority (GLA), a long-term 'vision' has been developed that requires the reconfiguration of energy production and consumption in London (Mayor of London, 2008, 2007; Hodson and Marvin, 2009a).

The vision of energy for London is to build a more self-sufficient and autonomous energy infrastructure through a strategy of reducing demand for energy while also promoting the development of decentralized forms of energy production, including combined cooling heat and power (CCHP), energy from waste, promoting the uptake of on-site renewable energy – including micro-wind, photovoltaic (PV) and solar thermal heating – and also pursuing large-scale renewable power generation through land-based wind, and tidal and wave power from the river Thames, and is predicated on a relative 'withdrawal' from national and regional provision. This, according to this view, is based on a recognition that the current organization of energy production and distribution to homes and offices fundamentally inhibits attempts to reduce carbon emissions in London. This is part of an attempt to reshape London's 'metabolism'; that is, the flows of energy resources into, within and out of the city (City Limits, 2002), and implies a much more autonomous London – less strongly connected to its existing regional and national infrastructure – with more localized, decentralized and renewable forms of infrastructure.

More specifically, the vision is that a quarter of London's energy will be produced by decentralized means by 2025, with the majority by 2050 – this includes combined cooling heat and power (CCHP) and on-site and larger renewables – and where, in relation to new developments, 10 per cent of energy needs must come from on-site renewable power wherever feasible (Mayor of London, 2007). Furthermore, behavioural change and energy efficiency are promoted as a means of addressing the 38 per cent of London's carbon emissions that are estimated to come from energy use in existing homes (Green Homes, 2008).

A critical part of these responses involves attempts to shape systemic change in the socio-technical organization of energy systems at the city–region scale. Yet, energy infrastructures are often organized regionally and nationally and, in an era of liberalization and privatization, control of energy 'systems' is distributed across multiple spheres and levels of governance. Very many social interests can lay claim to having an 'interest' in the way in which energy systems of production and consumption are organized. This can include political and policy actors and considerations at city–regional, local, national and supranational scales (regulators, industry, utilities, consumers, citizens and so on).

Building effective responses – 'visions' – and their realization therefore requires the *organization* of a multiplicity of social interests, forms of knowledge, financial resources and so on, in order to present a view of the future of the relationship of London to an energy system. Yet this is not pre-given, it has to be constituted. It must be done in the milieu of a plurality of forms of knowledge, expertise and new coalitions of social interests that are seeking to reshape the built environment, infrastructure and resource deployment of contemporary London.

The multilevel redistribution of governance responsibilities (Bache and Flinders, 2004) across scales needs to be acknowledged, and with it the possibilities and constraints upon action at an urban scale. This includes, for example, understanding the role of supranational and national energy and 'environmental' targets that are 'passed on' to regions and city–regions from national governments, and also the possibilities and constraints afforded by new decentralized and renewables technologies and demand-side options.

There are many pressures for the development of long-term visions and transitions for energy infrastructure and places. Yet, there are also many challenges in developing a notion of what an urban energy transition could and should look like. In particular, the issue of how the capacity to act is organized in constituting and realizing urban energy transitions, in such a fragmented context, is a fundamental one. Which social interests and/or their representatives are involved? How? What is the balance/relationship between experts and lay publics? How far does this and should this extend? Who leads such a process? These are fundamental questions in understanding attempts to develop visions of the future of London and energy, and the 'realization' of such visions. It is to these questions that our case study of the London Climate Change Agency (LCCA) and the London Green Homes programme is oriented.

The Emergence of Urban Energy Intermediaries as a Governance Fix

We are interested in the LCCA, as it appears to exemplify many aspects of an urban energy 'intermediary' (Hodson and Marvin, 2009c). 'Intermediaries' are important in the debate around reconfiguring urban energy, for various reasons. Notably, interventions in energy systems at an urban scale can potentially involve a wide array of social interests (urban political elites, regulators, technology providers, utilities, consumers, citizens and so on) across different scales (national, urban, local, household etc.). That requires understanding not only the governance relationships that constitute interventions in energy systems at an urban scale but also the relationships between the priorities they embody and their 'realization'.

This relationship 'in between' urbanism and energy is mediated by governance capacity and the capability to act. It is how this capacity and capability to act is organized in this space 'in between' that is critical to understanding the consequences of action in relation to urban energy. It is in this space that new 'intermediary' organizations seek to mediate between the priorities, purpose, targets and objectives of those social interests that provide its 'membership' and their 'implementation' in communities, organizations, buildings, households and so on. It is the practices of these energy intermediaries that contribute significantly to how it is that the relationship between urbanism and energy is thought about and acted upon. 'Intermediaries' operate within the opportunities and constraints afforded by the 'landscape' pressures, policy priorities and institutional frameworks within which they are located. There are, in short, many different 'types' of energy 'intermediary' – many of which would not characterize themselves as intermediaries – with a focus on urban energy issues.

The London Climate Change Agency and Green Homes

In this section we detail the emergence of an urban 'energy' intermediary. The development of the London Climate Change Agency (LCCA) (see LCCA, 2006a,b,c,d, 2008a,b,c) was a priority of the previous Mayor of London, Ken Livingstone, in his bid to be re-elected in 2004. It was launched in June 2005 and was established as a municipal company, chaired by the mayor and owned by the London Development Agency (LDA), in March 2006. The LCCA was viewed as fundamental to translating and 'implementing' the mayor's priorities around climate change, particularly in relation to energy, transport, waste and water in addressing ambitious CO_2 reduction targets, and was launched 'with the support of' BP, Lafarge, Legal & General, HSBC, Sir Robert McAlpine, Johnson Matthey, the Corporation of London, the Rockefeller Brothers' Trust, KPMG, Greenpeace, the Climate Group, the Carbon Trust and the Energy Savings Trust.

The LCCA was involved in developing and setting up numerous initiatives which included, for example, projects on a carbon accounting tool to report on the total emissions arising from GLA Group activities on an annual basis, aspirations to establish a London energy services company (ESCO), revolving funds for energy efficiency initiatives within GLA estate, 'flagship' projects largely in relation to GLA buildings (e.g. a project for the headquarters of the LDA and LCCA comprising an 84kW renewable energy system with 63kWp of photovoltaic panels on the roof and 21kW of building-integrated wind turbines also on the roof), various microgeneration and domestic energy efficiency initiatives, and so on. Furthermore, in addition to the demonstration and 'exemplar' function of these initiatives, the LCCA also sought to actively disseminate its work and achievements within the UK and internationally through the media, conferences and articles.

The LCCA's work aims to have a significant emphasis on the reconfiguration of London's energy metabolism through energy efficiency and decentralized and renewable energy initiatives. In particular, the London Green Homes programme was made a policy commitment in London's *Climate Change Action Plan* (CCAP) published in February 2007. The London CCAP was developed by the Greater London Authority (GLA) and launched by the (former) Mayor of London, Ken Livingstone. The programme is delivered by the Environment and Climate Change Unit of the London Development Agency.

The total budget of £7 million between 2007/8 and 2009/10 was from public sector budgets in the LDA, but it was envisaged that 'significant additional resources will also be leveraged in from national public and private sector energy programmes' (Mayor of London, 2007). This will primarily be used for generating public awareness, developing useful and readily accessible consumer information, and helping tradespeople to learn relevant skills. Funding was budgeted at £2.68 million in 2007/08 and £2.16 million in each of the following years. Initially the programme had a three-year time scale.

The LCCA and the Green Homes programme are symptomatic of the new organizational contexts that are being developed to create the capacity and capability to reconfigure urban energy systems. They are dominated by the forms of social interests detailed above, but little is understood about the relationships between these social interests, forms of knowledge and publics. In particular, the proposed forms and modes of public engagement and how these are practised and understood are in need of greater clarification, as are the consequences of this. We examine these issues here in relation to London Green Homes.

Green Homes: Modes and Media of Public Engagement

Green Homes is a relatively new initiative. As such, there is little or no academic literature in relation to it. In this section we use a range of documentary materials (LCCA, 2006a,b,c,d, 2008a,b,c) and five interviews with officials in the GLA. In doing this we sought to improve understanding of two issues: (1) how engagement with 'the public' is envisaged in Green Homes, and (2) how this was embodied in Green Homes' practices. The activities of Green Homes are organized around the following seven programmes:

1. Green Homes has an emphasis on marketing and behavioural change campaigns and, in so doing, attempts to explain and promote individual actions that can be taken in relation to energy savings. In this mode of engagement, 'education', explanation and representation are prioritized as a means

of awareness-raising to individuals and householders about changes that are required in domestic energy practices.

2. Green Homes also operates a single coordinated advice service which aims to build on the awareness-raising of marketing campaigns by providing practical information about specific actions that can be taken by individuals and households. This includes, for example, information on where individuals and householders can buy energy-efficient appliances; who can help install cavity wall insulation; how to get the most reliable micro-renewable products and who is qualified to install them. The mediation of advice between the priorities of the Green Homes programme and householders is through a website that includes information and advice and also a free telephone helpline.

3. Green Homes also offers a green concierge service. The self-stated aim of the service is to take the 'hassle factor' out of implementing energy saving improvements. The concierge service is a partnership between the mayor, the London Development Agency, the national Energy Saving Trust (EST), and a private provider, Ten UK. The concierge service is built on capacity that is both public and private, and includes national priorities and city–regional priorities. Practically, the service is a subsidized fee-based service (£199). The form of engagement with householders is through an energy audit and a report recommending ways to reduce emissions as well as project management for the implementation of the measures the home owner chooses.

4. Another facet of Green Homes is a social housing and fuel-poor programme. The aim of this is to address energy efficiency specifically for those in fuel poverty and in social housing; in particular through offering subsidized energy efficiency measures – free to those receiving state benefits – such as cavity wall insulation, loft insulation and interest-free credit. Through this, engagement is through a series of products and services oriented to very specific groups.

5. Green Homes also promotes skills training to provide a workforce and skills base that can 'implement', service and maintain new energy technologies and services. It 'actively' seeks to work in partnership to develop this skills base.

6. Green Homes also supported the undertaking of a feasibility study to examine the development of a 'green' landlord initiative. This was in recognition of the fact that rented dwellings are often difficult to target for energy efficiency due to the 'landlord–tenant disconnect'. The feasibility study aimed to assess the potential to partner with letting agents to introduce a joint voluntary green scheme that would motivate landlords to upgrade their properties, in exchange for being able to badge them as 'green properties'. Engagement here is through a partnership with letting agents to influence landlords to improve their proprieties, with implications for the energy-related practices of their tenants. This set of engagements is mediated through the symbolic representations of a green badge scheme.

7. Green Homes' aim with these initiatives is that by 2025 3.9 million tonnes of CO_2 per annum will be saved with energy savings totalling nearly £1 billion per year by 2025, or approximately £300 per year per average household.

Green Homes: Five 'Types' of Public Engagement

What is important here are the potential implications of these modes and media of engaging with publics in relation to energy in London. In particular, the issues of who is engaging whom and how, and the significance of this are critical. It is possible from our work on London Green Homes to sketch out the contours of five 'types' of engagement.

Engagement through awareness-raising

This is where the purpose of engagement is to raise levels of awareness of energy efficiency measures in the household and at an individual level and in relation to the installation of renewable energy systems and technologies. Engagement is viewed as being about representing the positive, potential benefits of energy efficiency and renewable energy. This focuses on engaging with a broad range of households and individuals – with highly variegated publics. Engagement is mediated in a variety of ways; particularly through a website and interactive sections on it such as a carbon calculator, which is 'blunt' in terms of the sophistication of its attempts to engage different publics. In doing this, primarily what is being mediated are forms of expert (technical and policy) knowledges embodied in representations to raise the visibility of 'the key messages' on household energy efficiency. The temporal orientation of this form of engagement is ongoing.

Engagement through advice and information provision

This envisages and practises engagement through providing information as to where individuals can access or locate certain types of expertise, products and services that allow them to act on the 'key messages' that are made visible through awareness-raising. Information provision is coordinated and seeks to engage a wide range of households. Relationships are mediated through a combination of a website and a telephone helpline. Through this process it is, again, forms of technical and policy knowledge, technologies and services that are mediated and 'received' by a wider variety of different 'publics'. This process of mediation, given the wide variety of publics it engages, can take the form of episodic or ongoing engagement.

Engagement through producing and consuming services

This anticipates that there are many complexities in negotiating the energy efficiency and renewables fields and that these are a significant constraint on individual action on energy production, consumption and efficiency. As a response to this anticipation, 'public engagement' is sought through the provision, and subsequent consumption, of energy efficiency services, in particular through the provision of an audit, a report of recommended actions and project management functions; these are packaged as services to be purchased. These services are broadly 'available' and seek to engage different publics. Given that there is a charge – and also charges attached to many of the associated recommendations – there is a degree of 'self-selection' in consuming these more 'individualized' services. The mediation of these services works at different levels, from a general awareness of their availability through a website and literature to more specific forms of interaction in the case of an audit. Primarily, again there is a predominance of technical and policy knowledges and also the possibilities this opens up for green business. In the case of activities such as the audit there is – differing between households – a negotiation of these different forms of knowledge and social interests with lay knowledges.

Engagement based on subsidy and redistribution

While there are efforts to engage with publics through producing and consuming services and the 'market opportunities' this offers, there are also attempts to engage with those in fuel poverty and social housing. There are efforts to provide some energy efficiency products – cavity wall insulation etc. – at subsidized rates or, for those on benefits, for free. This form of engagement is again premised on technical and policy knowledges and the negotiation of these with lay forms of knowledge, and usually begins only at the point where householders requiring 'products' engage with providers. This is, again, mediated through a combination of website, telephone and face-to-face interactions. The time scales of these interactions are variable, from one-off to ongoing.

Engagement at a distance

This is a further form of engagement that we can characterize as being at a distance. In the absence of being able to 'effectively' engage with absent landlords around energy efficiency and the technological responses that may be required, there are attempts to create a commonly recognized and symbolically visible validation of a set of standards with which rented houses should comply. This type of engagement, through creating a standard, is a way of engaging policy and technical knowledges at a distance from 'disinterested' landlords. The engagement aims to 'jump start' energy efficiency action and the upgrading of properties in a relatively non-compliant context. Engagement is initially through a feasibility report, which may also be seen as an attempt to make the scheme visible and build its legitimacy. It is the beginning of efforts to engage landlords through cultivating a common understanding. In this respect the process is ongoing.

Practical 'Public Engagement' as 'Delivery'

Overall, these different 'types' of attempts to engage publics contribute to a view of the Green Homes programme as one where the rationale for public engagement is to support the 'delivery' of a set of political priorities rather than being about the deliberation of an agenda in relation to energy efficiency. Engagement is thus about trying to 'localize' and embed energy efficiency in London households rather than assessing what the future of energy in relation to London households might look like.

Inherent in this is a view of 'publics' primarily not as citizens but as consumers. In this respect, engagement with publics is not viewed in terms of a dialogue and early involvement of various forms of expertise and lay publics in 'upstream' forms of public engagement (Wilsdon and Willis, 2004). Public engagement here, rather than taking place 'upstream', is something for *after* a set of fundamental decisions have been taken. In this respect it is concerned with 'how' public engagement should occur rather than 'why' it should. This is important, as it privileges the process of public engagement over public discussion of its purpose. It has an emphasis on 'educating', 'informing' and awareness-raising of a range of energy efficiency services, products and renewables technologies. It also starts to connect producers and consumers of these services and products through charging for them, through subsidizing them, and through creating legitimacy and a 'need' for them. Put in this way Green Homes (1) encompasses elements of a 'deficit' model (Wynne, 1991) view of publics, providing information and 'education'; and (2) it also operates as a 'conduit' for green business. Public engagement here is not citizen participation in the sense of a deliberative dialogue; rather, seen in these terms, it a form of *citizen* non-participation or 'manipulation' in that it is an illusory form of engagement (Arnstein, 1969) that provides cover for *consumer* engagement.

This needs to be viewed in its political context. There are clear limits to the power of the Mayor of London and the GLA, where there is a strong emphasis on working in 'partnership'. The importance of the strategic planning context for engagement also needs to be noted. The London Plan, the mayor's strategic planning framework for London, plays a critical role in setting the direction of travel for energy production, consumption and distribution in relation to London. It offers a very clear view of how it seeks to reshape London's energy 'metabolism': that is, the flows of energy resources into, within and out of the city. This implies a much more autonomous London – less strongly connected to its existing regional and national infrastructure – with more localized, decentralized and renewable forms of infrastructure in addition to behavioural change and demand-side reductions. This planning context forms a background within which the above forms of engagement take place.

Given its political context and the ways in which initiatives such as Green Homes are reliant on mayoral patronage and budgets, it is no surprise that in the context of mayoral change, Green Homes was strongly rumoured to be 'axed' in 2009 by the LDA.

Conclusions

In this chapter we have outlined how attempts are under way in urban contexts to reconfigure energy production, consumption and distribution. This 'affects' a wide range of social interests implicated in urban decision-making, energy systems and new actors who work at combining the two in reconfiguring urban energy. This wide range of interests operates in different governance spheres, often at different scales of governance. These interests – and the latent capacity that they signify – require an intermediary organizational context within which they can negotiate, so that their interests become aligned and coordinated in order to become 'active'.

We took the example of the LCCA – and Green Homes – to examine this intermediary, the social interests that constitute it and its agenda for energy efficiency, decentralized energy and renewables in relation to London households. In doing this we examined what role it envisaged for publics and how it would practically seek to engage with publics. From this we developed an analysis of five 'types' of public engagement and from this assessed the ways in which practical public engagement in this example was primarily concerned with the 'delivery' of technical, commercial and policy priorities. With this in mind, we wish to conclude by highlighting three further issues:

1. Public engagement being about 'delivery' means that it is conceived as being less about dialogue and more about the 'transfer' of a set of narrowly constituted policy and technical knowledges and assumptions to a wide range of different domestic contexts.
2. Implicit in this is a view of publics that is largely – though not totally, as one can see from the categorizations: landlords, fuel-poor, etc. – unvariegated, and that views of who constitutes different publics could be developed in a much more sophisticated manner.
3. To contribute to this it would be advantageous for intermediaries to engage with a wider variety of publics in the constitution of similar initiatives and their programmes of work prior to their 'delivery' rather than seeing the process of engagement as being solely about the embedding of such programmes.

Acknowledgements

The authors greatly acknowledge the suppor tof the EU Seventh Framework Funded CHANGING BEHAVIOUR project, Grant agreement no: 213217.

References

Arnstein, S. R. (1969) 'A ladder of citizen participation', *Journal of the American Planning Association*, vol 35, no 4, pp216–224

Bache, I. and Flinders, M. (eds) (2004) *Multi-Level Governance*, Oxford University Press, Oxford

City Limits (2002) 'Introducing City Limits: A resource flow and ecological footprint analysis of Greater London', www.citylimitslondon.com/download.htm

Clinton Climate Initiative (2010) 'C40 cities: An introduction', www.c40cities.org/

Green Homes (2008) 'Green Homes concierge service', www.greenhomeslondon.co.uk/ index.aspx

Hodson, M. and Marvin, S. (2009a) 'Urban ecological security: The new urban paradigm?', *International Journal of Urban and Regional Research*, vol 33, no 1, pp193–215

Hodson, M. and Marvin, S. (2009b) 'Cities mediating technological transitions: Understanding visions, intermediation and consequences', *Technology Analysis and Strategic Management*, vol 21, no 4, pp515–534

Hodson, M. and Marvin, S. (2009c) *Conceptualizing and Understanding Intermediaries in Context: Developing an Enhanced Understanding of Context, Actors and Transferability*, Changing Behaviour Project, European Commission, 7th Framework Programme

LCCA (2006a) London Climate Change Agency Briefing No. 1, February

LCCA (2006b) London Climate Change Agency Briefing No. 2, March

LCCA (2006c) London Climate Change Agency Briefing No. 3, August

LCCA (2006d) London Climate Change Agency Briefing No. 4, October

LCCA (2008a) Briefing No 5: *Delivering Sustainability in London*, LCCA Progress Report 07/08, February, LDA, London

LCCA (2008b) Briefing No 6: *Delivering a Low-carbon London*, Annual Progress Report 07/08, April, LDA, London

LCCA (2008c) Briefing No. 7: *London Climate Change Agency Progress Report Update*, August, LDA, London

Mayor of London (2007) *Action Today to Protect Tomorrow: The Mayor's Climate Change Action Plan*, GLA, London

Mayor of London (2008) *The London Climate Change Adaptation Strategy*, GLA, London

Wilsdon, J. and Willis, R. (2004) *See-through Science*, Demos, London

Wynne, B. (1991) 'Knowledges in context', *Science, Technology and Human Values*, vol 16, no 1, pp111–121

Chapter 8

Envisioning Public Engagement with Renewable Energy: An Empirical Analysis of Images within the UK National Press 2006/2007

Hannah Devine-Wright

Introduction

The UK Government is supporting a substantial increase in electricity generated from renewable energy sources, particularly offshore wind, in order to reduce carbon emissions. Renewable energy generation technologies vary considerably, not only in terms of their physical characteristics such as their scale or location, but also their salience and everyday familiarity. Public understanding of these renewable energy technologies is multifaceted and can be articulated in many ways: in speech, words, images or as behaviours (Sauter and Watson, 2007). However, the role of images in articulating beliefs is particularly under-researched, both theoretically and methodologically (van Leeuwen and Jewitt, 2001; Pauwels, 2006). Therefore, this study focused upon what images of renewable energy technologies occurred within newspaper images at a time of debate about future energy policy, and investigated how these images might contribute to collective sense using the theory of social representations. This theory focuses upon understanding the process by which beliefs about novel or unusual phenomenon are 'anchored' in pre-existing ideas. The particular focus was how, if at all, public engagement with renewable energy technologies was visually represented; for example, what kind of model(s) of the public were implied by the type of people represented and how these images might reinforce or contest modes of public engagement with renewable energy technologies, particularly NIMBYism ('Not in my back yard'-ism).

In order to reduce carbon emissions, the UK Government advocates a substantial increase in electricity generated from both nuclear and renewable energy sources, particularly offshore wind. During the last six years, the UK Government has embarked upon a series of initiatives to consult the public about future energy policy (e.g. *Energy White Paper*, 2003) that have resulted in similar views being expressed by the public, experts and policy-makers (Stagl, 2005). However, as Cass (2006) has noted, it is not clear whether these views are indicative of consensus, engagement or the steering of public opinion (Cass, 2006, p33). While direct experience, such as having personally seen a wind farm, and indirect experience, such as watching a programme about renewable energy technologies on TV, are the main sources of information about renewable energy mentioned by survey respondents, newspapers play a significant role in shaping public opinion (e.g. Scottish Executive, 2003; MORI Social Research Institute, 2004). In this chapter, it is argued that images of renewable energy technologies within newspapers provide a means of making visible those technologies that are often distant from everyday experience, and that the content of these images is a factor in the construction of public understanding about these technologies.

The daily readership of UK national tabloid newspapers is considerable, with *The Sun* achieving more than 7.5 million readers, compared with the most popular broadsheet, *The Times/Sunday Times*, which has one-third of this readership (almost 1.8 million). Empirical findings suggest that political beliefs are correlated with social acceptance of different low carbon technologies. For example, Populus (2005) found that 62 per cent of individuals indicating support for the Conservative party were supportive of new renewable energy developments compared with 86 per cent of Labour supporters and 84 per cent of Liberal Democrat supporters; while 37 per cent of Conservatives were supportive of new nuclear power stations compared with only 12 per cent of Labour supporters and 14 per cent of the Liberal Democrats. These figures suggest that pro-renewable articles and images are more likely to occur in centre/left-of-centre publications such as the *Independent* and the *Guardian* rather than right-of-centre publications such as *The Sun, Daily Telegraph* or *Daily Mail*.

Decision-making about the siting of renewable energy technologies is complex: questions arise about who and why a particular development occurs as well as where, what, when and how it occurs. Members of the public might respond to the siting of renewable energy technologies in different ways that can be typified as acceptance (e.g. Ekins, 2004), objection (e.g. Devine-Wright, 2008) or rejection. Rejection or objection on the basis of proximity is sometimes referred to as NIMBYism. This type of response can be conceptualized as stemming from a lack of knowledge or as an irrational and/or selfish response but this implies a deficit model of public understanding that has been countered by the finding that active opponents are typically more knowledgeable about a project than passive supporters. As Burningham and O'Brien (1994) have noted, it is often only by drawing attention to specific local and often personal impacts that objectors stand to win any victories at all. Opponents may not only be local people but may also be non-governmental organizations or industrialists with vested interests in opposing particular developments. The relationship between passive or active supporters or objectors and a particular renewable energy technology may be objectified within images that contain both people and the technology. At a time when energy policy is rapidly evolving, it is interesting to examine what type of people are portrayed, and to discuss how these human–technology–policy relationships might influence decision-making about the siting of renewable energy technologies.

Image theory and research

Visual aspects of social research is a rapidly developing area (Pauwels, 2006) in which it is assumed that images and image-making are an appropriate and valid means of both generating image data (e.g. Devine-Wright and Devine-Wright, 2009) and of data itself, since 'visual images can be powerful and seductive in their own right' (Rose, 2001, p10). Unlike text, images are a ubiquitous means of communicating ideas about events, persons or technologies. 'Often, images, although arising in specific social and cultural contexts, are presented, relatively unchanged in their meanings, in diverse spatial and temporal contexts' (de Rosa and Farr, 2001, p246). Their symbolic and affective content, which used to be associated with their being less 'rational' and therefore less valuable as a form of data (Hansen et al, 1998), is increasingly regarded as a positive attribute, particularly by social scientists, who argue that emotional responses are an important influence on beliefs, attitudes and behaviour (e.g. Bauer, 1995).

Within social research studies of energy issues, there are certain images that have become iconic e.g. the radioactive symbol or high voltage 'A-frame' electricity pylons (Devine-Wright and Devine-Wright, 2009). These images have a strong evaluative component; that is, they are highly positively or negatively regarded, are readily understood and easily communicated. It can be argued that such image-objects enable collective sense-making (Weick, 1995) and aid social remembering. However, the processes or mechanisms by which image-based sense-making occurs or develops is not always well articulated. A psychological starting point might be that the image and any associated textual content influences (and is influenced by) personal attitudes or opinions (points of view), although any image or stock of images will be neither the sole influence nor necessarily the main source of influence. This is particularly the case with an image within a newspaper that contains a variety of opinions (e.g. editorial content versus letters, special features or the main section). Thus, images might describe a variety of salient and contemporary viewpoints that a reader may or may not attend to and/or react to, that they may accept or reject, and which they may or may not communicate to others.

According to Moscovici (1984), 'thinking by images' or 'collective ideation' fulfils a communicative function and provides a means of objectifying thought processes; for example, when biotechnology is presented in the media as menacing (Joffe, 2003). Such mass media images are reported rather than personally experienced events, but in situations where technologies are unfamiliar or distant from everyday experience, images may become proxies of engagement and 'operate in a similar manner to experience' (Joffe, 2003, p64). In these situations, the symbolic content of images becomes an important factor affecting their influence on both individual and collective ways of thinking. Bauer (1995) has argued that 'resistance that is not communicated and symbolically elaborated, has a limited effect [on action]' (p408). This implies that images that are symbolic – that is, their form goes beyond the straightforward and conventional (Beloff, 1994) – are likely to affect behaviour to a greater extent than those that are simply descriptive. Such images do not communicate in a static or fixed manner, since their message will change over time as it is viewed by different people, the same people over time, or across different contexts or situations. However, there has been little empirical work studying either symbolic or affective aspects of renewable energy technologies (Devine-Wright, 2008). An exception has been Lee et al (1989), who found that 62 per cent of a sample of 1286 respondents associated wind turbines with a 'sign of progress', 15 per cent with 'harking back to the past', and 16 per cent a combination of both.

Images that invoke an emotional response are more likely to influence attitudes and behavioural intentions than those that do not. Advertisements are particularly likely to seek to establish or promote associations between an emotion and a brand name. While many advertisements have emotive content that is positive, some deliberately stimulate negative affective responses, e.g. Benetton advertisements (de Rosa and Kirchler, 2001), on the pretext that 'original and extreme points of view have much greater probabilities of exercising a strong attraction than of being rejected' (Moscovici, 1976). In a health context, Stuart and Blanton (2003) found that people underestimated the likelihood of positive health outcomes when presented with positively framed images of health, while they estimated that negative outcomes would be prevalent when negatively framed images were presented. They found that the effect of these 'prevalence estimates' was stronger for people who were initially more uncertain about 'behavioural norms'; that is, expectations about how they thought they should behave. This suggests that in relatively novel but rapidly developing policy areas such as energy policy, the framing of images as either positive or negative might have a significant effect upon climate change beliefs and behavioural intentions.

Images can be seen to be powerful in and of themselves, influencing our imagination (Devine-Wright, 1998) and stimulating symbolic affective responses that affect both individual and collective beliefs and behaviour. As the role of images in articulating beliefs is an under-researched area, both theoretically and methodologically (van Leeuwen and Jewitt, 2001; Pauwels, 2006), this study aims to examine representations of renewable energy technologies within national newspapers and to theorize about how images might 'position' the imagination (Corner et al, 1990) and act as proxies for modes of public engagement with these technologies. The meaning of an individual image was linked to its means of production (what type of image it was: e.g. a photograph or a cartoon), and how it might be understood given wider social discourse about engagement, participation and energy policy.

Method

Sample

Following Bauer et al's (1995) sampling procedure, hard copies of 588 of the following national, tabloid and broadsheet newspapers were collected: *The Sun/News of the World, Daily Mail/Mail on Sunday, Daily Mirror/Sunday Mirror, Daily Telegraph/Sunday Telegraph, The Times/Sunday Times,* the *Guardian/Observer* and the *Independent/Independent on Sunday.* A copy of each newspaper was collected for one week per month (8th to 14th) for a period of six months (April to September) across two years (2006 and 2007). The time frame for sampling was initiated by the launch of the UK Government's Energy White Paper consultation on 14 April 2006.

Procedure

Images (defined as photographs, cartoons, digital images, illustrations or drawings) were identified by manually scrolling through each of the newspapers. Initially, images were tagged that had 'energy-related' content (e.g. depicted nuclear power, energy efficiency, conventional fuels, electricity network technologies, renewable energy technologies, biofuels). In the second phase, the stock of images was reduced to 111 images (and attendant articles) that were 'renewable energy-related' (e.g. depicted wind, solar, tidal, biomass or marine technologies). A coding template was developed that detailed key attributes of the image (e.g. source, type, content and function: descriptive or symbolic). Although there was full agreement between two raters about the type of renewable energy technology depicted, there were nine images (representing 80 per cent agreement) for which the two raters differed in terms of their categorizing of the images as evidencing public engagement or not. These nine images were presented to a third rater for categorization and this process resulted in more than 99 per cent agreement between the three raters.

Results

The total number of images that contained renewable energy technologies (RETs) with or without people in 2006–2007 was 111. However, there was some duplication of images, particularly in 2007 when a series of advertisements was published by energy companies. Consequently, a detailed analysis of content was restricted to 72 different RET-related images. In 2006 there were 31 RET-related images and this increased to 80 images in 2007 (an increase of 158 per cent). However, 39 of the 80 images from 2007 were duplicates, principally advertisements produced by energy companies; for example, there were 20 adverts by E.ON depicting sycamore seeds being blown into a house occupied by a woman and child, and 11 of an advertisement by E.ON showing a man and three children standing on a cliff edge facing into a strong wind. Nevertheless, even taking duplication into account, there was a 42 per cent increase in the number of different RET-related images identified within the stratified sample from 2007 compared with 2006.

The day with the highest frequency of RET-related images was 8 July 2007 ($n=9$). However, this included five of the same advertisement by E.ON and two different advertisements by npower as well as two non-advertisement images (photographs with wind turbines). Otherwise, the highest frequency occurred on 12 July 2006 ($n=7$), which was the day after the Energy Review was announced. In 2006, the second highest daily frequency ($n=4$) occurred on 12 June and 12 August, which were one month before and after the announcement, respectively. These images were found mainly in feature sections. Energy policy consultation was especially salient in 2006 with the opening of consultation on energy policy in July. The political significance of this was reflected in the publication of three satirical cartoons: the first in the *Daily Mirror* one month prior to the consultation (14 June 2006), and the other two in the *Daily Mail* and the *Guardian* respectively (12 July 2006).

It was the daily broadsheets, particularly the right-of-centre *Daily Telegraph* ($n=15$) and *The Times* ($n=15$) and the left-of-centre *Guardian* ($n=15$), that carried the largest number of RET-related images, although a substantial propor-tion of these images were advertisements: *Daily Telegraph* (30 per cent), *The Times* (53 per cent) and the *Guardian* (40 per cent). By comparison, tabloids contained between four (*The Sun*) and ten RET-related images (*Daily Mail*), with five occurring in the left-of-centre *Daily Mirror*. With the exception of *The Sun*, where only one of the four images (25 per cent) was an advertisement, the percentage of advertisements amongst the tabloid images was higher than in the broadsheets, with 60 per cent categorized as advertisements in the *Daily Mail* ($n=6$) rising to 80 per cent ($n=4$) of those within the *Daily Mirror*.

The majority of the RET-related images appeared within the main section of the newspaper ($n=28$, of which ten were advertisements), while the second most frequent location was the business/finance section ($n=15$, where there was only one advertisement and the remainder were photographs). Three of the RET-related images were found in editorial sections, all of which were bespoke images, i.e. a cartoon, photomontage and drawing. Images in the property section ($n=7$) were predominantly of building-integrated renewables ($n=5$). There was only one RET-related image found on a *Guardian* letters page, and this was an iconic illus-tration of a wind turbine.

Only 14 of the images did not have an accompanying title and only 5 were not accompanied by text. The most common type of RET that appeared in the images was wind turbines ($n=48$) (of which 22 were from 2006 and 26 from 2007). The second most frequent RET depicted was solar (photovoltaics and solar thermal; $n=15$). Where multiple RETs were depicted ($n=5$), they would always include wind turbines and usually solar panels. Of the other RETs, tidal was depicted in three cases and there was only one example each of biomass and hydro facilities. The prevalence of wind turbines, and the use of images of wind turbines to illustrate articles about other energy technologies or climate change, supports the view of them as 'iconic' of renewable energy and strategies to address climate change. Members of the public tend to relate to specific renewable energy resources or technologies more than the general term; and wind, solar and hydro are the most widely recognized (e.g. awareness by over 70 per cent of respondents), in contrast to biomass (approximately 20 per cent awareness) (Scottish Executive, 2003; MORI Social Research Institute, 2004). However, the use of wind turbines to represent renewable energy in general may mitigate against the greater understanding of less familiar low carbon sources or technologies such as biomass or marine energy.

Multiple categorization was possible in terms of the function served by each image: impression formation, descriptive, symbolic, satirical or attention-getting: 31 of the 72 images were categorized as containing symbolic elements, while a further 3 (all in 2006) were satirical (a combination of symbolic and political). Almost all of the symbolic images were found in broadsheet newspapers, while descriptive images were evenly distributed within both broadsheet and tabloid newspapers. Of the 25 different images that contained people, 13 were either symbolic or satirical while only 5 were descriptive (one was both symbolic and descriptive). The majority of these images suggested that wind turbines were associated with 'progress'. Few of the images seemed to be associated with 'harking back to the past' (after Lee et al, 1989), an exception being a photograph of an eco-house built using traditional materials and methods of construction. More typically, eco-houses with building-integrated renewable energy technologies were 'futuristic' and 'technologically advanced'. Thus, 'green' renewable energy technologies were variously represented as traditional, everyday or futuristic technologies, depending upon the focus of the particular article.

Envisioning public engagement with renewable energy technologies

Initially, an image was categorized as 'public engagement' when it contained people; consequently, of 72 different images, 26 were categorized as 'public engagement' (35 per cent). Only one image (see Figure 8.1), from the 2006 sample, depicted members of the 'general public'.

The cartoon shows a shabbily dressed man seated on a wooden fence, at night, in driving rain, holding a small wind turbine that is generating enough electricity to power a single light bulb. The bulb is held by his wife who leans out of a cottage window to tell him about plans to build wind turbines in the area, which she has read about in a newspaper. There is no suggestion that local residents either have been or should have been consulted in any way about the building of turbines in their locality. The image describes a state of passive acceptance about government decision-making about the siting of onshore wind

'Great news, Denzil. Mr Blair's thinkin' of building some o' them great big ones up on the hill'

Figure 8.1 *Cartoon from the* Daily Mail, *12 July 2006*

turbines, albeit ambivalent/resigned acceptance (in the posture and expression of the man) and more positive acceptance (in the facial expression and enthusiastic communication of the woman).

Between 2006 and 2007, the prevalence of images with people and RETs increased substantially and there was a change in the type of people included in the images. Whereas in 2006, the type of people depicted were predominantly male (75 per cent), Caucasian (87.5 per cent) and technical experts (37.5 per cent); in 2007, the images included non-expert females and males of different ages. For example, the photograph in Figure 8.2 was typical, showing a technical expert standing below an onshore wind turbine.

By contrast, a series of advertisements for energy companies published in 2007 showed families, and young people in particular, as passive supporters of investment in 'green' technologies to 'protect their future'. In these images there was some suggestion of more formal processes of consultation, communication and participation, albeit with energy supply companies rather than planners or policy-makers.

Figure 8.2 *'Expert' engagement with renewable energy technologies*

Source: Daily Telegraph, 13 July 2006

Discussion

There was a significant increase in the prevalence of people within images of renewable energy technologies in the UK national press between 2006 and 2007. At the time of the launch of a review of UK energy policy on 12 July 2006, with the exception of a single Mac cartoon published in the *Daily Mail*, people – especially lay people – were absent from newspaper images containing renewable energy technologies. This may not be surprising given that the majority of RET-images were found within the business/finance section of broadsheet newspapers, where they were used to illustrate energy research, development and investment.

The absence of people, aside from technical experts or politicians, within the images from 2006 implied that decision-making about renewable energy technologies was an essentially technical/economic or political process that did not require substantial public engagement. The depiction of certain groups with renewable energy technologies, namely, 'informed' experts and members of an established elite, e.g. politicians, provided legitimacy for a model of the public as being deficient in knowledge or views about these technologies, as epitomized within the Mac cartoon (Figure 8.1).

Wind turbines were the most frequently depicted renewable energy technology and they had a variety of symbolic meanings: from lucrative financial investment to a means of protecting nature. While in 2006, it was politicians, investors and celebrities who were 'green', in 2007 'ordinary' people were photographed with 'green' technologies, especially within energy advertisements that depicted adults and children in a number of roles: as schoolchildren, parents or moral/planetary guardians. This suggested two ways in which engagement with renewable energy technologies was envisioned: firstly, through indirect contact, for example, through monetary transactions such as share prices, financial investment or paying 'green' energy bills; and, secondly, through identification with people and places affected (positively) by the installation of renewable energy technologies.

On the whole, decision-making about the siting of renewable energy technologies was represented as unproblematic. Where present within the sample of images, members of the public tended to be represented as indifferent or passively accepting of renewable energy technologies rather than as active supporters or objectors. There was no evidence of proximity (for example, 'in my back yard') being represented as a motivation for objection, despite proximity being emphasized, particularly within close-up photographs of wind turbines. While close-up shots of towering turbines had potentially negative symbolic associations, such as being monstrous, overbearing or noxious, on the whole, images of wind turbines were positive; symbolizing awe, power, technological progress and beauty. In this sense, there was little evidence of concern about the visual impact of wind farms either onshore or offshore. Instead, their striking, sentinel form was emphasized as a means of reinforcing rather than challenging the view that, at least for offshore wind developments, 'the ocean is special and humans should not intrude on it' (Kempton et al, 2005, p146).

Images containing members of the public, aside from advertisements, had relatively consistent meanings despite differences in the social, spatial, temporal and cultural context in which the images were created, and these meanings did not encompass discord or objection. Where impacts were specified, for example, within advertisements for energy companies, they were unlikely to be at the personal level. Rather, impacts were concentrated upon the local or wider community, e.g. a school, a church, or society more generally, for instance, as a means of addressing climate change. As opposition was not made visible, it increased the gap between norms of acceptability associated with renewable energy technologies generally and legitimate opposition to specific developments.

Although it was not possible to ascertain to what extent the images identified epitomized public views, not least because it was not possible to define who the public(s) were, it would seem reasonable to say that the newspaper images identified in this study reflected rather than 'distorted' public beliefs about renewable energy technologies. As such, these images are part of collective sense-making around renewable energy; they provide a means of envisioning, making concrete and familiar, technologies that are otherwise distant from everyday experience. However, the 2007 advertisements anchored renewable energy technologies to expressions of joy rather than the fear that might be associated with the potentially serious and threatening consequences of climate change. Furthermore, while some of the images illustrated the technical benefits or uses of micro-renewable technologies, e.g. solar panels installed on a church roof, they rarely provided any useful information about energy companies, renewable energy developers or the institutional structures that electricity supply operates within. This aggravates a situation whereby the institutions involved in planning decisions about the siting of large-scale renewable energy technologies, such as network operators, the electricity industry regulator OFGEM (Office of the Gas and Electricity Markets), or the Department for Energy and Climate Change (DECC), are seen as 'black holes'. Given that the energy policy debate initiated in 2006 focused upon all types of energy generation: conventional oil and gas, renewable sources and nuclear power; future studies might examine how public engagement with nuclear and conventional energy technologies was represented, particularly how risks and institutions associated with these technologies were communicated visually and how these differed from representations of engagement with renewable energy technologies.

Conclusions

Images are ubiquitous as a means of communicating information about unfamiliar and complex technologies or issues. The results of this study show that the content of newspaper images of renewable energy technologies has evolved such that members of the public are increasingly being represented alongside these technologies, replacing technical experts or politicians. However, they are typically represented as passive, individual supporters rather than as objectors and this may have the dual effect of delegitimating opposition and failing to acknowledge that opponents are likely to be collectives or institutions such as non-governmental organizations or industrialists with vested interests in opposing particular developments. Therefore, although an increase in salience of renewable energy technologies through a greater prevalence of images, albeit predominantly of wind turbines, is welcomed, increased public engagement with issues of energy policy and siting debates will require both a diversification in the type of technologies depicted and more detailed envisioning of the variety of roles that individuals can take in relation to public and private institutions involved in decision-making about the siting of renewable energy technologies.

Acknowledgements

This research was funded by the UK Research Council's Energy Programme under award number RES-152-25-1008. Thanks to Dr Yuko Heath for assisting with data collection and data analysis.

References

Bauer, M. (1995) (ed) *Resistance to New Technology: Nuclear Power, Information Technology, Biotechnology*, Cambridge University Press, Cambridge

Bauer, M., Durant, J., Ragnarsdottir, A. and Rudolfsdottir, A. (1995) S*cience and Technology in the British Press 1946–1992: The Media Monitor Project*, Vols 1–4, Technical Reports, Science Museum and Wellcome Trust for the History of Medicine, London

Beloff, H. (1994). 'Reading visual rhetoric', *Psychologist*, vol 7, no 11, pp495–499

Burningham, K. and O'Brien, M. (1994) 'Global environmental values and local contexts of action', *Sociology*, vol 28, no 4, pp913–932

Cass, N. (2006) 'Participatory-deliberative engagement: a literature review', Working Paper 1.2, Beyond Nimbyism project, www.geography.exeter.ac.uk/beyond_nimbyism

Corner, J., Richardson, K. and Fenton, N. (1990) *Nuclear Reactions: Form and Response in Public Issue Television*, Libbey, London

Department of Energy and Climate Change (DECC) (2003) 'Our energy future: Creating a low-carbon economy', www.decc.gov.uk/en/content/cms/publications/white_paper_03/white_paper_03.aspx

Devine-Wright, H. (1998) 'Conformation and individuation in social representation', PhD thesis, University of Surrey, Guildford, UK

Devine-Wright, H. and Devine-Wright, P. (2009) 'Social representations of electricity network technologies: Exploring processes of anchoring and objectification through the use of visual research methods', *British Journal of Social Psychology*, vol 48, no 2, pp357–373

Devine-Wright, P. (2008) 'Reconsidering public acceptance of renewable energy technologies: A critical review', in M. Grubb, T. Jamasb and M. Pollitt (eds) *Delivering a Low Carbon Electricity System: Technologies, Economics and Policy*, Cambridge University Press, Cambridge, pp443–461

de Rosa, A. S. and Farr, R. (2001) 'Icon and symbol: Two sides of the coin in the investigation of social representations', in F. Buschini and N. Kalampalikis (eds) *Penser la Vie, le Social, la Nature: Mélanges en Hommage à Serge Moscovici*, Les Editions de la Maison des Sciences de l'Homme, Paris, pp237–256

de Rosa, A. S. and Kirchler, E. (2001) 'Ambiguous images in advertising: An application of the associative network method', in C. Roland-Levy, E. Kirchler, E. Penz and C. Gray (eds) *Everyday Representations of the Economy*, WUV/Universitatsverlag, Vienna, pp49–65

Ekins, P. (2004) 'Step changes for decarbonising the energy system: Research needs for renewables, energy efficiency and nuclear power', *Energy Policy*, vol 32, no 17, pp1891–1904

Hansen, A., Cottle, S., Negrine, R. and Newbold, C. (1998) *Mass Communication Research Methods*, Palgrave, Basingstoke, UK

Joffe, H. (2003) 'Risk: From perception to social representation', *British Journal of Social Psychology*, vol 42, no 1, pp55–73

Kempton, W., Firestone, J., Lilley, J., Rouleau, T. and Whitaker, P. (2005) 'The offshore wind power debate: Views from Cape Cod', *Coastal Management*, vol 33, no 2, pp119–149

Lee, T., Wren, B. and Hickman, M. (1989) 'Public responses to the siting and operation of wind turbines', *Wind Engineering*, vol 13, pp188–195

MORI Social Research Institute (2004) 'Attitudes to renewable energy in Devon', for Regen SW, www.planningrenewables.org.uk/lib/liOtherDoc/336/Attitudes%20to%20renewable%20energy%20in%20Devon%20November%202004.%20Main%20report.pdf?CFID=587923&CFTOKEN=71725483

Moscovici, S. (1976) *La Psychanalyse, Son Image et Son Public*, Presses Universitaires de France, Paris

Moscovici, S. (1984) 'The phenomenon of social representations', in R. M. Farr and S. Moscovici (eds) *Social Representations*, Cambridge University Press, Cambridge, pp3–70

Pauwels, L. (2006) *Visual Cultures of Science: Visual Representation and Expression in Scientific Knowledge Building and Science Communication*, Dartmouth College Press, Hannover, Germany

Populus Ltd (2005) 'Energy balance of power poll', www.populus.co.uk/the-times-energy-balance-of-power-060705.html

Rose, G. (2001) *Visual Methodologies: An Introduction to the Interpretation of Visual Materials*, Sage, London

Sauter, R. and Watson, J. (2007) 'Strategies for the deployment of micro-generation: Implications for social acceptance', *Energy Policy*, vol 35, no 5, pp2770–2779

Scottish Executive (2003) 'Securing a renewable future: Scotland's renewable energy', www.npower-renewables.com/whyrenew/pdfs/srfe.pdf

Stagl, S. (2005) 'Multicriteria evaluation and public participation: The case of UK energy policy', *Land Use Policy*, vol 23, no 1, pp53–62

Stuart, A. E. and Blanton, H. (2003) 'The effects of message framing on behavioural prevalence assumptions', *European Journal of Social Psychology*, vol 33, no 1, pp93–102

van Leeuwen, T. and Jewitt, C. (2001) *Handbook of Visual Analysis*, Sage, London

Weick, K. E. (1995) *Sensemaking in Organizations*, Sage, London

Chapter 9

NIMBYism and Community Consultation in Electricity Transmission Network Planning

Matthew Cotton and Patrick Devine-Wright

Introduction:
The Electricity Network

In the UK, the Climate Change Act has established legally binding 'carbon budgets' aimed at cutting CO_2 emissions by 34 per cent by 2020 and at least 80 per cent by 2050 through investment in energy efficiency and low carbon energy technologies. Within the electricity sector, targets have been set to provide 40 per cent of UK electricity from low carbon sources such as renewables and nuclear power by 2020 (DECC, 2009). The development and deployment of new low carbon energy technologies requires significant infrastructural developments to the interconnected electricity transmission and distribution network systems that connect these power generation sources to industrial and domestic electricity users.

The primary focus of this chapter is upon the development of electricity transmission networks. The terms *transmission* and *distribution* denote electricity movement at different voltage levels and points of connection. Transmission is the bulk movement of electricity at high voltages (usually 400 or 275kV) from generating stations to distribution systems and to a small number of large industrial customers. Distribution is electricity provision to the majority of industrial and domestic customers through lower-voltage localized networks (typically 132kV to 230V) (Butler, 2001). There are three UK companies that hold a statutory licence under the Electricity Act 1989 to 'develop and maintain an efficient, coordinated and economical transmission system of electricity supply' (HMSO, 1989), and the National Grid Company (NGC) is the central focus here due to the fact that it owns the transmission network in England and Wales and operates the system across Great Britain, and is largest, both in terms of infrastructure assets and share of total transmission. The NGC invests in new infrastructure in order to connect new generating capacity (at one end of the system) and new customer connections from industry and the distribution networks (at the other end). It has a statutory duty to facilitate competition by offering to connect customers (generators, direct connectees and distribution network operators) to their systems, and hence the need for new network equipment is determined in the first instance by the locations chosen by their customers individually or collectively. The NGC is legally required to respond to customer requests by utilizing existing assets more efficiently or by building new infrastructure, including overhead lines and substations (National Grid, 2009c). Siting transmission infrastructure has, however, become increasingly difficult due to:

- the scale and technical complexity of the task;
- the changing industry structure;
- a regulatory environment that has turned publicly owned and vertically integrated electricity generation, transmission and supply companies into *de facto* regional monopolies (Graham and Marvin, 1994; Krapels, 2002);
- the changes in planning legislation that have placed a greater emphasis upon early public and stakeholder engagement (PSE) in infrastructure planning as part of the wider sustainable development framework and through the UK Planning Act 2008;
- the broader institutionalization of PSE in environmental planning and in science and technology decision-making contexts.

Environmental Impacts and Public Opposition

Infrastructure siting involves disparate risks, costs and benefits to diverse stakeholders, and affects local populations and the surrounding environment. Of critical importance is the fact that impacts are distributed asymmetrically, fuelling local opposition and compounding already complex engineering and economic considerations and project constraints (Vajjhala and Fishchbeck, 2007). Siting overhead lines, in particular, has often resulted in the formation of localized social 'technology movements' (Walsh et al, 1993) that bring diverse actors together to object to line siting in specific geographical areas, often resulting in significant planning delays (Jay, 2004). In the 1990s, for example, localized public opposition emerged towards proposals for the 50-mile 400kV Lackenby–Picton–Shipton overhead transmission line from Teesside to York in northeast England, whereby the affected local authorities formally objected, along with MPs, MEPs and approximately 8000 local residents along the designated route corridor (Sheate, 1995). Similarly, recently proposed upgrades to overhead lines from the Scottish towns of Beauly, north of Inverness, to Denny in Stirlingshire, from existing 132kV lines to the higher capacity 275kV and 400kV type, have been subject to such local opposition. The proposed 140-mile route has been met with widespread opposition, with over 17,000 objections to the application (Grant, 2009).

The motivations for public opposition are multifaceted. Overhead lines are locally unwanted land uses, due in part to emergent social and environmental impacts, in particular the visual intrusion into rural and suburban landscapes that has negative effects on local 'amenity value' and household property values (Priestley and Evans, 1996; Sims and Dent, 2005). Possible health concerns have been raised, such as the risk of childhood leukaemia arising from exposure to the electromagnetic fields emitted by overhead lines sited close to housing developments and other public areas (Draper et al, 2005). These localized factors highlight the asymmetrical distribution of electricity infrastructure impacts, whereby social benefits, risks and losses are unevenly distributed, particularly when losses and risks are 'concentrated' in areas in close proximity to line sites, and benefits are 'dispersed' across the broader society (Quah and Tan, 1998).

NIMBYism and siting

Where localized opposition to specific facility sites occurs, the 'Not in my back yard' (NIMBY) concept is often invoked to describe citizens' reactions. NIMBY labels characterize opponents as being able to recognize the value of an unwanted facility as long as it is not sited close to where they personally live (Fischer, 1995; Wolsink, 1996). In some cases, for example, Kuhn's (1998) study of nuclear waste repository siting, there is a correlation among those who support a proposed facility in principle, between the perception of risk and acceptable distance of the facility from their place of residence; although Devine-Wright (2005) notes that there is a general assumption within the literature on the NIMBY concept (particularly in relation to wind energy) that those living the closest to developments are likely to have the most negative attitudes when the empirical evidence is less conclusive. However, some studies have shown that individuals living closer to developments actually tend to have more positive attitudes towards infrastructure projects in comparison with those living further away (Braunholtz, 2003; Warren et al, 2005). With respect to overhead lines in particular, Priestley and Evans' (1996) survey of 236 residents living within 900ft of a transmission line in San Francisco illustrates how spatial proximity does not necessarily correlate with levels of concern about the lines, as their study showed no effect of distance or line visibility on perceptions of health and safety, house values or aesthetics. It appears that public concern over line siting cannot, therefore, be adequately explained by simply correlating the proximity of local citizens to the line, and then characterizing the opposition that arises as an attempt by individuals to protect 'local amenities' and household property values from negative local impacts.

Critique of the NIMBY concept

The NIMBY label is problematic, as it is often used by proponents of development projects as a means to discredit all forms of project opposition, regardless of its motivation (Davy, 1996), and wrongly characterizes local people as worried, irrational, ignorant of scientific and technical facts, and selfishly unwilling to support projects that benefit the broader society (Luloff et al, 1998; Burningham, 2000). Even if one were to accept this characterization of citizens opposed to line siting, NIMBYism is neither irrational nor necessarily unethical. Individuals behave rationally by rejecting personal disadvantage in order to achieve advantages for others, and in the context of potential health risks, the acceptance of personally elevated risks to help others is supererogatory, i.e. virtuous 'beyond the call of duty' (Peterson and Hansson, 2004). When members of a local community are required to accept risk exposure not imposed on others, they may legitimately ask why they and not others have been selected. Leaving aside the pejorative connotations of the NIMBY label, it does, however, raise significant questions about the spatial and power relationships involved in the distribution of project siting impacts.

Public opposition is partly rooted in the environmental justice implications of unevenly distributed risks and benefits between the transmission network operators (which are profit-making industries), electricity users, ecosystems and occupants of spaces subject to overhead line developments. There are, however, also fundamental socio-cultural factors that motivate public opposition, such as the lack of familiarity that citizens have with regard to the roles that network operators play in managing and developing the network, and hence a lack of trust in those organizations (Devine-Wright and Devine-Wright, 2009), and also a lack of expectation amongst local residents that network operators will implement community involvement in planning processes (Devine-Wright et al: 2010).

Understanding network operator communication with stakeholders and local communities

Given the aforementioned factors, it is necessary to understand that infrastructure siting impacts are influenced not just by the outcomes of line siting (i.e. the proximity of lines to houses and other occupied spaces) but by the nature of decision-making around line route selection and the attitudes of network industry actors towards opposition groups, local communities affected by line siting, and the stakeholder networks involved in planning. Implicit in this, therefore, are the mechanisms through which transmission network operators (TNOs) seek to communicate and engage with these different groups, and the ways in which heterogeneous social values are integrated into infrastructure siting processes. As such, it is necessary to understand the rationales and methods of TNO communication, consultation and engagement with these heterogeneous social actors affected by infrastructure siting and involved in project opposition, in order to illustrate how social constraints to network development are approached and resolved.

Interviewing Transmission Network Operator Actors

To explore these issues, a qualitative interview study was conducted with key actor representatives within the network transmission and distribution industry. The results draw upon six in-depth interviews (and one shorter solely public engagement-focused interview) with TNO representatives, taken from a larger study across the networks industry (22 interviews with TNO, DNO and OFGEM representatives; see Cotton and Devine-Wright, 2010); it also examines recent policy and consultation documents released by the NGC regarding their stakeholder and community consultation strategies. The participants were chosen for their respective expertise in land use planning, environmental assessment, electric and magnetic field risks, research and development, and public consultation. A 'snowball' sampling strategy was used, where information gained from the earlier interviews was used to access other key participants. A standardized interview protocol was used, structured around themes of perceived future technology and infrastructure developments; how network actors constructed the concept of 'the public', 'stakeholders' and 'local communities'; the legislative and policy context of public engagement in network infrastructure siting; and the rationales and methods of communication and engagement employed. The interview data were transcribed and coded using MaxQDA software, based upon a constructionist epistemology and 'thematic' coding structure (Coffey and Atkinson, 1996) to inductively draw together emerging themes from the data set for further analysis and discussion. Quotations are anonymous and the participants are numbered for differentiation.

Network infrastructure siting processes

First and foremost, TNO respondents recognized that public consultation is an important aspect of network infrastructure siting due to the long-term changes to local landscapes that occur as the network expands:

> TNO3: *'Electricity has done more consultation historically, because, well, not that we build them very often, but when we do, power lines stick up above ground and they're in the local community's conscience for the next 60 years.'*

The siting of overhead lines and substations follows a specific process involving multi-actor engagement throughout. As mentioned previously, the primary reason for new infrastructure development begins with an electricity generation developer-led application for a connection. Once an application has been submitted, the planning process is multi-phased. At the point at which TNO1–6 were interviewed, respondents noted that network planning was approached on a 'high' or 'strategic' level first – whereby a broad 'route corridor' is proposed:

> TNO1: *'We're [TNO] coming to a view about where we think this thing ought to, in the general sense, be generally routed. And that's a broad corridor, about a kilometre wide, for arguments sake, it isn't a precise alignment and a precise route.'*

TNO respondents stated that, at the initial planning stages, input from external technical consultants and internal TNO personnel factors into the technical design, followed by input from 'key stakeholders' who can take a 'national, regional or strategic view'. These include:

> TNO1: *'Countryside Council for Wales, Natural England, English Heritage, Environment Agency, DECC [Department for Energy and Climate Change], National Assembly for Wales: organizations that are capable of seeing what our problem is, understanding what our need is and then we can consult at that level with them about the scope and the methodology of how we're going to go about this task of finding where's the best place to route this new line.'*

TNO respondents categorized this stage as 'strategic' or 'high-level' consultation. The second involves consultation with local planning authorities, and then:

> TNO1: *'Once you get to a point where you've got a broader consensus at that strategic level … then toward the end of that process … we would contemplate holding public exhibitions and opening the doors to absolutely everybody … and only then start canvassing opinion.'*

> TNO2 [in reference to a potential line-siting project in Mid-Wales]: *'On the really big projects, we've got to start [with]… where do we sensibly think we should be building it and then get to what's the right stage to start talking to communities, and that tends to be when we're getting to the stage of actually, "We think it's going to be coming through your community here," as opposed to engaging with people who are never going to be bothered about it or impacted by it ultimately.'*

At the first stages of assessing the broader route corridor for a line, it is clear that technical and geographical criteria are of primary importance, and these criteria are evaluated firstly by the TNO and associated consultants, then by strategic or 'high-level' stakeholders, followed by local planning authorities and then 'the public'. Implicit in this statement is an assumption about both the capacities of non-institutionally affiliated citizens to take a high-level, or 'strategic' viewpoint, and an explicitly ethical motivation for excluding citizen consultation at this early stage. As interviewee TNO1 continues:

> *'We've got a great big study area here, and the thing [overhead line] is going to end up being in one place; we don't think it's right that we worry*

and upset everybody in this 314 square kilometres about, "Are they going to end up building it in my back yard, and in my area?" which is what happens. We think it's right that we start talking to the public once we're drawing some firmer conclusions about where this thing should appropriately be built.'

At the time of interview, once specific route corridors are established across specific geographical areas, then the affected citizenry within these routes become involved in a consultative capacity on 'route alignment' further 'downstream' in the decision-making process. Implicit in this planning strategy are specific NIMBY assumptions that characterize the NGC's attitude towards local communities along the route corridor. Inherent in the conceptualization of NIMBY objectors were assumptions that the proximity of housing developments to lines was the primary motivating factor, as TNO 4 states:

'A NIMBY objector is somebody who was either rural or semi-rural who had the line passing in proximity and just didn't want it.'

TNO5 [in relation to a line-siting example in Scotland]: *'Although there was a wealth of objection round about the area it came from … and fundamentally there was an argument there on routing of the line to the east or west of the village and the line ultimately went to the east and that became the subject of the local community's or that community council's involvement in objecting. But very much driven by people who are not in the centre of the village by any manner or means, or anybody to the west of the village who was extremely pleased that it wasn't there. It tended to be the people in closest proximity to the route of the line.'*

This categorization of NIMBY responses to line siting influences the manner in which TNOs engage with local communities. Citizens from affected site communities are excluded from 'upstream' decision-making (see Wilsdon and Willis, 2004) at the 'high' level because they are characterized as concerned by the proximity of the line to their town/village and incapable of input into the broader strategic planning processes due to being concerned primarily with the protection of local spaces, even from within their own community. Implicit in this strategy, therefore, is a strategic rationale to consult with communities as a means to ameliorate public opposition to line siting following a proposed route, rather than to share decision-making power, or build local partnerships in choosing the appropriate route:

TNO2: *'You need to get it [public engagement] right, to get it as quick as possible, to get it as cheap as possible. What you don't want to do is be wasting money. So it's a bit like putting up a planning application for whatever; it's worth doing a bit of lobbying to make it smoother. It's that sort of scenario, and it's information. It's informing … you typically come*

> *up against people who are going to be very antagonistic. You need to get*
> *over the information so that people can go on fact, rather than hearsay*
> *and whatever.'*

> TNO6: *'We're very much more of an open and consulting company than*
> *we used to be ... one of the things that National Grid has become quite*
> *passionate about is the importance of involving people in the process*
> *because you are far more likely to get informed decisions made by the*
> *public if you treat them with respect in the first place and give them as*
> *much information as you can to help them understand why it is you need*
> *to do something and then how it's going to be built.'*

Although these statements allude to public involvement throughout the stages of the planning process, it is clear that engagement strategies emphasize information provision and placation rather than the integration of diverse social values into the decision-making process. These characterizations display 'deficit model' thinking (Wynne, 1982), which portrays citizens as passive, ignorant and worried, and technical specialists as knowledgeable experts. By working under these assumptions, the goal becomes more and better communication of expert knowledge to the public in order to allay misinformed, 'irrational' objections, and to encourage them to adopt a more positive attitude towards technical proposals (Irwin and Michael, 2003). This statement illustrates how infrastructure siting decisions are problematized by the prioritization of the *bounded rationality* that TNO experts possess (and can effectively communicate to lay people) over the *social rationality* of the 'lay' public (Perrow, 1999); whereby 'hard' technical and scientific expertise is communicated in order to ameliorate an antagonistic public that bases its decisions upon 'soft' lay knowledge, moral values and emotions.

Changes to infrastructure planning legislation

It is important to note that changes to the NGC's planning processes have occurred in light of the Planning Act 2008, which establishes new criteria for large infrastructure projects, intended to speed the handling of these developments through the planning system. The Act brings in a new two-stage process to address the need for new infrastructure in a National Policy Statement (NPS), and then the local impacts of a specific proposed development are assessed by a new Infrastructure Planning Commission (IPC) rather than by Ministers and their inspectors. The development of new high-voltage power lines (of 132kV or above) will be covered by the Act and, at the time of writing, a new draft National Policy Statement is being prepared for consultation which details how these new legislative requirements are to be implemented. TNO respondents were keen to stress that the PSE is an important and valued aspect of their infrastructure planning processes, and that the IPC creates new challenges for TNO engagement with local communities in a way that can effectively incorporate public values and knowledge into decision-making processes:

TNO3: '*One of the big concerns that's been raised is whether or not the arrival of the IPC means that there'll be less public say in major new infrastructure projects because of the effective removal of local planning authorities from the decision-making process. So we've been very concerned because we've been very strong advocates of the creation of the IPC and the removal of local authorities from the planning process of major schemes, but we're also very conscious of the fact that we need to make sure that the public do have an opportunity to have their say at a stage where they can influence the design of the project itself not just, you know, what colour the gates are going to be, if you see what I mean?*'

In reference to this challenge, the NGC released a draft consultation document on their stakeholder, community and amenity policy (National Grid, 2009c) which, among other things, details a commitment to community and stakeholder consultation involving the following commitments:

- to identify and understand the views and opinions of all the stakeholders and communities who may be affected by our works;
- to provide opportunities for engagement from the early stages of the process, where there is the greatest scope to influence the design of the works;
- to endeavour to enable constructive debate to take place, creating open and two-way communication processes;
- to ensure that benefits, constraints and adverse impacts of proposed works are communicated openly for meaningful stakeholder and community comment and discussion;
- to be clear about any aspects of the works that cannot be altered;
- to utilize appropriate methods and effort in engaging stakeholders and communities, proportionate to the scale and impact of the works;
- to provide feedback on how views expressed have been considered, and the outcomes of any engagement process or activity.

To illustrate these principles in practice, at the time of writing the NGC is implementing community consultation processes in advance of applications to the newly constituted IPC for a development consent order for new 400kV overhead electricity transmission line connections in southwest England, and for new transmission upgrades along the line from Bramford (East Anglia) to Twinstead (southeast England). In both cases, following 'strategic-level' consultation and detailed route corridor studies (National Grid, 2009a) for these network connections, a community consultation is carried out, with options for community feedback on the proposed route corridors. This occurs first through opportunities for public inspection and commentary on proposals at various locations throughout each of the proposed routes, or through online responses; and second, through a series of open exhibitions where local participants can view the proposals, talk to project team representatives, and record their comments at venues at approximately 6km intervals within the consultation zones along the length of each route and, where such venues are available, in the consultation zones surrounding the proposed substations. The National Grid proposes the following public engagement strategy:

- No fewer than 14 public meetings are being held for the Hinkley Point project, and 19 for the Bramford to Twinstead project, at about 6km intervals along the proposed routes.
- All those living within 1km will be mailed directly. Briefings are being offered to Parish and Town Councils, and other organizations can invite the National Grid to brief them.
- Specific community forums may also be created.
- Project updates will be distributed at least every six months to those organizations and others who request them.
- Comments can be made online, to freepost addresses, or by telephone.

At the exhibitions, feedback forms are available for members of the public to record their comments. The NGC will also offer project briefings with Parish and Town Councils in the vicinity of the proposed works, followed by project updates as the proposals progress (National Grid, 2009b). These methods form the basis of the public engagement strategy that the NGC plans to adopt in all future large-scale infrastructure projects.

The crucial difference between previous public consultation processes illustrated in the above quotes and the new public consultation strategy mandated by the IPC is, as TNO7 states:

> *'[NGC public consultations are] going out a lot earlier than before; at the route corridor stage. Before we would have run public exhibitions at the 'alignment stage' where the towers go within that corridor.'*

In light of new planning legislation, the consultation processes have evolved towards more 'upstream' public engagement in the sense that now local communities have opportunities to give feedback on the choice of route corridor, rather than just to the siting of pylons within a preselected corridor. The public exhibitions, however, focus upon informing the communities of proposed works and allowing opportunities to ask questions and provide written feedback which will be summarized in a consultation report submitted to the IPC (National Grid, 2009b). Though ostensibly moving upstream, this new strategy still raises a number of questions about the framing of public responses. It is unclear from their consultation strategy documents how issues raised by community participants are selected as being important or appropriate. Although the NGC fulfils its stated aim to identify and understand the views and opinions of stakeholders and local communities, as their consultation document states:

> *'feedback and comments made at all stages of the consultation process will be recorded and carefully considered by the project team. Where appropri-*

ate, our project team will respond directly on the points that people make. Should other potentially viable options be raised during our consulta-tions, we will consider their relative merits and report on them' (National Grid, 2009b).

This raises a problem of 'framing' effects on public responses, as what is consid-ered 'important' is decided by the industry representatives, not citizen consultees. They also imply in their public engagement aims that moving the public exhibi-tion to an earlier stage in the planning process allows the local communities 'the greatest scope to influence the design of the works' (National Grid, 2009b), although this influence amounts to allowing citizens to choose their preferred option (presented as corridor option A or B) and no opportunity to contest the 'need' for new electricity infrastructure or the designated area of the route corri-dor, raise issues of compensation or benefits to affected communities, or assert different options for (for example) undergrounding lines and hence potentially reducing long-term environmental and community impacts.

Conclusions

The TNO characterizations of community engagement processes illustrate a number of significant challenges. A rhetoric of thorough and transparent commu-nity engagement is evident throughout both the respondents' statements and the NGC's consultation documents; however, community engagement is limited to feedback stating a preference for one of two preselected options, and so affected citizens effectively wield little decision-making power. Communities are portrayed by TNO respondents as NIMBYs who lack both the technical expertise and the strategic viewpoint necessary to have useful input into regional siting strategies, and hence are engaged in a capacity where their decisional influence is limited. One of the NGC's stated public engagement aims is 'to utilize appropriate methods and effort in engaging stakeholders and communities, proportionate to the scale and impact of the works'; however, the strategy of public exhibitions around route corridor selection is not necessarily 'appropriate'. The strategy of public exhibitions as a consultation method reveals a design primarily geared towards legitimizing agency decisions that have already been made (Fiorino, 1990). Such methods have been criticized for placing participants in the position of reacting to proposals rather than providing input into their development, and thus force participants to engage with predefined plans for siting, rather than providing opportunities to holistically evaluate the project's feasibility, or present alternative options (Gariepy, 1991). It would behove TNO organizations, there-fore, to be mindful of the fact that public exhibitions themselves can become a focal point for proposal opposition to agencies' *de facto* decisions, suggesting that their use as a tool to 'enable constructive debate to take place, creating open and two-way communication processes' (National Grid, 2009b) will be likely to serve the opposite purpose: reinforcing public opposition rather than ameliorating it, which could lead to project delay or, in extreme cases, ultimately force the TNO to abandon its proposals (Chess and Purcell, 1999), thus leading to planning failure and potentially causing damage to local community trust in the network operator organizations involved.

References

Braunholtz, S. (2003) 'Public attitudes to windfarms: A survey of local residents in Scotland', Scottish Executive Social Research and MORI Scotland, Edinburgh

Burningham, K. (2000) 'Using the language of NIMBY: A topic for research, not an activity for researchers', *Local Environment*, vol 5, no 1, pp55–67

Butler, S. (2001) 'UK Electricity Networks: The nature of UK electricity transmission and distribution networks in an intermittent renewable and embedded electricity generation future', Parliamentary Office of Science and Technology, London

Chess, C. and Purcell, K. (1999) 'Public participation and the environment: Do we know what works?' *Environmental Science and Technology*, vol 33, no 16, pp2685–2692

Coffey, A. and Atkinson, P. (1996) *Making Sense Of Qualitative Data: Complementary Research Strategies*, Sage, Thousand Oaks, CA

Cotton, M. and Devine-Wright, P. (2010) 'Making electricity networks "visible": Industry actor constructions of "publics" and public engagement in infrastructure planning', *Public Understanding of Science*, doi: 10.1177/0963662510362658

Davy, B. (1996) 'Fairness as compassion: Towards a less unfair facility siting policy', *Risk: Health, Safety and Environment*, vol 7, no 2, pp99–108

DECC (2009) *The UK Low Carbon Transition Plan: National Strategy for Climate and Energy*, Department of Energy and Climate Change, London

Devine-Wright, P. (2005) 'Beyond NIMBYism: Towards an integrated framework for understanding public perceptions of wind energy', *Wind Energy*, vol 8, no 2, pp125–139

Devine-Wright, H. and Devine-Wright, P. (2009) 'Social representations of electricity network technologies: Exploring processes of anchoring and objectification through the use of visual research methods', *British Journal of Social Psychology*, vol 48, no 2, pp357–373

Devine-Wright, P., Devine-Wright, H. and Sherry-Brennan, F. (2010) 'Visible technologies, invisible organisations: An empirical study of public beliefs about electricity supply networks', *Energy Policy*, vol 38, no 8, pp4127–4134

Draper, G., Vincent, T., Kroll, M. E. and Swanson, J. (2005) 'Childhood cancer in relation to distance from high voltage power lines in England and Wales: A case-control study', *British Medical Journal*, vol 330, no 7503, pp1290

Fiorino, D. (1990) 'Citizen participation and environmental risk: A survey of institutional mechanisms', *Science, Technology and Human Values*, vol 15, no 2, pp226–243

Fischer, F. (1995) 'Hazardous waste policy, community movements and the politics of Nimby: Participatory risk assessment in the USA and Canada', in: F. Fischer and M. Black (eds) *Greening Environmental Policy: The Politics of a Sustainable Future*, Paul Chapman Publishing, London

Gariepy, M. (1991) 'Toward a dual-influence system: Assessing the effects of public participation in environmental impact assessment for hydro-Quebec projects', *Environmental Impact Assessment Review*, vol 11, no 4, pp353–374

Graham, S. and Marvin, S. (1994) 'Cherry picking and social dumping: Utilities in the 1990s', *Utilities Policy*, vol 4, no 2, pp113–119

Grant, J. (2009) 'Expert warns case for Beauly-Denny power line is flawed', John Muir Trust, Edinburgh, www.jmt.org/news.asp?s=2&cat=Beauly%20Denny&nid= JMT-N10345

HMSO (1989) 'Section 9, The Electricity Act 1989', HM Stationery Office, London

Irwin, A. and Michael, M. (2003) *Science, Social Theory and Public Knowledge*, Open University Press, Maidenhead, UK

Jay, S. (2004) 'The forces shaping local planning policy on high voltage electricity installations', *Journal of Environmental Policy and Planning*, vol 6, no 3, pp207–226

Krapels, E. N. (2002) 'Stimulating new transmission investments', *Electricity Journal*, vol 15, no 3, pp76–80

Kuhn, R. G. (1998) 'Social and political issues in siting a nuclear-fuel waste disposal facility in Ontario, Canada', *Canadian Geographer*, vol 42, no 1, pp14–28

Luloff, A. E., Albrecht, S. L. and Bourke, L. (1998) 'NIMBY and the hazardous and toxic waste siting dilemma: The need for concept clarification', *Society and Natural Resources*, vol 11, no 1, pp81–89

National Grid (2009a) 'Detailed route corridor study', National Grid, Warwick, www.nationalgrid.com/uk/Electricity/MajorProjects/HinkleyConnection/ RouteCorridorStudies/index.htm

National Grid (2009b) 'Hinkley Point C connection project: Consultation strategy', National Grid, Warwick

National Grid (2009c) 'National Grid's commitments when undertaking works in the UK: Our stakeholder, community and amenity policy', National Grid, Warwick

Perrow, C. (1999) *Normal Accidents: Living with High Risk Technologies*, Princeton University Press, Princeton, NJ

Peterson, M. and Hansson, S. O. (2004) 'On the application of rights-based moral theories to siting controversies', *Journal of Risk Research*, vol 7, no 2, pp269–275

Priestley, T. and Evans, G. W. (1996) 'Resident perceptions of a nearby electric transmission line', *Journal of Environmental Psychology*, vol 16, no 1, pp65–74

Quah, E. and Tan, K. C. (1998) 'The siting problem of NIMBY facilities: Cost–benefit analysis and auction mechanisms', *Environment and Planning C*, vol 16, no 3, pp255–264

Sheate, W. (1995) 'Electricity generation and transmission: A case study of problematic EIA implementation in the UK', *Environmental Policy and Practice*, vol 5, no 1, pp17–25

Sims, S. and Dent, P. (2005) 'High-voltage overhead power lines and property values: A residential study in the UK', *Urban Studies*, vol 42, no 4, pp665–694

Vajjhala, S. P. and Fishchbeck, P. S. (2007) 'Quantifying siting difficulty: A case study of US transmission line siting', *Energy Policy*, vol 35, no 1, pp650–671.

Walsh, E., Warland, R. and Clayton Smith, D. (1993) 'Backyards, NIMBYs, and incinerator sitings: Implications for social movement theory', *Social Problems*, vol 40, no 1, pp25–38

Warren, C. R., Lumsden, C., O'Dowd, S. and Birnie, R. V. (2005) '"Green on green": Public perceptions of wind power in Scotland and Ireland', *Journal of Environmental Planning and Management*, vol 48, no 6, pp853–875

Wilsdon, J. and Willis, R. (2004) *See-through Science: Why Public Engagement Needs to Move Upstream*, Demos, London

Wolsink, M. (1996) 'Dutch wind power policy: Stagnating implementation of renewables', *Energy Policy*, vol 24, no 12, pp1079–1088

Wynne, B. (1982) *Rationality and Ritual: The Windscale Inquiry and Nuclear Decisions in Britain*, British Society for the History of Science, Chalfont St Giles, Bucks, UK

Part 2

CASE STUDIES OF PUBLIC BELIEFS AND RESPONSES

Chapter 10

Turning the Heat On: Public Engagement in Australia's Energy Future

Peta Ashworth, Anna Littleboy, Paul Graham
and Simon Niemeyer

Introduction

In Australia, climate change is bringing society face to face with issues that go right to the heart of the Australian economy, if not their psyche. Blessed to date with cheap energy, abundant coal reserves and extensive mineral resources for local use as well as export, Australia now finds itself a global contender for the highest rates of energy consumption and greenhouse gas emissions per capita (IEA, 2006).

Deep cuts in Australia's greenhouse gas emissions will only emerge through a combination of technological innovation, economic reform and societal change. Recognizing this, the Commonwealth Scientific and Industrial Research Organization (CSIRO) convened an Energy Futures Forum (EFF) to identify and assess a range of plausible scenarios for the future of energy in Australia. A diverse range of key stakeholders were brought together over two years to develop the scenarios and identify the likely impacts of action or inaction towards climate change. The scenarios generated by this group were also used as a vehicle for discussions and deliberation at three citizens' panels that were held with members of the general public.

This chapter discusses the use of scenarios as a vehicle for stakeholder dialogue and participatory decision-making around energy by examining the outcomes of these citizens' panels. The following section sets the context for this case study by outlining the energy landscape in Australia and an initiative of CSIRO's Energy Transformed Flagship (ETF) to apply both futures-oriented and deliberative research concepts to generate a range of plausible energy scenarios for detailed impact analysis. In the section entitled 'The use of scenarios as a vehicle for public deliberation on Australia's energy future', the use of these scenarios to engage in deliberation with members of the public is discussed and then analysed in the section entitled 'Overview of the results from the citizens' panels'. Finally, the chapter draws conclusions about the use of a scenarios-based approach for stakeholder deliberation and dialogue.

Australia's Energy Futures Forum

Energy in Australia

Energy is big business in Australia, with energy-related sectors such as electricity, mining and transport accounting for some 11 per cent of Australian gross domestic product (GDP) and around half of the total AU$190 billion in Australian exports each year (DRET, 2008). The sector has installed much of the nation's long-lived capital infrastructure such as electricity plants, transmission links, refineries and production facilities, pipelines, wind farms and smaller-scale wholesale and retail distribution sites. About 120,000 Australians are directly employed in 'energy', primarily through the production and supply of stationary energy (such as electricity and gas), transport energy (mainly petroleum-based fuels) and energy for export.

Australia is well endowed with energy resources (DRET, 2008). It is the world's fourth largest producer and exporter of coal (IEA, 2006), contends with Canada for supremacy in the export of uranium, and has substantial natural gas and oil resources. There is significant potential for renewable energy in the form of geothermal, wave, solar and wind. The potential for large-scale hydropower has largely been exploited although some potential for smaller-scale systems remains.

A small nation in terms of population, Australia spends AU$50 billion on energy each year. The largest uses are electricity generation, transport and manufacturing processes, which together account for some 75 per cent of Australia's energy consumption. Residential and commercial services consume 50 per cent of the country's generated electricity, with the remainder used in industry. Although it has a sophisticated energy infrastructure, the dominance of coal-fired power stations, the presence of established but energy-intensive primary industries, and the easy availability of relatively cheap energy means that Australia has the second highest greenhouse gas emissions per capita on the planet (DRET, 2008).

As a result of the energy landscape described above, Australians are familiar with a wide range of differing energy technologies and are used to accessible, secure and relatively cheap electricity. These factors have been critical in establishing the competitiveness of Australian industry in a global marketplace, but are under threat as Australia shifts to an energy system appropriate for a climate-altered world.

Responding to climate change is, by any reckoning, a 'wicked' problem (Funtowicz and Ravetz, 2001) – one that involves highly complex, uncertain interactions between technology, society and the environment, often with little or no precedent in documented history. Increasingly, diverse bodies of academic literature ranging from decision theory (Keeney, 1996), strategic foresight (Reidy, 2008), risk (Fischoff, 1995), public policy (Funtowicz and Ravetz, 2001) and communication are advocating concepts such as deliberation, consultation and participation as key components of determining a course of action in the face of such uncertainties. Recognizing this, and the rising priority on futures-oriented research, the CSIRO created the concept of an EFF in 2004. This forum provided a means of engaging a wide set of stakeholders from the energy and transport sectors – energy suppliers, generators, distributors, researchers, government and community representatives – in developing and assessing pathways for the future of energy in Australia and, in doing so, considered the implications for the nation's future.

The Energy Futures Forum

The EFF was conceived as a participatory process bringing together energy sector stakeholders to determine plausible scenarios and their implications for the future of Australia's energy sector (CSIRO, 2006). The forum went through a five-stage analytic-deliberative process to identify, refine and analyse a range of future scenarios over a period of two years. The five stages were:

1. developing detailed qualitative scenarios about how the future might unfold for the Australian energy sector;
2. social mapping to assess how public reactions to different aspects of Australia's energy future are likely to evolve, and to test the plausibility and comprehensiveness of the qualitative scenarios;
3. quantitative analysis of key scenario assumptions;
4. modelling of climate change impacts, risks and the benefits of mitigation;
5. deliberation on the implications.

Central to the EFF process was the development of scenarios for the future of energy in Australia (stage 1). Nine qualitative scenarios were developed – describing many possible interactions in the way that national and global situations could develop based on the availability and application of technology options and policy instruments. Developing qualitative scenarios is an art rather than a science. The scenario should quickly capture a lot of complexity and leave a lasting message with the reader. Scenario narratives should stretch thinking to challenge conventional wisdom and show futures that could diverge widely, whilst staying close enough to the present to maintain relevance and credibility. The details of their initial narrative content are less important than the types of conversation that they start. For this reason, the EFF scenarios were used as thought starters for multi-stakeholder dialogue, both between participants in the forum (stage 1 of the process) and also with the public (stage 2).

Table 10.1 summarizes the key attributes of the nine scenarios: Power to the People; Blissful Indifference; Rough Ride; Cultural Revolution; Clean Green Down Under; The Day After Tomorrow; Atomic Odyssey; Centralized Failure; and Technology to the Rescue (CSIRO, 2006). For each scenario, an indication of the consequential changes in technology were also identified.

Table 10.1 *Key attributes of the nine scenarios*

Blissful Indifference	*Business as usual policy settings leading to no new implementation of greenhouse gas emission reduction policies. Technological development and government policies progress along known paths.*
Rough Ride	*Geopolitical instability and conflict leading to global resource constraints, and lack of global agreement on addressing climate change. Technological change is limited.*
Centralized Failure	*Late action by all countries due to failure to reach a global agreement. When the scheme does commence the emission reduction rate is very high, with a full range of abatement technologies. However, nuclear power not adopted in Australia.*
The Day After Tomorrow	*Late and moderate action by all countries due to a failure to implement clear and comprehensive greenhouse gas mitigation policies. Moderate technological change.*
Cultural Revolution	*Early action by all countries following development of a China–US agreement. High rates of technological change. Nuclear power not adopted in Australia.*
Technology to the Rescue	*Early action by all countries is motivated by a desire to take part in a greenhouse gas abatement technology boom. High rates of technological change.*
Clean Green Down Under	*Early action by all countries and renewable energy prevalent. Carbon capture and storage is unavailable globally and nuclear not adopted in Australia.*
Atomic Odyssey	*Early action by all countries. Carbon capture and storage technology unavailable globally. Consequently Australia adopts nuclear power.*
Power to the People	*Early action on climate change and major restructure in the way in which Australians obtain their energy supply through distributed generation.*

The Use of Scenarios as a Vehicle for Public Deliberation on Australia's Energy Future

Objectives

The scenarios initially generated by the EFF were used as the vehicle for dialogue between the forum and members of the public. The purpose of this dialogue was to assess attitudes and perspectives of members of the public to the different scenarios and the different combinations of energy technologies contained therein at early stages in their development. In this way, forum participants sought to augment their own knowledge with information from public citizens. By initiating the dialogue at these early stages, the forum sought to adopt principles of early engagement, which has now been strongly advocated in many fields of public policy interaction with science. Deliberative democracy provided the primary theoretical framework on which this public consultation process was founded (Mendelberg, 2002).

Deliberative democracy involves group discussion on a given topic with a view to coming to some conclusion, having had access to expert information (Dryzek, 2000). Therefore, it was important to provide a group of people with the opportunity to engage with the issues facing the energy sector in an information-rich, but safe and respectful, environment. Critical parameters for understanding the dynamics of public perspectives on energy included:

- the recruitment of participants from a diversity of perspectives;
- definition of a clear remit, or task, for participants to address;
- the provision of sufficient information to address the remit;
- research methods that track and measure perspectives to identify how they change as a result of the process (Cooke, 2000; Dryzek, 2000; Mendelberg, 2002).

Having reviewed potential deliberative processes that would fulfil these criteria (Littleboy and Niemeyer, 2005), a citizens' jury or a 'planning cell' was selected as the appropriate way forward. In general, these processes encourage discussion and deliberation, based on information provided to the panel during and leading up to the process (Lovel et al, 2004). However, to accommodate the open-ended nature of the scenarios component of the forum, the process was modified somewhat to limit any expectation that concrete recommendations and preferences would be implemented. This resulted in the citizens' jury approach being modified to a citizens' panel.

Overall approach

The citizens' panels were conducted across three states of Australia in two discrete phases, with a period of time in between to review and revise the approach (Figure 10.1).

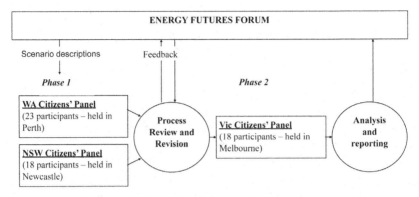

Figure 10.1 *Research approach*

Participants were recruited by stratifying 180 responses from 2000 letters sent to randomly selected citizens in each of the three states. This resulted in 23 participants in Perth and 18 in both Newcastle and Melbourne after some attrition. Descriptive representation of the participants was achieved using random stratification for gender, age and reduction, which were benchmarked against the distribution within the Australian population. Participants were provided an incentive to participate in the form of a relatively small stipend. This was done both to improve the response rates during recruitment and to compensate participants for their time and incidental costs.

The task of each of the citizens' panels was to consider a range of technologies that might be part of a future energy system for Australia and to make suggestions for a secure and sustainable energy future. The facilitator of the process guided the participants through a series of exercises, including providing feedback about what they considered to be the main issues in relation to energy, before being given any specific information, discussing how they felt about different scenarios for the future proposed by the EFF; assessing different energy technologies having heard from experts on climate change and technology; and finally working in small groups to make suggestions about a preferred energy future. Table 10.2 summarizes the main elements of the citizens' panel process.

Following analysis and review of the Perth and Newcastle panels using exit survey feedback and follow-up interviews with participants, some process modifications were made prior to the second phase of the project. These included:

- providing more time for deliberation, as there was evidence of incomplete deliberation in Perth, where some aspects of deliberation were still exploratory at the end of the three days;
- providing more information on social and economic modelling that became available between phase 1 and phase 2;
- allowing participants the opportunity to ask questions about climate change;
- providing more background information to all participants prior to attending the process.

Table 10.2 *The Energy Futures citizens' panel process*

Day	Phase 1: Perth and Newcastle			Phase 2: Melbourne		
	Focus	Questions to consider	Information provided	Focus	Questions to consider	Information provided
1	Orientation	None	The remit of the citizens' panel	Orientation	None	Remit and background reading from AGO and Victorian Government literature
	Mind mapping exercise	What are the issues facing Australia's energy future?	None	Mind mapping exercise	What are the issues facing Australia's energy future?	None
	EFF scenarios	How plausible are the energy scenarios? How comprehensive are the scenarios?	CSIRO presentation on current energy context; EFF Chair presents potential scenarios	Climate change and environmental risk	None	Presentation by leading Australian climate scientist
	Climate change and environmental risk	None	Dinner presentation on the impacts of climate change by leading Australian climate scientist	Potential social and economic impacts	None	Presentation of Business Roundtable findings by CSIRO
2	Energy technologies	What criteria are important for evaluating technologies?	Presentations by CSIRO describing different technologies	EFF scenarios	How plausible are the energy scenarios? How comprehensive are the scenarios?	Presentation by EFF Chair on potential scenarios for the future
	Technology preferences	How do the different technologies stack up against different criteria?	None	Australia's energy system and energy technologies	What criteria are important for evaluating technologies?	Presentations by CSIRO on current energy context and available energy technologies
3	Mapping technologies and scenarios through group deliberation	What are your suggestions for Australia's energy future?	None, but interactive sessions and feedback presentations were used to ensure that feedback from participants was accurately represented	Mapping technologies and scenarios through group deliberation	What are your recommendations for Australia's energy future?	None, but interactive sessions and feedback presentations were used to ensure that feedback from participants was accurately represented

Measurement and monitoring

Both quantitative and qualitative data were generated by all panels and used to monitor shifts in perspectives during the process. Monitoring of underlying attitudes was achieved by using Q methodology, a form of quantitative discourse analysis (Brown, 1980; Dryzek, 1990) designed to maintain robustness and external validity with small participant samples. Participants completed three surveys, known as 'Q sorts' – one at the start of the process, one midway through the process (after information and discussion), and one at the end of the process (after deliberation). The Q sorts entailed participants initially indicating their level of agreement or disagreement on 45 statements representing different positions on energy futures, which were drawn (verbatim in most cases) from secondary sources covering debate regarding energy futures in Australia – newspaper articles and reports. Many were also drawn directly from the EFF discussions that were recorded and transcribed during the process. Participants then sorted or ranked their responses according to a predetermined distribution. At the same time, participants were also asked to rank nine energy technologies in order of preference according to how resources should be invested, providing another source of quantitative data to monitor changing preferences.

The results from this exercise were used to track the shifts in discourses during the panel meetings. This was done using a similar approach to that adopted by Niemeyer (2004), by measuring the extent to which participants 'agreed' with each of the discourses, where the discourses were derived using inverted factor analysis. This produced four 'discourses' in the form of an array of typical responses to the 45 statements. Level of agreement was measured in the form of factor loadings, which is analogous to a simple correlation with the typical response to each statement for the four factors.

A third source of quantitative data was a technology assessment exercise in which participants were asked to rank the nine technologies according to specific criteria including greenhouse gas emissions, social impact and the costs of the technology.

Direct records of the dialogue and written input from the participants were kept through the use of different media, the writing up of breakout group material, and the completion of a post-process questionnaire. This all formed part of the citizens' panel record and was used in the subsequent analysis.

Overview of the Results from the Citizens' Panels

In qualitative terms, all panels advocated a paradigm shift towards a more synergistic society where goods are shared, wastes are reduced, reused and/or recycled, and services are provided on the basis of life cycle management. This was not seen as necessarily being detrimental to the economy if we can think differently about how to run our businesses. The panels indicated a preparedness to pay more in taxes to make this happen, but wanted reassurance that the money raised was going to encourage immediate change to conserve energy and reduce use; to establish education systems to equip the upcoming generation with the knowledge to manage a different energy system; and to appoint an independent arbiter for apportioning research and development funds appropriately.

Plausibility of the EFF scenarios

Perspectives on the plausibility of the forum-generated scenarios emerged from qualitative information elicited following a presentation on the scenarios. The panels in general confirmed the following:

- Late action on climate change and greenhouse gas mitigation is considered very plausible. A number of the forum scenarios resulted in this late action ('Rough Ride', 'Blissful Indifference', 'Centralized Failure', and 'The Day After Tomorrow'), although for different reasons.
- Scenarios involving early action with distributed energy engendered the maximum interest from all three panels – particularly in terms of the opportunities they presented for localized (distributed) generation and the requirements they imposed for additional regulation. 'Power to the People' and 'Clean Green Down Under' were the scenario examples that most obviously conformed to this perspective.
- At the Melbourne panel, the business costs of early action were discussed much more. This was because the Australian Business Roundtable on Climate Change (2006) had just released their report showing positive support for early investment in mitigation options. The economic modelling from the Australian Business Roundtable report was presented in the modified process and obviously influenced the deliberations. However, overall participants still gravitated towards the early action scenarios ('Clean Green Down Under', 'Power to the People', 'Technology to the Rescue', and 'Cultural Revolution').
- Some of the assumptions implicit in the early action scenarios were considered implausible, most notably the notion of free global trading and commerce – most obvious in the 'Cultural Revolution' scenario.

Comprehensiveness of the scenarios

While no additional scenarios were identified by the panels, all three panels made suggestions about how to bring about the scenarios, with an emphasis being placed on public education and the establishment of an independent body to administer revenue from a carbon tax back into energy research and development.

Prevalent public 'discourses' concerning energy futures

Factor analyses of the quantitative data obtained from the participants during the panel process revealed five different types of 'discourses' or factors. These were loosely characterized using the following labels:

A. Broadscale reform
B. Centralized energy generation
C. Orderly reform
D. Technologically conservative
E. Radically alternative.

These discourses represent the major subjective groups embodying the values and beliefs of the panel participants in relation to energy technologies. The main prevailing attitudes of the emerging factors are summarized in Table 10.3, while Figure 10.2 shows the overlapping spheres containing statements representative of each discourse and their interrelation.

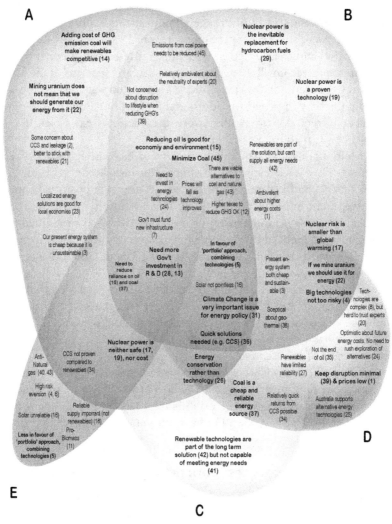

Figure 10.2 *Prevalent public discourses and typifying statements*

Table 10.3 *Prevailing attitudes towards energy technologies*

Attitude	Attractive technologies
A Broadscale reform – associated with 'whole energy approach' and a belief that all technologies can compete once externalities are factored in.	Renewable/decentralized technologies such as wind, solar, biomass and geothermal.
B Centralized energy generation – emphasis on centralized generation and distribution of energy and technology intensive approaches for greenhouse gas reductions.	Centralized technologies such as coal (only if combined with carbon capture and storage), natural gas, and in some cases nuclear.
C Orderly reform – concern about energy policy and how it might drive the system to evolve. Technology innovation over demand management is seen as the primary solution for greenhouse gas abatement.	Wide portfolio of technologies with emphasis on minimizing disruption and costs.
D Technologically conservative – most technology-conservative and price-sensitive. Cynicism towards experts. Greater emphasis on demand and behaviour to mitigate greenhouse gas emissions.	Averse to radical technological change.
E Radically alternative – concern about many of the large-scale technologies because of risk involved. Technology should follow the lead rather than driving change.	Low-risk technologies with minimum supply disruption such as natural gas, solar power, wind power and hydroelectric power.

Shifts in perspective during the panel process

Significant shifts in the strength of these discourses were identified as deliberation progressed (Figure 10.3). *Discourse A* reflects concern about climate change and the risks associated with large-scale solutions and, to a lesser extent, the social impacts. This led to increased interest in renewable sources of energy based on their potential to reduce greenhouse gas emissions. *Discourse A* remained strong through deliberation.

Two other strong trends were observed. The first trend occurred in relation to *Discourse B*, where interest in renewable energy was offset by an emphasis on current limitations such as meeting peak energy demand and high costs, thus tending to favour large-scale centralized solutions. The second trend was a shift towards *Discourse C*, which occurred mainly in Victoria, where there was a greater concern with the short-term viability of renewable energy which needed to be augmented by transition technologies. *Discourses D* and *E* both declined during the deliberation process.

All three of the large discourses (factors) shared serious concern about greenhouse emissions and climate change, which manifested itself in different energy

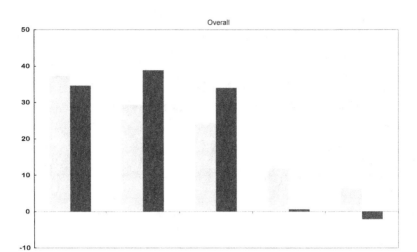

Figure 10.3 *Shifts in perspectives as a result of the panel process*

technology trajectories. Concerns about climate change, combined with a desire for certainty in energy supply, were the main distinguishing features, and also, to a lesser extent, concerns about the resulting shape of society.

Technology perspectives

A number of attributes were used to assess each of the technologies. The ability to reduce greenhouse gas emissions clearly dominated as the preferred attribute of energy technologies, followed by other environmental impacts and reliability and sustainability of energy supply (Figure 10.4). Other important attributes included

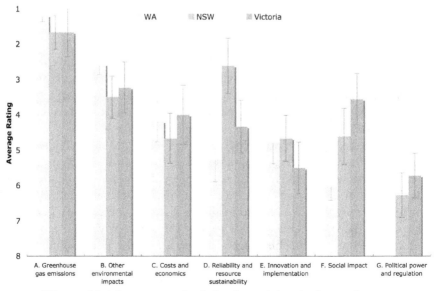

Figure 10.4 *Important criteria for determining the future of energy*

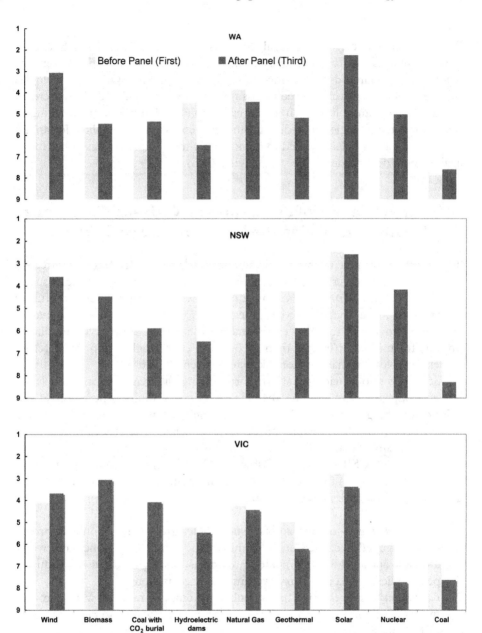

Figure 10.5 *Average technology priority rates before and after dialogue*

cost, social impact and the ease of implementation. The Victorian panel was more concerned with social impact (possibly as the result of an increased profile of this issue politically within the state) and New South Wales exhibited a significantly higher concern for reliability and resource sustainability, which can be expressed as a desire for a 'keeping the lights on' perspective.

Technology preferences

Similar to other studies (Reiner et al, 2006; Ashworth et al, 2007, 2008; Sola et al, 2007), when asked to individually rank their preferences for specific energy technologies, solar and wind tended to be the most popular. Other technologies that were more positively viewed across most of the panels included geothermal, gas-fired power and biomass. It is interesting to note that the more emerging or less familiar technologies, including geothermal, coal with carbon dioxide capture and storage, and nuclear tended to demonstrate more rapid swings either for or against them depending on the state (Figure 10.5).

The Effectiveness of Scenarios and Citizens' Panels as a Means of Engaging the Public on Energy Futures

The results from the citizens' panels demonstrate that the process is an effective way of engaging a diverse audience in discussion around such a complex issue as the global warming/energy nexus, particularly when trying to identify a future energy mix for a specific geographical location or country. The scenarios approach provides a tool that easily enables the presentation of a portfolio of options for mitigation rather than focusing in on a single solution: therefore presenting solutions that are more likely to be deemed plausible.

Scenarios also provide a platform for engaging all levels of society and stakeholder groups on a similar issue, therefore allowing for multiple perspectives and solutions to be generated and compared, which can provide a critical aid for policy-makers' decision-making processes – especially when they are grappling with such complex issues.

From earlier CSIRO research, Ashworth (2009) identified four key audiences to stratify stakeholders for engagement and information provision around climate and energy. These include the following:

1. *Influential others* – comprising key stakeholder groups that should be proactively engaged because they have the ability to influence policy and wider industry action. This can include politicians, managing directors, industry peak bodies, media and non-governmental organizations.
2. *Community* – representing the lay public who may or may not want to proactively engage on the topic but for the most part are willing to participate and provide their viewpoints.
3. *Education* – focusing on all levels from primary through to tertiary. Deemed an essential component for the longer-term acceptance and understanding of such complex issues requiring action.
4. *Project-specific* – in the energy domain it is clear that many of the solutions will involve acceptance of new technologies in certain geographical locations, and these require their own level of engagement to ensure positive outcomes for all concerned.

Often each of the audiences above would require a specific engagement process to elicit viewpoints on a particular issue, with the outcomes being difficult to compare. The scenario process, on the other hand, with its rich narrative and story-telling elements, can be used with all of these groups. This allows for effective and meaningful engagement and discussion of the problem, which generates results that are much more easily compared and contrasted.

Although this easy comparison of results is often evidenced with scenario processes, one of the major drawbacks of the EFF was the eventual lack of integration of the lay public citizens' panels' results into the larger forum process with influential stakeholders. In a review conducted after the two-year process ended, it was apparent there were mixed feelings in relation to the social modelling component. Some of the EFF participants praised the citizens' panel work; however, others felt that it was not adequately integrated into the results.

Much of this lack of integration was due to the processes running in parallel, with not enough time to share the findings of each of the panels as they were completed. This was also exacerbated because the formal forum involved high-level organizational representatives who were already time-challenged. Participation in the forum already required considerable additional time, which although participants were happy to give more time for the integration of the citizens' panels on top of this workload might have been negatively perceived. To overcome this problem, it was concluded that it is important to ensure that there is adequate time for the researchers of the citizens' panel social modelling process to report more frequently back into the overarching forum process and that time is allocated accordingly across the whole process.

Limitations and drawbacks

Although the citizens' panels provided the rich deliberation so useful for dealing with complex issues, there were some limitations to using them. The first is that for the panels to be successful you need to limit the number of participants in each panel. Although drawn from a representative sample, the numbers are always small, and it was therefore difficult to draw significant conclusions from such deliberations.

The other limitation is scenario planning processes; citizens' panels are very costly to run in terms of financial resources. The financial investment required can often result in alternative methodologies being the default process. In addition to financial resources, the time investment required is another resource that can critically impact on the success of such a process. Three days of each individual's time is a big ask for anyone participating voluntarily in such a panel. As such, this often resulted in last-minute drop-outs of participants because of external issues outside the control of the researchers.

This can also be exacerbated when panels are run over a period of time, as in the study reported in this chapter, because it can be difficult to have all the same experts available for each of the processes. However, this is critical in order to ensure good experimental design and being able to make direct comparisons whenever possible. Even within this process, we had to modify it slightly, learning from the earlier sessions, but of course this does impact on the overall results.

Conclusions

Despite these limitations, the overall process of citizens' panels provides an excellent framework for addressing complex issues that can be applied in various contexts at the local, national or international level. The rich deliberation that participants were exposed to was well received and it was apparent from the analyses that shifts in perspectives occurred due to the opportunity to experience having information presented from credible, trusted experts as well as the opportunity to interact with other peers within each of the panels to hear the range of viewpoints that individuals held. This, in turn, tended to challenge the underlying assumptions that many held about the various technology solutions.

Within Australia, this work has provided a strong foundation for helping to understand how the Australian lay public perceive climate change and the range of energy technologies required to achieve a low carbon economy. As a result, it has been welcomed by industry, policy-makers and researchers alike. The CSIRO ETF is continuing to build on these findings using a range of social processes to understand how perspectives shift when presented with objective information on the latest developments in low carbon emission energy solutions. In addition, the overall forum process has been used to examine the future of Australian transport fuels and will possibly be applied to examine the challenges currently being faced by the aviation industry as well. In addition, the concept is being used to examine other complex issues in different domains. For example, what is the future of Australia's mineral industry? As such, other countries could equally adapt the process to address issues being faced by policy-makers around the world.

References

Ashworth, P. (2009) 'Challenges and needs of industry when communicating the science of climate change', Paper presented at the Australian Science Communicators' Conference: Communicating the Challenge of Climate Change: Is It All Hot Air?, Brisbane, Australia, 19 August

Ashworth, P., Reiner, D., Gardner, J. and Littleboy, A. (2007) 'Kyoto or non-Kyoto People or Politics: Results of recent public opinion surveys on energy and climate change', Paper presented at Greenhouse 2007, Sydney, 1–5 October

Ashworth, P., Carr-Cornish, S., Boughen, N. and Thambimuthu, K. (2008) 'Engaging the public on carbon dioxide capture and storage: Does a large group process work?', Proceedings of the 9th International Conference on Greenhouse Gas Control Technologies (GHGT-9), 16–20 November, vol 1, no 1, pp4765–4773

Australian Business Roundtable on Climate Change (2006) 'The business case for early action', www.businessroundtable.com.au/html/documents.html

Brown, S. R. (1980) *Political Subjectivity: Applications of Q Methodology in Political Science*, Yale University Press, New Haven, CT

CSIRO (Commonwealth Scientific and Industrial Research Organization) (2006) *The Heat is On: The Future of Energy in Australia*, CSIRO Publishing, Canberra, Australia

Cooke, M. (2000) 'Five arguments for deliberative democracy', *Political Studies*, vol 48, no 5, pp947–969

DRET (Department of Resources, Energy and Tourism) (2008) 'Key facts on Australia's energy industry', www.ret.gov.au/energy/facts/Pages/EnergyFacts.aspx

Dryzek, J. S. (2000) *Deliberative Democracy and Beyond: Liberals, Critics, Contestations*, Oxford University Press, Oxford

Dryzek, J. S. (1990) *Discursive Democracy: Politics, Policy and Political Science*, Cambridge: Cambridge University Press

Fischoff, B. (1995) 'Risk perception and communication unplugged: Twenty years of process', *Risk Analysis*, vol 15, no 2, pp137–145

Funtowicz, S. O. and Ravetz, J. R. (2001) *Uncertainty and Quality in Science for Policy*, Theory and Decision Library, series A, vol 15: Philosophy and Methodology of the Social Sciences, Kluwer Academic Publishers, Dordrecht, The Netherlands

IEA (International Energy Agency) (2006) 'World energy outlook', www.worldenergyoutlook.org/2006.asp

Keeney, R. L. (1996) *Value-focused Thinking: A Path to Creative Decision Making*, Harvard University Press, Cambridge, MA

Littleboy, A. K. and Niemeyer, S. J. (2005) *Literature Review: Technology and Society*, CSIRO Exploration and Mining Report No. 232, CSIRO Publishing, Pullenvale, Australia

Lovel, R., Katz, E. and Solomon, F. L. (2004) *Participation Processes for the Minerals Industry*, CSIRO Minerals Report No. DMR-2375, CSIRO, Melbourne, Australia

Mendelberg, T. (2002) 'The deliberative citizen: Theory and evidence', in M. D. X. Carpini, L. Huddy and R. Y. Shapiro (eds) *Research in Micropolitics*, vol 6, Political Decision-making, Deliberation and Participation, JAI Press, London

Niemeyer, S. J. (2004) 'Deliberation in the wilderness: Displacing symbolic politics', *Environmental Politics*, vol 13, no 2, pp347–372

Reidy, C. J. (2008) 'Citizen participation in decisions about Australia's climate change response', Paper presented at the 4Rs Conference: Rights, Reconciliation, Respect, Responsibility. Sydney, 30 September–3 October

Reiner, D., Curry, T. E., de Figueiredo, M. A., Herzog, H., Ansolabehere, S., Itaoka, K., Akai, M., Johnsson, F. and Odenberger, M. (2006) 'An international comparison of public attitudes towards carbon capture and storage technologies', Paper presented at the 8th International Conference on Greenhouse Gas Control Technologies (GHGT-8), Trondheim, Norway, 18–22 June

Sola, R., Oltra, C. and Sala, R. (2007) *Public Perception of Energy Policy and Climate Change in Spain*, Social Research Technical Unit, CIEMAT

Chapter 11

Shaping People's Engagement with Microgeneration Technology: The Case of Solar Photovoltaics in UK Homes

Dana Abi-Ghanem and Claire Haggett

Introduction

Renewable energy technologies (RETs) are an important component in the effort towards meeting the challenges of climate change in the UK (Elliot, 2000; Ekins, 2004). In recent years, national energy strategies have included steps to promote the development and implementation of various types of RETs (Haas et al, 2004), including microgeneration technologies for the domestic sector. The benefits of microgeneration (which include solar photovoltaics, micro-wind, micro-CHP, ground source heat pumps, small hydro power and fuel cells) have been emphasized as a measure to mitigate the ever increasing energy demand of the sector (BERR, 2007) while providing a source of green electricity. In the UK, a review of the government's Energy White Paper (DTI, 2007) asserts their importance in achieving the country's target of a 60 per cent reduction in carbon emissions.

According to the Energy Saving Trust (EST, 2005), there will have to be significant increases in the deployment of microgeneration for it to have an impact on the UK's electricity system. The study by the EST emphasizes the need for a decentralized approach to energy policy and planning, but also points to the need for a 'new understanding of the likely interaction between microgeneration technology and its multitude of potential end users (the general public)' (EST, 2005, p4). However, the deployment of microgeneration technologies in the UK is still lagging behind other European countries such as Germany, Austria and Spain. Moreover, of the 4.6 per cent of the total electricity generated from RETs in the UK, 93 per cent of it is produced from large-scale technologies such as hydropower and wind (BERR, 2007). This suggests that much needs to be done to improve the diffusion of microgeneration technologies if the UK is to reach its carbon reduction targets.

In view of the urgent need to increase the uptake of RETs in the domestic sector, the government has set up various programmes that provide financial assistance for households willing to install new renewable energy sources; indeed, the levels of microgeneration installation are closely correlated with grant funding (EST, 2005). Moreover, field trial schemes were designed to promote, implement and monitor various microgeneration technologies, such as the Major Demonstration Programme, which aimed to install photovoltaic technologies in large building projects; and the Photovoltaic Domestic Field Trial (PV DFT) for the housing sector (DTI, 2006). Both these programmes resulted in an increase of over 60 per cent in the deployment of photovoltaic (PV) technology in the UK (International Energy Agency, 2004). The PV DFT aims to promote solar photovoltaic technology in the housing sector on new-build projects and existing building stock as part of refurbishment projects.

Deploying Microgeneration Technologies: The Photovoltaic Domestic Field Trial

This chapter presents in-depth qualitative research on two projects that took place in the north of England as part of the PV DFT scheme. Table 11.1 summarizes the elements of the two case studies, including the number of households, their size, the type of PV system installed and its final design within the building. A closer look at the trial scheme reveals that the aim of the programme was not only to examine the feasibility of the technology, but to use the installation project as a learning opportunity for utilities, building developers and other key players in the area of design, construction and monitoring of photovoltaic installations. The purpose, therefore, as the name suggests, was 'to take a systematic approach to the assessment of the domestic application of photovoltaics in the UK' (Pearsall and Butterss, 2002, p1497), resulting in best practice recommendations as well as information regarding system performance, maintenance, reliability, buildability and user satisfaction (BRE, 2005). In effect, knowledge from the trial would benefit the UK's construction industry in the hope of stimulating the PV market and furthering the deployment of this type of RET. In practice, the scheme involved coordination between the government, the PV industry and other stakeholders such as local authorities, private developers and energy consultants. The particular role that the energy consultants played was their responsibility in monitoring and handling the data generated on the performance of the PV

Table 11.1 *Project details of the two case studies*

Characteristics	Case 1	Case 2
Development type	Social housing	Private development
Dwelling type	1 and 2 bedroom flats	3 and 4 bedroom houses
Number of households	25	12
Installation process	Retrofit	New build
PV system type	Roof-integrated panels	Roof-integrated tiles; Bolt-on 'sun in a box'
Location of display monitor	Ground floor communal hallway in building block	Utility room or entrance hall/staircase cupboard

systems for two years after the installation. Accordingly, the trial is the first widespread monitoring of PV systems in the domestic sector in the UK and also includes feedback from developers and occupants through post-occupancy surveys. The scheme resulted in the installation of 470 PV systems on 28 different projects, covering different types of residential buildings (private, social housing and mixed use).

Both projects involved energy consultants and engineers, as well as PV installers, and as in all other trial projects, they were contracted with the Department for Trade and Industry (DTI) to implement and monitor the PV's performance. The first case study involved the installation of 25 roof-integrated PV panels on a social housing block of flats. The project took place as part of the building's refurbishment, was managed by the local authority, and resulted in the deployment of PVs with a total capacity of 38.25kWp (kilowatt peak). The display monitors – which indicate to the users the amount of electricity produced – were installed in the ground floor communal hallway next to the meter cupboards, as shown in Figure 11.1. As a result, the installation was completed in a relatively short time, hence avoiding the need to enter individual flats (which requires permission and can cause delays) to install individual display monitors. The project also included re-roofing the property for the installation of the PV panels and the required energy monitoring equipment.

The second case study consisted of a private housing development that included a range of sustainability measures as part of a planning authority requirement. The project comprised 12 houses and the trialling of two different types of PV systems: roof-integrated tiles and bolted-on 'sun in a box' systems. In this case, however, the project managers installed the display monitors in individual homes – which indicated, in this case, the amount of electricity produced as well as the percentage consumed in real time, as shown in Figure 11.2 – and distributed PV information packs to households as part of a home visit by the energy consultant.

By exploring the two case studies above, the research highlights two processes: the way in which the actors involved in the PV installations in the two case studies imagined the PV users, consequently influencing the PV installation

Figure 11.1 *Display monitors encased in the social housing project*

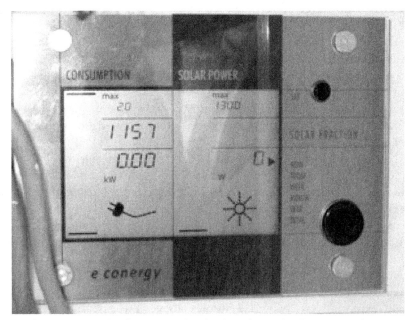

Figure 11.2 *The display monitor in the private development project*

Source: see BRE 2006, p15

process and design; and the ways in which users engaged with the technology, assigning to it different meanings as they integrated it into their everyday lives. Generally, the study adopts the view that energy and its associated technologies and services constitute a complex socio-technical system (Shove et al, 1998; Guy 2006). Building on this literature, it examines the role of PV users from the perspective of science and technology studies (STS), which can be useful in highlighting how meanings and practices surrounding technologies influence design traditions, their diffusion in society, and related cultural expectations (Bijker, 1995; Oudshoorn and Pinch, 2003; Guy, 2006).

In the next section, a critique of current literature on the diffusion of micro-generation technology is presented, highlighting its heavy dependence on socio-psychological models of attitudes and behavioural change. It argues instead for a socio-technical exploration of RETs and their users, emphasizing the co-construction dynamics taking place between technologies, users and related actors. This study involved the analysis of interviews conducted with the stake-holders and users of the two projects, as well as related documentation produced during the installations (such as memos, email exchanges, press releases and user guides) that were made available to the researcher, as well as documents and reports from the DTI on the PV DFT. The resulting analysis presents a typology of four different types of users – conscious, opportunistic, interested and non-users. The chapter concludes with an appeal to a more sophisticated analysis of energy users; one that takes into consideration the social and cultural nature of the technology's development and diffusion, and the socially shaped nature of its use. In doing so, the study avoids the limited views of the techno-economic approach, which assumes a linear process of technological diffusion based on a technical and economic understanding of technology in society (Guy and Shove, 2000), and calls for a more central role of social science research, questioning the various conceptualizations regarding the barriers to technology diffusion and behavioural change (Shove et al, 1998).

Analysing Users and Technology: The View from STS

Studies in STS have explored the way in which users are constructed and config-ured during technological innovation and diffusion. The analytical approach used in this research draws on two main theories on users and technologies: the config-uration of users based on the analysis of *technology as text* (Woolgar, 1991), and the concept of *script*[2] and the inscription of users and technologies stemming from actor–network theory (Akrich, 1992). The metaphor *technology as text* emphasizes the design processes that configure how users interpret and engage with technology; hence technologies – like texts – are written with particular users in mind, consequently assuming certain capacities attributed to both technology and user. Equally, these technologies can be read in various ways – in some cases quite differently from how the designers originally imagined (Woolgar, 1991).

Therefore, a technological artefact's capability is 'not transparently obvious and necessarily requires some form of interpretation' (Grint and Woolgar, 1997, p32). An implication of this anti-essentialist view of technology is the importance of studying and analysing interpretation processes concerning technology, instead of assuming that society is persuaded purely by a technology's effectiveness or its technical efficiency. Similarly, ideas developed from actor–network theory argue that technological artefacts carry 'scripts' (Akrich, 1992, p208) through which a framework of action is defined, shaping the space in which technologies and their users act. Technological artefacts can therefore create new 'geographies of responsibilities', where competencies or actions are distributed according to the script inscribed in the technology (Akrich, 1992, p207). Importantly, this concept contends that users may play a different role from that envisaged by the designers, effectively 'de-scripting' technologies during use (Akrich and Latour, 1992, p261).

Indeed, a similar argument can be made regarding people's engagement with microgeneration technologies. The study presented here illustrates how users engaged with photovoltaics in their homes in different ways, and argues that this dynamic was influenced by the socio-technical processes that took place during their installation, the ensuing PV system design, and the various meanings attributed to the technology by the end-users. In doing so, the research builds on previous work by STS scholars on the socio-technical nature of technology adoption (Kline and Pinch, 1996; Rohracher, 2003, 2005), unpacking the processes to reveal various social, technological, political and cultural interactions that shape the meaning, design and use of technologies. These studies have highlighted the socially shaped nature of technologies, and have shown the roles that users play in reinterpreting the meaning and function of technologies by employing them in different ways than intended, or tinkering with their design for various purposes. Alongside work on the diffusion of technologies, studies have also looked at the consumption of energy in the home, indicating how energy consumption takes place within a wide socio-technical landscape, consisting of complex and interconnected everyday practices (Aune et al, 2002; Guy, 2002; Shove, 2003).

Shove (1998) argues that the debate on energy matters concerning conservation and carbon reduction has failed to grasp the logic of everyday energy use. The dominant discourse focuses on energy conservation and financial savings, while ignoring the perspectives of households where the logic of energy use centres on other issues, such as comfort and convenience (Shove, 2003). Moreover, electricity consumption in the home is distinctive because it is not consumed directly; rather it is the services that the availability of electricity makes possible that are important. As a result:

> *'the extent of electricity consumption is mediated by all sorts of domestic technologies; patterns of use are typically inconspicuous and householders are only dimly aware of the social and technical infrastructures of electricity'* (Shove and Chappells, 2001, p55).

The authors add that the practice of daily routines around the household shape and are shaped by the existence of different domestic technologies and, more importantly, that 'we might reach for similar narratives of co-evolution were we to consider the introduction and diffusion of other products and services' (Shove and Chappells, 2001, p55).

Imagining PV Users

Therefore, if we are to consider the effect of introducing a PV system into the built environment, it is important to think of the socio-technical nature of electricity consumption, paying attention to the daily habits and routines that individuals establish in relation to PV technology, their preferences and attitudes, as well as existing material infrastructures (Aune, 2007). In particular, the focus is on the interaction with the PV through its user interface – the display monitor. The image of PV users in the literature tends to be framed around the classic deficit model (Owens, 2000), which calls for energy education and environmental awareness about the externalities of electricity from fossil fuels; moreover, there is an assumed economic rationality when it comes to energy consumption and related policy, which dismisses the social nature of energy consumption as noted earlier (Shove, 1998). With respect to RET implementation, such technologies tend to be seen as 'technological fixes' (Brand, 2005, p5) for the climate change problem. PV technology, in particular, is usually constructed as a 'tacit technology' (Brand, 2005, p8), which can be integrated into buildings 'without needing the cooperation of users after the technology has been implemented' (Rohracher and Ornetzeder, 2002, p73). As such, users are imagined as passive, weakening any notion of engaging with technologies such as photovoltaics. The work presented in this chapter, therefore, argues that the way that the projects' managers (consultants, installers, engineers, local authority officers, etc.) imagine the user (as passive, economically rational or ignorant of the importance of RETs in tackling climate change), as well as the technical and institutional constraints, such as the requirements for PV installation and the stakeholders' preferences discussed below, impact on the way in which users engage with PV technology.

Engaging with Photovoltaics

When exploring how people use PV in their homes, different types of users emerge: the *conscious* user, which is a grounded notion from the residents' reported engagement with the technology; the *opportunistic* user, whose intention is to consume free electricity; the *interested* user, who shows interest in the technology itself, and the *non-user* group, who did not engage with the technology. These distinctions are not meant to divide users into different groups; neither does it uncover the 'truth' about the users as opposed to how the project stakeholders imagined them. Rather, the four types of users are presented as analytical

Table 11.2 *Summary of the different types of PV users*

Type of user category	Description
The 'conscious' user	These users are more aware of their energy consumption and seek (by employing the display monitor) to change or modify their energy use habits.
The 'opportunistic' user	These users consume more electricity during the times when the PV system is generating the most energy (such as midday or on sunny days in summer). Their excess consumption is related to their requirements for convenience and comfort.
The 'interested' user	This user is fascinated by the technology itself, its workings and general performance.
Non-users	
Passive non-users	Non-users who were designed-out of the PV system implementation. This research argues that this mode of user is 'scripted' in the design of the installation, especially in the case of the social housing project.
Active non-users	Non-users who chose not to engage with the technology due to disinterest or the belief that it is not suitable or effective for tackling climate change in the UK.

categories or constructions that can suggest the various (and sometimes unexpected) ways in which users can engage with photovoltaic energy technology. As reported by Aune (2007), these analytical categories:

> *'convey an understanding of a complexity that is far from the "rational consumer". Economy matters, but economical considerations are integrated into an everyday life setting'* (Aune, 2007, p5464).

As such, these categories of users are set against the imagined users dominant in research and policy on energy and RETs, echoing Akrich's (1992) call for analysing the 'real' as well as the 'projected' user (Akrich, 1992, p209). Table 11.2 summarizes the user types derived from this research.

The conscious user

> *'I think it makes you more conscious of how much electricity you use, and as a result you take steps to reduce it'* (Resident 1, private development).

The notion expressed by this resident represents several respondents in the case of the private development. In some cases, the presence of the panels on the roof was sufficient to make them think about the energy they consumed in their home. As one resident put it:

'It made me a bit more conscious of the energy I use during different times of the day. It probably made me a little bit more careful for heating and lights on timers not to come on unless it is absolutely necessary' (Resident 8, private development).

However, the majority of the residents became increasingly aware of their energy consumption as they were provided with this information through the display monitor. Previous studies into the behaviour of householders living with photovoltaics (Keirstead, 2007) and other renewable energy technologies (Haas et al, 2004; Bahaj and James, 2007) suggest that such microgeneration technologies can create 'opportunities for consumers to become more aware of their energy use and its impacts, thereby encouraging demand management' (Keirstead, 2007, p4129). While these studies point to an interesting use of renewable technologies and give a new meaning to microgeneration, their analysis remains based on a behavioural model, which assumes that energy consumption is a rational activity isolated from the surrounding socio-technical landscape. This study argues that the impact of the technology on behaviour is influenced by the PV system's design, which is manifest in the design and location of the display monitor within the home. As such, residents who had the monitor installed in a visible part of the house related PV energy generation to their everyday use of energy, compared with others who had it installed in a cupboard, and to those in the social housing block of flats, where the monitors were downstairs in the communal area.

The conscious users reported their acquired knowledge on consumption levels in their homes after looking at their display monitor. Indeed, according to Darby (2006), feedback on energy consumption can achieve the anticipated benefits in terms of reducing energy demand and lowering carbon emissions. While the visibility of the display monitor played a major role in the formation of this knowledge, it was contingent in nature. In most cases, the residents had 'by chance' looked at the monitor owing to its location in the house, and as a result were able to conceptualize how much energy they consumed at different times of the day, suggesting the influence of everyday social practices on engaging with the technology (Shove, 2003). While the presence of the photovoltaic panels on the roof had, in some cases, reminded the householders of their energy use, as noted by Bahaj and James (2007), in most cases the reference to the PV system and their energy consumption related to the display monitor. The conscious user, therefore, was likely to take steps to eliminate unnecessary or unwanted energy consumption. Their interest was not only economic, but was also related to their attitudes towards wastage and their preferences regarding what constitutes a comfortable and welcoming home. Their action was facilitated, we argue, by the existing design of the PV system at home.

Similarly, this research shows the residents' use of energy in the context of the provision of comfort and convenience. In the context of being conscious of energy consumption, the residents' views on what is considered necessary for the normal functioning of their homes determined their behaviour. As one interviewee added:

> *'[The photovoltaic technology] makes you think about being economic without the house being cold and without necessarily sitting in the dark. It makes you stop and think whether we need all the lights on at a certain hour, so I turn them off. It gives you a mindset which you never had before'* (Resident 8, private development).

The example of the resident below shows that this notion was not experienced prior to living with the photovoltaic technology, especially regarding hidden types of energy consumption, such as mobile phone chargers left plugged in and on. This type of experience with regards to the photovoltaic system can be described as a mode of use, and we can thus conceive of a conscious user in relation to the technology in focus. The quotation below best summarizes this view, contextualizing it within everyday practice:

> *'It makes you very aware of things like charging your mobile phone, because quite often you plug the mobile charger in and you might leave it "switched on" on the wall, but your phone is now charged and you go off to work. However, it is still drawing electricity out. It makes you more aware of things like that, and I didn't know that until we moved in and started using the panels'* (Resident 2, private development).

The opportunistic user

The other mode of use evident from this research involves the operation of specific household appliances in relation to the performance of the PV panel. With an understanding that on sunny days the generation of the photovoltaic panel is greater, which is also indicated by the reading on the display monitors in the private development, these residents reported using additional electrical appliances to aid them in their housework. For example, one resident admitted using her tumble dryer at those times, justifying it by her increased laundry needs as she had recently given birth. Responding to my question on what she thought about the technology, one resident expressed their satisfaction:

> *'It was excellent. I think it is generating about a third of my electricity so now I can use appliances like the tumble dryer and the dishwasher when I am generating electricity'* (Resident 3, private development).

This 'opportunistic' mode of use has occurred in the context of maximizing convenience while benefiting from the technology. Another resident had shifted the time for performing housework in the interest of maximizing economic gain. As she explained:

> *'When I have to do the washing and it is raining cats and dogs outside, and if I have enough clothes in my wardrobe, I wait until it is sunny before I would do my washing because that way it is for free'* (Resident 9, private development).

The 'opportunistic' user can sometimes reduce their energy consumption if they use their household appliances during the day, while the panels are generating more energy, without increasing their normal consumption levels. However, as shown above, that is not always the case. In some cases, the presence of the photovoltaic panels helped to maintain a high consumption of household electricity. The expectation that such behaviours are now possible without an increase in the energy bill was perceived as a positive aspect of having photovoltaics on the roof. As a resident from a household with children pointed out:

> *'It is nice to have two or more computers on, as well as a television and other kitchen appliances that were [switched] on at the same time while the system is generating'* (Resident 5, private development).

Load shifting, whereby users change their behaviour by using the appliances they need during the day, is encouraged in the literature on photovoltaics in order to maximize the benefit from the technology and, as a result, increase returns. Keirstead (2007) discusses load shifting as a behavioural change related to people's rational economic interest, while Denholm and Margolis (2007, p4432) talk about 'a number of 'enabling technologies' that could potentially utilize excess PV production, such as timers on appliances and smart metering technologies, thereby ensuring the correct use of photovoltaic technology. The focus of this literature is in obtaining a 'double dividend', the result of lower energy consumption (Keirstead, 2007, p4129) and reduced carbon emissions from RETs. This study points out that such behaviour was reported from residents but has not always been in the interest of reducing electricity bills. In fact sometimes the same opportunistic users reported load shifting for different reasons, depending on the situation that they found themselves in, and the needs they had to satisfy in terms of running a home with children or a large family.

The interested user

The category of an interested user pertains to the respondents' reported fascination with the technology itself, independent of its meaning with respect to electricity generation and utility bills. This is in contrast to the assumed passive nature of user engagement with PVs. Such interest is expressed in the residents' gaze at the display monitor as it reads the amount of electricity generated by the system. The 'interested' user was more likely to be interested in electronics, the functioning of a technology such as photovoltaics, or the novelty of having a modern electric device in the home. One resident commented on the 'sleek, modern reader' as a positive aspect of having photovoltaic technology, making it a favourable choice compared with other microgeneration technologies. When asked what she liked about the technology, another resident mentioned the display monitor before anything else:

> *'It was quite interesting to see because it would have a picture of the sun when the system was generating. The monitor clocked up the number of*

*units that had been created by the panels so you know exactly what units
had been created that week and that month'* (Resident 9, private development).

For those users, the display monitor was useful in demystifying the workings of
the technology, allowing them to feel part of the system as they used different
appliances around the house to see how much energy they generated. They
expressed satisfaction in knowing the way in which the photovoltaic system
functions, how much energy different devices consume, and which settings would
use more or less electricity because it was simply interesting to know. As one
resident explains:

> *'It is useful sometimes when you put on certain electrical appliances to see
> which ones use the most; for example, when you put the kettle on you can
> see the difference it makes in terms of the energy it uses'* (Resident 7,
> private development).

While such modes of use are less prevalent than the two former categories, it is
nonetheless important to conceive of such a user. As mentioned earlier, this aspect
of the user–technology relationship challenges the projected user in the literature
and policy on PV technology. The dominant discourse on the use of photovoltaics
limits the user's space to that of consuming energy and relating such use to the
technology. The design of the PV systems in the two case studies is in keeping
with this idea, where the actions and interests of the users were limited to energy
consumption, and the performance of the technology is presumed to be uninter-
esting to the everyday practices of the residents. In fact, one of the perceived
advantages, as echoed by the project managers in this study, is that the users of the
photovoltaics do not have to do anything with the system and do not have to
change their behaviour. However, when thinking about the interested user, one
can start to imagine different modes of use outside the expectations of designers
and mediators (Kline, 2003).

The 'non-user'

Having discussed, so far, three different types of users emerging from this
research, this section describes the case of non-users. Historically, users have been
neglected in technology studies (Mackay and Gillespie, 1992), and including
them is important in order to avoid the focus on the powerful actors in the development and diffusion of technology. However, as Wyatt (2003, p69) argues,
focusing on use and users alone introduces another problem, as 'we implicitly
accept the promises of technology and the capitalized relations of its production',
and she thus urges her readers to study users in relation to non-users. It could be
said that all (or the majority) of the residents in the social housing project were
non-users because they were prevented from interacting with the photovoltaic
technology during the installation, and that was compounded by the project

managers' decision to mount the display monitors in the communal area, as noted earlier. Hence, we argue that their non-use was configured in the design of the technology. By dissociating the domestic spaces from the system components of the PV system, the tenants in the social housing were unable to use the PV technology, as such. Moreover, the tenants were not able to relate their electricity consumption to the electricity generated by the PV panels. One respondent expressed this view:

> 'The letter from the housing association said that [the PVs] will benefit us by cheaper electricity bills, I didn't see any difference. I think I looked at [the display monitor] once when they were put there and that was it' (Resident 1, social housing).

As a result, the perceived benefits of the technology, such as lower electricity bills, were never apparent. Even as residents compared their utility bills with those received in other dwellings they had resided in, they did not perceive significant savings. The usefulness of the display monitor and its potential in facilitating energy awareness or reduced energy consumption, as the examples above show, was lost. As one resident responded:

> 'I moved from a three bedroom house to this [two bedroom house]. My bills are still the same. The [display monitor] shows the electricity, I suppose, but where do you go from there' (Resident 5, social housing).

It is argued in this chapter that the project managers at the social housing installation effectively designed-out their users, resulting in what is referred to in this study as a *passive non-user*. In this case, the imagined *passive user* resonates with the category of non-users as it highlights the process of scripting that took place in the design of the PV system. The construction of an image of the user as being unwilling or finding it difficult to engage with RETs and associated behaviours of reduced energy consumption was reflected in the project managers' decision that effectively separated the user from the technology's interface and prevented useful forms of interaction.

Another category, or subcategory, of non-use is that of an *active non-user*. These residents were living in the private development project, where householders were more likely to engage with the technology and where residents were given sufficient information about the PV system. However, these non-users chose not to engage with the technology. In one case, their decision was related to their general disinterest in technologies such as photovoltaics. As this resident pointed out:

> 'It doesn't really bother us to be honest. It is only that we get so much money at the end of the year. We don't mind having it but we don't have anything to do with it' (Resident 7, private development).

Another resident believed in reducing energy consumption and deploying RETs, but believed that the choice of solar photovoltaics was not suitable for the UK climate and that the development would benefit more from other energy efficiency technologies.

Conclusions

This study has shown that users varied with respect to their interaction with the PV technology: from householders becoming increasingly conscious of their energy consumption, to opportunistic users who wanted to benefit from 'free electricity'; and from interested users who were fascinated by the technology in their homes, to others who did not relate to its presence or performance. This study does not suggest that a static typology of PV users exists; on the contrary, it argues for a wider understanding of how users can engage with microgeneration technologies in their home. More importantly, the study highlighted the intricate nature of PV use and the everyday energy consuming activities experienced by the user. In particular, it sought to delineate the different interactions with the technology as a product of users' pursuit of convenience in their daily social practices. This can be significant, as a more engaged use of microgeneration technologies requires its embeddedness into the socio-technical landscape constituting the home.

Moreover, it is apparent from the analysis of the two case studies that residents of the private development were more capable of engaging with the technology, in some cases realizing energy savings and becoming increasingly aware of their energy consumption and general electricity use. This can have potential benefits in the context of reducing energy consumption in the domestic sector. Perceived energy savings and a more conscious consumption of energy were, unfortunately, not realized in the social housing case. The configuration of the social housing users as passive and separated from the technology resulted in a lack of perceived benefits and a general ambivalence about the performance of the PV system and the purpose of the display monitor.

Consequently, this study argues that during the installation of microgeneration technologies in the domestic realm, attention should be paid to the ways in which users can engage with the technologies. This can be achieved through providing users with information on the technology and its design during installation (through clear documentation, home visits, etc.), as well as including in the design an intuitive interface that can enable such user engagement. It is also important to consider the context in which this engagement is possible, allowing for ease of use and generating an interest in energy consumption, as well as environmental and other potential benefits.

Acknowledgements

This chapter is based on doctoral research funded by the Natural Environment Research Council (NERC) and Scottish Power studentship. The author would like to thank all those interviewed in the case studies for their cooperation. Thanks are also due to Dona Abi Ghanem's PhD supervisors, Professor Simon Guy, Dr Geoff Vigar and Dr Claire Haggett, for their help and encouragement.

Notes

1. In this system, the PV panels are contained in an aluminium frame, and can be fixed onto a roof and fastened without penetrating the roof membrane. The installation is quick and can easily be removed if necessary (Bahaj, 2003).
2. The term 'script' describes the vision of the world materialized in the object and expressed in its design as well as the programme of action it presumably leads to. Hence 'the technologists define the characteristics of their objects ... and make hypotheses about the entities that make up the world into which the object is to be inserted. A large part of the work of innovators is that of "inscribing" this vision of (or prediction about) the world in the technical content of the new object. I will call this a "script" or a "scenario"' (Akrich, 1992, p207).

References

Akrich, M. (1992) 'The de-scription of technical objects', in W. E. Bijker and J. Law (eds) *Shaping Technology/Building Society*, MIT Press, Cambridge, MA, pp205–223
Akrich, M. and Latour, B. (1992) 'A summary of a convenient vocabulary for the semiotics of human and nonhuman assemblies', in W. E. Bijker and J. Law (eds) *Shaping Technology/Building Society*, MIT Press, Cambridge, MA, pp259–264
Aune, M. (2007) 'Energy comes home', *Energy Policy*, vol 35, no 11, pp5457–5465
Aune, M., Berker, T. and Sørensen, K. H. (2002) 'Needs, roles and participation: A review of social science studies of users in technological design', A report within the research program: Smart Energy-Efficient Buildings, NTNU and SINTEF, Department of Interdisciplinary Studies of Culture, Trondheim, Norway
Bahaj, A. S. (2003) 'Photovoltaic roofing: Issues of design and integration into buildings', *Energy Policy*, vol 28, no 14, pp2195–2204
Bahaj, A. S. and James, P. A. B. (2007) 'Urban energy generation: The added value of photovoltaics in social housing', *Renewable and Sustainable Energy Reviews*, vol 11, no 9, pp2121–2136
BERR (2007) *Digest of United Kingdom Energy Statistics 2007*, A National Statistics Publication, The Stationery Office, London
Bijker, W. E. (1995) 'Sociohistorical technology studies', in S. Jasanoff, G. E. Markle, J. C. Peterson and T. Pinch (eds) *Handbook of Science and Technology Studies*, Sage Publications, Thousand Oaks, CA
Brand, R. (2005) *Synchronizing Science and Technology with Human Behaviour*, Earthscan, London

BRE (2005) *DTI Photovoltaic Domestic Field Trial: Third Annual Report*, DTI, London

BRE (2006) *PV Domestic Field Trial Good Practice Guide. Part II: System Performance Issues*, DTI, London

Darby, S. (2006) 'The effectiveness of feedback on energy consumption: A review for Defra of the literature on metering, billing and direct displays', Environmental Change Institute, University of Oxford, Oxford, www.eci.ox.ac.uk/research/energy/downloads/smart-metering-report.pdf

Denholm, P. and Margolis, R. M. (2007) 'Evaluating the limits of solar photovoltaics (PV) in electric power systems utilizing energy storage and other enabling technologies', *Energy Policy*, vol 35, no 9, pp4424–4433

DTI (2006) *Photovoltaic Domestic Field Trial: Final Technical Report*, Department of Trade and Industry, London

DTI (2007) *Meeting the Energy Challenge: A White Paper on Energy*, Department of Trade and Industry, London

Ekins, P. (2004) 'Step changes for decarbonising the energy system: Research needs for renewables, energy efficiency and nuclear power', *Energy Policy*, vol 32, no 17, pp1891–1904

Elliot, D. (2000) 'Renewable energy and sustainable futures', *Futures*, vol 32, no 3/4, pp261–274

EST (2005) 'Potential for microgeneration: Study and analysis', Energy Saving Trust, London, www.berr.gov.uk/files/file27559.pdf

Grint, K. and Woolgar, S. (1997) *The Machine at Work: Technology, Work and Organisation*, Polity Press, Cambridge, UK

Guy, S. (2002) 'Sustainable buildings: Meanings, processes, users', *Built Environment*, vol 28, no 1, pp5–10

Guy, S. (2006) 'Designing urban knowledge: Competing perspectives on energy and buildings', *Environment and Planning C: Government and Policy*, vol 24, no 5, pp645–659

Guy, S. and Shove, E. (2000) *A Sociology of Energy, Buildings and the Environment: Constructing Knowledge, Designing Practice*, Routledge Research Global Environmental Change, London

Haas, R., Eichhammer, W., Huber, C., Langniss, O., Lorenzoni, A., Madlener, R., Menanteau, P., Morthorst, P. E., Martins, A., Oniszk, A., Schleich, J., Smith, A., Vass, Z. and Verbruggen, A. (2004) 'How to promote renewable energy systems successfully and effectively', *Energy Policy*, vol 32, no 6, pp833–839

International Energy Agency (2004) 'Photovoltaics Power System Programme', IEA, www.iea-pvps.org

Keirstead, J. (2007) 'Behavioural responses to photovoltaic systems in the UK domestic sector', *Energy Policy*, vol 35, no 8, pp4128–4141

Kline, R. and Pinch, T. (1996) 'Users as agents of technological change: The social construction of the automobile in the rural United States', *Technology and Culture*, vol 37, no 4, pp763–795

Kline, R. (2003) 'Resisting consumer technology in rural America: The telephone and electrification', in N. Oudshoorn and T. Pinch (eds) *How Users Matter: The Co-construction of Users and Technology*, MIT Press, Cambridge, MA, pp51–66

Mackay, H. and Gillespie, G. (1992) 'Extending the social shaping of technology approach: Ideology and appropriation', *Social Studies of Science*, vol 22, pp685–716

Oudshoorn, N. and Pinch, T. (eds) (2003) *How Users Matter: The Co-construction of Users and Technology*, MIT Press, Cambridge, MA

Owens, S. (2000) 'Engaging the public: Information and deliberation in environmental policy', *Environment and Planning A*, vol 32, no 7, pp1141–1148

Pearsall, N. M. and Butterss, I. (2002) 'The UK Domestic Photovoltaic Systems Field Trial: Objectives and initial results', presented at Photovoltaics Specialists Conference 2002, Conference Record of the 29th IEEE

Rohracher, H. (2003) 'The role of users in the social shaping of environmental technologies', *Innovation*, vol 16, no 2, pp177–192

Rohracher, H. (ed) (2005) *User Involvement in Innovation Processes: Strategies and Limitations from a Socio-technical Perspective*, Profil, Vienna

Rohracher, H. and Ornetzeder, M. (2002) 'Green buildings in context: Improving social learning processes between users and producers', *Built Environment*, vol 28, no 1, pp73–84

Shove, E. (1998) 'Gaps, barriers and conceptual chasms: Theories of technology transfer and energy in buildings', *Energy Policy*, vol 26, no 15, 1105–1112

Shove, E. (2003) 'Users, technologies and expectations of comfort, cleanliness and convenience', *Innovation*, vol 16, no 2, pp193–206

Shove, E. and Chappells, H. (2001) 'Ordinary consumption and extraordinary relations: Utilities and their users', in A. Warde and J. Gronow (eds) *Ordinary Consumption*, Routledge, London, pp45–58

Shove, E., Lutzenhiser, L., Guy, S., Hackett, B. and Wilhite, H. (1998) 'Energy and social systems', in S. Rayner and L. E. Malone (eds) *Human Choice and Climate Change: Volume 2: Resources and Technology*, Battelle Press, Columbus, OH, pp291–325

Woolgar, S. (1991) 'Configuring the user: The case of usability trials', in J. Law (ed) *A Sociology of Monsters: Essays on Power, Technology and Domination*, Routledge, London, pp57–99

Wyatt, S. (2003) 'Non-users also matter: The construction of users and non-users of the internet', in Oudshoorn, N. and Pinch, T. (eds) (2003) *How Users Matter: The Co-construction of Users and Technology*, MIT Press, Cambridge, MA, pp23–40

Chapter 12

Siting Solar Power in Arizona: A Public Value Failure?

Martin J. Pasqualetti and Cynthia Schwartz

Introduction

Rapid growth, rising demand for electricity, and abundant sunlight make Arizona the quintessential location for solar power development. There are many ways to use the sun to generate electricity, but at present, concentrating solar power (CSP) has the leading role. Private investors are forging ahead with plans to locate the 280MW Solana Solar Generating Station near Gila Bend, 70 miles southwest of Phoenix, Arizona (Figure 12.1). This development, like any other, requires many stages of preparation, including engineering design, transmission arrangements, and agreements for the sale of the electricity. However, during these stages of preparation, private developers may overlook the differentiated publics' interests. A pragmatic viewpoint argues that it is crucial to consider the communities' instrumental and intrinsic public values during decision-making. Its absence can raise social barriers to intended projects and create unwelcome impediments for renewable energy, as it already has for wind power (Pasqualetti et al, 2002; Pasqualetti, 2004, 2008). This might be happening at the Solana project as well.

Approach

John Dewey's (1927) public interest theory, a *pragmatic approach* to analysing situation-dependant public values, supplies this study's theoretical foundation. Bozeman's public value mapping model, based on elements of Dewey-inspired deliberative democracy, offers a dynamic view of civic preferences, 'recognizing

Figure 12.1 *Location of the Solana generating station*

Source: Abengoa Solar

the opportunities for social learning in deliberative settings' (Bozeman, 2007, p111). As phrased by Bozeman (2007, p13), 'A society's 'public values' are those providing normative consensus about (1) the rights, benefits, and prerogatives to which citizens should (and should not) be entitled; (2) the obligations of citizens to the state, and one another; and (3) the principles on which governments and policies should be based'. Public value (PV) failure occurs 'when neither the market not the public sector provides goods and services required to achieve public values' (Bozeman, 2007). We use Bozeman's public value failure criteria to assess the Solana project as the first of several dozen proposed solar projects for the Arizona desert.

We argue that affording 'public values' is not simply a governmental responsibility. Many of the values held by the differentiated publics are bestowed by private enterprises. We consider that 'publicness' judges an organization 'public' if it 'exerts or is constrained by political authority ... [I]t is 'private' [if] it exerts or is constrained by economic authority' (Bozeman, 1987, pp84–85). Our approach is to use public value criteria to analyse the issue or controversy during the civic engagement processes, looking for occasions of public value failure. As such, we avoid prescriptive procedures or particular process steps; our approach does not present a checklist for agency-level stakeholder decision-making. We seek to investigate the civic engagement activities and social culture required to meet the various publics' core values. We agree that 'only direct participation of each concerned party permits the complexity of its values to be expressed, considered, and incorporated' (Whitlatch, 1991, p112). Much of the public participation literature assumes that organized interest groups or responsible stakeholders represent the affected publics during knowledge creation. In our study, the publics' capability to engage in decision-making about energy policy becomes a crucial aspect of participation.

'Capacity of the community' serves as an overarching explanatory mechanism for public value failure. We argue that the 'capacity of the rural community' lens affords a prominent element relative to public engagement effectiveness for power plant siting. This 'community capacity' rationale includes factors of 'representativeness' (Beierle and Cayford, 2002), 'local knowledge' (Scott, 1998), 'political culture' (Jasanoff, 2005), 'power inequity' (Lahsen, 2005) and 'distributional inequity (Cozzens, 2007).

The literature examining the influence of public participation activities is uneven. Substantial scholarly literature examines the influence of public participation activities upon environmental decision-making by US federal agencies (HDGC, 2008). There is little literature that evaluates whether public engagement has met the communities' values. No studies were identified that regard issues of public participation in the siting of solar power plants in Arizona. Our purpose here is to take a state-level view of how public engagement has satisfied Arizona's imputed public values relevant to siting central solar plants.

Government Involvement with Public Engagement

During the last decade, energy security remained a prevailing public value, especially by politicians after the 9/11 attacks (Simon, 2007). Funding for nuclear research and clean coal development were given high priority. In 2002 the Department of Energy proposed that 1000MW of concentrating solar power (CSP) technology could be implemented, given adequate governmental incentives (US Department of Energy, 2007). However, the conservative right disdained subsidies for renewable energy, preferring that matters such as solar energy development be delegated to the states (Udall, 1977; Laird, 2001). In addition, strong federal resistance to mitigating climate change, coupled with muscular coal and nuclear lobbies, hampered efforts to support renewable energy strategies. This attitude suffocated legislative efforts in that direction. Without political will, the US could not develop an effective national energy plan for renewable energy.

In response to these developments, Western state leaders strived to seize forward momentum towards renewable energy. Testifying at a US House hearing, Governor Napolitano stated,

> *'In the absence of meaningful federal action, it [was] up to the states to take action to address climate change and reduce greenhouse gas emissions in this country'* (Napolitano, 2007).

She joined the Western governors in their support for state-level climate change initiatives (Arizona Climate Action Initiative, 2006). The governor tenaciously backed rule-making for climate change initiatives and supported the increased generation of renewable energy in Arizona (Napolitano, 2007). She utilized two influential public entities; the Climate Change Advisory Group for policy identification and the Arizona Corporation Commission for rule-making promulgation. Civic decision-making propelled enactment of strategic instrumental values relating to the adoption of CSP. In parallel, business interests pushed the Arizona Department of Commerce's efforts towards defining an industry-friendly Solar Roadmap (Arizona Department of Commerce, 2007). Over three years, four influential groups championed public engagement that was to lead up to the Solana plant announcement.

The first was the Western Governors' Solar Task Force Report stakeholder process. In addressing environmental challenges as vital public values, the Western Governors Association (WGA) believed that a 'clean, diverse, reliable and affordable energy supply' was one of America's top priorities (Western Governors Association, 2004). They established the Solar Task Force to study the possibility of using central solar plants as one means of meeting public value objectives. The committee stated that, 'the continued prosperity of the West depends on strong economic growth, which in turn requires a secure and predictable energy supply' (Solar Task Force, 2006). The multi-state committee's stakeholders, representing municipal administrators, solar executives, government consultants, utilities, national laboratories, solar advocates and industry associations, noted that solar energy could make a major contribution to the 2015 goal of 30,000MW of clean energy. They suggested that Arizona had the largest solar energy resource potential and that the state should pursue 2000MW of solar thermal by 2015 (Solar Task Force, 2006). Economic values, however, outweighed essential public values. Market barriers were noted as particularly problematic, whereas policy and regulatory measures were expected to suffice. The report gives short shrift to the idea that the 'availability of water is a significant issue' (p19). No social barriers were delineated. In addition, there was no notice taken of the need to include the general public in the discourse around using centralized solar as a future energy source.

Another stakeholder process was the Arizona Climate Change Advisory Group (CCAG) established by Governor Napolitano. The CCAG consisted of 35 stakeholders representing environmental groups, Arizona Indian communities, universities, utilities, major corporations, solar advocate associations, mining, farming/ranching and public administration. They were tasked with preparing a renewable energy action plan for Arizona. The Arizona Department of Environmental Quality (ADEQ) coordinated the stakeholders' input and technical committees' actions during the year. The CCAG recommended 49 policy options, 3 of which constituted 80 per cent of carbon emission savings. The proposed option yielding the largest greenhouse gas (GHG) reduction required an increase in the renewable percentage each year through to 2025 (Climate Change Action Plan, 2006). The Governor accepted the report's proposals and identified solar technology as an instrumental value which enables the 'bigger picture' intrinsic value of energy independence. In agreement with CCAG recommendations, the Governor signed Executive Order 2006-13, 'to establish a statewide goal to reduce future GHG to the 2000 level by 2020 and to 50% below the 2000 level by 2040' (Arizona Climate Action Initiative, 2006). The effectiveness of this order is questionable, however, as we found no evidence of media notification. Who was to know about this momentous civic participation activity? The plan identified many problems but included negligible prescriptions for who would have to make adjustments and how it was to be done. Another shortcoming was the lack of legislative representation on the committee, despite the proclaimed need for state legislation or rule-making. There were no measurable outcomes or strategies for moving the solar agenda forward, and no mention of the push for large solar plants. The executive directive emerged as the primary output.

A third stakeholder process resulted in the development of the Arizona Solar Electric Roadmap Study (ASERS). The Commerce and Economic Development Commission (CEDC), having responsibility for mapping Arizona's economic plan, commissioned a project to 'accelerate the use and adoption of solar technologies and to increase energy efficiency, enhance energy security, and protect the environment' (Arizona Department of Commerce, 2007). Study members included solar businessmen, public administrators, university leaders, home developers and key figures from Arizona's major utilities, with the Department of Commerce (and its internal Arizona Energy Office) supplying advisory consultants. The Roadmap defined five initiatives: establishing an outreach programme, a solar zone, a Solar Centre of Excellence, 'Sustainable partners', and – *most important* – constructing and operating large central solar plants. The stakeholders' stated ambitions included 1000MW of solar power, an accompanying 3000 new jobs, and the reduction of CO_2 emissions by 400,000 tons per year, all by 2020 (Arizona Department of Commerce, 2007). This committee's public engagement process ostensibly affirmed public values of good jobs and reduced emissions as the underlying means to accomplish the overall goal of energy cost containment. However, these values seemed to be swathed in commercial opportunities. Many of the proposed policies assumed promulgation of critical legislation or rule-making (e.g. tax credits, rebates, incentives). 'Big Solar' had gripped the Department of Commerce stakeholders' imagination: they envisioned an expanding market reality, seeing shiny solar fields as sparkling dollar signs. The question of water usage, which was to become a highly visible worry within two years, received little mention. There were, despite the best intentions, several deficiencies. For example, the intended beneficiaries were unclear, the committee membership did not represent common citizen values, and the study was not instructive for characterizing and addressing the social implications of transformative change due to CSP technology. The link between this study and the creation of the Solana project remains cloudy.

The fourth activity to address renewable energy during this period was the development of rules by the Arizona Corporation Commission (ACC). After two years of diligent efforts towards negotiated rule-making by renewable energy advocacy groups, and after rounds of sincere haggling within the ACC, the Commissioners voted 3 to 2 to approve the enhanced Arizona Renewable Energy Standard (RES) (Mayes, 2008). The ACC approved rules 'requiring utilities to generate 15% of their total energy from renewable energy technologies by 2025' (Arizona Corporation Commission, 2006). The rule amendment process included open workshops – including testimony, research and written correspondence. The working groups witnessed presentations from suppliers of central solar products, wind generation, distributed photovoltaics, fuel cells, landfill gas, solar thermal, biomass, geothermal and solar electric cars. Each wanted to ensure that the standard would carefully consider incentives for their particular technology. Many individuals and enterprises – from mining, cattle ranchers and tribes, to solar companies and electricity providers – provided their comments on possible changes to the evolving Environmental Portfolio Standard (Arizona Corporation Commission, 2008). The solar energy industry wanted a solar set-aside and encouragement of solar power plants, while other advocates argued for acceptance of out-of-state energy sources and demand-side management (DSM). Ecologists focused on regulations assuring a sustainable future. One commissioner mentioned costs and reliability as deal-breaking factors. Three commissioners and the pro-solar special interest groups believed that, given the higher price of renewable energy, the market alone would not drive demand. The public values of caring lobbyists, consumers and corporations were carefully incorporated into the final version as regulatory mandates. The Commissioners expected the RES incentive to spur solar industry growth for manufacturers, installers, large-scale projects and roof-top solar product suppliers, and this has happened, although not on a wide scale. For example, the solar incentive enterprise of the Salt River project stimulated the installation of fewer than 500 roof-top residential systems (Hayslip, 2009). This number of solar installations is out of a total of about 838,000 residential customers.

Questions remain about engagement with the wider public, including the rural citizen. The countryside, where the best plant sites were to be located, heard little of the vision of merchant 'central solar plants', and the incipient need for land and water. There was little expression of rural community values, and the request for proposals from a large solar facility was not given wide publicity. Confidentiality agreements prevented an intelligence leak. Six months after the Attorney General's final approval of the new RES ruling, the world learned the news.

The Solana Generating Station Project

In front of the Arizona Science Center on 21 February 2008, Governor Napolitano lauded Arizona's largest electric utility's endeavours:

> 'This is a major milestone for Arizona in our efforts to increase the amount of renewable energy available in the United States. Arizona is

Figure 12.2 *Parabolic trough concentrators at Kramer Junction, California, similar in design and operation to the installation planned for the Solana Project in Arizona*

Source: National Renewable Energy Laboratory

leading the way in protecting our world for future generations through combating climate change' (APS, 2008).

A news release confirmed plans for a 280MW concentrating solar power plant – 'one of the world's largest solar facilities' – to be built 70 miles southwest of Phoenix, near Gila Bend, Arizona. Arizona Public Service (APS) signed a power purchase agreement (PPA) with supplier Abengoa Solar to buy 100 per cent of the plant's energy output. With operation scheduled for the beginning of 2012, the plant design called for parabolic trough technology and thermal storage using molten salts. At full capacity, the generating station was advertised to supply clean power to 70,000 APS customers and eliminate around 400,000 tons of CO_2 (Abengoa Solar, 2008).

Solana will use CSP technology (Figures 12.2 and 12.3). It will employ 2700 trough collectors to gather and concentrate the heat of sunlight onto a tube filled with a 'working fluid'. The heat in this fluid will be transferred to water and then used in conventional steam turbines. The solar field will cover 3sq.miles, with each trough collector measuring about 25ft wide, 500ft long, and 10ft in height. Thermal storage, using molten salts, will allow up to six hours dispatchable

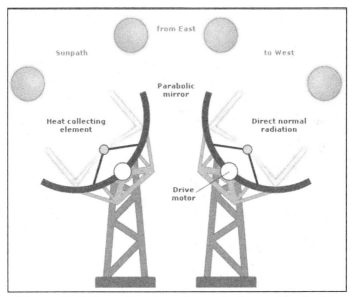

Figure 12.3 *Operating scheme for parabolic trough technology*

Source: Abengoa Solar

energy. Along the way to full operation, the project should create about 1500 construction jobs. After completion it is expected to produce 85 skilled permanent jobs. Studies have estimated the total dollar impact during construction of a project like Solana to be roughly equal to the total capital investment in the plant plus the creation of an additional 11,000–15,000 jobs. In total, the Solana project was expected to bring more than US$1 billion in economic benefits to the state of Arizona (APS, 2008).

The local media reacted to the news with the enthusiasm of pent-up expectation. They asked questions about the decision to employ innovative technology, its costs and contributions, its environmental effects and how it might stimulate other projects. Four metropolitan radio stations hyped the announcement on the evening news bulletin, and some posted the Governor's comments via streaming video on their website (Solana Generating Station Project, 2008). The story hit the front page of the *Arizona Republic*. An information website was listed. Was the Gila River Indian community aware of the plans to build this new-fangled solar plant? Hearing details about the decision to install vast numbers of long metal troughs seemed to be a big deal … or was it? Who cared about placing 3sq.miles of mirrors on farmland in Gila Bend?

Gila Bend: Crossroads of the Southwest

The tiny derelict town of Gila Bend has hovered on the edge of death for years. Gila Bend has found a way to survive in spite of a harsh, hot climate and a rundown economy. Romig's (2006) eloquent geographical analysis describes the dichotomous town as being 'on the road to somewhere else'. For 150 years it had been the essential spoke of a central transportation hub; a key place in the settling of the Southwest. The booms and busts of people-moving – the stage coach, railway and interstate highway – left the town an ill-fated destiny. Through traffic bypassed the town; it was being propelled towards social decline. Demographics denote the sad reality: 25 per cent of the 1831 residents live below the poverty level (more than half are destitute); per capita income is one-half of the Arizona average; and only 55 per cent of adults have graduated from high school. Hispanic and American Indians comprise 65 per cent of the population: 23 per cent are foreign-born (from Latin America). Agriculture, construction, administration and trucking comprise the main male jobs (Gila Bend Arizona, 2009).

Notwithstanding such glum economic indicators, the town's leaders continue to attract jobs to the area by welcoming unappealing enterprises. Gila Bend seems 'willing to accept environmental and social risk to keep the town viable' (Romig, 2006). Three miles south of town is located the Barry M. Goldwater Air Force Range, a 2 million acre combat training site acquired in 1941, still in operation. In the 'bend' of the Gila River valley, state and federal agricultural officials in the 1950s used new technology (DDT) to eradicate the cotton bollworm throughout the area's farms. Today, the contaminated run-off still gathers at the Painted Rock dam, one of the most toxic sink holes of pesticide contamination in the country, located just 12 miles north of the proposed solar energy site (Dougherty, 2005). Four decades later, town officials worked to catch the attention of profitable businesses. Gila Bend's economic development programme supported a 66,000sq.ft hazardous materials plant built to incinerate contaminated soil. However, piles of dirt remain, due to a lack of clean-up funding (Romig, 2006). State money was always welcomed: a juvenile correction facility now sits 20 miles away. The biggest success has been utilization of the local brackish, salty ground-water, employed as a growth medium for profitable shrimp aqua-farming: the 'sweet white' variety is a local delicacy and tourist draw (Desert Sweet Shrimp, 2009).

Electrical power generation emerges as the community's most lucrative industry. In the mid-1970s, the Gila Bend community watched the siting challenges of Palo Verde, the largest nuclear generating facility in the US, 40 miles due north. It is the only nuclear plant in the world not adjacent to a large volume of surface water, instead consuming treated sewage water from Phoenix municipal plants. Thirty years later, two combined cycle gas-fired plants with a total capacity of 3145MW, now dwell just east of the town. Power is sold onto the grid and transmitted to any consumers willing to pay the asking price, usually California. Now, the prospect of the country's largest solar facility has again excited the community. Ironically, history has shown no link between power generation and an appreciable or sustained improvement in local economic conditions.

Part of what attracts power producers to Gila Bend is its water. The Gila River is the last major tributary to merge with the Colorado River, and the town of Gila Bend is nearby. Beneath the surface is even more water. Irrigated agriculture, as long as the water is inexpensive, is a profitable enterprise, most predominantly for the production of cotton. More important, Gila Bend's agricultural precedent may weigh profoundly in its salvation, as water rights are doled out to first land settlers under the doctrine of 'prior appropriation' (Worster, 1985). Since water rights are legally attached to the land, water follows the land with any change of title. This provision, under Arizona's 'appropriation doctrine', means that the farmland near Gila Bend can be an especially valuable attractant to new enterprises. However, in order to keep such privileges, the owner must use up their allocation or lose their appropriated amount. The value of land in most of rural Gila Bend is based on continued water usage. This doctrine attracts power producers to the area and was a critical factor in siting the Solana project. It was one of the principal topics of discussion during the stages of public engagement once the Solana project was announced.

The public engagement process

In Arizona, much public engagement occurs during the ACC's transmission line and plant siting open hearings. Solana 'initiated a public involvement program for the [project] which included extensive outreach efforts on distributing information and soliciting input from the public and interested stakeholders' (Arizona Corporation Commission, 2008). These stakeholders included representatives from such groups as environmentalists, farmers, town council, historic preservation organizations, the military, corporation commissioners and water rights owners. Targeted briefings facilitated two-way communication. Some spoke of the Air Force Base safety officers' concerns regarding the mirror's up-facing orientation. Base managers wondered about the possibility of bright reflections negatively interfering with the test pilot's vision. Flight testing experiences from a similarly mirrored landscape dismissed any worry about visibility, as the mirrors are all focused near the group. Stakeholder meetings helped to air local concerns about proposed alternatives for line siting locations.

Solana consultants issued communiqués and posted notices requesting local participation in the public process. A town official noted that APS held two open meetings at the Gila Bend Elks Lodge, with 150 people in attendance. A few residents looked forward to potential jobs and hoped for a positive impact to the local economy. The intrinsic value of job creation appeared to be the major focus of concern for the town's citizens. Two additional open public forums in Glendale, Arizona allowed for a wider representation of Phoenix area residents to voice their opinions. Examination of the lists of attendees revealed that almost all of the responses exhibited positive comments 'for' the new centralized power plant.

Apprehension expressed in these meetings over land and water issues was allayed. The decision to use irrigated fields for the 3sq.mile plant seemed to represent a 'win–win' result for many publics. According to a Sierra Club spokesperson,

> *'The proposed facility site is not an environmentally sensitive area, it is on private land that has been used for agricultural purposes and will actually use less water than the current use'* (Bahr, 2008).

The Executive Director of the Sonoran Institute testified,

> *'Solana will be built on private lands ... Solana will not involve the scraping of our precious natural environment ... transmission lines will not be on sensitive desert lands ... [and] Abengoa's public outreach has been effective and inclusive'* (Propst, 2008).

One participant observed that the land owner will receive a good price for his alfalfa field and the Paloma Irrigation and Drainage District (PIDD) will get an equitable deal for part of their allotment of Colorado River water. Local context reveals hidden knowledge. The developer's attorney, Mr. Campbell, tried to understand the logic,

> *'it would be a burden on the district [if the] applicant will be using less water than current agricultural use, and you will lose the revenue from the current agricultural user?'* (Arizona Corporation Commission, p363).

Mr Zimmerman of the PIDD responded,

> *'Selling water is like selling anything else. If you are not able to deliver it, you are not making any money. [PIDD has] the rights to regulate all use of water out there'* (Campbell, 2008; Zimmerman, 2008).

The PIDD wanted Solana to agree to buy the same amount of water previously required for irrigating the site's alfalfa fields. They expected the developer to pay the difference, even if additional water was not needed for plant operation. In this way, water becomes a saleable commodity, with the PIDD water district seeking to maintain their approved allocation while ensuring a profit.

Line siting approval was characterized as a tricky hurdle to negotiate. During the hearing, the developer's attorney, Mr Campbell, stated to the Commission Chairman,

> *'Anytime you can put a transmission line down a road [named] Powerline Avenue, I'm not sure that I've ever seen a case so straightforward'* (Campbell, 2008).

It turned out that it was not as simple as that. The neighbouring cotton farmer could not assent. Taller power lines would prevent crop dusting planes from flying close to the cotton fields. Understanding local context was crucial. Having heard about the 'done deal' for line siting during the site tour, the two farmers who resided alongside the proposed site argued their preference for 'Alternative #1' at the hearing. One farmer declared:

> *'Powerline Road, I believe, is just being called Powerline Road because we put a sign out there ... I hope you don't just put power lines on it because we put that name out there.'*

The farmer continued to talk about

> *'a big pole over our methane digester ... lines over our cattle sheds ... there will be static. We have several thousand cows and they can get shocked by the metal fences'* (Arizona Corporation Commission, 2008, pp356–347).

Another farmer said:

> *'[there are] hardships ... with lines in the middle of your crops ... Crop dusting is a vital part of our business ... It is going to significantly impact our crop process and our efficiency and our effectiveness to produce crops ... [and] limit methods of irrigation. [But] we know it is green. It is the way to go. It is the future of energy. But we also have to take into consideration impacting everybody else along the way ... The things will be there ... for generations to come'* (Arizona Corporation Commission, 2008, pp349–351).

An effective public process that seeks to understand and appreciate the rural community public values appears critically important in plant siting. Obtaining rural input receives much less attention than all other steps in the process, which is something that is suggested by the timing of the hearing well after the announcement of the Solana project.

The imperative query asks: Have the various public values accepted by the community been supplied or guaranteed via the public engagement process? We hypothesize how each of the differentiated publics framed their criteria for success as part of their involvement in the Solana project. State and local legislation and agency strategic plans were searched for the highest-level value proclamations relating to society's general desire for CSP projects. Exploration of the literature yielded the entities' public value frames (Table 12.1), where the last column considers relevant instrumental mechanisms for satisfying the imputed values.

Public Value Failure

The study's analysis utilizes public value failure criteria – similar to market failure criteria – according to the analytical framework of Bozeman (2007). As he describes it, a public value failure occurs 'when neither the market nor the public sector provides goods and services required to achieve public values' (Bozeman, 2007, p16). Our goal is to explore the extent to which public engagement activities for the Solana Generating Plant have satisfied the public values of interested and affected publics. One way to evaluate such failure is to view the Solana process from each public value failure criterion lens (Bozeman, 2007). The following criteria are 'neither necessary nor sufficient' conditions, but they offer useful indicators for understanding private–public responsibilities.

Table 12.1 *The differentiated publics and their values*

The interested or affected publics	Representing whom?	Their public value frame	In what way?
AZ Governor Napolitano	Arizona –Executive	Climate change is real	Show leadership and issue directives for reducing GHG
AZ Department of Commerce (ADOC)	Arizona – Business	Economic growth to Arizonans	Attract business, increase power and contain costs
AZ Corporation Commission (ACC)	AZ utility regulators	Ensure affordable electricity	Keep electricity rates down; and enforce renewable share
Arizona Public Service (APS)	Private utility	Satisfy demand for peaking load	Keep customers, shareholders and ACC satisfied
Abengoa Solar	Electricity supplier	Profitability and sustainability	Use solar to create GHG-free power and make money
Sierra Club and Sonoran Institute	Environmental groups	Conservation and sustainability	Protect the world for future generations; do no harm
The town of Gila Bend	Rural community	Create jobs for community	Embrace any industry to provide local employment
Paloma Water District	Water rights owners	Use water and continue flow	Ensure water delivery to water district users
Rural citizens of Gila Bend	Local farmers and ranchers	Way of life and efficiency	Agree with green – but don't impact farm/rural life

Interest aggregation or articulation

A public value (PV) failure can occur if there are insufficient means of ensuring articulation and effective communication of core values, or, if processes for aggregating values lead to distortions:

* *Who represents the values of the rural folk?* It is highly probable that the stakeholders attending the task force/ committee meetings leading to the Solana decision did not represent the aggregate public values of Gila Bend citizens. The decision-making process did not involve an appropriate sample from the affected community. For example, none of the participants in any of the three stakeholder meetings met the criteria for 'affected community' since they didn't live in or represent Gila Bend. Without such representation, there was a public value failure.

- *To what extent does the ACC represent the public?* The values expressed by the ACC's decision in imposing renewable energy mandates may not represent the strongly libertarian viewpoint that is characteristic of Arizona's rural areas. Nor were those who live in rural areas as readily able to attend protracted hearings, most of which took place in Phoenix. A lack of mechanisms for democratic engagement by voters regarding the decision for central solar may be perceived as a PV failure.

Imperfect monopolies

A PV failure can occur due to a breakdown of a government's legitimate monopoly in the delivery of goods and services:

- *How are the efforts of public process consultants responsible to the government?* The consultants sell a service to the solar plant supplier, who, in turn, will sell energy to a regulated private utility. Each entity acts in a public role, as delegated by ACC's political power: they must follow Arizona statutes. Even though no PV failure was identified for public engagement, some in Arizona doubt the political authority of the ACC (Bolick, 2009).

Imperfect public information

A PV failure can occur if transparency is insufficient to permit citizens to make informed judgements:

- *To what extent is public engagement visible?* The three stakeholder meetings were by 'invitation only': information was not widely publicized. In contrast, the ACC's RES amendment process was well-attended and transparent. But, in both cases, the general public was not aware of the social implications of the new solar technology. None of the lists of stakeholders included a representative from Gila Bend. The head of the Gila Bend Economic Development Initiative did not know that something was being proposed until the APS told them that they were buying land in the area to put a solar plant on. If those 'affected' (rural or central solar) were not involved in the decision-making process, and the process lacked full transparency, there was a PV failure.

Distribution of benefits

A PV failure can occur when there are public domain benefits – which should be freely shared amongst all – are not distributed.

- *Does participation in the process result in less hoarding?* The general public is not aware of the large volume of water for power plant operations (typically about 800–1000 gallons per megawatt-hour), much less of the idea that Arizona's allocated water (marketable commodity) will be used for merchant plants such as the Solana project. The public should be aware and involved in the knowledge-creation process for apportioning water for solar electricity generation use. If the water is used for out-of-state energy and is not available to the state's participating public, there may be a PV failure.

Provider availability

A PV failure can occur because there is a deficit of providers for a core public value, or because providers prefer to ignore public values:

- *In what ways did civic engagement assist in providing central solar?* APS issued an open RFP for CSP plant bids: only one supplier from Spain met the capacity and energy storage parameters. Contracting out yielded a scarcity of providers. The participation process was not known to the general public due to confidentiality concerns. A sole source solution might be considered a PV failure.
- *How does the public engage in deciding renewable mandates?* The ACC RES mandated that utilities provide a certain percentage of renewables in retail electricity. But, significantly, their regulations do not require it be from Arizona. The public was not engaged in the process of deciding where the energy is derived. If 'home-grown' is a core value, then there is a PV failure.

Time horizon

A PV failure can occur if decision-making actions are calculated on short-term horizons:

- *Does the engaging public have the capacity to compel long-term planning?* Utilities follow simplistic rate-setting processes which adversely affect their ability to plan in the long term. The public needs to engage and push the commissioners towards a longer view, other than just 'low cost' (Knowledge, 2008). The public does not appear to have the capacity to alter the commissioner's view without sufficient political support. This situation yields a PV failure.
- *How does the public participate in long-term planning for CSP?* There is no federal policy or coordination mechanism for organizing governmental layers (regional, state, county and city) when deciding central solar needs. No pre-decision deliberation and planning venue exists for the public to discuss the siting of CSP plants in Arizona. The forecasting process is in the hands of private industrialists, representing a PV failure.

Substitutability/conservation

A PV failure can occur when resources are not seen as distinctive or highly valued, and instead, are treated as substitutable:

- *How does the participating public view CSP's need for water?* Gila River Valley's deeded 'private' water will be substituted with solar electrical energy, often sold to the highest bidder. Future water availability is questionable. Arizona publics have not shown much of an interest in considering water a public value (Pasqualetti and Kelley, 2008). Lack of civic engagement for safeguarding a core resource reveals this as a PV failure.

Subsistence and human dignity

A PV failure can occur when human beings, especially the vulnerable, are not treated with dignity, and if their subsistence is threatened:

- *Who speaks for the rural communities?* Gila Bend's disadvantaged publics will probably not garner benefits due to Solana. The imposition of CSP plants may threaten their future way of life. The community may lack the capacity to robustly engage with public agencies and assist in decision-making. Farms and ranches are being pushed out further towards the fringes. No public engagement venue exists for dispossessed publics. This problem imparts a PV failure.

Conclusions

If energy is indeed tied to everything we do, then a shift in where we get it will influence us in every way. As we start to fully accept the closeness of this relationship, we are realizing its influence on how we feel about renewable energy. While, in the theoretical sense, we have been supporting the idea of a renewable energy future, we are finding that the more it becomes a possibility, the more care we are giving to its implications. We have already seen this sequence with public resistance to the proposed wind projects near Palm Springs, California, among many others, and we are beginning to witness the same reactions for solar plants proposed for many places in the Southwest US. The emergence of such barriers to renewable energy has come as something of a surprise to developers, given their assumption of public acceptance. That they tended to miss this evolution of reaction is not surprising; while they well understood barriers that were technical in origin, social barriers were less familiar. What they are learning is that such obstacles have the power to slow, or even derail, renewable energy development because they vary widely with time, group, location and culture. Every proposed project is a different case.

One of the challenges to renewable energy is how to integrate the public into the planning process. There are disagreements about this question. There is no consensus about how much effort should be taken to inform those directly affected, how to reach affected parties, how to integrate their views into planning implementation, how much detail to provide each group, when discussions should commence, or how attitudes should be evaluated, monitored and incorporated into planning and design.

A key element in winning public support is the assessment of public values. In applying the Bozeman analytical criteria to the Solana project, it appears there has been a public value failure at every level. Whether this will be significant to the overall success of the project is as yet unknown, but one suspects that failures of this type could impede the successful spread of solar energy, as it has for other renewable energy resources such as wind power.

Solana is but the first of several similar solar projects proposed for Arizona. All of them are so-called 'merchant plants', where the generated electricity is sold to whoever wishes to buy it. In the case of Solana, Arizona Public Service has agreed to buy all the electricity, because the company needs to satisfy the renewable energy requirements of the Arizona Corporation Commission. Future plants of similar design are likely to transmit their electricity to California, where the utility rates are almost double those in Arizona. For these plants especially, one must ask why power plants are being sited in Arizona when the customers are in California. It must be that, collectively, conditions in Arizona make it more profitable. Certainly many factors are involved in such a decision, including the price and availability of land, the availability of water, community support for economic development, the regulatory atmosphere and the presumption of public acceptance.

Were there to be more complete and earlier public involvement, what would this do to future plans for renewable energy? Would it enhance and speed renewable energy plans or would it slow their implementation? The answer is not yet clear, but as public acceptability attracts more attention, developers will be wrestling with many remaining questions. For example, they will need to identify how much to tell the public, which part of the public to involve, when to do it, and what means to use in disseminating information. In general, the earlier the information is provided, and the more detailed it is, the more completely the public can be involved in the planning and construction of every project.

References

Abengoa Solar (2008) 'Abengoa Solar: Solar power for a sustainable world', www.abengoasolar.com/corp/web/en/index.html

APS (Arizona Public Service) (2008) 'APS announces new solar power plant, among world's largest', www.aps.com/general_info/NewsRelease_ARCHIVED/NewsReleases/NewsRelease_440.html

Arizona Climate Action Initiative (2006) 'Executive Order 2006-13', Arizona Climate Change Action Initiatives, http://azclimatechange.gov/initiatives/index.html

Arizona Corporation Commission (2006) 'Commissioners approve rules requiring 15 percent of energy from renewables by 2025', *Commission News*, www.cc.state.az.us

Arizona Corporation Commission (2008) 'Environmental compatibility and line siting', Docket #L-00000GG-08-0407-00139/00140, eDocket website, http://edocket.azcc.gov/

Arizona Corporation Commission (2009) 'Court affirms Commission's authority to set renewable energy standards for Arizona's utilities', www.cc.state.az.us

Arizona Corporation Commission (2009) 'Renewable Energy Standard and Tariff', Renewable energy, www.cc.state.az.us/divisions/utilities/electric/environmental.asp

Arizona Department of Commerce (2007) 'Arizona Solar Electric Roadmap Study: Full report', www.sfaz.org/Common/Files/az_solar_electric_roadmap_study_full_report.pdf

Arnstein, S. R. (1969) 'A ladder of citizen participation', *Journal of the American Institute of Planners*, vol. 35, no 4, pp216–224

Bahr, S. (2008) 'Witness Testimony: Sierra Club: Grand Canyon Chapter', filed in ACC Docket #L-00000GG-08-0407-00139/00140, 17 September, Arizona Corporation Commission

Beierle, T. and Cayford, J. (2002) *Democracy in Practice: Public Participation in Environmental Decisions*, Resources for the Future Press, Washington, DC

Bolick, C. (2009) 'Solar subsidies: Or a better economic climate for all?', Goldwater Institute, www.goldwaterinstitute.org/article/2788

Bozeman, B. (1987) *All Organizations are Public*, Jossey-Bass, San Francisco, CA

Bozeman, B. (2007) *Public Values and Public Interest: Counterbalancing Economic Individualism*, Georgetown Press, Washington, DC

Campbell, T. (2008) 'Attorney for Solana, Lewis and Roca', Docket # L-00000GG-08-0407-00139/00140.p.363,368, October 14, Arizona Corporation Commission

Climate Change Action Plan (2006) 'Arizona Climate Change Advisory Group's response to Arizona Executive Order 2005-02', www.azclimatechange.gov/download/O40F9347.pdf

Cozzens, S. (2007) 'Distributive justice in science and technology policies', *Science and Public Policy*, vol 34, no 2, pp 85–94

Desert Sweet Shrimp (2009) 'Website homepage', www.desertsweetshrimp.com/about.html

Dewey, J. (1927) *The Public and its Problems*, Holt, New York

Dougherty, J. (2005) 'Contaminated splendor', *Phoenix New Times*, 10 March, www.phoenixnewtimes.com/2005-03-10/news/contaminated-splendor/

Dryzek, J. (2005) *The Politics of the Earth: Environmental Discourses*, 2nd edn, Oxford University Press, Oxford

Firestone, J., Kempton, W. and Krueger, A. (2008) 'Delaware opinion on offshore wind power: Final report', January 2008, University of Delaware College of Earth, Ocean, and Environment

Gila Bend Arizona (2009) 'Demographic data for Gila Bend, Arizona' from City-Data website, www.city-data.com/city/Gila-Bend-Arizona.html

Hayslip, R. (2009) 'SRP sustainable portfolio principles', SRP Resource Planning Workshop, 5 August 2009, www.srpnet.com/about/pdfx/SustainablePortfolioPrinciples.pdf

HDGC (Committee on the Human Dimensions of Global Change) (2008) 'Public participation in environmental assessment and decision making', National Academies Press, www.nationalacademies.org/gateway/international/1107.html

Jasanoff, S. (2005) *Designs on Nature*, Princeton University Press, Princeton, NJ

Knowledge (2008) 'Public utility regulation, planning for long-term costs, and transitions to cleaner energy technologies', Knowledge W. P. Carey, Arizona State University, http://knowledge.wpcarey.asu.edu/article.cfm?articleid=1667

Lahsen, M. (2005) 'Technocracy, democracy, and US climate politics: The need for demarcations', *Science, Technology, and Human Values*, vol 30, no 1, Special Issue, pp137–169

Laird, F. N. (2001) *Solar Energy, Technology Policy, and Institutional Values*, Cambridge University Press, New York

Mayes, K. (2008) 'Renewable energy in Arizona', speech given at Arizona Workshop for Renewable Energy, 19 November, Arizona State University

Napolitano, J. (2007) 'State leadership towards a low carbon energy future', US House of Representatives Hearing, 14 November, www.globalwarming.house.gov/tools/assets/files/0204.pdf

Pasqualetti, M. J. (2004) 'Wind power: obstacles and opportunities', *Environment,* vol 46, no 7, pp23–38

Pasqualetti, M. J. (2008) 'Social barriers to renewable energy', Paper presented at Arizona Workshop on Renewable Energy, 17–19 November, www.aire.asu.edu/presentations/Pasqualetti.pdf

Pasqualetti, M. J. and Kelley, S. (2008) 'The water costs of Arizona electricity', Arizona Water Institute, www.azwaterinstitute.org/media/Cost%20of%20water%20and%20energy%20in%20az

Pasqualetti, M. J., Gipe, P. and Righter, R. (eds) (2002) *Wind Power in View: Energy Landscapes in a Crowded World,* Academic Press, San Diego, CA

Propst, L. (2008) 'Supportive testimony for Solana', Sonoran Institute, Filed in ACC Docket #L-00000GG-08-0407-00139/00140, 18 August, Arizona Corporation Commission

Romig, K. (2006) 'Gila Bend Arizona: on the road somewhere else', *Yearbook of the Association of Pacific Coast Geographers,* vol 68, no 1, pp33–52

Scott, J. C. (1998) *Seeing Like a State: How Certain Schemes to Improve the Human Condition Have Failed,* Yale University Press, New Haven, CT

Simon, C. A. (2007) *Alternative Energy: Political, Economic, and Social Feasibility,* Rowman & Littlefield Publishers, Lanham, MD

Solana Generating Station Project (2008) 'Abengoa Solar' (includes news station videos), www.solanasolar.com/default.cfm

Solar Task Force Report (2006) 'Clean and diversified energy initiative', www.westgov.org/wga/initiatives/cdeac/Solar-full.pdf

Udall, M. (1977) 'Solar energy: A ray of hope', *Congressman's Report,* US House of Representatives, vol XV, no 3

US Department of Energy (2007) 'Assessment of potential impact of concentrating solar power for electricity generation', www.nrel.gov/csp/troughnet/pdfs/41233.pdf

Western Governors Association (2004) 'Clean and Diversified Energy Initiative', Resolution 04-13, www.westgov.org/wga/initiatives/cdeac/Solar-full.pdf

Whitlatch, E. E. (1990) 'Public participation in energy facility siting II: Future directions', *Journal of Energy Engineering,* vol 116, no 2, pp111–122

Wolsink, M. (2000) 'Wind power and the NIMBY-myth: Institutional capacity and the limited significance of public support', *Renewable Energy,* vol 21, issue 1, pp49–64

Worster, D. (1985) *Rivers of Empire: Water, Aridity, and the Growth of the American West,* Pantheon, New York

Zimmerman, J. (2008) 'Attorney for Paloma Irrigation and Drainage District (PIDD)', Docket # L-00000GG-08-0407-00139/00140.p.363,368, Arizona Corporation Commission

Chapter 13

Socio-environmental Research on Energy Sustainable Communities: Participation Experiences of Two Decades

Petra Schweizer-Ries

Introduction

This chapter presents the knowledge and approaches of social and behavioural sciences to develop inter- and transdisciplinary models of energy sustainable communities, expanding the often purely technical viewpoints. A systemic and transactional model explains how energy communities may be analysed and transformative knowledge developed to transform them into energy sustainable communities. Participative instruments and more public engagement are the crucial factors in the action-oriented research process. The three case studies represent typical examples of energy communities installing a solar technology: a technically driven integration lacking participation of the communities; a socially driven one featuring technical deficiencies; and a participative integration that functioned properly and helped to further develop the community. The chapter concludes by presenting criteria for the successful realization of a sustainable energy community.

Energy Sustainability and Energy Sustainable Communities

The sustainable production and use of energy is widely discussed in the technical sciences, but is now also receiving more attention in the social sciences. From the sustainable development point of view, the topic includes ecological, social and economic aspects. Thanks to the implementation of sustainability science (Clark, 2008), which acts as a value orientation and encompasses sustainable development, the topic has become even more interesting. It stimulates inter- and transdisciplinary research and the inclusion of social and behavioural sciences, thus showing that the time has come to develop and add social science models of energy-sustainable communities to the predominant, purely technical, definitions.

In this chapter, communities are defined as organisms that have a joint identity and act as a whole. They can be described on different levels such as households, villages, regions, states, and even the world community. Ideally, energy-sustainable communities participate in and benefit from changes in energy supply and consumption changes (like the 'Type C' communities described by Walker and Devine-Wright, 2008). In these research projects, the term 'community' comprises a wide range of formations from single households with various participants, organizations like business companies or universities, to geographical regions. The definition follows the socio-technical system approach that always contextualizes communities that consume and sometimes even produce energy and technology (Schweizer-Ries, 2004). These socio-technical energy communities can range from a single household with a solar home system (Schweizer-Ries and Preiser, 1997; Fitriana et al, 1998; Kansteiner et al, 1998) or a village with mini-grid (Schmid et al, 2003) to a whole region connected to the national electricity grid. The energy can be produced either nearby or far away. Its consumers may be aware of its origin (e.g. when using a solar system on their roof) or unaware of it, as in most grid-connected cases. Research into the latter is often concerned with the acceptance of renewable energy systems, such as wind power stations, large photovoltaic systems or biomass plants (Schweizer-Ries and Linneweber, 2004; Wemheuer et al, 2006; Zoellner et al, 2008), which may be constructed either near the village (with the inhabitants being able to see the technology) or far away (the inhabitants merely consume 'green' electricity).[1] This chapter concentrates on the first cases, in which the energy production directly belongs to the communities, and where the socio-technical units, such as charge controllers in solar home systems or technical distribution systems in village power supplies, are visible signs (cultural artefacts) in the houses. In any case, the world of energy is changing. Following the 'smart grid' approach (Lugmaier and Brunner, 2008), which states that the energy demand should be better adapted to the energy production, it is necessary to further improve the interchange between consumers and producers at the level of national and international grid networks (Bendel et al, 2008).

Energy-sustainable communities are often defined as communities that cover more than 50 per cent of their total energy demand from renewable energy

(Schweizer-Ries, 2008) and that are energy efficient. However, energy-sustainable communities should not only be defined by means of energy production and consumption. Instead, they should be actively involved in the process of energy sustainability, which is only one of many other important fields concerned with sustainable development. This chapter describes the sustainability field of energy consumption and production, combining it with principles of sustainable development as well as community development. It introduces a model for analysing energy application systems and making them change into becoming more sustainable. This needs public engagement, which is often missing in technically driven processes. The examples presented will show that community participation is crucial for an integral change.

Socio-technical Energy Systems

The underlying model used to describe the energy system is based on the open systems theory (cybernetic, second order) and, more specifically, on the socio-technical systems design (van Eijnatten, 1990; van Eijnatten et al, 1992; Emery, 1993; Pasmore, 2002), in which technologies and humans influence each other and evolve in cooperation over time.

The corresponding studies presented below follow the principles of action research (Peters and Robinson, 1984; Aguinis, 1993; Dickens and Watkins, 1999; Reason and Bradbury, 2002). They include the idea of social and participative design derived from architecture (Sommer, 1983). The aim of these research studies is to support societal change as described in sustainability science (Clark, 2008).

A special phase model has been developed in order to analyse the different phases of the introduction of energy technology. In all phases, communities have to be actively involved, as the following examples show. Ongoing research investigates the various forms of participation.

Figure 13.1 shows the phase model, which has been applied to different processes of technology introduction (Schweizer-Ries et al, 2002; Schweizer-Ries, 2004) and which can be compared with Sommer's social design approach (1983).

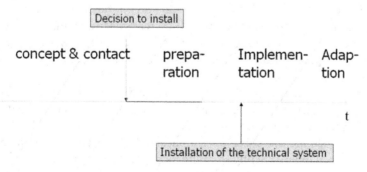

Figure 13.1 *Phase model*

According to the phase model, the development of energy communities over time can be described, using two aspects that are important for environmental psychology (see also McKenzie-Mohr, 2002):

- The '*social construction process*' can be seen as an active perception process in which people jointly construct realities and share wishes such as preserving resources for future generations and distributing them fairly between the individuals of today.
- The '*development of behaviour*' refers to behaviours that change the perception process and its physical, legal and infrastructural contexts, which are then again perceived and interpreted by individuals and social groups.

Both are dominated by habits (mental as well as behavioural) that help individuals and organizations to structure a complex world and to carry on with their daily routines as much as possible. The process of change towards energy sustainability has to overcome these daily routines and exchange them – where necessary – for new, more sustainable ones.

In order to emphasize the different starting points of change both inside and outside the community, Kaufmann-Hayoz and Gutscher (2001) and Kaufmann-Hayoz (2006) developed a model which is used as a basis to describe energy systems and produce system knowledge (knowledge about how the system functions today), target knowledge (how it should function in future), and transformation knowledge (how it can be changed), as described in the field of transdisciplinary needs for sustainable development.

Figure 13.2 shows the model that is permanently adapted to new research findings and in which central concepts are investigated and developed in fieldwork with local actors (Schweizer-Ries, 2004, 2008, 2010), according to Kaufmann-Hayoz and Gutscher (2001).

With this model it is important to be aware that the investigation process artificially separates the investigated system (e.g. a person, family, organization or village) from its environment. This is called the 'change system', stating that an investigation of a system is also a kind of intervention (Willke, 1996). From the perspective of sustainability science, the change should result in a better (more sustainable) state of the system (known as target knowledge, see above). This kind of intervention can change both the perception and appraisal of reality, and the manner of action in this world. The socio-technical system changes over time. Especially when a new energy technology is introduced, there is a change that may be utilized to produce new and more energy-sustainable habits regarding behaviour and thoughts.

In this approach, the socio-technical system is defined according to the introduction of the new technology. The research in all the case studies presented here focuses on communities at the level of villages, which can be seen as subdivisions of regions and which include sublevels of households, for example. Social structures cannot be seen independently from the technical realization and the existing and permanently developing cultures[2] of the production, distribution and use of

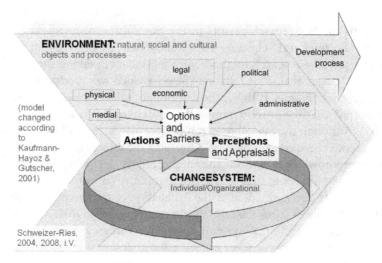

Figure 13.2 *System model*

energy. There are mutual relationships between the environment and the embedded system that can be examined (Willke, 2000).

The 'change system' defined here (see Figure 13.2) is regarded as being separate from the environment. It describes the developing socio-technical system. An introduction of technology starts with the social system that develops during the installation (see Figure 13.1 in the installation phase, when the technology is installed in the village and the household, respectively) and finally becomes a socio-technical system at the end.

According to this model, the following methodology focuses on the socio-technical systems involved, including single actors, organizations or representatives with designated roles. All data presented are derived from multi-, inter- and even transdisciplinary work.[3]

Socio-technical Energy Communities

The three cases described were chosen from an overall work with villages of between 12 and 3000 inhabitants in Europe, Latin America, Africa and Asia. Over 30 cases have been studied intensively using the concept of socio-technical systems (Emery, 1993), social or participative design (van Eijnatten, 1990) and the joint use of a limited resource (Ostrom et al, 1994). Although all research methods had been constantly developed and improved in later investigations, they all followed the same principles: the researchers came into direct contact with the community for some time, conducting participative observations and collecting qualitative and quantitative data with open interviews and semi-standardized questionnaires. The underlying research concepts and quantifiable constructs, such as community orientation, acceptance, knowledge of energy systems etc., were derived from or designed by using test-theoretical design (Zoellner, 2010).

In all cases, interactive actions, such as designing presentations and organizing discussions of the research results in the communities, involved community members (Zoellner and Schweizer-Ries, 2008). In a few cases, photo documentation was used as a research method; with the villagers taking the photographs themselves (Jaeger et al, 2006). In one village, a video was produced in collaboration with the inhabitants. It shows the community's development and the changes that occurred after the introduction of the new energy system (Schweizer-Ries et al, 2001). Although the overall research project also includes impact studies, the work presented here concentrates on describing the energy system when it was set up (system knowledge) and on the interventions designed together with the citizens to establish a sustainable energy community (transformation knowledge) or to support its development after the installation of the technical system (target knowledge). In most cases, researchers were invited to do their studies after the installation of the technical system, except for three cases in Latin America, Europe and Africa. In those three cases the social design was introduced from the beginning, even though the realization was only possible in one case, since the technological side dominated the introduction process.

The third example given (in the section entitled 'The socio-technical approach') describes the introduction of a solar system in a village and the transdisciplinary process, while the section entitled 'The technical approach' presents a very typical example of an introduction with a technical focus, which is a situation that can be found in many places and is difficult to avoid, since the technical part is often regarded as the most important aspect of the whole energy system. An alternative trend tends to prefer a more technical solution with a social focus. The section entitled 'The social approach' shows that technical functioning is important as well. Once the technical focus has been abandoned and technical solutions that meet the people's and societies' requirements have been developed, the way has been paved for the development of an energy-sustainable community all over the world.

The three examples presented in this chapter are neither quasi-experimentally tested nor representative for other villages in the world, but nevertheless they highlight some general features. It was possible to further develop the model of system theory on sustainable energy systems, which explains how they develop and, moreover, what constrains their development towards sustainable production and use of energy. The presentation of the cases in the following three sections includes part of the results, which are typical of the reflexive rather than the linear research process (Patterson, 1977; Willke, 1987).

The technical approach

The first example presents a very typical technology introduction process with a strictly technical point of view. An innovative or approved technology was applied and implemented for further testing or permanent use. The devices installed in these projects were often paid for by an external body like an NGO (non-governmental organization), a technical research project or a sponsor. Sometimes it was not clear who was going to pay for the maintenance costs after the installation, and it seemed as if nobody even cared. In this example, the planners took care of financing and social experts were even hired to accompany the introduction process, thus exceeding a purely technical approach. However, the process turned out to be dominated by the technological aspects.

Concurrent with the implementation of the village's energy supply and the social study, the points of view of the researchers involved were analysed. The results of this analysis highlighted the main reason for the project's failure in becoming an accepted and sustainable energy use and supply.

The introduction process

The different phases of the introduction process were carried through according to the social design approach. A needs analysis had been done before the system was designed, and there was also interchange with the villagers. A European NGO paid for the technical system. A joint decision was made to install the system in the village to supply the local health centre first and the village later. A contract was set up, called a 'memorandum of understanding', which unfortunately was not signed before the installation of the technical system.

At a higher level, cooperation between the research institutes involved and local organizations such as universities, schools, research centres etc. were planned. Both the Ministry of Education and the Ministry of Energy were involved almost from the beginning.

Several meetings took place in the village in order to prepare a special approach for introducing the technology. During the installation, three carefully selected local technicians received professional training. Only the key, which had been in possession of a European technician living near the village, was not handed over to the local operator.

The system's inauguration was celebrated with officials from the capital. Later on, the system was used for different purposes that were partly planned (e.g. one refrigerator) and partly not planned (e.g. charging batteries for the villagers). The system's operation was monitored by a satellite connection, allowing European technicians to observe the energy consumption 24 hours a day. A priority system of supplying different appliances was proposed and realized by the European partners: when the system's battery status was very high, the battery's display was green for all planned appliances, yellow for reduced appliances when the system's battery status was only medium, and red when the battery status was even lower, only enough for the refrigerator containing the vaccine. The battery's colour display, and thus its status, could be observed in different rooms of the health centre.

Unfortunately, the recommendations of social scientists to hand over full responsibility to the locals from the beginning were ignored, and the ownership of the system was not given to the villagers. The responsibility for this decision lay with one of the project's European NGOs, as it was convinced that an uncontrolled technical system would not work. When the European technician left the project, the system's operation was at risk. The villagers complained about the fact that the electricity did not supply their houses directly, but only the local health centre.

Main results

During the whole process, social scientists were involved, which was exceptional for a project with such a technical focus, but showed the general tendency to include social and behavioural aspects, e.g. in European programmes. The participants involved did not proceed in a participative manner that would have considered the villagers as partners and, moreover, as steering agents in this newly installed socio-technical system, as necessary in participative design processes (Königswieser and Exner, 1998).

A qualitative analysis was carried out, studying the structures that had surfaced in the open interviews; the results of which are presented here. A follow-up study is in progress. The interview partners were selected by theoretical sampling and the interviews were conducted and analysed according to the steps of the grounded theory approach (Strauss and Corbin, 1990/1996). Seven open interviews were taken in the following sequence: one female social scientist, one male engineer, one male member of the NGO, one female social science professor, one male engineering professor and two students with a social science background (Schwark, 2008).

The analysis showed that the categories of the different perspectives on the project were very contradictory. Especially in the field of participation, three different approaches became evident: the theory-driven social scientists' idea of the value of participation, the theory-driven and experience-driven rejection of participation of the engineer, and participation seen as sacrifice of control and power by the member of the NGO. With these different perceptions of reality and evaluations of participation, it was difficult – if not impossible – for the project to succeed. As the NGO is expected to leave the project, new opportunities for further development may arise. Still, the engineers have to adapt their view of participation and even then only time will tell whether real participation, with full control for the end-users, as described in the participative approach (see, for example, Villalobos Montoya and Schweizer-Ries, 2004) will take place, and whether this will ultimately lead to the development of an energy-sustainable community.

The social approach

The second type of case study was a very rare one. It dealt with a village that had organized the production and consumption of energy on its own. Thus, the villagers were involved and actively engaged from the beginning, while the social scientists joined the process later on. Searching for a technical solution, the village found a company 800km away that was willing to support them. The following sections reconstruct this socio-technical process.

The introduction process

The village consisted of about 70 reconstructed houses. Before the installation of the technical system, its inhabitants established in the village committee a subdivision responsible for energy supply. In 1997 the technical system was installed by the aforementioned company. It was a newly developed system, with the

European Commission funding a large part of the cost of the technology: the rest was financed by the villagers. The system included a special technology that allowed the equal distribution of electricity so that every household would get its exact intended share. Several social studies took place between 1998 and 2008. The results showed that even though the villagers were extremely interested, committed and involved, they didn't fully understand the technology and how it functioned. They complained about the company being so far away and that it had not installed the system in a comprehensive manner. As one result of the study's recommendations, workshops were prepared in cooperation with the villagers and the company in order to explain the operation of the system and to promote its correct use. For the same purpose, the villagers, supported by the team of social scientists, organized a solar festival for all target groups such as children, women and men.

The whole process, including the village's development and the change in people's living situation because of the new energy system, was documented on video. In 2008, a follow-up study took place and ten households were surveyed in detail. It turned out that the system could not always meet the demand completely, especially in summer when the village (mainly a summer residence) was fully populated. The system had been maintained, but some faults had been detected, like the batteries not having been exchanged as scheduled after eight years of operation, which would have been crucial for the proper functioning of the technical system. Villagers were already thinking of the possibility of connecting the village to the national electricity grid.

Main results

This village can be characterized as using the technical system in a fully integrated, autonomous and responsible way. It used energy-efficient appliances where possible and the energy demand was adapted to the supply. People felt constricted by the energy supply, but at the same time described it as an advantage to become aware of the limitations in supply, even starting to apply some energy-saving habits also to their main residences connected to the national electricity grid.

The main problems with this project lay in the deficit of the solar system's technical functioning, closely followed by the distance between the technical staff and the technical system, which could have been prevented by contracting a local maintenance service. Since this never happened, technical parts, such as distributors, that functioned badly were not replaced in time, thus causing problems.

Most of the villagers could be described as very sensitive and aware of the system, but the system's technical functioning was nevertheless reduced mainly due to a lack of correct maintenance and the timely replacement of technical parts. The system's technical performance was therefore quite low. Due to the villagers' regular payments, funds were available for the renewal of the batteries. However, expecting to become the beneficiaries of future projects of infrastructural improvements as being connected with the national electricy grid, the users' association decided to postpone the purchase.

The socio-technical approach

The third example deals with a village in which social and technical experts were involved from the beginning and the introduction process was planned and realized participatively. The village was selected, which means that the village did not take the initiative at the beginning of the project, which is a very typical example of the processes of technical introduction in developing countries. The following sections trace the successful introduction process and the measures for developing a sustainable energy community.

The introduction process

First the different researchers from various disciplines and countries (namely a European State and a Latin American State) that were involved in the project discussed the technical concept and the best way to introduce the new energy supply in a Latin American village. An interdisciplinary research team was assembled, which agreed to apply the human development approach combined with the socio-technical approach, taking into account social as well as technical aspects and putting the people at the heart of the technology development.

The project group also informed and involved the government, since the whole project was organized as a cooperation between the two States. Although the project's budget included the costs of the scientists running the project, the financing of the follow-up phase was not taken into account by the research project and had to be organized by the villagers.

Immediately after the start of the project, the researchers and the government selected a village from a number of villages that had applied to participate in the project for village electrification with solar energy. Different studies, including an analysis of the people's needs, were done before the system was designed. Therefore the social scientists were able to take into account the social reconstruction and description of the village structures.

The scientists paid special attention to the preparation of the contract and its signature before the actual installation. During this process, people learned about the costs, the general advantages, and the system's probable impact on daily life, including special instructions for the proper use of the available, yet limited, energy. The project group prepared presentations at the local school for different groups such as women, men and children. Two local technicians, who also supported the installation process, underwent technical training.

After the system had been installed, researchers and villagers prepared a special festival. The technical systems installed were to supply individual households with energy. All the individual systems were installed and inaugurated at the same time.

One year after the installation, the first evaluation study took place and some adaptations were made. A special research task was to solve the problem that the charge controllers interfered with radio frequencies. The first study demonstrated that the village had changed considerably not only because of the supply of electricity for light, radios and TVs in the houses, but also because of the water supply, which was organized by the villagers in cooperation with one of the researchers. Gardens grew and people expressed hope, which was not the case at the beginning of the project (Preiser et al, 1997; Parodi et al, 1998).

Ten years later, another study revealed that the systems were still running, the batteries had been regularly changed, and the village prospered; its inhabitants staying and not emigrating like so many others from small Latin American villages (Schweizer-Ries et al, 2006).

Main results

Previous sections have touched upon the results for community development, which can also be studied elsewhere (Pontoriero et al, 1994). This chapter points to the fact that the joint approach and the creation of an interdisciplinary research team required a lot of effort, and that many team discussions were necessary in order to come together. The whole process saw a range of meta-communication both inside and outside the village. The project's strength lay in the very open-minded technical partners, who invited the social scientists to join the project and took them as seriously as the inhabitants. During the realization of the initial project, one central point of the whole process was the agreement to a human-centred approach for the introduction of the technology – the so called socio-technical systems approach.

Lessons Learned

The world is still a long way from having many energy-sustainable communities. The introduction process of technical innovations has to be accompanied by social adaptations, the involvement of end-users, for example, realized through public engagement and the building of a good infrastructure. It is also important to train all the actors involved in communication, real partnership and mutual acceptance.

The following principles of transdisciplinary research (Sieber and Braunschweig, 2005) can also be applied to this work:

- *Commitment*: It is important that the people involved feel committed through-out the whole process and that researchers are present in the field, working closely with locals and following mutual targets. The former can be supported by public engagement at the beginning; the latter can be implemented by applying elements of participative research.
- *Communication*: It is not easy to understand each other and work together when coming from different cultures and subcultures (different states, disci-plines and living conditions etc.). A cautious yet clear communication and mutual understanding provide the most relevant basis for a successful public engagement process. It is the social facilitator's task to initiate and support activities of cooperation and unity. The communication process has to be followed up during and after the project.
- *Continuity*: The processes involved in the introduction of innovative technolo-gies take time. Several years may pass from an initial idea to the project's

inauguration. Personal continuity is an advantage, because the partners can get to know each other, their contact persons and their respective backgrounds and institutions. This can create an atmosphere of trust and assurance. Since researchers are not external figures but a part of the project team, it is imperative that they are present during the whole process and that they cultivate their contacts even between field studies. Because the methodology of action research includes all these principles, this approach has proved to be very useful in the field and thus was applied in all further studies.

Outlook:
What Else Is Necessary?

The role of social scientists in projects of technical innovation has changed greatly during the last decade. Today, an increasing interest in involving social partners can be observed. One example is the promotion of this involvement by the European Commission in its recent project frameworks, although it sometimes seems that social partners are only included due to formal requirements. There is still much to be learned about the capacities of social scientists and the added value of a socio-technical partnership and cooperation with local stakeholders. Future efforts, focusing on common interests and goals, may contribute to an improved mutual professional understanding and valorization in order to develop successful interdisciplinary and transdisciplinary strategies of work that target public engagement.

The overall task for social scientists dealing with energy issues and sustainability is to contribute to a change of energy culture by developing a broader sense of consumption culture in order to apply the sufficiency strategy (Schweizer-Ries and Villalobos Montoya, 2002). This change requires a modification of values and socially shared beliefs; including those about status symbols, for example. Therefore, a transformation process at all levels of society is necessary for the construction of new models of responsible consumption and for defining new values regarding concepts such as quality of life, welfare and comfort. On the one hand, society's shared beliefs and 'common sense' can be shaped by the mass media and the education of the younger generation. On the other hand, social scientists should closely cooperate with the technical staff in order to develop optimal combinations of all three sustainability strategies (consistency, efficiency, sufficiency, see also Schweizer-Ries, 2008) for each target area, and to use synergetic effects instead of moving in different directions. Villagers need to be involved in a proper participative way and have to be regarded as equal partners in the processes of research and development as conceptualized in the public engagement process. The road towards energy-sustainable communities is long and difficult, but promising examples do exist as well as an increasing knowledge that this is the possible direction.

Notes

1. 'Green' electricity is produced from renewable energy sources such as wind, water or sun.
2. In this context, culture refers to the way in which people evaluate and create their environments, and how they establish rules about how to act in daily life and thus establish spatio-temporal action patterns typical for their culture (see also, for example, Bösch, 1980).
3. As defined by Max-Neef (2005), for example, multidisciplinarity refers to the aspect of bringing together perspectives from different disciplines; interdisciplinarity describes the process of disciplines working together and agreeing on one model; and transdisciplinarity transcends the boundaries between the disciplines and also between researchers and the stakeholders/citizens/persons concerned.

References

Aguinis, H. (1993) 'Action research and scientific method: Presumed discrepancies and actual similarities', *Journal of Applied Behavioral Science*, vol 29, no 4, pp416–431

Bendel, C., Nestle, D. and Ringelstein, J. (2008) 'Bidirektionales Energiemanagement im Niederspannungsnetz: Strategie, Umsetzung und Anwendungen', *Elektrotechnik and Informationstechnik*, vol 125, no 12, pp415–418

Bösch, E. E. (1980) *Kultur und Handlung: Einführung in die Kulturpsychologie*, Hans Huber, Bern, Switzerland

Clark, W. C. (2008) 'Sustainability science: A room of its own', *Proceedings of the National Academy of Science*, vol 104, pp1737–1738

Dickens, L. and Watkins, K. (1999) 'Action research: Rethinking Lewin', *Management Learning*, vol 30, no 2, pp127–140

Emery, F. (1993) 'Characteristics of socio-technical systems', in E. L. Trist and H. Murray (eds) *The Social Engagement of Social Science: A Tavistock Anthology. Vol. II: The Sociotechnical Perspective*, University of Pennsylvania Press, Philadelphia, PA pp157–186

Fitriana, I., Kantosa, E., Sudradjat, A., Kuhmann, J., Preiser, K. and Schweizer-Ries, P. (1998) 'On the way from Sukatani to the 50 MW programme: A socio-technical analysis of solar home systems in Indonesia', Paper presented at the 2nd World Conference and Exhibition on Photovoltaic Solar Energy Conversion, Vienna

Jaeger, M., Schweizer-Ries, P. and Villalobos Montoya, C. (2006) 'Process management and participation in rural electrification projects', in *3rd European Conference on PV Hybrid and Minigrids*, Aix en Provence, France (CD-ROM)

Kansteiner, B., Strauss, P., Preiser, K., Schweizer-Ries, P. and Aulich, H. (1998) 'Rural electrification project with photovoltaic-hybrid systems and solar home systems for Vietnam', Paper presented at the 2nd World Conference and Exhibition on Photovoltaic Solar Energy Conversion, Vienna

Kaufmann-Hayoz, R. (2006) 'Human action in context: A model framework for interdisciplinary studies in view of sustainable development', *Umweltpsychologie*, vol 10, no 1, pp154–177

Kaufmann-Hayoz, R. and Gutscher, H. (2001) 'Transforming towards sustainability: An interdisciplinary, actor-oriented perspective', in R. Kaufmann-Hayoz and H. Gutscher (eds) *Changing Things – Moving People: Strategies for Promoting Sustainable Development at the Local Level*, Birkhäuser, Basel–Boston–Berlin, pp19–25

Königswieser, R. and Exner, A. (1998) *Systemische Intervention: Architekturen und Designs für Berater und Veränderungsmanager*, Klett-Cotta, Stuttgart, Germany

Lugmaier, A. and Brunner, H. (2008) *Leitfaden für den Weg zum Aktiven Verteilernetz*, Bundesministerium für Verkehr, Innovation und Technologie, Vienna

Max-Neef, M. A. (2005) 'Foundations of transdisciplinarity', *Ecological Economics*, vol 53, no 1, pp5–16

McKenzie-Mohr, D. (2002) 'The next revolution: Sustainability', in P. Schmuck and W. Schultz (eds) *Psychology of Sustainable Development*, Kluwer, Boston, MA, pp19–36

Ostrom, E., Gardner, R. and Walker, J. (1994) *Rules, Games, and Common-pool Resources*, University of Michigan Press, Ann Arbor, MI

Parodi, O., Preiser, K., Schweizer-Ries, P. and Wendl, M. (1998) 'When the night falls on Balde de Leyes: The success story of an integrated approach in PV Rural electrification', Paper presented at the 2nd World Conference and Exhibition on Photovoltaic Solar Energy Conversion, Vienna

Pasmore, W. (2002) 'Action research in the workplace: The socio-technical perspective', in P. Reason and H. Brandbury (eds) *Handbook of Action Research*, Sage Publications, London–Thousand Oaks–New Delhi, pp38–47

Patterson, A. H. (1977) 'Methodological developments in environment-behavioral research', in D. Stokols (ed) *Perspectives on Environment and Behavior*, Plenum Press, New York, pp325–344

Peters, M. and Robinson, V. (1984) 'The origins and status of action research', *Journal of Applied Behavioral Science*, vol 20, no 2, pp113–124

Pontoriero, D., Blasco, I., Hoesé, E., Serpa, L., Morales, R., Avila, E. et al (1994) 'Proyecto "Pequeñas aplicaciones fotovoltáicas en zonas aridas"' (Informe de Avance)', Universidad Nacional, San Juan

Preiser, K., Schweizer-Ries, P. and Parodi, O. (1997) 'Balde de Leyes: La manera integrada hacia la luz eléctrica', *Energía y Desarrollo*, vol 11, no 1, pp7–11

Reason, P. and Bradbury, H. (2002) 'Introduction: Inquiry and participation in search of a world worthy of human aspiration', in P. Reason and H. Bradbury (eds) *Handbook of Action Research: Participative Inquiry and Practice (1-14)*, Sage Publications, London–Thousand Oaks–New Delhi

Schmid, J., Strauss, P. and Schweizer-Ries, P. (2003) 'Photovoltaics: Minigrids for rural development and economic growth', *Renewable Energy World*, July–August, pp192–199

Schwark, S. (2008) *Partizipation: Zwischen Anspruch und sozialer Wirklichkeit: Eine Einzelfallanalyse zur Einführung erneuerbarer Energien in Entwicklungsländer*, Otto-von-Guericke-Universität, Magdeburg, Germany

Schweizer-Ries, P. (2004) 'Nutzung von Solarstromanlagen: ein umweltpsychologisches Thema', *Magdeburger Wissenschaftsjournal*, vol 1, no 9, pp27–34

Schweizer-Ries, P. (2008) 'Energy sustainable communities: Environmental-psychological investigations', *Energy Policy*, 36, no 11, pp4126–4135

Schweizer-Ries, P. (2010) 'Nachhaltige Konsummuster aus umweltpsychologischer Sicht: Ein Verhaltensmodell zum Umdenken und Umlenken', in *Loccumer Protokoll Nr*, Eigenverlag, Rehburg-Loccum, Germany

Schweizer-Ries, P. and Linneweber, V. (2004) 'Social acceptability and implementation of renewable energy', *Journal of Applied Psychology*, 5(3/4), pp157–166

Schweizer-Ries, P. and Preiser, K. (1997) 'Socio-technical analysis of solar home systems in the Nepalese Himalaya', Paper presented at the 14th European Photovoltaic Solar

Energy Conference and Exhibition, Vienna
Schweizer-Ries, P. and Villalobos Montoya, C. (2002) 'Utilizing social knowledge to convert PV systems into sustainable energy communities', in J. L. Bal, R. Vigotti, G. Ivestrini, M. Gamberale, A. Grassi, P. Helm and W. Palz (eds) *Conference and Exhibition 'PV in Europe: From PV Technology to Energy Solutions'*, Vol 1, pp1234–1237
Schweizer-Ries, P., Vogt, G. and Casper, C. (2001) 'Mensch-Technik-Organisations (MTO): Analyse von netzunabhängigen Dorfstromanlagen', Paper presented at the Tagungsbeitrag zum 16. Symposium Photovoltaische Solarenergie, Vol 10, pp287–292
Schweizer-Ries, P., Casper, C., Djuwita, R., Ramirez, E. and Hidalgo de Ávila, E. (2002) 'Social interventions to achieve success with off-grid village power supply systems: Case studies from Indonesia, Spain and Argentina', Paper presented at the Proceedings of the 17th European Photovoltaic Solar Energy Conference and Exhibition, Vol 17, pp1951–1955
Schweizer-Ries, P., Hidalgo, E., Luther, K. and Schulze, A. (2006) 'Sozio-technische Einführung von Solar Home Systemen in Balde de Leyes: die 10-Jahres-Evaluation', Paper presented at the Tagungsbeitrag zum 21 Symposium Photovoltaische Solarenergie, Staffelstein, Germany
Sieber, P. and Braunschweig, T. (2005) *Choosing the Right Projects: Designing Selection Processes for North–South Research Partnership Programmes*, Swiss Commission for Research Partnerships with Developing Countries, KFPE, Bern, Switzeland
Sommer, R. (1983) *Social Design: Creating Buildings with People in Mind*, Prentice-Hall International, Spektrum Books, Englewood Cliffs, NJ
Strauss, A. L., and Corbin, J. (1990/1996) *Grounded Theory: Grundlagen qualitativer Sozialforschung*, Psychologie Verlags Union, Weinheim, Germany
van Eijnatten, F. M. (1990) 'Classical socio-technical systems design: The socio-technical design paradigm of organisations', Research Memorandum No. 90-005, Eindhoven University of Technology, Limburg, The Netherlands
van Eijnatten, F. M., Hoevenaars, A. M. and Rutte, C. G. (1992) 'Holistic and participative (re)design: Contemporary STSD modelling in The Netherlands', Reprint No. BDK/397, Eindhoven University of Technology, Graduate School of Industrial Engineering and Management Science, Limburg, The Netherlands
Villalobos Montoya, C. and Schweizer-Ries, P. (2004) 'Getting people involved: The relationship between community participation and project sustainability', Paper presented at the Proceedings of the 18th European Photovoltaic Solar Energy Conference and Exhibition
Walker, G. and Devine-Wright, P. (2008) 'Community renewable energy: What does it mean?' *Energy Policy*, 36, 497–500.
Wemheuer, C., Zoellner, J. and Schweizer-Ries, P. (2006) 'Public acceptance of PV ground-installed systems: Key factors of a successful process', Paper presented at the 21st European Photovoltaic Solar Energy Conference and Exhibition
Willke, H. (1987) 'Systemdiagnose, Systemintervention: Weisse Löcher in schwarzen Kästen?', in G. Schiepek (ed) *Systeme erkennen Systeme*, PVU, Weinheim, Munich
Willke, H. (1996) *Systemtheorie II: Interventionstheorie. Grundzüge einer Theorie der Intervention in komplexen Systemen*, UTB, Stuttgart, Germany
Willke, H. (2000) *Systemtheorie I: Grundlagen*, 6th edn, Lucius and Lucius, Stuttgart, Germany
Zoellner, J. and Schweizer-Ries, P. (2008) 'Nur eine Frage der Technik? Akzeptanz Erneuerbarer Energien und sozialwissenschaftliche Fragen', *Eta-Energie*, vol 2, pp26–28

Zoellner, J., Schweizer-Ries, P. and Wemheuer, C. (2008) 'Public acceptance of renewable energies: Results from case studies in Germany, *Energy Policy*, vol 36, no 11, pp4136–4141

Zoellner, J. (unpublished) 'Akzeptanz von Windkraftanlagen in Deutschland: eine umweltpsychologische Studie', (in preparation)

Chapter 14

Yes In My Back Yard: UK Householders Pioneering Microgeneration Technologies

Sally Caird and Robin Roy

Introduction

Following the 2008 Climate Change Act, in its first carbon budget the UK government set demanding targets to reduce the nation's CO_2 and other greenhouse gas emissions by 34 per cent by 2020 and 80 per cent by 2050 from 1990 levels. Households alone contribute 27 per cent of UK carbon emissions, with approximately three-quarters of these emissions arising from space and water heating (DTI, 2007). Increasing low carbon and renewable energy supplies is a key element of the government strategy to achieve its carbon reduction targets. Also in 2008, the European Commission set the UK a target that 15 per cent of electricity, heat and transport energy should come from renewable sources by 2020, including small-scale microgeneration technologies in homes and other buildings (HM Government, 2009).

The government's microgeneration strategy suggested that the widespread adoption of microgeneration technologies – defined as the small-scale production of heat and/or electricity from a low carbon source – could reduce domestic carbon emissions by up to 15 per cent by 2050; a worthwhile contribution to the carbon reduction targets (DTI, 2006). But household adoption in the UK of microgeneration technologies has been slow compared with other countries, despite government grant schemes such as the Low Carbon Buildings Programme (LCBP). A recent detailed report on the potential for microgeneration estimated that by 2007 there were only 95,000–98,000 installations in UK homes, with solar thermal hot water (STHW or solar water heating) systems accounting for over 92 per cent of them. Even rarer are other microgeneration technologies, including heat pumps, wood-fuelled stoves and boilers, solar photovoltaic (PV) and micro-wind systems. It is estimated that there were only about 5000 such domestic systems in 2007 (Element Energy, 2008).

The total number of microgeneration systems installed therefore represents only a tiny percentage of the potential market. Element Energy (2008) calculated that the UK market for domestic microgeneration could reach 9 million installations by 2020 given an ambitious policy support framework, such as a subsidy of 2p/kWh for microgenerated heat, and prohibiting all off-site (non-renewable) electricity for zero-carbon homes except for low carbon systems such as heat pumps.

Before such policies can be effective, more needs to be known about public perceptions of, and engagement with, microgeneration; why so few UK consumers are currently installing the technologies; and what would help boost their uptake. Existing studies have tended to focus on financial, regulatory and informational barriers to account for the slow adoption of microgeneration. For example, a survey of enquirers to a solar thermal hot water (STHW) promotion scheme in London showed that they were deterred by high capital cost, lack of trustworthy information, and difficulties knowing which brands were reliable (SEA/RENUE, 2005). Another UK study of the potential of solar PV, micro-CHP and micro-wind also identified the barriers of high upfront costs, long payback times and lack of information, in addition noting consumer scepticism regarding the performance and reliability of these technologies (Watson et al, 2006). Inadequate grants and subsidies to alleviate high costs are another main obstacle to adoption (DTI, 2006; Element Energy, 2008). Other reports point to the low level of consumer awareness, restrictive planning laws, and the complexities of selling electricity back to the grid (EST, 2007). Similar obstacles were identified in a UK Parliamentary Trade and Industry Committee report, which also highlighted the considerable technical knowledge required to decide whether to invest in microgeneration (House of Commons, 2007).

The government's Microgeneration Strategy progress report claims that many of the planning and technical barriers, plus consumer demand for independent certification of microgeneration technologies, have been addressed (BERR, 2008). This is important for extending the microgeneration market beyond the pioneer enthusiasts and 'early adopters' to many more consumers.

This chapter draws on two Open University-led collaborative projects that surveyed consumer perceptions and experiences of several microgeneration technologies for generating heat or electricity at the household level. These included:

* solar thermal hot water (STHW) systems;
* ground source heat pumps (GSHPs);
* simple wood-burning stoves;
* wood-fuelled boilers and automatic biomass stoves;

- solar photovoltaic (PV) systems;
- micro-wind turbines.

The focus in this chapter is on how householders who have seriously considered purchasing a microgeneration system for their home – and the pioneer adopters who have actually installed one – engage with these technologies, what made them adopt or reject microgeneration, and what would encourage these already interested consumers and the broader public to adopt these technologies more widely. The respondents to our surveys were self-selected and, not unexpectedly, were 'greener' and from higher socio-economic groups than the general UK population. Our respondents' reasons for rejecting microgeneration systems, and any problems experienced by those who did adopt them, thus represent significant issues that need to be addressed before the less wealthy, less 'green', general UK population will decide to install microgeneration and thus achieve the worthwhile carbon reductions estimated to result from their widespread adoption.

Aims, Methods and Outline

The two projects on which this chapter is based are outlined below.

People-centred ecodesign (PCED)

This project involved a survey of the UK public who in 2006 had viewed a BBC/OU TV series on climate change and then accessed an Open University (OU) online questionnaire via the BBC/OU or Energy Saving Trust (EST) websites. This produced 390 responses from people who had adopted, or had seriously considered but decided against adopting, a microgeneration system. The responses covered STHW systems (39 adopters; 151 non-adopters); solar PV (12 adopters; 130 non-adopters), micro-wind turbines (7 adopters; 128 non-adopters) and simple wood-burning stoves (63 adopters; 65 non-adopters). The project also involved in-depth telephone interviews with a different group who had sought advice from a National Energy Foundation scheme called 'Energy for Good': 15 who had adopted and 13 who had considered but rejected a STHW system (see Caird and Roy et al, 2007).

The YIMBY generation (Yes in my back yard! UK householders pioneering microgeneration heat)

The OU and the Energy Saving Trust (EST) collaborated to conduct one of the largest surveys to date of UK householders in the process of purchasing or considering a microgeneration space heating and/or hot water system. The surveys covered four technologies, all eligible for government grants under the Low Carbon Buildings Programme (LCBP) – namely STHW, ground source heat pumps (GSHP), wood-fuelled boilers (WFB) and biomass stoves with automatic pellet feed (BS) (see Roy et al, 2008).

Online questionnaires produced over 900 responses from members of the public who accessed the EST or BBC/OU websites in mid-2007. The first survey covered 314 householders seriously considering buying one of these technologies (named 'Considerers'; of which 221 were considering STHW, 50 GSHP, 28 WFB and 15 BS) and 64 householders who had considered but decided against purchase ('Non-adopters'; of which 50 rejected STHW, 7 GSHP, 2 WFB and 3 BS).

Further surveys were conducted with 546 UK householders who had been awarded a LCBP grant to install a microgeneration heat technology (named 'Adopters'; of which 413 had adopted STHW, 89 GSHP, 36 WFB and 8 BS): 285 of these adopters had already installed and had experience of using their system. The LCBP grant-holders also included 70 householders who were counted as non-adopters of a microgeneration technology that they had rejected in favour of another, for which they received the grant.

Outline

This chapter outlines selected results and conclusions of these two studies focusing on the following questions:

- Who is interested in adopting microgeneration technologies?
- What motivates the pioneers who adopt microgeneration?
- What influences the adoption process?
- How do microgeneration adopters engage with their system?
- Why do most people decide against adopting microgeneration?
- What measures would encourage more people to adopt microgeneration?

Further results, including more detailed feedback from the pioneer adopters on their experiences of using their system and ideas for improving it, may be found in the final reports on these projects (Caird et al, 2007; Roy et al, 2008).

Who Is Interested in Adopting Microgeneration Technologies?

The people-centred ecodesign (PCED) project found that people interested in microgeneration (both adopters and non-adopters) are typically from environmentally concerned households where the main earner's occupation is professional, managerial or in education/medical services, with a significant proportion being retired. The adopters are mainly older couples living in three or four bedroom houses and only about a quarter had children under 16 years living at home (Caird et al, 2007).

The YIMBY generation surveys provided similar results. Two-thirds (66 per cent) of all surveyed households (considerers, adopters and non-adopters) included a main earner with (or retired from) a professional or senior managerial occupation. Over 60 per cent of respondents lived in households without children or where the children had left home. Up to half of respondents from all groups claimed that they usually took actions to reduce their environmental impacts; such as walking, cycling or using public transport instead of driving, whenever possible.

The YIMBY surveys show that, unsurprisingly, microgeneration adopters are a wealthier group than considerers and non-adopters. But although they had above-average household incomes, most adopters were not especially wealthy; just over a quarter had an annual household income more than twice the £30,000 UK average, and fewer than 10 per cent had a household income above £100,000. They were also an older group, with 71 per cent of adopters aged over 45 years and a quarter retired (compared with 14 per cent of considerers and non-adopters).

One notable result is that over half of the microgeneration heat adopters lived in detached homes with four or more bedrooms and large gardens, located in rural areas, and off the mains gas network. This is not surprising, given that currently GSHPs, wood boilers and biomass stoves are only cost-effective in properties previously heated by oil, electricity or solid fuel, and are suited to larger properties with space for the equipment; heat pump ground loops or wood fuel stores.

STHW systems have a wider appeal, with only about half of installations being without mains gas, and about a third of the adopters surveyed living in smaller suburban properties. This reflects the fact that STHW is a lower-cost, more compact and familiar technology, which is worthwhile for properties with or without mains gas.

Generally our results show that existing UK consumer demand for microgeneration is largely confined to a niche market of environmentally concerned, older, middle-class householders, often living in larger properties off the mains gas network. By comparison, although considerers and non-adopters have similar occupational characteristics and environmental attitudes, more live in suburban homes in areas with mains gas supplies, and were more often considering retro-fitting rather than installing a system in a new-build project.

What Motivates the Pioneers Who Adopt Microgeneration?

The PCED survey identified the three most frequently cited reasons for adopting STHW, solar PV and micro-wind systems:

- saving energy;
- reducing fuel bills;
- concern for the environment.

For people buying simple wood-burning stoves, saving energy, money and the environment are important, but they are mainly bought because they offer the warmth and appearance of a real fire.

Table 14.1 *YIMBY generation: What motivates householders to seriously consider or adopt microgeneration heat technologies?*

Reason(s) given for serious consideration or adoption	Percentage
To reduce carbon dioxide emissions	75%
To save money on fuel bills	72%
I wanted to use low carbon energy and will get pleasure from doing so	61%
Allows me to visibly demonstrate my environmental commitment	34%
The low carbon technology forms part of a heating system replacement or upgrade	23%
Related to my job, hobby or interests in the environment/ low carbon technologies	21%
Being innovative, a pioneer in using low carbon energy technology	21%
The low carbon technology forms part of other home improvements e.g. home extension; loft conversion; new build	20%
Total responses: 'considerers' and 'adopters'	*859*

These findings were reinforced by the YIMBY study (see Table 14.1). This showed that the main reasons why some UK householders are seriously considering or have adopted microgeneration heat are environmental (to reduce carbon emissions) and/or financial (to reduce fuel bills). However, the survey showed that they desired a microgeneration system for the pleasure of using a low carbon energy source. A fifth of these considerers and pioneer adopters had jobs or hobbies related to the environment or low carbon technology and were often technology enthusiasts. Another fifth said that they were using the opportunity of a new build or another major home improvement project to seriously consider or install microgeneration heating.

What Influences the Adoption Process?

Information and advice

Only a minority (fewer than 10 per cent) of PCED respondents said they wanted better information and advice to help them decide whether and how to invest in microgeneration. However, several commented that the information provided by existing advice bodies is too generalized, with the technical details of installations left up to the installers. A single body to guide people through the details of technology choice, grant applications, planning permission, installation, use and maintenance were suggested as ways of facilitating adoption.

The YIMBY surveys found that uncertainty about system performance and payback is one of the main barriers to adopting microgeneration (see Table 14.3); indicating the need for better impartial information for people considering investing in these technologies. Over 90 per cent of considerers first looked on the internet for information, and then over half obtained manufacturers' or other literature. Advice from family, friends and neighbours was drawn on by a third – again indicating the difficulties consumers have in finding impartial and informed advice – and from installers by a quarter. Many tried to find information on more than one technology and gradually narrowed down their choice to what may be suitable for their home. This can be difficult, as installers tend to specialize in a single technology or supplier. When choosing between technologies, purchasers generally chose the one perceived to be less risky, better established, and more compatible with their existing or new property. Together with their lower initial cost, this favours STHW systems.

Grants

Grants are a significant factor and there is evidence that potential adopters are deterred after their initial consideration of microgeneration because of the high cost and relatively small UK grants available at the time of the survey, which typically cover only 10–15 per cent of the price. Most who decided against purchase did so after looking at the grants information and then decided not to apply. For the pioneers who did proceed with the LCBP grants, although 70 per cent said the grant was an important factor in their decision to purchase ('The grant is the sugar that sweetened the pill') many down-played its importance in retrospect. Even so, the majority of adopters criticized the grants for being too small. A substantial minority (44 per cent) of the pioneer adopters said they probably would have decided to purchase their system without an LCBP grant, but the same is unlikely to apply to the wider market of considerers.

How Do Microgeneration Adopters Engage with their System?

Pioneer microgeneration adopters tended to be enthusiasts for green technologies and so most wanted to use their system to reduce their household energy use and emissions as much as possible. It is known that the way in which people use microgeneration affects the performance of the system (e.g. Guy and Shove, 2000). For example, the times when hot water is drawn from a STHW system or the pattern of demand from a heat pump can affect system efficiency (EST, 2001; Parker, 2007). The PCED results showed that nearly half (47 per cent) of inter- viewed STHW adopters tried to use solar heated water when it was available, for example showering in the afternoon or evening, when the water is hot, or in the morning if there was hot water from the previous day and a sunny day was expected. But more than half (53 per cent) said that they made no changes to their behaviour, perhaps needing better feedback from the system to enable its most efficient operation (Caird and Roy, 2008).

In the YIMBY survey, the most common problems experienced by adopters, affecting about a third, were uncertainty about how best to operate the system to make the most efficient use of fuel or energy (37 per cent), and difficulties in understanding the system's, often complex, controls (28 per cent). It is therefore not surprising that the main design improvements desired by the adopters were more user-friendly controls, better instructions on their operation, and improved feedback displays. For example, nearly half (48 per cent) of STHW adopters wanted easier to understand controls that minimize back-up water heating requirements and provide feedback on money and energy savings. Over half of GSHP (53 per cent) adopters would like controls that give more feedback on operating efficiency and energy saved – rather like a car computer. Such improvements should help users understand how to maximize energy, carbon and financial savings.

One of the most promising findings of the YIMBY surveys is the fact that the majority of 272 adopters with experience of microgeneration use claimed that they are more aware than before of their household's energy use (74 per cent) and make greater efforts to save energy (72 per cent). It is perhaps less surprising that, having gone to such efforts to research and install their new technology, 71 per cent also said that they are adapting their behaviours to make the most efficient use of the hot water or heat generated.

Why Do Most People Decide against Adopting Microgeneration?

The PCED survey found that just 20 per cent of those who seriously considered getting microgeneration actually installed a system. Like previous studies, the PCED survey found that high initial cost was the main reason for rejection of solar PV (85 per cent of non-adopters), STHW (73 per cent) and micro-wind turbines (53 per cent) (see Table 14.2). However, simple wood-burning stoves were more often rejected because of anticipated difficulties in finding the space to store fuel (45 per cent), controlling their heat output (43 per cent), and the extra dirt and labour they involve (40 per cent), rather than their cost (35 per cent).

As Table 14.2 shows, there were other deterrents to adoption, some technology-specific. For non-adopters of STHW, solar PV and micro-wind, an obstacle for about a quarter was the difficulty in finding a trustworthy installer. Indeed several commented that there was a need for regulation to control 'cowboy' installers. This is being addressed by providing installer accreditation, for example, through the Solar Trade Association and the government's Microgeneration Certification Scheme. More than one-fifth of non-adopters were also uncertain about the performance, reliability and durability of solar and wind systems, and half were deterred by the low price paid for solar electricity exported to the grid. Additional obstacles to micro-wind adoption included getting planning permission, finding a suitable location, and worries about noise and vibration.

The YIMBY surveys again found that financial barriers – high cost (86 per cent), long or uncertain payback (68 per cent) and relatively small grants (60 per cent) – were major deterrents for the microgeneration heat non-adopters (Table 14.3).

Table 14.2 *People-centred ecodesign: Barriers to the adoption of microgeneration*

Reason(s) given for non-adoption*	Solar thermal hot water	Solar PV	Micro-wind turbine
Too expensive	73%	85%	53%
Likely fuel savings not worth the cost	36%	40%	21%
Difficulty in finding trustworthy installer	25%	24%	25%
System not likely to last long enough to pay back	24%	28%	15%
New technology with uncertain performance and reliability	23%	19%	21%
Gaining planning permission	13%	13%	37%
Difficulty in finding space or suitable location for unit	17%	16%	33%
Insufficient electricity produced	n/a *	28%	19%
Noise /vibration	n/a	n/a	26%
Total responses: non-adopters	*149*	*123*	*126*

Notes: * Results for the 69 non-adopters of simple wood-burning stoves are presented in the text.
n/a = not asked/applicable.

Table 14.3 *YIMBY generation: Barriers to the adoption of microgeneration heat*

Non-adopters responding that the following issue(s) are 'very' or 'fairly' important	Solar thermal hot water	Ground source heat pump	Wood-fuelled boiler	Total non-adopters*
Purchase price	87%	95%	76%	86%
Pay back on the investment is uncertain or long	75%	70%	48%	68%
Grant(s) only cover 10–20% of the purchase price	65%	58%	57%	60%
Performance and reliability uncertainties	57%	63%	57%	58%
More cost-effective ways to reduce carbon emissions	58%	51%	57%	56%
Possible major modifications to existing heating, hot water or electrical systems required	55%	51%	67%	54%
Difficulties finding space or suitable location	38%	49%	62%	50%
Time and effort involved in investigating and installing	42%	51%	62%	47%
System unlikely to provide all household's heating/hot water demand	42%	42%	38%	42%
Uncertainties how much energy/CO_2 system will save	33%	44%	52%	42%
Difficulties getting a grant	48%	28%	43%	40%
Difficulty finding a suitable installer	22%	28%	43%	26%
Total responses: non-adopters	*60*	*43*	*21*	*132**

Note: * results for non-adopters of automatic biomass stoves are not presented separately because there were only eight responses.

Table 14.4 *People-centred ecodesign: Improvements that would encourage the more widespread adoption of microgeneration*

Improvement(s) chosen by non-adopters	Solar thermal hot water	Solar PV	Micro-wind turbine
Lower-cost systems	60%	80%	82%
System financed by energy supplier paid back via fuel bills	56%	55%	59%
Mandatory standards for performance, reliability and durability	47%	46%	48%
Total responses: non-adopters	149	123	126

Table 14.3 also shows that, apart from the cost, there are other major reasons for non-adoption, especially the lack of consumer confidence in the performance and reliability of unfamiliar technologies (58 per cent), the frequent need to modify existing properties and heating systems when installing microgeneration (54 per cent), a lack of space to install equipment (50 per cent) and the time, effort and technical knowledge involved in choosing between technologies, selecting a system and getting it installed (47 per cent).

What Measures Would Encourage More People to Adopt Microgeneration?

Responses to both the PCED and YIMBY surveys identified a need for a variety of measures to lower the financial and other barriers to the wider consumer uptake of microgeneration systems. Table 14.4 shows some of the improvements that the non-adopters of domestic solar and wind systems in the PCED online survey considered would encourage them and/or others to purchase a system.

Cost reduction

Reducing upfront costs is a clear priority. A majority of PCED respondents would like incentives to reduce costs, such as tax breaks, increased subsidies and grants, and reduced council tax for adopters. Energy suppliers have a role to play in reducing initial costs. In particular, more than half of non-adopters of STHW, solar PV and micro-wind systems said they would be encouraged to adopt if energy suppliers offered schemes to install systems with repayment via (reduced) fuel bills (Table 14.4).

The YIMBY surveys found price thresholds below which many more considerers and non-adopters said they would purchase. For example, £2500–3000 rather than the £4000 average price for a retrofit STHW and a maximum of £10,000 for a ground source heat pump system. Microgeneration systems have already benefited from a 5 per cent VAT rate, and costs could be brought down further by larger grants, through lower-cost production (e.g. from Chinese and

Table 14.5 *YIMBY generation: preferred financial measures to encourage the purchase of microgeneration heat technologies (if all of equivalent value)*

Financial measure	Percentage choosing
Annual reduction in council tax after installation	53%
Government or local authority grant	39%
Reduced price system from an energy supplier	32%
System installed free by an energy supplier and paid back via fuel bills	24%
Low-interest loan for the full cost paid back over several years	18%
Number of responses: total sample	*914*

Indian suppliers), or by subsidies from energy suppliers as required under the government's Carbon Emissions Reduction Target (CERT). However, the most popular financial incentive was council tax relief – favoured by over half of all respondents (and three-quarters of considerers) – and the least popular was low-cost, long-term loans (Table 14.5).

Regulation

In the PCED survey, just under half of non-adopters of STHW, solar PV and micro-wind would like long-term guarantees if they bought a microgeneration system, including a stronger government role in establishing mandatory standards for product performance, reliability and durability (Table 14.4). Many respondents would also welcome the phasing out of inefficient domestic heating and electrical technologies, as proposed in policies such as the Code for Sustainable Homes and Zero Carbon Homes.

The YIMBY surveys found that two-thirds (69 per cent) of all respondents would support tighter building regulations that required householders to install low carbon energy technologies when undertaking major refurbishments or home extensions. However, only one-third (35 per cent) of all YIMBY respondents would support a carbon rationing scheme (e.g. in which each citizen is given an equal carbon ration and can buy and sell unused rations).

Information and advice

The PCED survey respondents pointed to improvements in information and advice that should help those considering microgeneration to make confident purchasing decisions. These include online comparisons of equipment specifications and independent assessments of how different manufacturers' systems perform.

The YIMBY surveys also found that increasing consumer understanding and confidence in the technologies is needed in order to promote wider adoption (Table 14.6). Nearly three-quarters (71 per cent) of all YIMBY respondents would therefore welcome *Which?*-style independent tests showing the performance and payback of different manufacturers' equipment and systems. Such comparative information is becoming more widely available

Table 14.6 *YIMBY Generation: Desired information and advice measures*

Information and advice measure	Percentage choosing
Independent information on the performance and payback of different manufacturers' systems	71%
One-stop shop assisting process of technology choice, grant applications, planning permission, installation, use and maintenance, and effective use	69%
Online information to help assess suitability of home for low carbon energy technologies	50%
More opportunity to see low carbon energy technologies installed in people's homes and public buildings	46%
Installers who supply different low carbon energy technologies and advice on the most suitable	41%
Number of responses; total sample	*914*

under the government's Microgeneration Certification Scheme, beginning with the publication of accredited manufacturers' ratings of wind-turbines. YIMBY respondents also cited difficulties in finding trustworthy installers, underlining the importance of accreditation and the value of a 'one-stop shop' for independent advice and information on the whole process of choosing, buying, installing and using a microgeneration system – something that the Energy Saving Trust is rolling out through its 'ActOnCO$_2$' advice service.

There will always be properties that are unsuitable for microgeneration. For example, monitoring has shown that micro-wind turbines are generally unsuited to urban areas (EST, 2009) and STHW systems only suit properties that have a mainly south-facing roof and space for a larger water cylinder. Improved online information to assess a home's suitability for microgeneration would thus be welcomed by half of all YIMBY respondents, and especially by the considerers. Multi-skilled installers able to advise on and install the different technologies are also desired by over 40 per cent of respondents, as is more opportunity to see working microgeneration systems in action (Table 14.6).

Conclusions

The widespread adoption of microgeneration technologies in existing and new homes could make a significant contribution towards achieving the UK's carbon reduction targets. Current demand is largely confined to a niche market of environmentally concerned, older, middle-class householders, often those living in larger rural properties off the mains gas network. This niche market applies especially to ground source heat pumps, wood-fuelled boilers and biomass stoves. This is not surprising, given that these technologies are better suited to larger properties with space for the equipment, ground heat collectors, or wood fuel stores. Microgeneration space heating systems are currently only cost-effective in properties previously heated by oil, electricity or solid fuel. STHW systems have a wider appeal because they are based on a lower-cost, more compact and familiar technology, and are worthwhile for rural, urban and suburban homes with or without mains gas.

Solar PV also has the potential for widespread adoption, given the government introduction of a generous feed-in tariff in 2010 for UK householders who generate renewable electricy for their own use and for export to the National Grid; similar to the highly effective German scheme. This is something that 50 per cent of solar PV non-adopters in the PCED survey wanted. The planned introduction of a UK renewable heat incentive in 2011 should give a similar boost to STHW, heat pump and biomass systems.

Our surveys reveal that, despite considerable public interest – indeed serious consideration – in adopting microgeneration, the UK market is still at an early phase of the diffusion curve, mainly attracting 'pioneers' who are driven by conviction to reduce carbon emissions coupled with the hope of saving money and enjoying the pleasure of using low or zero carbon energy. Nevertheless, there is considerable potential to widen the appeal of microgeneration beyond the small niche of technology pioneers. With the exception of the small sample of micro-wind turbine adopters, both the PCED and YIMBY surveys showed generally high levels of satisfaction among householders who have installed a microgeneration system. Market segmentation by the EST of applicants to the LCBP shows that there are potentially 4.8 million homes (20 per cent of UK households) that could be targeted for installing microgeneration; namely affluent, middle-aged and professional couples, many who live in off-gas areas. Government standards and policies should widen this niche significantly, as low and zero carbon technologies are increasingly required for new housing under the Code for Sustainable Homes and Zero Carbon Homes.

The government's Microgeneration Strategy Progress Report outlines the relevant actions needed to achieve the market transformation required for the more widespread adoption of microgeneration (BERR, 2008), which our survey findings complement. For microgeneration to expand beyond its current market niche, at least the following issues need to be addressed:

- *Capital cost reduction*: as the greatest barrier, this is probably the main way of widening appeal. It could be achieved with a range of measures including council tax relief for adopters, more generous government grants, financial incentives from energy suppliers such as the feed-in tariff and the renewable heat incentive, or via manufacturing solutions.
- *Better advice*: potential adopters want 'one stop', independent, trustworthy advice that offers comparative information on the suitability, performance and payback of the different technologies and manufacturers' systems.
- *Independent information* on the performance and energy-saving of different microgeneration technologies to increase consumer confidence in installing innovative or unfamiliar technologies.

- *Improved system designs* that are less disruptive to install, and which require fewer modifications to existing buildings, heating, hot water and electrical systems.
- *User-centred design improvements to controls*, with improved feedback displays showing the energy generated, emissions and money saved.

Although the above measures should increase the adoption of all microgeneration systems, our surveys also indicate that a strategy tailored to the different technologies is needed. An Energy Saving Trust report found that 'no single policy will encourage the kind of mass adoption of microgeneration that is needed to get results' (EST, 2007). The views of adopters, those considering purchase, or people merely interested in microgeneration can inform government policies, industry strategies and installer practices so as to increase the uptake of these technologies, and help tackle the challenges of climate change.

Acknowledgements

This chapter draws on the Open University (OU) 'People-Centred Ecodesign' project on consumer adoption of household renewables, conducted in collaboration with the National Energy Foundation and the Energy saving Trust (EST), and the OU and EST 'YIMBY' project, which evaluated microgeneration heat technologies for UK households, part-funded by the Higher Education Innovation Fund's 'Carbon Connections' programme administered through the University of East Anglia. The YIMBY project forms the background for a technical field trial and user evaluation by the EST and OU of heat pumps in real UK domestic installations to be completed in 2011 with an interim EST report in Autumn 2010. We would like to thank the following organizations for collaboration and support for this research: The National Energy Foundation, Milton Keynes Energy Agency, The Energy Saving Trust and Carbon Connections.

References

BERR (2008) 'Microgeneration strategy progress report', Department of Business and Regulatory Reform, London, June, www.berr.gov.uk/whatwedo/energy/sources/sustainable/microgeneration/index.html

Caird, S. and Roy, R. (with Potter, S. and Herring, H.) (2007) *Consumer Adoption of Household Renewable Energy Technologies*, Report DIG-10, Design Innovation Group, The Open University, Milton Keynes, UK, December, www.design.open.ac.uk/research/research_dig.htm

Caird, S. and Roy, R. (2008) 'User-centred improvements to energy efficiency products and renewable energy systems: Research on household adoption and use', *International Journal of Innovation Management*, vol 12, no 3, pp327–355

DTI (2006) *Microgeneration Strategy: Power from the People*, Department of Trade and Industry, London, March

DTI (2007) *Meeting the Energy Challenge: A White Paper on Energy*, CM 7124, Department of Trade and Industry, The Stationery Office, Norwich, May

Element Energy (2008) *The Growth Potential for Microgeneration in England, Wales and Scotland*, Report commissioned by the Department of Business, Enterprise and Regulatory Reform, NGOs, Energy Saving Trust and Industry, Cambridge, June, www.berr.gov.uk/energy/microgenerationresearch

EST (Energy Saving Trust) (2001) *Solar Hot Water Systems in New Housing*, Report GIR88, The Energy Saving Trust, London

EST (Energy Saving Trust) (2007) *Generating the Future: An Analysis of Policy Interventions to Achieve Widespread Microgeneration Penetration*, Commissioned by Department for Business, Enterprise and Regulatory Reform (BERR), London, November

EST (Energy Saving Trust) (2009) *Location, Location, Location: Domestic Small-scale Wind Field Trial Report*, The Energy Saving Trust, London, July

Guy, S. and Shove, E. (2000) *A Sociology of Energy, Buildings and the Environment: Constructing Knowledge, Designing Practice*, Routledge, London

HM Government (2009) *The UK Renewable Energy Strategy*, Cm 7686, The Stationery Office, Norwich, July

House of Commons (2007) 'Local energy: Turning consumers into producers', HC 257 First Report of Session 2006-7, The Stationery Office, Norwich, January

Parker, J. (2007) 'Calorex domestic heat pumps: GSHP monitoring research by Calorex', www.calorex.com/Product_range/Domestic_ground_source_heat_pumps/introduction2.htm

Roy, R., Caird, S. and Abelman, J. (2008) *YIMBY Generation: Yes in My Back Yard! UK Householders Pioneering Microgeneration Heat*, The Energy Saving Trust, London, June, http://open.ac.uk/oro10828/1/24660_EST.pdf

SEA/RENUE (2005) 'Barriers to installing domestic solar hot water systems', Sustainable Energy Action/Renewable Energy in the Urban Environment, London, September

Watson, J., Sauter, R., Bahaj, B., James, P. A., Myers, L. and Wing, R. (2006) 'Unlocking the power house: Policy and system change for domestic microgeneration in the UK', Universities of Sussex and Southampton and Imperial College London, October, www.sussex.ac.uk/sussexenergygroup/documents/unlocking_the_power_house_report.pdf

Chapter 15

Socio-environmental Impacts of Brazil's First Large-scale Wind Farm

Rafaella Lenoir Improta and José Q. Pinheiro

Introduction

The adoption of renewable sources of energy is becoming more and more prevalent in some wealthy nations, while not so in the developing world. In both cases, however, the decisive option for 'alternative' forms of energy seems to depend upon a combination of economic access to scientific and technological innovations, political will and public participation, especially when the last two are motivated by sustainability ideals; something not so common among citizens of emerging economies.

Brazil, a country endowed with a plethora of natural resources, has largely used hydroelectric power from river water reservoirs to meet its electricity needs. Such hydroelectric plants, however, are typically too large and may cause serious environmental and social impacts, including deforestation, the need to remove the residents from their homes, hydrological alterations, and the emission of heat-trapping gases. Some specialists, in fact, criticize the size of these dams, defending similar alternatives on a smaller scale (Filgueiras and Silva, 2003; Bermann, 2007). At the same time, the country massively utilizes petroleum for transportation and industrial activities. Despite a flirtation with sugarcane ethanol as a fuel for vehicles over the last few decades, there have been no committed and widespread official efforts related to research and development into other sources of renewable energy (Bermann, 2001).

When focusing on the wind energy option, it is worth noting that Brazil is favoured in several respects. As well as its extensive coastline and reasonably flat terrain, the winds become stronger during the drought season, when the river dams receive less water; a scenario that conforms with contemporary recommendations about the consortium of complementary sources of renewable energy (Dutra, 2007). In addition, the country presents one of the best wind energy potentials in the world; and several of these privileged locations are in states with no other sources of electricity generation (Agência Nacional de Energia Elétrica – ANEEL, 2004).

Despite all these favourable aspects, the history of wind energy in Brazil is quite recent when compared with other countries. The first large-scale wind farm connected to the national network of electricity distribution was built in 2007, under the name of the municipality in which it is located: Parque Eólico de Rio do Fogo (or PERF; the Portuguese equivalent to Rio do Fogo Wind Farm), in the state of Rio Grande do Norte (RN). The state, located in northeastern Brazil, has no previous history of locally generated electricity for public consumption on a large scale.

The northern part of the Atlantic coast of Brazil, especially the coast of RN state, is known as one of the world's regions best served by winds (Centro de Pesquisas de Energia Elétrica – CEPEL, 2001; see Figure 15.1). Even so, and despite all the information collected during the planning stage of the PERF project, the plant operators still admit to being surprised at the directional stability and reliable persistence of local winds, systematically coming from the southeast, from ocean to land, and with practically no interruptions.

Parque Eólico de Rio do Fogo (PERF) and the village of Zumbi

PERF is located in the municipality of Rio do Fogo, near Natal, the capital of the state of Rio Grande do Norte (RN), in northeastern Brazil. Within an uninhabited area of 850ha, the wind farm comprises 62 'towers' (as called by locals) each 80m high – a height equivalent to a 26-floor building – while the local residents live in simple houses, only a few of which are two-storey. The plant generates a total of 49MW that is sent into (and sold to) the national system of electricity distribution (Centro de Referência para Energias Solar e Eólica Sérgio de Salvo Brito, 2006).

As part of a large series of projects concerning wind plants approved (but only partially implemented) by federal government authorities, the construction of PERF began in April 2004, as a joint endeavour of private capital and government funds. During the construction stage, 400 temporary jobs were offered, the majority filled by local residents.

PERF was built near the community of Zumbi, a small beach village with 4500 inhabitants, traditionally attached to subsistence agriculture and fishery as the main economic activities. In the last two decades or so, Zumbi has seen the proliferation of a 'predatory' form of tourism that does not value the local culture, exploits the natural resources and forces the population to move from their traditional occupations to new forms of earning their living, providing bars and similar

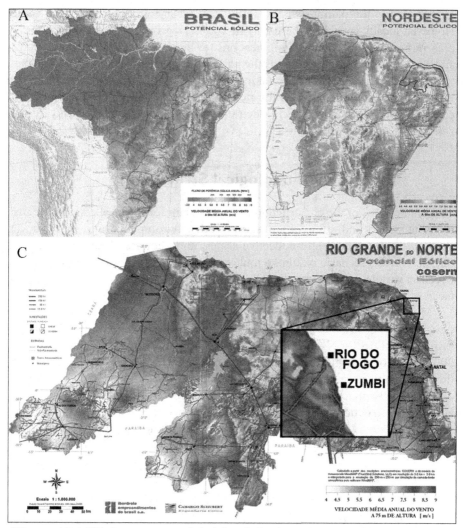

Figure 15.1 *Wind energy potential of the whole of Brazil; (a) its northeastern region (b) (from Centro de Pesquisa de Energia Elétrica, 2001); and the state of Rio Grande do Norte (c) (Companhia Elétrica do Rio Grande do Norte, 2003)*

services. The village is now characterized by a serious unemployment problem, in addition to the low income of those with regular jobs, an uneducated population, precarious health services, unpaved roads and streets and, as an ironic paradox, no streetlights to provide illumination at night in the streets near the wind farm.

Purpose of the study

The implementation of wind farms has been increasing around the world and even greater growth is expected throughout the next decades. Globally speaking, people are typically pro-renewable energy because it is a clean source and it contributes to the planet's sustainability, thus carrying a positive social value. However, locally speaking, there may be conflicts, given that the wind farm may present practical and financial implications for locals and/or affect their symbolic and affective relationships towards the place. The purpose of our study was, then, to analyse the socio-environmental impact of that wind farm (Parque Eólico de Rio do Fogo; or PERF) upon the neighbouring residents – representing two contrasting realities: a 'high-tech' electricity plant practically in the backyard of a community with no streetlights.

Methodological Strategies

The implications of the construction of a wind plant for the local community may be quite varied and complex, involving both environmental and psychosocial aspects, the individual and collective scales, and short- and long-term conse-quences. Such a scenario requires a multi-method approach, as an attempt not only to collect various types of data but also to favour the integration of complementary facets of the same reality (Sommer and Sommer, 1997; Günther et al, 2008).

More specifically, and consistent with that multidimensional approach, the design of our study was based on the international literature on the theme and inspired by DIS/BCN (Social Impact Detection/Barcelona; Pol and Moreno, 2002); a set of strategies theoretically and methodologically devoted to the detec-tion of possible social impacts before the intervention takes place. We could not develop a full application of DIS/BCN because our investigation took place only after the construction of the plant. Due to the pioneering character of our psycho-social approximation to the topic in Brazil, we could not take into account other national studies of the same kind.

Participants

We tried to contact different types of local people somehow related to PERF, since our approach was necessarily exploratory in its nature and we wanted to collect all possible kinds of viewpoints related to the installation of the plant. Zumbi residents – both adults and children – were our main focus. Such a group included people with some importance in the community and/or who had worked directly in the construction of the plant or in indirect jobs during that time (restaurants, inns and grocery stores).

All the adults had been living in Zumbi for at least seven years – we estab-lished this minimum time–place relationship in order to include some years of their life in the village without the presence of PERF. These interviewees were 17 females and 13 males, with an average age of 43.8 years. The educational level of the majority (20) of them fell between illiteracy and incomplete high school; one had incomplete college level education, and two had finished a university course.

Additionally, representatives of the municipal and state governments were interviewed, as well as workers for the company that operates the plant. Altogether (residents, local authority and PERF workers) 47 people were interviewed.

Procedures and instruments

The study comprised three stages, each preceded by pilot applications whenever applicable. Ethical considerations followed the standards of psychological research (American Psychological Association, 2002), implying that we had participants' agreement and in all circumstances their participation was voluntary and anonymous.

Phase 1: Collecting preliminary information

We started by establishing the limits of the site to be studied, in its physical, administrative, sociological and symbolic aspects. For this, we scanned various documentary material, including regional newspapers, national magazines and public archives, in search of relevant material related to wind energy, Parque Eólico de Rio do Fogo (PERF), and the residents of Rio do Fogo and Zumbi village. At this point in the study, we also began field observations aimed at the characterization of patterns of relationship between locals and PERF. Since no fences separate PERF from the village, allowing free access to the plant property, we analysed spatial usage of the space by villagers, employing techniques such as walk-through (Horelli, 2002) and *place centred behavioural mapping* (Sommer and Sommer, 1997; Pinheiro et al, 2008).

Phase 2: Children's point of view – visual and verbal information

We invited students from the local school to take part in the study and, with the help of the teachers, two boys and three girls agreed to participate. They were residents of the neighbouring settlement, Conjunto Novo Horizonte, and their ages were between 9 and 12 years. Applying the *autophotography* technique (Neiva-Silva and Koller, 2002), a disposable camera was given to each child, with instructions to photograph, over the space of a week, up to six places in their community that they liked most and six places that they liked least. Afterwards, the five children were individually interviewed, and were asked to comment on the photos they had taken. We encouraged them to make comments about the content present in the pictures and also the process of taking them.

Following this, a group interview with all five children was carried out, alongside a panel mounted with the pictures taken by all the children. This was exposed to the children during the meeting in order to motivate additional comments about the relationships between the community and the wind farm, also allowing for the observation of their reactions to the pictures and to the comments. The conversation was purportedly directed to the theme of PERF. It is important to mention that during the individual and group interviews, the participants had no knowledge of the purposes of the study.

Phase 3: The viewpoint of the adult population

Adult residents of the community were individually and sequentially interviewed, until the provided information reached the point of saturation, repeating information that had already been gathered. The interviews were audio-recorded and were later transcribed. They were carried out at residents' homes, in a semi-structured vein that allowed for the occasional intervention of other members of the family.

These interviews were augmented with a number of photographic panels. The choice of photographs for each panel followed two criteria: their thematic similarity and their potential for eliciting verbal comments from the interviewees (Neiva-Silva and Koller, 2002). We adopted such a strategy because of the open informational richness of a graphic/non-verbal stimulus. The first panel contained old photographs of the community, dating from 15 years before the construction of PERF; the second set comprised pictures of the construction site; the third panel combined PERF views and scenes of the community; and the last set presented images of the aerogenerators and the whole wind farm. Their main purpose was to let us learn locals' own words for those elements in the photographs. Additionally, the photographs taken by the children were also presented to the adults, and we asked them for the possible reasons why the children had chosen to photograph those images as the best or worst scenes of their community.

We also interviewed the group of people who had been in charge of implanting the project: executives, clerical staff and technicians of the managing company, and representatives of the municipal and state governments. A special questionnaire was designed for each of the interviews, aimed at investigating the relationships between the company and the community, and between the company and the local authorities.

Data analysis

We adopted four axes (big themes) for the analysis of the interviews: old Zumbi; Zumbi during the construction of PERF; the relationship between present-day Zumbi and PERF; and social aspects of Zumbi. Content analysis was performed (Bardin, 1977; Bauer, 2002) and more detailed categories were identified in the transcripts.

Results and Discussion

The five children demonstrated a positive image associated with the wind farm, as they all included these farms among the photographs taken as one of the places they liked most in their environment (see Figure 15.2). During the group interview, the children pointed out that PERF is used to produce energy but, to our surprise, they failed to say how that energy was produced. They also explained that during the construction period they did not know what was being built, but they described the hustle and bustle of people and machinery and commented that they visited the site to see the building work. Thanks to the individual and group interviews, it became clear that the visual aspect of PERF is what the children most positively appreciated, possibly because it is something quite different from their daily life.

Figure 15.2 *Examples of the photographs taken by the children as positively valued parts of their daily life environment*

Positive perceptions help in the acceptance of the enterprise

We were able to verify that the Zumbi adults also showed a positive visual assessment of the wind farm. They appreciated its size and beauty, which confirms the indications of the literature. According to Wolsink (2000, 2007), the visual assessment of the impact of a wind farm is the dominant factor when explaining the opposition or support of a community to a wind farm, as well as determining the general attitudes.

Apart from the visual aspects, another factor that may lead communities to oppose such enterprises is noise pollution (Wolsink, 2000; Devine-Wright, 2005b; Loring, 2007). No complaints have been found about the noise produced by the aerogenerators. Inhabitants living close to PERF said that they sometimes heard the noises produced by the turbines, but they stated that they did not find it uncomfortable.

The contrast between technology and the importance of the enterprise, on one hand, and the humble housing conditions, on the other, is found in the positive impact the wind farm has had on the inhabitants' perceptions, as a symbol of development, of something new; absolutely different from what these people are used to. In other words, PERF represents the development of the place and, therefore, becomes a synonym for progress and improvement. The same result was found in a study by Lee et al (1989; in Devine-Wright, 2005b) on the analysis of the symbolic dimension of perceptions of wind farms in the UK, in which 62 per cent of the interviewees stated that the wind turbines symbolized a 'sign of progress'.

The company managing PERF confirmed that they had left the site as a free area for local inhabitants, as they wanted to keep interference with people's lives to a minimum. Thus, the site of the wind farm is still being used by locals as a recreation area, as pasture for animals, and as a road to other communities.

It is worth mentioning that, as evidence of the emotional value added to the site, some of the interviewees told the story of a 'ball of fire' that is often seen at night, growing bigger and running after people venturing into that deserted area. This being – which they called '*Batatão*'– is reminiscent of stories about '*Boitatá*' or '*Batatá*' told in other parts of the country (Gallucci, 2007).

When setting up a wind farm implies the promotion of new jobs, local inhabitants show no opposition at all (Pol et al, 2006). Similarly, people who are economically involved with wind farms show a more positive attitude to wind power than those who are not (Devine-Wright, 2005a). In the Zumbi-PERF case, this effect was verified as a form of economic compensation of employment (not related to the present employment, as the farm maintenance requires qualified people, but at the time of the construction of the farm). Many Zumbi locals got a job in PERF – even fishermen who were going through a fishing crisis had their sustenance thanks to the building of the wind farm.

There were about 400 people working, some from other cities and even from abroad, which eventually led to the creation of many indirect jobs at inns, restaurants and markets for over a year. The new job demand and the great unemployment rate encouraged locals to let their houses for rent to foreigners. Such cultural exchange had never been seen before in this village, which became famous and appeared on TV in advertisements and interviews about the wind farm.

Lack of affiliation and participation

The completion of the construction of PERF brought Zumbi's busy everyday life, as well as job opportunities, to an end. At present, only three locals work for PERF and indirect jobs are virtually nil.

Locals currently perceive PERF as something neutral and alien to their lives. However, the closeness between each other shows almost no permeability in the PERF–Zumbi relationships (or vice versa). Locals and businessmen unanimously perceive PERF and Zumbi as two different worlds, coexisting next to each other. Local inhabitants feel that there is no further influence of the enterprise on Zumbi. Basically, taking into account the time aspect, locals' reactions to PERF were related to the job opportunities. As there are no more jobs on offer, there is no longer a positive or negative perception.

Therefore, there is no other long-lasting change that locals perceive other than the visual one. The wind farm does not embody the symbolic dimension of the area beyond the visual dimension. In spite of its proximity, it does not belong to the daily life of the community. But there is more evidence that proves the lack of a reciprocal relationship between PERF and Zumbi.

According to the interviewees, the only formal contact of the population with the enterprise managers took place during a meeting to introduce the wind farm project, organized by the PERF managing company, before the beginning of the construction. Interviewees stated that on that occasion the managers explained how the farm would work, showed how other wind farms worked in other parts of the world, commented on the potential tourist attraction, and made it clear that there would be an abundance of jobs for the locals, although only during the construction period, as they would later need a specialized workforce.

Another factor that shows the great distance and the lack of affiliation existing between PERF and the closest locals is the fact that none of the children interviewed, unlike most of the adults, knew the name of the company run by PERF or could say whether the enterprise was generating power or not. It was clearly demonstrated that locals are relating to the site but not to the enterprise located there.

In addition to this, the locals' speech revealed certain confusion in relation to the production of energy in a wind farm. Some of them believed that the energy from PERF was not produced only by the wind. Others thought that wind power was another type of energy different from the one that supplied them, or was more expensive and thus unavailable in their area. This clash of ideas shows a clear lack of knowledge with respect to the production of power in a wind farm and a lack of integration of this enterprise with the community life, as well as ignorance about national power policies.

This indifference and ignorance may be related to the fact that this was the first large-scale wind farm established in the country. In a previous foreign study, Wolsink (1988) researched the impact of a major wind turbine set in a town in Holland. As in Zumbi, this study showed the low level of precise information about the applications of wind power and the little knowledge people had about the amount of energy the aerogenerator produced. Our interviewees' answers revealed curiosity about the PERF operation. They related that during the construction period they would go to the site to ask for details about the building, mostly to locals working there, as there was no close contact between the community and the technicians.

Moreover, only four interviewees were aware of the global environmental benefits of wind power. However, none of them linked the topic of renewable energy to climate change, at least explicitly. It should be mentioned that those 4 interviewees belonged to the group with at least 12 years schooling.

Another four interviewees did not associate PERF with global environmental issues, although they expressed their opinions on the positive and negative consequences of the enterprise on their town. Wolsink (1988) obtained the same results, since he believes that the environmental advantages of using wind power have a global nature. Because the population mainly perceives the changes at a local level, there is difficulty in understanding or making use of the general advantages of wind power due to the question of scale.

Authors who have analysed the socio-environmental impacts of wind farms point out the need to take preventive measures on this aspect. It is worth noting that despite the lack of measures prior to the implantation of PERF, there was no rejection. No NIMBY effect nor any other type of rejection was expressed by the locals. If there were signs of rejection, these could be due to the apathy that the community showed towards the project, as their lack of involvement in the decisions was one of the main causes for the rejection of enterprises, unanimously mentioned by the sources consulted (Wolsink, 2000; Devine-Wright 2005a,b; Ek, 2005; Pol, 2006; Loring, 2007).

Concluding Remarks

The use of photographic resources as an innovative methodology in research of this type deserves to be continued, because when the participants were stimulated by the pictures, they provided additional information and opinions on topics already dealt with. It is worth mentioning that this resource proved to be useful in this exploratory research, especially when combined with the question 'Why do you think the child photographed this?', as this exempted the participant from stating his own personal opinion.

Among the factors that favoured the community's acceptance of PERF we can mention: the positive aesthetic assessment, the implied idea of 'progress' in the enterprise, the free movement of locals through the site, and the lack of use of this site before the PERF construction. As the site was well chosen, negative implications were kept to a minimum (Wolsink, 1988), the enterprise was non-invasive (Devine-Wright, 2005a) and there was no interference with the symbolic dimension attributed by locals (Pol et al, 2006). Added to this, during the construction period there was a wide selection of jobs on offer for a population with a high unemployment rate. The fact that there are presently no posts for locals is justified, as the company had previously informed the villagers that they would need a specialized workforce, which was non-existent in the community. The possibility of education and training was not considered as part of the agreements for setting up PERF.

Among the reasons that contribute to the non-negative perception of PERF and its acceptance by the villagers without major criticisms were the low level of their schooling and the absence of social organizations within their community. The quality of the answers of the (few) people with a higher level of schooling contrasted with those of the rest of the interviewees, as the former criticized the wind farm and the associated social problems. Successful community opposition requires strong social networks (Loring, 2007), but we have not been able to identify any signs of significant social networks in the village. We could not find organized opposition because the villagers do not count on civil associations as the nuclei of their social structures (Pol, 2002).

This 'neutrality' in the Zumbi–PERF relationships can also be found in the following aspects: the enterprise is not part of the community's everyday life; locals do not know the name of the companies in charge; and the community states they have no contact either with the workers or with the managing company. The interaction found between locals and PERF refers to the site though not to the enterprise.

Zumbi locals have shown no signs of rejection towards PERF. However, it would be interesting to continue analysing this situation, as suggested by Devine-Wright (2005b), since with the passing of time, conflict may arise in the PERF–Zumbi relationship. Likewise, there may be conflicts relating to other wind farms yet to be built, if they are set up in the same way that PERF was established in Zumbi.

This is why it is important to turn to the literature consulted in this research, as it comes from developed countries that have been coexisting with wind power for decades and have gathered scientific contributions for the analysis of the socio-environmental impacts of their wind farms. While renewable energy becomes part of the technological, political and economic scenario of developing countries, it is important to internationalize knowledge in this field (Devine-Wright 2005b), given that this is what the ideals of sustainability advocate.

This study suggests that future research on the impact of wind farms on neighbouring communities, at least in the Brazilian case, should take into account the socio-economic and schooling levels of the participants, as well as criticisms of the enterprise, since technological innovations seem to play an alluring role in uninformed and unorganized populations. Without addressing the structure of local social relations, it would be pointless to consider sustainability issues such as participation and equity.

The managing company brought its knowledge of high technology for generating electric power and its international experience in handling the socio-environmental problems when setting up wind farms, which was particularly easy in the case of this old fishing village, with high levels of unemployment and confusion in the face of the uncertain prospects of 'the industry of tourism' for the region. The ethics involved in the case reported here (even if some form of local power supply were provided for street lighting) does not suggest an appropriate model to take forward with other energy entrepreneurship in Brazil, or in other developing countries more generally. Of course, government action – even if only in the signing of contracts – will be required in order to assure the social and economic benefits to local communities, especially considering that wind farms are usually built far from large population centres.

Also confused at the national level, the Brazilian authorities hesitated to define their position at the Global Climate Change Conference at Copenhagen in late 2009, and have just approved the construction of another nuclear power station. A country that is supplied by renewable sources of hydroelectric energy, and with the possibility of expansion in wind and ethanol-based energy, is presently debating how to exploit the huge oilfields recently discovered in the pre-sal layer.

It is still important and necessary to widen the options for renewable energies, as is the case for wind power, which has a softer impact on the environment than other forms of energy. Nevertheless, this development must be followed by the provision of better information and greater participation of the community in general regarding the national power policies. Additionally, in the case of communities such as the one studied here, it is necessary to narrow the gap between advanced energy technologies and the general living conditions of the people who coexist alongside the wind farm.

Acknowledgements

Some parts of this chapter were presented at the 20th Conference of International Association for People–Environment Surroundings Studies (IAPS), in Rome, 28 July–1 August 2008. The study was developed while the first author was receiving a scholarship from CAPES Foundation, Brazilian Education Ministry.

References

Agência Nacional de Energia Elétrica – ANEEL (2004) *Atlas de Energia Elétrica do Brasil*, 2ª edição [*Atlas of Brazilian Electrical Energy*, 2nd edition], www.aneel.gov.br/aplicacoes/Atlas

American Psychological Association (2002) 'Ethical principles of psychologists and code of conduct', *American Psychologist*, vol 57, no 12, pp1060–1073

Bardin, L. (1977) *Análise de conteúdo* [*Content Analysis*], Edições 70, Lisbon

Bauer, M. W. (2002) 'Análise de conteúdo clássica: uma revisão' ['Classical content analysis: A review'], in M. W. Bauer and G. Gaskell (eds) *Pesquisa qualitativa com texto, imagem e som: um manual prático* [*Qualitative Researching with Text, Image and Sound: A Practical Handbook*], Vozes, Petrópolis, Brazil

Bermann, C. (2001) *Energia no Brasil: Para quê? Para quem? – Crise e alternativas para um país sustentável* [*Energy in Brazil: What for? To Whom? – Crisis and Alternatives for a Sustainable Country*], Livraria da Física, São Paulo

Bermann, C. (2007) 'Impasses e controvérsias da hidreletricidade' ['Hydroelectricity's impasses and controversies'], *Estudos Avançados [Advanced Studies]*, vol 21, no 59, pp139–153

Centro de Pesquisas de Energia Elétrica – CEPEL (2001) *Atlas do Potencial Eólico Brasileiro* [*Atlas of Brazilian Wind Potential*], Rio de Janeiro

Centro de Referência para Energias Solar e Eólica Sérgio de Salvo Brito – CRESESB (2006) 'Parques eólicos do PROINFA entram em operação' ['Wind plants of PROINFA start operating'], *Informe*, no 11, pp10–11

Compania Elétrica do Estado do Rio Grande do Norte (2003) 'Atlas do Potencial Eólico do Estado do Rio Grande do Norte' ['Atlas of Rio Grande do Norte wind potential'], www.cosern.com.br

Devine-Wright, P. (2005a) 'Local aspects of UK renewable energy development: Exploring public beliefs and policy implications', *Local Economy*, vol 10, no 1, pp57–69

Devine-Wright, P. (2005b) 'Beyond NIMBYism: Towards an integrated framework for understanding public perceptions of wind energy', *Wind Energy*, vol 8, pp125–139.

Dutra, R. M. (2007) 'Propostas de políticas específicas para energia eólica no Brasil após a primeira fase do PROINFA' ['Proposal of specific politics for wind energy in Brazil after the first phase of the PROINFA programme'], PhD Thesis, Universidade Federal do Rio de Janeiro, Brazil

Ek, K. (2005) 'Public and private attitudes towards "green" electricity: The case of Swedish wind power', *Energy Policy*, vol 33, pp1677–1689

Filgueiras, A., and Silva, T. M. V. (2003) 'Energia eólica no Brasil – presente e futuro' ['Wind energy in Brasil – present and future'], in H. M. Souza, P. C. Silva and R. M. Dutra (eds) *Coletânea de artigos energias solar e eólica* [*Solar and Wind Energy Articles Compilation*], vol 2, pp263–271, CRESESB, Rio de Janeiro

Gallucci, D. R. (2007) 'Mitos que metem medo' ['Legends that cause fear'], *Brasil Almanaque de Cultura Popular* [Brazil, Popular Culture Almanac], vol 102, pp14–17

Günther, H., Elali, G. A. and Pinheiro, J. Q. (2008) 'A abordagem multimétodos em Estudos Pessoa-Ambiente: características, definições e implicações' ['Multi-method approach in person–environment studies: Characteristics, definitions and implications'], in J. Q. Pinheiro and H. Günther (eds) *Métodos de pesquisa nos estudos pessoa-ambiente* [*Research Methods in Person–Environment Studies*], Casa do Psicólogo, São Paulo

Horelli, L. (2002) 'A methodology of participatory planning', in R. B. Bechtel and A. Churchman (eds) *Handbook of Environmental Psychology*, John Wiley and Sons, New York

Loring, J. M. (2007) 'Wind energy planning in England, Wales and Denmark: Factors influencing project success', *Energy Policy*, vol 35, no 5, pp2648–2660

Neiva-Silva, L. and Koller, S. H. (2002) 'The use of photography in psychological research [in Portuguese]', *Estudos de Psicologia* (Natal), vol 7, no 2, pp237–250, www.scielo.br/epsic

Pinheiro, J. Q., Elali, G. A. and Fernandes, O. S. (2008) 'Observando a interação pessoa-ambiente: vestígios ambientais e mapeamento comportamental' ['Observing person–environment interaction: Traces and behavioral mapping'], in J. Q. Pinheiro and H. Günther (eds) *Métodos de pesquisa nos estudos pessoa-ambiente* [*Research Methods in Person–Environment Studies*], Casa do Psicólogo, São Paulo

Pol, E. (2002). 'The theoretical background of the City–Identity–Sustainability Network', *Environment and Behavior*, vol 34, no 1, pp8–25

Pol, E., Di Masso, A., Castrechini, A., Bonet, M. R. and Vidal, T. (2006) 'Psychological parameters to understand and manage the NIMBY effect', *Revue Européenne de Psychologie Appliquée / European Review of Applied Psychology*, vol 56, pp43–51

Pol, E. and Moreno, E. (2002) *DIS/BCN Detecció d'impactes socials [SID/BCN Social Impact Dectection]* [Interactive CD], Publications Universidad de Barcelona, Barcelona

Sommer, B. and Sommer, R. (1997) *A Practical Guide to Behavioral Research*, 4th edn, Oxford University Press, New York

Wolsink, M. (1988) 'The social impact of a large wind turbine', *Environment Impact Assesssment Review*, vol 8, pp323–334

Wolsink, M. (2000) 'Wind power and the NIMBY-myth: Institutional capacity and the limited significance of public support', *Renewable Energy*, vol 21, no 1, pp49–64

Wolsink, M. (2007) 'Planning of renewable schemes: Deliberative and fair decision-making on landscape issues instead of reproachful accusations of non-cooperation', *Energy Policy*, vol 35, no 5, pp2692–2704

Chapter 16

Perceptions and Preferences Regarding Offshore Wind Power in the United States: The Leading Edge of a New Energy Source for the Americas

Jeremy Firestone

Introduction

The emission of CO_2 into the atmosphere presents ever increasing threats to wildlife, ecosystems and low-lying coastal and other vulnerable populations. In the US, approximately 40 per cent of the CO_2 released into the atmosphere comes from the burning of fossil fuels to generate electricity, with the transportation sector contributing the next largest share at 30 per cent. Given that the US accounts for approximately 25 per cent of the globe's greenhouse gas (GHG) emissions, roughly 10 per cent of worldwide CO_2 emissions come from US electricity consumption alone. If the international community, generally, and the US, specifically, is serious about addressing climate change, it is thus prudent to begin any discussion about GHG reduction with a consideration of the US electricity market; in particular, the means to reduce consumption and alternatives to fossil fuels. Moreover, given the related phenomena of ocean acidification, which results from the increasing concentration of CO_2 in the world's oceans (Caldeira and Wickett, 2003), any strategy that considers GHG reduction must separately focus on and limit CO_2 emissions into the atmosphere.

In the US, electricity is used for lighting, heating and cooling, cooking, powering devices and other functions. Although the importance of energy efficiency measures in reducing electricity generation cannot be overstated, even after such measures are adopted, there will still be a large residual demand for electricity and further growth in consumption is predicted. This suggests that alternatives to the present fossil fuel-dominated electricity sources must be considered, and in particular, alternatives to coal, which is a notoriously large contributor to CO_2 emissions. There would also be other benefits from such a 'fuel switch' in terms of ecosystem health (e.g. avoidance of mountain top mining) and human health (e.g. avoidance of mercury).

In considering renewable alternatives to the present means of generation, three factors are of prime consideration: location, size of the resource and price. While land-based wind has its place in windy areas of the US such as western Texas, and concentrating solar in areas such as Arizona; in the densely populated mid-Atlantic and northeastern US, running from Virginia to Massachusetts, there is negligible utility-scale land-based wind. Fortunately, there are tremendous offshore wind resources that can be converted to power with the technology available today, given high wind speeds and a gentle, sloping continental shelf (Kempton et al, 2007). Indeed, the US Atlantic wind resource is much larger than the area's oil and gas resources, or wave and tidal resources, for that matter (Kempton et al, 2007). The offshore wind resource is, in fact, so large that it could power not only all of the electricity needs of the states bordering the Atlantic, but automobile transportation and heating and cooling needs as well (Kempton et al, 2007). With high electricity prices in these states, due to a relative lack of generation assets and a need to import electricity from coal states such as West Virginia, offshore wind power has the potential to be a large component of generation in those states in the years to come. Although there are presently no offshore wind turbines supplying the US, development proposals are advancing off the coasts of Delaware, New Jersey, New York, Rhode Island and Massachusetts, while others are advancing in the Great Lakes.

Offshore wind development in the US, however, has been hampered by several factors. First, development has been slowed by the lack, until very recently, of a regulatory regime in both federal (Firestone et al, 2004) and state-controlled waters (Dhanju and Firestone, 2009).[1] Second, a related policy framework providing the appropriate economic incentives and political support for development has yet to materialize. Third, the industry has been reluctant to invest in offshore wind power because of concerns over public opposition to offshore wind farms as epitomized by the long-standing dispute over the Cape Wind (Nantucket Sound) wind farm.

This chapter focuses on citizens' perceptions of, attitudes towards and preferences concerning offshore wind power in the US, with my understanding of such cognitive and behavioural responses primarily drawn from several mail surveys that my colleagues and I conducted.

Background on Surveys and Summary of Results

Prior to undertaking our survey work in Cape Cod, Massachusetts, and in Delaware, we conducted approximately 20 semi-structured interviews in each locale, and published our Cape Cod findings (Kempton et al, 2005). We conducted mail surveys in 2005 of a probability sample of Cape Cod, Martha's Vineyard and Nantucket Island residents (hereinafter jointly 'Cape Cod' residents or 'Cape Cod and Island' residents) regarding their opinions, knowledge and attitudes towards a proposed 450MW wind farm in Nantucket Sound off the coast of Massachusetts (Firestone and Kempton, 2007), and in 2006 of a stratified probability sample (with coastal residents over-sampled) of public preferences and perceptions of Delaware residents (Firestone et al, 2009). We also undertook an in-person probability survey of out-of-state visitors to Delaware beaches in the summer of 2007 (Lilley et al, 2010).

There are similarities and differences between Cape Cod and Delaware that may be relevant to understanding the differences in public opinion. The areas have comparable population densities and, while both areas rely on coastal tourism, Delaware's economy is much more diverse. Interestingly, both Cape Cod and coastal Delaware have antiquated fossil fuel plants located within about 20–25km of coastal residents who would be most affected by an offshore wind farm. Delaware's coast is adjacent to the open ocean as well as to the estuarine area known as Delaware Bay. Cape Cod, Nantucket Island and Martha's Vineyard, which is also an island, create a semi-enclosed sea known as Nantucket Sound. Nantucket Sound is unusual in that there is a doughnut-shaped hole in the middle of the sound that is controlled by the federal government, entirely surrounded by waters controlled by the state (Massachusetts).

In general, we found mixed results among Cape Cod residents, with slightly more opposed than supportive, although those opposed were much more firm in their opposition than supporters were in their support (a much higher percentage of those categorized as supporters were leaning towards support rather than firm in their support, as compared with those opposed); in contrast, among Delaware residents, we found only token opposition statewide (4 per cent), less than 20 per cent opposed in coastal communities and, even among those who had a view of the ocean, supporters outnumbered opponents by more than two to one (Firestone, et al., 2009).

We attribute the stark contrast in support for offshore wind in the two areas to differences in the desire for electric rate stability, concern over the air quality impacts of fossil fuel generation, and in how individuals feel about semi-enclosed bodies of water such as Nantucket Sound or Delaware Bay as compared to the vast open ocean (Firestone, et al., 2009). As I explain below, we interpret the concern over aesthetics to be more a question of attachment to place than a concern over the viewshed. In addition, residents of Cape Cod articulated a concern over the private use of public waters; an expression that was not manifest in Delaware (Firestone, et al., 2009). This suggests that the developer of the Cape

Cod project was not wholly successful in engaging the public or that its efforts were muted by well-funded opponents to the project.

It is important to caution that these findings are snapshots in time – public opinion can be fickle at the best of times, and public acceptance of wind power has been shown to change over the course of development (Devine-Wright, 2005; Wolsink, 2007). Bearing that in mind, we undertook new surveys in Cape Cod and Delaware in 2009 and included an expanded enquiry into place attachment and public engagement. We can report preliminarily that a majority now support the cape wind project and that a plurality in both Cape Cod and Delaware feel that the process has been fair and the respective developer transparent.

NIMBYism, Viewshed Disamenities, Attraction and Attachment to Place

As noted above, we began our work to understand the public's perceptions and preferences by conducting a series of semi-structured interviews. We observed that opposition to development projects in general and wind projects specifically is often labelled as NIMBY ('Not in my back yard'), although little analysis typically accompanies such labelling. The problem with the term 'NIMBY' is that while it is descriptive of an outcome – local opposition – it does not explain the reasons why individuals are opposed, and thus tends to generate more heat than light (Kempton et al, 2005). The term NIMBY is often used despairingly to imply that an individual's opposition is based on selfishness, or at the very least self-interest, while there may be other reasons for opposition, such as concern for marine wildlife, unfamiliarity with the technology, unhappiness with the process, concern over industrialization of the ocean, and so on (Firestone and Kempton, 2007).

Our subsequent mail surveys also provide little support for a NIMBY hypothesis. Indeed, individuals in both Cape Cod and Delaware indicated that they would be more supportive of offshore wind farm development off their respective coast if the wind farm was the 'first of many' such wind farms (see discussion below, in the section entitled 'Transformative offshore wind power'). This contrasts with what we would expect local citizens' reactions to be towards a proposed landfill or waste dump and other proposed noxious developments. We would not expect one of those development proposals to garner increased local support if it were billed as the 'first of many' (Firestone and Kempton, 2007). Moreover, given that of those who are opposed to offshore wind power development in each locale, we find that a higher percentage of Delawareans who live near the coast than Cape Cod residents indicate that 'aesthetics' is one of the top three reasons for their opposition (Firestone et al, 2009), an emphasis on the viewshed for its own sake would appear misplaced.

Furthermore, in real estate, the mantra is 'location, location, location'. In contrast, we infer from our offshore wind power research that topography probably trumps location. Indeed, individuals appear to feel differently about, and have greater attachment to, semi-enclosed seas (bays and sounds) than they do to the open ocean. We come to this conclusion by comparing public opinion of Cape Cod residents concerning a wind farm in a sound to that in Delaware concerning a wind farm in the ocean, and in Delawareans' preference for the installation of wind turbines in the open ocean over than in a bay (Firestone, et al., 2009).

Subjectively, it would seem that semi-enclosed seas are less pristine than the open ocean, yet the public appears to perceive a greater intrusion in those semi-enclosed ecosystems. In contrast, on land, one would think that the opposite would be true – that the public would perceive the greatest intrusion to be in large, pristine natural areas such as national parks and wilderness areas as opposed to regional environmental features that are often broken up by roads, buildings, electrical wires, and the like (Firestone, et al.,2009). Thus, 'symbolic, affective and socially constructed aspects' as noted by Devine-Wright (2005), such as how residents come to make sense of the impact that an unfamiliar technology has on the place in which they live, would appear to have particular resonance for sea-based wind turbines in semi-enclosed seas. Thus, in these sea areas there may be a 'public sense of angst', brought about by the potential for rapid changes in the seascape, that may lead some to feel 'expelled from their homeland' (Schwahn, 2002). In others words, at sea, place attachment (Vorkinn and Riese, 2001; Short, 2002) appears to resonate with the public more than the viewshed itself.

That the focus of policy-makers, developers and social scientists should be on place attachment and the disruption to cultural practices (such as recreational boating and navigation) rather than on the viewshed or the much mentioned NIMBY phenomena is underscored by the fact that many simulations of proposed offshore wind farms probably exaggerate the impact that wind turbines (if ultimately installed) would have on the ocean view. First, and I must admit that we have been complicit, survey respondents are often asked for their opinions (both support and opposition as well as on other matters such as whether they think an offshore wind farm will negatively impact aesthetics) based on photo-simulations of wind farms where the wind turbines encompass most, if not the entire, ocean horizon (see, e.g., simulations of Cape Wind, www.capewind.org). I call this the 'blinkered racehorse' view.

In an attempt to better understand how photosimulations can affect public perceptions, in our 2009 survey of public opinion in Cape Cod and Delaware, we provided half of the sample with simulations that were 7inches wide and half with simulations that were 16inches wide. It is worth noting that even in this attempt to provide a more realistic image we had to compromise for reasons of practicality. To provide photosimulations of the entire field of a human's view, where a person stands in one place and moves his or her head from side to side, would have required photosimulations that were twice as wide again; something that was not feasible in a mail survey. As noted by Global Insight (2008) in its report of offshore wind power development off the New Jersey coast, a wind farm would occupy only 22.5 per cent of the ocean vista if it was located 10km from the coast.

In addition, visual impacts are overstated when a potentially affected individual has only clear-day photosimulations on which to base his or her opinion. As noted elsewhere, visual impacts may decrease or disappear on hazy or cloudy days (Bishop and Miller, 2007). The photosimulations that we used, which depict stationary turbines, also may result in greater perceived visual impacts than if we had administered the survey on the internet using rotating turbine blades (we prefer mail surveys because web-based surveys require individuals to have high connection speeds, which either creates practical/expense issues or survey sampling bias). In summary, if a picture is worth a thousand words, an inaccurate one is likely to provoke many more, and we as researchers have to be careful when designing studies and interpreting results.

The 'collective wisdom' also is that the public will not support in-view developments. Our survey results lead us to question that 'wisdom'. Of particular note is the 2006 Delaware residents' survey, where we employed choice experiments and modelling. Choice experiments are based on the proposition that the utility that an individual derives from a good comes from the characteristics (or 'attributes') of that good, not from the good itself (Lancaster, 1966). To understand choice experiments, think of toothpaste. The theory, which comes from marketing, is that people do not buy toothpaste; they buy the attributes related thereto. Is it a paste or a gel? If, a paste, is the paste white or striped? Is it wintergreen/cinnamon or spearmint flavoured? Does it have extra whiteners or not? Does it come in a tube that you squeeze and roll or is it encased in a hard plastic container that stands upright on the bathroom shelf?

Returning to the world of offshore wind power development, attributes of interest could include distance from shore, wind farm location (e.g. adjacent to Delaware Bay, to a large coastal town, or to a less developed coastal community), the amount of revenues that will be raised from leasing, and the premium that households would have to pay over and above their current monthly electricity bill (see also Ladenburg and Dubgaard, 2007, who considered size of wind farm). For the Delaware survey, different 'wind farms' were assembled, and each survey respondent was asked to choose between two wind farms and the 'status quo' option of new coal or natural gas generation (Figure 16.1). In order to generate enough variation in responses for statistical analysis, the question was repeated twice in the survey instrument, but each time with different wind farm attributes, and 25 different versions of the survey were prepared. Survey respondents were also shown simulations of what a wind farm might look like at various distances, with the closest being 0.9 miles (1.5km) and the furthest being out of sight (Krueger et al, 2010).

Although Delaware residents were highly supportive of offshore wind power (Firestone et al, 2009), they do consider wind turbines to be a visual disamenity and, as a result, they are willing to pay to move them further from shore. Importantly, however, we found that the marginal societal benefits of installing wind turbines an additional mile further from shore are small after about 10km and have all but vanished by around 15km. Although those residents who lived near the ocean were willing to pay more to have wind turbines placed further from the shore than those who lived either near Delaware Bay or inland, ocean residents likewise saw little benefit in moving turbines entirely out of view. Furthermore, when we

18) Now for which option would you vote?

Refer to the Delaware map insert for the 'wind farm location.' Refer to the ocean photo insert for simulated views of the wind farm at different distances.

	Option A	Option B	Option C
Wind farm location	Ocean (South)	Ocean (North)	No wind power
Distance from shore	0.9 km	6 km	
Annual rent/royalty	$1 million to Beach Nourishment Fund	$8 million to Beach Nourishment Fund	Expansion of coal or natural gas power
Renewable energy fee on your monthly electricity bill for 3 years	$1	$20	

I would vote for …
- ☐ Option A
- ☐ Option B
- ☐ Option C

Figure 16.1 *Sample choice experiment question*

Source: Krueger et al, 2010

modelled how close the turbines could be located to the shore before ocean residents (those living within a kilometre of the beach) would prefer a new coal or gas plant somewhere in Delaware (which could be more than 150km away) we found that the answer was pretty close – indeed, less than 2km! It thus appears that, while a great deal of focus in the US is on the social acceptability of offshore wind power, at least among Delawareans, it is new coal development rather than in-view offshore wind power that is socially unacceptable.

As noted, we also undertook a survey of more than 1000 out-of-state tourists at three Delaware state park beaches, three tourist town beaches and two board-walks in Delaware in 2007, and achieved a response rate of over 80 per cent (Lilley et al, 2010). To systematically sample individuals on the beach, surveyors walked parallel to the shore and then at regular, predetermined intervals, walked perpendicular to the shore. The closest individual in each group within 2 metres of each transect was then asked to participate in the survey (Lilley et al, 2010).

We found some reported tourism loss with an offshore wind farm at 22km (6.3 per cent), and more loss at 10km (26.1 per cent) (Lilley et al, 2010). With wind turbines at 1.5km (closer than any planned US development), 44.7 per cent reported that they would stop visiting the same beach, with most tourists saying that they would then visit a different beach in Delaware, as opposed to a beach in another state (e.g. New Jersey or Maryland) (Lilley et al, 2010). This stated inten-tion to visit another beach would be a substantial concern for coastal communities, if not for a countervailing effect – the ability of a beach community with wind turbines off its coast to attract tourists and create a new tourism industry. Indeed, when we asked beachgoers about the effect of a wind farm 10km from shore at a beach they did not usually visit, the percentage attracted to the beach (65.8 per cent) – that is, that would visit a new beach at least once – is over twice the percentage reporting that they would not visit the same beach (26.1 per cent) and more than nine times the percentage reporting that they would have switched to an out-of-state beach (Lilley et al, 2010). Moreover, 44.4 per cent of survey respondents indicated that they would be likely to take a boat tour of an offshore wind farm, further indicating the positive effect of such a development. Thus, although not proven by Lilley et al (2010), it is at least plausible that the attractive effects of in-view offshore wind development are greater than the negative effects.

Needed Context: Wind Power and Its Alternatives (Comparative Impacts)

There should be no dispute that environmental impacts of proposed offshore wind farms should be assessed and that projects should be located to minimize negative environmental impacts on avian and marine wildlife (Lilley and Firestone, 2008). But, as we have argued elsewhere, there is a need for a re-conceptualized environmental assessment process that places more emphasis on consideration of trade-offs and alternatives to offshore wind power than alternative locations for offshore wind (Lilley and Firestone, 2008). By this I mean that the environmental impacts of offshore wind power need to be considered in context. Although the choice among offshore locations A, B and C is important and not without consequence, it pales in comparison to the choice among means of electricity generation (coal, natural gas, nuclear, hydro, solar, wind, biomass etc.). Regulators have long made price comparisons between these choices (neglecting, however, in most instances, the external costs associated with those means); it is time to make explicit comparisons in the environmental assessment process.

Likewise, it is important for individuals to understand the environmental impacts of offshore wind power, the avoided health consequences associated with non-fossil fuel energy resources, and the environmental impacts of other means of generation (e.g. the impingement and entrainment of fish and thermal pollution associated with hydropower and nuclear, and the mountain top mining associated with West Virginia coal). With surveys of public opinion, sometimes researchers desire to provide this context and determine the value of information; at other times, they wish to understand what the public knows and believes, and why. But in either instance, it is useful if those responding to a survey understand that trade-offs have to be made – that their electricity has to come from somewhere and that there are no free lunches. Unfortunately, in Cape Cod, the Cape Wind project appears to be understood as a choice between offshore wind power development in Nantucket Sound or nothing, when the real choice is between offshore wind and coal, etc., and that may explain some of the mixed feelings towards the project. That is why, in our Delaware resident survey, when asking individuals to make a choice, we included the status quo choice of coal or natural gas.

Interestingly, in Delaware, when the choice of offshore wind was subsequently presented to state regulators and citizens, it was in the context of an all-source bidding process that also included natural gas and coal gasification. The victory for offshore wind in Delaware and the subsequent power purchase agreement (PPA) between Bluewater Wind and Delmarva Power, which was the result of an open process expertly managed by the state's electricity regulatory commission and a public that was uniquely engaged with the bidding process, fervently supported the offshore wind power option for reasons of public health and concerns over climate change, and led state decision-makers towards the final resolution, underlines the importance of providing a forum for involving citizens in public processes as well as realistic options when attempting to gauge and understand public perceptions and opinions of new technologies.

Transformative Offshore Wind Power

Finally, I want to return to a theme I mentioned at the beginning of this chapter – transformative offshore wind power. In order to understand whether the public might support something like what is unfolding in Europe, where the European Union and the member countries have tied their energy future to offshore wind (EWEA, 2009), we asked each Cape Cod and Delaware resident how his or her support or opposition ('more likely to support,' 'less likely to support' or 'no effect') would change if the project was the first of 300 such projects off the US mid-Atlantic and northeast Atlantic coasts. The question noted that this would result in supplying half of coastal states' electricity, with concomitant environmental benefits (and increased impacts as well). Table 16.1 presents the results for Cape Cod, Delaware as a whole (statewide) and for the Delaware ocean group discussed earlier who live, on average, 1km from the beach.

With this larger plan, we see a large shift among residents towards being more supportive, with a comparatively much smaller shift towards opposition (Firestone, et al, 2009). Among those opposed to a wind farm in 'their backyard,' a net 15–20 per cent among those living in Cape Cod or near the Delaware shore and almost 40 per cent statewide in Delaware (Firestone, et al., 2009) would be more likely to support their backyard project if it was the 'first of many'. Among those who were unsure, there were large net gains in increased support of 43 per cent across Delaware, 60 per cent among those Delaware residents living near the coast, and 55 per cent of Cape Cod residents. We also see supporters becoming more fervent with wide-scale implementation (Firestone, et al., 2009).

These results suggest that citizens are ready for a transformation that mirrors the policies that have been adopted in Europe. In the US, while the Obama administration has made great strides in advancing offshore wind power through regulation and research and development funding, such a transformation will require bolder action that considers feed-in-tariffs; internalization of externalities, including pricing carbon; long-term investment; and tax policies that recognize that, like nuclear power, offshore wind power has long planning horizons.

Table 16.1 *Shift in support (more or less than previously) for a larger project plan*

Alternative project	Survey area	Supporters		Unsure		Opponents	
		More	Less	More	Less	More	Less
First of	Cape Cod	61%	5%	67%	12%	35%	16%
many projects	DE Ocean	75%	1%	63%	3%	29%	14%
	DE Statewide	75%	1%	55%	12%	47%	9%

Notes: For Cape Cod, 'supporters' and 'opponents' include both those who expressed a firm opinion and those who leant in that direction, while 'unsure' includes all those initially undecided (as there were only four respondents who were not firm or leaning). Thus, for Cape Cod there is some overlap in the categories; that is not the case for the Delaware results.
Source: adapted from Table 6 in Firestone et al., 2009

Conclusions

Sitting in a somewhat cramped coach seat, reflecting on the 2009 European Offshore Wind (EOW) Conference which I had just attended in Stockholm, it occurred to me that the transformation in the US that our research suggests could occur has already been realized in Europe. When I attended the last EOW conference in 2007 in Berlin, social acceptance, the political will, and the policies that were then being contemplated and starting to be put into place were much on the mind of the conference attendees. In contrast to a focus on social and political considerations, at the 2009 EOW conference, the delegates were drawn to technical sessions that focused on an offshore transmission grid to facilitate transmission of offshore wind power among northern European nations, wind turbine technology, and offshore foundations for wind turbines. Indeed, the conference organizers had to scramble mid-conference and move the technology sessions to the largest room, given the interests of the delegates, while sessions addressing policy formulation and implementation were sent to the side rooms.

The term 'social acceptance' was almost entirely absent from the 2009 conference, relegated to a couple of posters (mine being one of them) and a few comments from speakers. Interestingly, to the extent that social acceptance was mentioned by those speakers, the concern related not to wind turbines being placed in the ocean or even offshore transmission, but to transmission/transformers on land as offshore wind power becomes integrated with the land-based grid. That wind turbines would be placed in the ocean and offshore wind power would become a substantial fraction of energy supply in northern Europe was taken as a given. Why was this? In part, I surmise, it was because of communities' experience with offshore turbines, citizens' understanding of the limited environmental effects, and a plan for the future that relies more on installations at some distance from shore. But, much also appears to be the result of political leadership.

This does not necessarily mean that the northern European citizenry supports and will support every offshore project. Rather, it may suggest that national governments have become more accustomed to public objections, comfortable with opposition, and savvy at addressing the public's concerns. It also may be that national governments in Europe have simply assumed a larger role in decision-making at the expense of local control, particularly with regard to large-scale projects that are characteristic of offshore development. The question of the conference thus was not whether offshore wind, but how to accomplish the objective of offshore wind becoming a significant fraction of supply at the lowest cost and greatest benefit.

Developers need to be sensitive to communities' attachment to place and should not promise that wind farms will engender no negative tourism and environmental impacts. That said, the US public is ready to embrace offshore wind power and to even accept in-view developments. The public also perceives offshore wind farms to be as much, if not more, tourist attractions than disamenities, and is anxious to participate in a transformation in how the US generates electricity, with wind power at its centre. It is time for the politicians in the US to lead, as they have in Europe.

Acknowledgements

It would be remiss of me if I did not acknowledge the work of my co-authors, in particular Willett Kempton, Meredith Blaydes Lilley, Andrew Krueger and George Parsons, without whom the underlying data analysis and interpretation would not have been possible.

Notes

1. As a general rule, US states have primacy over development in the first three nautical miles (5.5km) from shore, while the federal government controls the remainder of the US continental shelf.

References

Bishop, I. D. and Miller, D. R. (2007) 'Visual assessment of off-shore wind turbines: The influence of distance, contrast, movement and social variables', *Renewable Energy*, vol 32, pp814–831
Caldeira, K. And Wickett, M.E. (2003) 'Oceanography: Anthropogenic carbon and ocean pH', *Nature*, vol 425, p365 (2003)
Dhanju, A. and Firestone, J. (2009) 'Access system framework for regulating offshore wind power in state waters', *Coastal Management*, vol 37 no 5, pp441–478
Devine-Wright, P. (2005) 'Beyond NIMBYism: Towards an integrated framework for understanding public perceptions of wind energy', *Wind Energy*, vol 7, pp125–39
EWEA (European Wind Energy Association) (2009) *Oceans of Opportunity: Harnessing Europe's Largest Domestic Energy Resource*, www.ewea.org/fileadmin/ewea_documents/documents/publications/reports/Offshore_Report_2009.pdf

Firestone, J. and Kempton, W. (2007) 'Public opinion about large offshore wind power: Underlying factors', *Energy Policy*, vol 35, no 5, pp1584–1598

Firestone, J., Kempton, W., Krueger, A. and Loper, C. E. (2004) 'Regulating offshore wind power and aquaculture: Messages from land and sea', *Cornell Journal of Law and Public Policy*, vol 14, no 1, pp71–111

Firestone, J., Kempton, W. and Krueger, A. (2009) 'Public acceptance of offshore wind power projects in the United States', *Wind Energy*, vol 12, no 2, pp183–202

Global Insight (2008) *An Assessment of the Potential Costs and Benefits of Offshore Wind Turbines*, Report for The State of New Jersey, www.njcleanenergy.com/files/file/Renewable_Programs/Economic%2520Assessment%2520of%2520NJ%2520OSWT-03Sept08.pdf

Kempton, W., Firestone, J., Lilley, J., Rouleau, T. and Whitaker, P. (2005) 'The offshore wind power debate: Views from Cape Cod', *Coastal Management Journal*, vol 33, pp119–149

Kempton, W., Archer, C. L. Dhanju, A., Garvine, R. W. and Jacobson, M. Z. (2007) 'Large CO_2 reductions via offshore wind power matched to inherent storage in energy end-uses', *Geophysical Research Letters*, vol 34, pL02817, doi:10.1029/2006GL028016

Krueger, A. D., Parsons, G. R. and Firestone, J. (2010) 'Valuing the visual disamenity of offshore wind power projects at varying distances from the shore: An application on the Delaware shoreline', *Land Economics*, vol 87, no 2

Ladenburg, J. and Dubgaard, A. (2007) 'Willingness to pay for reduced visual disamenities from offshore wind farms in Denmark', *Energy Policy*, vol 35, pp4059–4071

Lancaster, K. (1966) 'A new approach to consumer theory', *Journal of Political Economy*, vol 74, pp132–157

Lilley, M. B. and Firestone, J. (2008) 'Wind power, wildlife, and the Migratory Bird Treaty Act: A way forward', *Environmental Law*, vol 38, pp1167–1214

Lilley, M. B., Firestone, J. and Kempton, W. (2010) 'The effect of wind power installations on coastal tourism', *Energies*, vol 3, pp1–22; doi:10.3390/en3010001, www.mdpi.com/1996-1073/3/1/1/pdf

Schwahn, C. (2002) 'Landscape policy in the northern sea marshes', in M. Pasqualetti, P. Gipe and R. W. Righter (eds) *Wind Power in View: Energy Landscapes in a Crowded World*, Academic Press, San Diego, CA, pp133–150

Short, L. (2002) 'Wind power and English landscape identity', in M. Pasqualetti, P. Gipe and R. W. Righter (eds) *Wind Power in View: Energy Landscapes in a Crowded World*, Academic Press, San Diego, CA, pp43–58

Vorkinn, M. and Riese, H. (2001) 'Environmental concern in a local context: The significance of place attachment,' *Environment and Behavior*, vol 33, no 2, pp249–263

Wolsink, M. (2007), 'Wind power implementation: The nature of public attitudes: Equity and fairness instead of "backyard motives"', *Renewable and Sustainable Energy Reviews*, vol 11, pp1188–1207

Chapter 17

The Limits of Upstream Engagement in an Emergent Technology: Lay Perceptions of Hydrogen Energy Technologies

Rob Flynn, Paul Bellaby and Miriam Ricci

Introduction

Contemporary discourse about public engagement has rejected the 'public under-standing of science' (PUS) model, in which lay people were thought to be inadequately informed or irrational about science (or risk) and therefore needed to be 'educated' by experts. The assumption that 'the public' has a 'knowledge deficit' has been challenged, mainly because it presumes that expert scientific knowledge is always objective and superior to lay knowledge. To overcome the weaknesses of the deficit model, deliberative methods have been devised to explic-itly involve the public in discussions of science and technology, and to elicit their beliefs and preferences (see, for example, Irwin and Wynne, 1996; Rowe and Frewer, 2004, 2005; Rowe et al, 2004; Irwin, 2007; Renn, 2008). 'Upstream' deliberative engagement implies an active role for citizens throughout the entire process of scientific research and development. In this process, citizens are not merely passive recipients of an established body of expert knowledge which nulli-fies their contribution to decisions about the desirability or feasibility of a technology. However, there are many different types of engagement, all of which have various limitations on their practice.

We discuss three of the most important limitations on attempts to engage the public in emergent technologies below. First, despite the critique of the PUS and deficit model, it is still likely that the highly technical and complex nature of the information available may make it difficult for citizens to make reasonable assessments about the merits and disadvantages of certain proposals. Even allowing for different methods of communication to reach a population characterized by educational, cultural and socio-economic differentiation, some proposed innovations and their attendant risks may still be difficult to understand. Where the science is uncertain, or is dealing with unknown risks (for instance, nanotechnology) attempts to engage the public, however genuine and systematic, are bound to be problematic (see Horlick-Jones et al, 2007a). Second, in undertaking public engagement, a major question arises about whom to engage – the whole population or representative samples, or purposive samples of those most likely to be directly affected? Obviously this depends on the nature of the issue and its immediate relevance to different social groups, but 'the' public – or rather 'publics' – are segmented into different social groups, with different interests, which affect the saliency of the emergent technology and its perceived risks. Some may be positive about the technology, some may be hostile, some may be indifferent, and some may not even wish to be consulted (see Burningham et al, 2007) and because of this, it is difficult to design a participatory programme which accommodates these varying levels of engagement. Thirdly, it is worth emphasizing that, irrespective of governments' or stakeholders' desire to secure public *acceptance* of an emerging technology, any engagement procedure must anticipate the possibility of rejection, or only obtaining conditional and limited approval. Engagement, in itself, does not necessarily result in social acceptance or endorsement – and arguably, nor should it, if it is open-ended and enables alternative options to be debated.

Public Engagement Surrounding Technological Innovation

There is a large and multidisciplinary literature about the relationship between expert risk assessment and public perceptions of technological innovation (see Slovic, 2000; Pidgeon et al, 2003; Mythen and Walklate, 2006; Pidgeon et al, 2006; Taylor-Gooby and Zinn, 2006; Flynn, 2007). Risk analysts have acknowledged that citizen participation is a vital element in risk assessment and management, and have recommended the adoption of 'analytic-deliberative' methods (Renn, 1999, 2008). Governments faced with distrustful and questioning publics – alarmed by controversies over scientific and technological innovations such as nuclear power, genetically modified organisms and nanotechnologies – have gradually adopted an alternative public engagement approach (Horlick-Jones et al, 2007a; Irwin, 2007; Mohr, 2007).

Others have also advocated including lay people in debates about science and technology as early as possible in the research and development process. Grove-

White et al (2000) specifically criticized the 'one-way' nature of conventional information provision in science (and risk communication), and argued for greater transparency. Wilsdon and Willis (2004) further argued in favour of moving public engagement 'upstream', to 'ask deeper questions about the values, visions and vested interests that motivate scientific endeavour' (Wilsdon and Willis, 2004, p18). Noting that public participation (and risk assessment) usually occurs when a technology is almost ready for implementation, and attention is focused on its 'downstream' impact, Wilsdon and Willis proposed a radical shifting of engagement 'upstream' in order to shape the objectives and priorities of the innovation from its inception. Such upstream public engagement (UPE) should be 'substantive', that is, it must *shape* decisions, rather than coming after the event; it should 'open up' debate and the public should help decide which issues and what questions should be addressed.

Commentators, having observed recent UPE exercises (such as those about GM food and nanotechnologies in the UK) are now cautious about their validity and usefulness (see Abelson et al, 2003; Petts, 2004; Rowe et al, 2004; Rowe and Frewer, 2005; Renn, 2008). Leach et al (2005) observed that citizen involvement through deliberative processes was still based on a 'liberal' theory of citizenship, in which citizens are only given a passive role. Leach and Scoones (2005) argued that deliberative forums remain framed within a scientistic discourse. Wynne (2005) criticized the 'extravagant optimism' surrounding recent participatory exercises, and claimed that the commitment to engage the public is 'something of a mirage' (Wynne, 2005, p68). Similarly, Stirling (2005) questioned whether new participatory discourses used in the social appraisal of technology 'open up' or 'close down' public debate. For example, in two of the most significant recent public consultation exercises in Britain, about genetically modified (GM) organisms and nanotechnologies, critical observers have raised doubts about the impact and value of the engagement process (see Doubleday, 2007; Horlick-Jones et al, 2007a,b; Pidgeon and Rogers-Hayden, 2007). There are two main concerns about the adequacy of analytic-deliberative processes and upstream engagement exercises. First, there is still an asymmetrical relationship between the experts and citizens, and the agenda for debate may be pre-empted (Chilvers and Burgess, 2008). Secondly, there are doubts about how widely adopted UPE really is in government policy-making and in the private sector where environmental risks are paramount (Burningham et al, 2007). Thus, despite the ambitious and radical expectations surrounding UPE (see Cornwall, 2008), there are major difficulties in implementing it and continuing questions about its impact on policy (Irwin 2007; Lidskog, 2008; Petts, 2008).

The fundamentally important issue is how far UPE can be undertaken in what may appear to be highly uncertain or *emergent* technologies. There are some embryonic innovations where the scientific knowledge base is still evolving, which pose particular problems for engaging the public. In the case of GM food, studies of public perceptions reveal a deep-rooted ambivalence about biotechnology and its long-term effects (see Pidgeon et al, 2005; Horlick-Jones et al, 2007a; Bickerstaff et al, 2008). Ambivalence has also been consistently reported in studies of public attitudes towards nanotechnologies (Royal Society and RAE, 2004; Doubleday, 2007; Mohr, 2007; Pidgeon and Rogers-Hayden, 2007). Such ambivalence is not simply a reflection of a lack of knowledge or information. Rather, it signifies reluctance by people to make unequivocal statements about these innovations, and the wider socio-technical systems in which they might be embedded, until they are directly experienced and/or it is shown how they might connect with their everyday lives. Thus, the cautious and provisional nature of public attitudes towards emerging technologies is to be expected.

To illustrate some of the practical problems of carrying out upstream public engagement in an emergent technology, we will now consider evidence from an ongoing study of lay perceptions of, and attitudes towards, hydrogen energy technologies. First, some brief information about hydrogen and hydrogen energy technologies is presented.

Hydrogen and Hydrogen Energy Technologies

Only a very brief and simplified summary of hydrogen energy can be given in this chapter (but see United Nations, 2006; Ricci et al, 2007a, 2008). Hydrogen is an energy *carrier* not a primary energy source – although it is the most abundant element in the universe. Hydrogen is produced commercially for various industrial uses by re-forming natural gas (or methane from biomass) and also by electrolysis of water using electricity from any source (nuclear, solar, wind, wave). Proponents of hydrogen see it as a supplement or even an alternative for fossil fuels; they stress it is 'green' and non-polluting. Hydrogen can be used in fuel cells – in transport (such as vehicles), in stationary applications (such as combined heat and power systems for buildings) and even in portable devices (such as laptops). Radical and ambitious claims have been made about hydrogen's potential to 'democratize' energy production. Rifkin (2002) suggested that consumers in a new 'hydrogen economy' could become their own hydrogen energy producers (using their own cars and houses). Many countries have invested large sums in the research and development of hydrogen. Both in the US and Europe, demonstration projects have been introduced, such as fuel cell buses and trials of hydrogen refuelling stations, and many motor car manufacturers are reaching an advanced stage in producing hydrogen fuel cell cars.

There are, however, many critics who challenge hydrogen's 'green' credentials and question whether it is sustainable. Most hydrogen is currently reliant on fossil fuels, and to replace this poses problems in terms of the quantity (and reliability) required from renewable energy sources. Many commentators have identified severe safety hazards and risks with hydrogen – it is highly explosive, and the gas must be stored at extremely high pressures and at extremely low temperatures in liquid form. How hydrogen is to be produced, stored, transported, distributed and used raises major safety (as well as economic) questions. The European Commission identified safety, regulatory and public acceptance issues as important 'non-technical barriers' to the development of hydrogen as an energy carrier

(European Commission, 2006). A recent report also highlighted institutional and economic barriers to the widespread introduction of hydrogen infrastructure in transport in the UK (AEA, 2008). Industrial and scientific stakeholders have differing views about possible alternative future scenarios. Eames and McDowall (2006) and McDowall and Eames (2006) have used deliberative mapping among stakeholders and identified six separate hydrogen 'visions', with very different characteristics and interests. Ekins and Hughes (2007) have questioned whether the 'hydrogen economy' is economically feasible.

Here then, is an emergent or embryonic technology, surrounded by many scientific and economic uncertainties, whose advocates claim will solve some of our contemporary energy problems. But are the general public aware of it, and what are their attitudes towards it? Evidence about these important questions is relatively sparse, the methodology for investigating them is varied, and the evidence is mixed. For example, Fuhrmann and Bleischwitz's (2007) review of the literature found very little attention given to the question of public awareness and acceptance of hydrogen. Heinz and Erdmann (2008) analysed public attitudes towards hydrogen, but in the context of eight cities where an experimental hydrogen bus was operating; they found broad acceptance but also a substantial minority with neutral or negative views. Roche et al (2009) have also reviewed different studies and found quantitative evidence indicating low awareness but generally positive attitudes, whereas qualitative studies displayed a more complex, mixed pattern. Similarly, Ricci et al (2008) noted the methodological predominance of quantitative research using questionnaire surveys, and a concentration on transport applications, often with non-representative samples. Against this background, this chapter offers insights drawn from the authors' recent and ongoing work using a variety of methods in different case-study areas.

Lay Perceptions of Hydrogen Energy Technologies

The data (mainly qualitative) derive from two interlinked projects. The first is part of the Engineering and Physical Sciences Research Council (EPSRC) programme on sustainable energy and the UK Sustainable Hydrogen Energy Consortium (UKSHEC, 2003 onwards: see www.uk-shec.org.uk and www.psi.org.uk/ukshec/publications.htm). Within this programme, the authors (with other colleagues) have carried out case studies in three areas of England and Wales where there are already existing hydrogen production facilities and infrastructure, or plans for developing them, and/or early stage demonstration projects using hydrogen fuel cell vehicles and other hydrogen energy applications: Teesside (northeast England), Wales and London. Two phases of focus group meetings were carried out (in October–December 2005 and October–November 2006) with members of the public sampled from local authorities' own consultation panels. In the first phase there were nine groups, and in the second there were seven groups; each group was mixed in gender, age and socio-economic group (group size varied between six and eight people). Focus group participants were deliberately recruited on the basis that they had no direct involvement in the hydrogen industry. At the first meetings, their general awareness of environmental and energy issues was discussed, and then various types of information about hydrogen were provided. At the second meetings, more detailed information about hydrogen was presented and participants were invited to debate alternative scenarios. These discussions were digitally audiotaped, transcribed and then thematically analysed by the research team.

A series of Citizens' Panels were carried out in Teesside and Wales (November 2008 and April–May 2009), when members of the public participated in two meetings with experts, questioned and challenged those experts, and debated various alternative scenarios for hydrogen energy. Panel members were again selected from local authorities' own public consultation panels, which are statistically representative of the local population. At the first Teesside event, 19 people (8 female, 11 male) attended an all-day meeting facilitated by the research team and, from the same group, 18 people attended the second all-day meeting three weeks later. Two scientists from the UK Sustainable Hydrogen Consortium, together with an expert stakeholder from the region and a representative from the Health and Safety Executive, gave talks and participated in discussions with the panel. All of the presentations, questions and discussions were digitally recorded and the transcripts have been analysed thematically. Here, findings are summarized from the *second* meetings of the focus groups, and then from the Teesside citizens' panel only; material from the Wales citizens' panel is reported separately elsewhere.

The other project was carried out for the UK Department for Transport about public engagement with hydrogen infrastructure in transport (Bellaby and Upham et al, 2007). This assembled 12 focus groups in three areas of England where there were *no* existing or embryonic hydrogen infrastructures: Norwich, Sheffield and Southampton. These areas were also deliberately selected because they comprise different types of labour markets and have very different travel networks. A research company carried out a telephone questionnaire survey of a representative sample of the local populations ($n=1003$), and from this recruited four focus groups in each area. These groups contained between eight and ten participants and were mixed in terms of age, gender and socio-economic group. A professional facilitator convened the group discussions; after general discussion of climate change and other environmental and energy issues, a specially produced DVD about hydrogen energy and its transport applications was shown, and participants were invited to express their opinions. These focus group discussions were digitally audiotaped, transcribed and thematically analysed by several team members and an independent researcher.

Findings from each of these studies are now presented: as usual in reporting focus group qualitative data, a summary or overview is given, together with selected illustrative quotations (Barbour and Kitzinger, 1999; Bloor et al, 2001).

Focus group views on hydrogen energy technologies

All of the groups were very aware of issues such as climate change and global warming, and the crisis over fossil fuels. Many participants were concerned that action should be taken by national governments to address these problems and acknowledged that significant changes in consumer behaviour (over energy use) were also required. In common with other studies of public perceptions of hydrogen, our focus group members had very little awareness of hydrogen energy and its possible uses (see Ricci et al, 2007b, 2008).

However, after being presented with various types of information about hydrogen, there was neither enthusiastic acceptance nor complete rejection – rather, people maintained a determinedly agnostic view. Participants raised fundamental 'whole system' questions about how hydrogen and its associated infrastructure might work, and wanted more information about its relative benefits, costs and risks compared with conventional energy sources and carriers. Thus, for example, one man commented:

> *'We can all contribute to overall energy saving in small ways. But hydrogen energy as an alternative energy? Until somebody comes up with a proven, cost-effective, efficient, economical device, none of us knows which way to go'* (Carmarthen).

Another man in Teesside remarked:

> *'The facts have got to be there to tell us it's a viable concept, and all that comes into viable: safety, economy, cost effectiveness.'*

Many questioned how hydrogen technologies related to the local economy and environment, and their employment implications. Very few cited potential safety hazards of hydrogen as an overwhelming concern; it was widely believed that risks would have been minimized to safe levels and 'engineered out' before such technologies were introduced. Cost and convenience were the overriding concerns from a consumer perspective.

Throughout the discussions, questions signalled uncertainty and ambivalence about hydrogen (see Flynn et al, 2008). Many participants asked basic questions about how the hydrogen was going to be produced, and whether, if the major source was still fossil fuels there were any environmental advantages. They were unsure (or unconvinced) that renewable energy sources could generate sufficient hydrogen on a large scale. They asked for much more detailed information than was currently available from official sources, and identified issues which are still the subject of ongoing scientific research. Thus:

> *'But which one [hydrogen production method] has the most potential? Because I think that is the one people want to know about. Which is the one we should be going for because it is the cleanest, because it is reasonably cheap, and less impact on the environment'* (Man, Teesside).

When they discussed possible hydrogen technologies such as fuel cell vehicles, domestic combined heat and power (CHP) systems and other portable applications using hydrogen, safety issues figured more prominently. As a man in Teesside commented:

> *'I think if people were thinking about putting hydrogen in their own back yard, they would want it to be very, very, safe.'*

Participants also stressed that everyday routines meant that they were effectively 'locked-in' to existing technologies: consequently, they thought it would be difficult to persuade people to change their behaviour until there were fewer uncertainties surrounding hydrogen. As one woman in London observed:

> *'People can embrace things which are good for the planet, good for your health ... but only if it is not going to disrupt their lifestyle too much* [and] *if it is not going to be too costly for them.'*

Focus group participants were asked for their views about consultation with the public about hydrogen energy. In all of the groups, people interpreted 'involvement' and 'engagement' *not* as a dialogue, but as a one-way communication of information from experts and stakeholders to citizens. This may partly be explained by their unfamiliarity with more deliberative and interactive forms of consultation, and their more usual experience of simply receiving communication through the media or by completing questionnaires. Some participants expressed deep cynicism about consultation processes, and suggested that public policy about hydrogen was already a 'done deal'. However, several participants suggested that most people were uninterested, unable or unwilling to become 'engaged'. This raises challenging and critical questions about the objectives of upstream engagement.

Participants emphasized that the issues had to be presented to them in ways which were relevant to their immediate everyday lives. Several pointed out that realistic judgements about whether the hydrogen economy was desirable or needed could only be given when they could experience hydrogen energy technologies 'in action'. They also stressed that information had to be communicated by spokespersons who could be trusted; people were distrustful of 'vested interests' and many were particularly critical of business, industry and government.

Overall, public perceptions of hydrogen were broadly neutral, but were also highly conditional and context-driven. Most importantly, people expected to be able to see practical demonstrations of the technologies in use, and also wanted greater knowledge about the wider socio-technical system which might emerge. They were unable and unwilling to voice positive or negative opinions until they received much more information, and, in particular, wished to be shown how hydrogen would materially benefit them as individuals as well as bringing environmental benefits.

Hydrogen and transport infrastructures

In the Department for Transport project there were 12 focus groups; here, only a highly selective and condensed summary of findings can be given (see Bellaby and Upham et al, 2007). In all of the groups there was little awareness of hydrogen energy, but considerable interest in being provided with detailed information about its future uses. After being shown a DVD and given other information, participants stressed that they needed to know how it might connect with their own daily routines and lifestyles. They also asked questions about how hydrogen compared with existing energy carriers and what its overall costs and benefits might be. Importantly, there was consistent opposition to using fossil fuels and nuclear power to generate hydrogen. Attitudes towards renewable energy sources were more favourable; while some supported wind power (subject to aesthetic and noise conditions) many were unaware of the possibility of biomass for hydrogen, and had varied opinions about it. People talked about the difficulty of imagining a large-scale infrastructure for the production, distribution and storage of hydrogen. They also identified the complexity of the safety and regulatory aspects of such a new system as problematic. Many asked questions about the relative costs and efficiency of hydrogen as compared with other energy sources and carriers. But across the groups generally, there was also widespread support for the view that the public would accept a new infrastructure if the benefits were demonstrated.

While safety concerns did not result in extensive or serious opposition to hydrogen, many participants (in all groups) raised questions about potential hazards. As one woman in Norwich said:

> *'I suppose what I'm asking is, in terms of the risk assessment of the sort of accident that's likely to occur – say, the turning over of a container – is the risk of harm more than we're used to, or less than we're used to?'*

People wanted to know how hydrogen would be handled, and how their own behaviour (e.g. in using cars) might have to change. Many people were unable or unwilling to express definite opinions about the possible configurations of hydrogen infrastructure and a possible 'hydrogen economy' without much more information from what they regarded as trustworthy sources. Their views were also conditional on knowing much more about the specific technologies envisaged, and the context in which the infrastructure would be developed. Another woman in Norwich commented:

> *'In order to make a judgement about relative energy sources here, you actually need to have quite a lot of technical information. Or you have to – you either have to do that, or you have to make a much more personal decision about which scientist you trust, and how much.'*

Frequently, participants emphasized that to discuss hydrogen in isolation was unrealistic: they constantly referred to the need to consider hydrogen in relation to our dependence on fossil fuels and doubts about the value of renewable (wind, wave, solar) energy sources. In all the focus groups, people also expressed the view that if there was to be a major transition to hydrogen it would need to be justified in terms of improvements in cost and performance over existing technologies, and would also necessitate large-scale demonstration projects to convince the public of its practicality. A woman in Southampton remarked:

> 'Unless you can actually make a hydrogen car that is going to be some sort of equivalent to the cars we've got today, people aren't going to go en masse and buy these cars.'

Regarding the value of public engagement, there were mixed views. Most people believed it was necessary and important for the public to be informed of potential changes in the energy infrastructure, but many also questioned the nature of the engagement process. There was widespread scepticism about whether public opinion would be influential in decision-making, and how people might know whether it had affected policy.

In summary, what the findings from all these focus groups (from both projects) indicate is that, while knowledge of hydrogen is limited, attitudes are agnostic. People are keen to learn more about hydrogen energy technologies, but reluctant to express explicit approval – or outright rejection – until more information is available about the relative costs, benefits and risks as compared with existing systems. Frequently, participants asked questions about what several of them referred to as 'the bigger picture' and most people found it difficult to comprehend the large-scale and radical changes in the energy system envisaged by proponents of the 'hydrogen economy'. Many also voiced doubts about the impact of public consultation exercises, suggesting that engagement was of little consequence to policy and decisions.

Teesside citizens' panel deliberations

From the two meetings with experts, several themes emerged. First, general awareness of hydrogen and its potential applications was low. People asked detailed questions about how hydrogen compared – especially in terms of efficiency and costs – with other energy sources and energy carriers. They also asked about how accessible these new technologies would be or whether the price would deter people. Secondly, questions were also asked about how hydrogen fuel cell technologies would be maintained and serviced (in a domestic setting), as well as the environmental impact of hydrogen production facilities. Safety surfaced as an issue but it was not overwhelmingly important – although questions were asked about the potential hazards of storing large quantities of gas in refuelling stations, pumping it through pipelines, or transporting it by road tankers. Third, many of the participants favoured obtaining greater familiarity with hydrogen technologies through demonstration projects, although most were actually unaware of some existing local demonstration projects. Fourth, generally positive views were expressed in support of continued research and development, particularly where this was linked with regional economic regeneration and employment opportunities.

When debating the role played by the citizen or consumer in technological innovation, most people believed that usually there was little public input, and that public opinion was often ignored by government and was weak in relation to market forces. Having questioned the experts, panel members debated the difficulties of assimilating technical information and raised the issue of how to deal with conflicting and complex science. Trust became central, but there was no agreement about who might be the most trusted provider of information. Participants nevertheless urged that impartial information must be presented which enabled them to consider different options, and which would identify advantages and disadvantages in an unbiased way. But when asked directly about the significance of public engagement, most people expressed cynical views. Some argued that certain groups would *not* be interested and that others would be unable to become engaged for practical reasons (the time and cost of becoming involved is a deterrent). While welcoming the chance to participate in these citizens' panel meetings, and having the opportunity to meet and discuss matters with experts, most were sceptical about how influential public engagement might be. A few even argued that important policy decisions should be largely left to the experts rather than being subject to public consultation. This group at least seemed to regard the principle of upstream public engagement as attractive but ultimately ineffectual.

Conclusions

Expecting lay people to imagine future technological developments and to make judgements about their desirability and feasibility is always fraught with difficulty. Involving members of the public in upstream engagement about emerging technologies in the energy field is particularly challenging. The case study of hydrogen energy technologies discussed here indicates some of the important constraints on upstream public engagement where the technology is still embryonic or nascent. It is not simply the difficulty of communicating information about the basic science, or conveying differences in scientific opinion about alternative methods of production and storage, or presenting expert risk assessments of safety to an 'uninformed' public which is at issue. Rather, it is about providing citizens with a meaningful and realistic appreciation of the environmental and personal benefits, costs and risks which might result from a transition to a hydrogen economy. This necessarily entails providing a description of alternative scenarios embodying choices and consequences. But this requires a 'whole systems' perspective which is currently absent or unimagined. Asking citizens or consumers to express preferences among vague and uncertain possibilities when so little is known about how the technology will be used operationally in everyday life, let alone about what kind of institutional and regulatory system is required, is unlikely to yield significant improvements in public engagement. Upstream public engagement in an emergent technology like hydrogen does not simply have to address one decision or one policy, but multiple options with different systemic features. Inevitably, then, upstream public engagement will continue to be a contested concept in theory and practice. It may be a democratically valuable endeavour, but its achievement is always likely to be limited and incomplete.

Acknowledgements

The research on which this chapter is based was funded by the EPSRC (UK Engineering and Physical Sciences Research Council) through the UK Sustainable Hydrogen Energy Consortium (UKSHEC: see www.uk-shec.org.uk and www.psi.org.uk/ukshec) and by the UK Department for Transport's Horizons Research Programme (PPRO4/54/2). The views expressed in this chapter are those of the authors alone. We are grateful to all those who participated in the focus groups and to the various agencies who assisted in recruiting the participants.

References

AEA Energy and Environment (2008) *Removing the Economic and Institutional Barriers to a Hydrogen Future*, Report to the Department for Transport, February, www.dft.gov.uk/pgr/scienceresearch/futures/horizons/june08

Abelson, J., Forest, P. G., Eyles, J., Smith, P., Martin, E. and Gauvin, F. P. (2003) 'Deliberations about deliberative methods: Issues in the design and evaluation of public participation processes', *Social Science and Medicine*, vol 57, pp239–251

Barbour, R. and Kitzinger, J. (1999) *Developing Focus Group Research*, Sage, London

Bellaby, P. and Upham. P., with Flynn, R., Dresner, S., Fish, R., Goldring, J., Hughes, N., Ricci, M., Speakman, D. and Tomei, J. (2007) *Public Engagement with Hydrogen Infrastructures in Transport*, Report for the Department for Transport, UK, contract number PPRO4/54/2, wwww.dft.gov.uk/pgr/scienceresearch/futures/horizons/june08

Bickerstaff, K., Simmons, P. and Pidgeon, N. (2008) 'Constructing responsibilities for risk: Negotiating citizen–state relationships', *Environment and Planning A*, vol 40, pp1312–1330

Bloor, M., Frankland, J., Thomas, M. and Ronson, K. (2001) *Focus Groups in Social Research*, Sage, London

Burningham, K., Barnett, J., Carr, A., Clift, R. and Wehrmeyer, W. (2007) 'Industrial constructions of publics and public knowledge: A qualitative investigation of practice in the UK chemicals industry', *Public Understanding of Science*, vol 16, no 1, pp23–43

Chilvers, J. and Burgess, J. (2008) 'Power relations: The politics of risk and procedure in nuclear waste governance', *Environment and Planning A*, vol 40, pp1881–1900

Cornwall, A. (2008) *Democratising Engagement: What the UK Can Learn from International Experience*, April, Demos, London

Doubleday, R. (2007) 'Risky public engagement and reflexivity: Alternative framings of the public dimensions of nanotechnology', *Health, Risk and Society*, vol 9, no 2, pp211–227

Eames, M. and McDowall, W. (2006) *Transitions to a UK Hydrogen Economy*, UKSHEC Social Science Working Paper No.19, Policy Studies Institute, London

Ekins, P. and Hughes, N. (2007) *The Prospects for a Hydrogen Economy*, UKSHEC Social Science Working Paper, Policy Studies Institute, London

European Commission (2006) *Introducing Hydrogen as an Energy Carrier: Safety, Regulatory and Public Acceptance Issues*, Report for the Director-General for Research Sustainable Energy Systems, EUR22002, Luxembourg

Flynn, R., Bellaby, P. and Ricci, M. (2008) 'Environmental citizenship and public attitudes to hydrogen energy technologies', *Environmental Politics*, vol 17, no 5, pp766–783

Flynn, R. (2007) 'Risk and the public acceptance of new technologies', in R. Flynn and P. Bellaby (eds), *Risk and the Public Acceptance of New Technologies*, Palgrave-Macmillan, Basingstoke and New York

Fuhrmann, K. and Bleischwitz, R. (2007) 'Existing acceptance analysis in the field of hydrogen technologies', Work Package 1, Task 1, Deliverable 1.6, College of Europe, *Roads2HyCom* (R2H1007PU), www.roads2hycom/Downloads/Roads2HyCom

Grove-White, R., Macnaghten, P. and Wynne, B. (2000) *Wising Up: The Public and New Technologies*, Centre for the Study of Environmental Change, University of Lancaster, Lancaster

Heinz, B. and Erdmann, G. (2008) 'Dynamic effects on the acceptance of hydrogen technologies: an international comparison', *International Journal of Hydrogen Energy*, vol 33, no 12, pp3004–3008

Horlick-Jones, T., Walls, J., Rowe, G., Pidgeon, N., Poortinga, W., Murdock, G. and O'Riordan, T. (2007a) *The GM Debate: Risk, Politics and Public Engagement*, Routledge, London and New York

Horlick-Jones, T., Rowe, G. and Walls, J. (2007b) 'Citizen engagement processes as information systems: The role of knowledge and the concept of translation quality', *Public Understanding of Science*, vol 16, pp259–278

Irwin, A. (2007) 'Public dialogue and the scientific citizen', in R. Flynn and P. Bellaby (eds) *Risk and the Public Acceptance of New Technologies*, Palgrave-Macmillan, Basingstoke and New York

Irwin, A. and Wynne, B. (1996) 'Introduction', in A. Irwin and B. Wynne (eds) *Misunderstanding Science?*, Cambridge University Press, Cambridge

Leach, M. and Scoones, I. (2005) 'Science and citizenship in a global context', in M. Leach, I. Scoones and B. Wynne (eds) *Science and Citizens: Globalization and the Challenge of Engagement*, Zed Books, London and New York

Leach, M., Scoones, I. and Wynne, B. (2005) 'Introduction', in M. Leach, I. Scoones and B. Wynne (eds) *Science and Citizens: Globalization and the Challenge of Engagement*, Zed Books, London and New York

Lidskog, R. (2008) 'Scientised citizens and democratised science: Re-assessing the expert–lay divide', *Journal of Risk Research*, vol 11, nos 1/2, pp69–86

McDowall, W. and Eames, M. (2006) 'Forecasts, scenarios, backcasts and roadmaps to the hydrogen economy: A review of the hydrogen futures literature', *Energy Policy*, vol 34, pp1236–1250

Mohr, A. (2007) 'Against the stream: Moving public engagement on nanotechnologies upstream', in R. Flynn and P. Bellaby (eds) *Risk and the Public Acceptance of New Technologies*, Palgrave-Macmillan, Basingstoke and New York

Mythen, G. and Walklate, S. (2006) 'Introduction: Thinking beyond the risk society', in G. Mythen and S. Walklate (eds) *Beyond the Risk Society*, Open University Press, Maidenhead, UK

Petts, J. (2004) 'Barriers to participation and deliberation in risk decisions: Evidence from waste management', *Journal of Risk Research*, vol 7, no 2, pp115–133

Petts, J. (2008) 'Public engagement to build trust: False hopes?' *Journal of Risk Research*, vol 11, no 6, pp821–835

Pidgeon, N. and Rogers-Hayden, T. (2007) 'Opening up nanotechnology dialogue with the publics: Risk communication or "upstream engagement"?' *Health, Risk and Society*, vol 9, no 2, pp191–210

Pidgeon, N., Poortinga, W., Rowe, G., Horlick-Jones, T., Walls, J. and O'Riordan, T. (2005) 'Using surveys in public participation processes for risk decision-making: The case of the 2003 British GM Nation', *Risk Analysis*, vol 25, no 2, pp467–479

Pidgeon, N., Kasperson, R. and Slovic, P. (2003) 'Introduction', in N. Pidgeon, R. Kasperson and P. Slovic (eds) *The Social Amplification of Risk*, Cambridge University Press, Cambridge

Pidgeon, N., Simmons, P. and Henwood, K. (2006) 'Risk, environment and technology', in P. Taylor-Gooby and J. Zinn (eds) *Risk in Social Science*, Oxford University Press, Oxford

Renn, O. (1999) 'A model for an analytic-deliberative process in risk management', *Environmental Science and Technology*, vol 33, no 18, pp3049–3055

Renn, O. (2008) *Risk Governance*, Earthscan, London

Ricci, M., Newsholme, G., Bellaby, P. and Flynn, R. (2007a) 'The transition to hydrogen-based energy: Combining technology and risk assessments and lay perspectives', *International Journal of Energy Sector Management*, vol 1, no 1, pp43–50

Ricci, M., Bellaby, P. and Flynn, R. (2007b) 'Stakeholders' and publics' perceptions of hydrogen energy technologies', in R. Flynn and P. Bellaby (eds) *Risk and the Public Acceptance of New Technologies*, Palgrave-Macmillan, Basingstoke and New York

Ricci, M., Flynn, R. and Bellaby, P. (2008) 'What do we know about public perceptions and acceptance of hydrogen? A critical review and new case study evidence', *International Journal of Hydrogen Energy*, vol 33, no 21, pp5868–5880

Rifkin, J. (2002) *The Hydrogen Economy*, Tarcher/Putnam, New York

Roche, M.Y., Mourato, S., Fischedick, M., Pietzner, K. and Viebahn, P. (2009) 'Public attitudes towards and demand for hydrogen and fuel cell vehicles: A review of the evidence and methodological implications', *Energy Policy*: doi:10.1016/j.enpol.2009.03.029

Rowe, G. and Frewer, L. (2004) 'Evaluating public participation exercises: A research agenda', *Science, Technology and Human Values*, vol 29, no 4, pp512–556

Rowe, G. and Frewer, L. (2005) 'A typology of public engagement mechanisms', *Science, Technology and Human Values*, vol 30, no 2, pp251–290

Rowe, G., Marsh, R. and Frewer, L. (2004) 'Evaluation of a deliberative conference', *Science, Technology and Human Values*, vol 29, no 1, pp88–121

Royal Society and Royal Academy of Engineering (2004) *Nanoscience and Nanotechnologies*, The Royal Society, London

Slovic, P. (2000) *The Perception of Risk*, Earthscan Publications, London

Stirling, A. (2005) 'Opening-up or closing down? Analysis, participation and power in the social appraisal of technology', in M. Leach, I. Scoones and B. Wynne, *Science and Citizens: Globalization and the Challenge of Engagement*, Zed Books, London and New York

Taylor-Gooby, P. and Zinn, J. (2006) 'The current significance of risk', in P. Taylor-Gooby and J. Zinn (eds) *Risk and Social Science*, Oxford University Press, Oxford

United Nations (2006) 'The hydrogen economy: a non-technical review', www.uneptie.org/energy/publications/pdfs/Hydro_Econ_final.pdf

Wilsdon, J. and Willis, R. (2004) *See-through Science: Why Public Engagement Needs to Move Upstream*, Demos, London

Wynne, B. (2005) 'Risk as globalizing discourse? Framing subjects and citizens', in M. Leach, I. Scoones and B. Wynne (eds) *Science and Citizens: Globalization and the Challenge of Engagement*, Zed Books, London and New York.

Chapter 18

Public Engagement with Wind–Hydrogen Technology: A Comparative Study

*Fionnguala Sherry-Brennan, Patrick Devine-Wright and
Hannah Devine-Wright*

Introduction

Public engagement with renewable energy technologies (RETs) has received much research focus in recent years given the proliferation of these technologies in compliance with energy policy targets for 20 per cent of all energy produced by 2050 to be from renewable sources (DTI, 2003). As described by Walker et al (Chapter 1, this volume) diverse public and developer expectations and contexts influence all aspects of renewable energy technology development. As one of the less familiar technologies, wind–hydrogen energy technology has been seen as a novel means of providing a non-intermittent, low carbon, renewable energy supply. With intermittent energy provided by wind, any excess is used to convert water into hydrogen which is stored; the hydrogen then being available for use as electricity when the wind stops blowing. However, both wind turbines and hydrogen technology have been associated with controversy, either in relation to siting or uncertainties about the technologies themselves (Ricci et al, 2007). As research on public acceptance and understanding of new technology often revolves around the assessment of attitudes, Devine-Wright (2008) has suggested using social-psychological theory to move beyond this to further our knowledge of the psychological and social process of understanding.

In order to gain a deeper awareness of public engagement with wind–hydrogen technology, social representations theory was used to explore how the public made sense of wind–hydrogen technology. Focusing predominantly on public rather than industry actors from the framework proposed in Chapter 1, the role of the locality, previous knowledge and experience, and the perceived impacts of the technology on the community were highlighted as important considerations for future deployment of wind–hydrogen energy technology. This chapter explores the social representations of wind–hydrogen technology in two different case studies contrasting location, scale of development and developer.

Theoretical Framework

The theory chosen to provide the framework for research was social representations theory (SRT) (Moscovici, 1976/2007). The theory explores the emergence and transformation of knowledge as it passes from the unknown to the familiar. Focused originally on the transformation of scientific knowledge as it becomes integrated into common sense, the theory has since been applied in various research areas (e.g. biotechnology, Wagner et al, 2002; energy, Devine-Wright and Devine-Wright, 2006; health, Joffe and Washer, 2007) as it is able to provide a means of looking at how and why certain knowledge becomes integrated into common sense. The processes of anchoring and objectification are used to describe how previously acquired knowledge and experience is used to anchor something new or unfamiliar, how it meets expectations and anticipations, and how, through objectification, this knowledge becomes concretized as part of the real world. Although a degree of consensuality is often found in representations, their social construction often leads to pluralistic ways of thinking, leading to diverse understandings which may vary in different contexts.

Case Studies

Finding an everyday experience where hydrogen might be salient was reflected by adopting a research strategy in which actual developments were used. With this in mind, a case study approach was adopted using two wind–hydrogen projects at different stages of development (Table 18.1). The first, based in Unst, Shetland, has a generating capacity of 30kW coupled with a 5kW hydrogen fuel cell and has been running since May 2005. This project is called PURE (Promoting Unst's Renewable Energy). The second, a 48MW wind farm, has been proposed for installation in Clyde Muirshiel Regional Park (CMRP), west of Glasgow, Scotland, with a 5MW hydrogen facility intended for installation in a small industrial park three miles from the wind farm in the small town of Kilbirnie. This project is referred to as the Wings Law project after the name of the region in the park intended for development. Although the technologies for both projects are similar, there are essential differences regarding scale, location, type of developer, and connectivity, which distinguish them. The following sections provide descriptive detail about the projects and the places with which they are associated.

Table 18.1 *Case study summaries*

	PURE project	Wings Law
Location	Unst, Shetland	Clyde Muirshiel Regional Park, Scotland
Scale	30kW wind, 5kW hydrogen	48MW wind, 5MW hydrogen
Developer	Community-owned	WHL Ltd
Engagement by the developer	Newsletters, open days, radio interview	Public exhibitions, leaflet, public survey
Local opposition group?	No	Yes

Research Design

Exploring the right-hand side of the framework for understanding public responses to RETs (see Chapter 1, Figure 1.5), a combination of interviews, focus groups and surveys were employed to look at understanding of the project generally and also about hydrogen itself in relation to the local project. Between cases, comparable survey items included level of project support, the perceived impacts of the project, and questions about place, familiarity with place, how they felt about the locality, and how important it was to them. A free association task with the word 'hydrogen', designed to access less-reflexive responses to contrast with the more discursive, reflexive responses from interviews and focus groups, was used to investigate the ways in which the public engaged with the technology. The results of this research are presented below, project by project, under a series of headings arranged around the main thematic areas found in describing how hydrogen and the projects were represented.

The PURE Project

The PURE project is a community-owned project, devised by a local graduate and developed in conjunction with local and regional funding. The project aims to produce electricity for the project offices on the small industrial estate where they are based, as well as electricity from hydrogen being used to help power the offices and a small electric car. The wind turbines and hydrogen facility form an inter-connected, stand-alone system and have no connection with the larger electricity grid through which electricity for the island as a whole is provided.

Local historical background

The island has approximately 600 residents. In the north, close to the village of Haroldswick, was an RAF radar base, Saxa Vord, established in 1940, but closed completely in 2005 following a partial drawdown in 1999, with a concomitant loss of jobs and people from the island. Population figures for Unst from the 2001 census cited 720 compared with estimates of 590 from doctor registration records in 2006, illustrating an 18 per cent decrease in population in five years. Departing RAF personnel and their families left behind fewer people to support local businesses and schools, and an urgent need to find ways and means of supporting the island population and economy. A response to the closure of the base was the creation of the Unst Partnership, whose aim was to promote and regenerate Unst and to provide support for local initiatives such as the PURE project.

Results from the PURE project

Interviews for the PURE project were conducted in May 2005 following the launch of the project (stakeholders $n=4$, public $n=15$) and the survey was carried out in April 2006 ($n=156$). The interview sample comprised eight males and seven females representing members of the general public, and three males and one female representing project stakeholders. The survey sample comprised 50.3 per cent males ($n=81$) and 46 per cent females ($n=74$) with an age range of 81 years and 63.4 per cent ($n=102$) of the sample being aged 41 years or above. At the time of data collection, the estimated population of Unst was 590, therefore, the 156 responses collected represented 26.4 per cent of the population. Compared to the *Shetland in Statistics* data (SINS, 2004) the sample was considered representative of gender but biased in age, with a greater proportion of the sample being aged 61 years or over. This can, in part, be explained by the recent closure of the RAF base and subsequent loss of employment, causing migration of the working population from Unst, leaving behind an ageing population.

Free associations with hydrogen revealed that the most frequent association, made by 38.8 per cent ($n=54$) of the survey sample, was 'science', which included terms such as, 'gas', 'first element in the periodic table', and the compound with which it is commonly associated, 'water' (H_2O). Regarding knowledge of hydrogen more generally, the largest proportion of the sample expressed a low or very low knowledge (57.2 per cent, $n=92$), followed by those who gave a neutral response (28.0 per cent, $n=45$). Other associations made with hydrogen are discussed in the following sections. Support for the project was rated as high or very high by 59.1 per cent ($n=94$), with 24.5 per cent ($n=39$) providing a neutral response.

Energy

The second largest category in the free association task from the survey described associations of 'energy' with hydrogen (9.2 per cent, $n=13$). Although this was the second most frequent association with hydrogen, the difference between the two most common associations, 'science' and 'energy', was noticeably large. All interviewees acknowledged the relationship. Energy associations identified hydrogen as an 'energy source', being able to provide 'unlimited power'. Interviewees engaged with hydrogen through the PURE project, although it was stakeholders, rather than members of the general public (although there were exceptions), who had a well-developed understanding of the role of hydrogen as a storage device within the system:

> *'to ... er ... divide it say in water, you split it up using electrolysis and so it, it requires power to get your hydrogen stored, but once it's stored then you can use it to produce power, so therefore it's really viewed as a storage device ... it's a portable storage device then ... like a battery, but better'* (Stakeholder interview).

Generally, members of the general public had a less technical understanding of storage but were able to discuss hydrogen storage within the context of intermittency:

> *'one of the problems they were having with the windmills was when the wind was low there was no electricity so, and that tends to be when it's cold as well, but because now they've got the hydrogen cell then that actually's the back-up'* (Public interview).

Having hydrogen stored at the site raised some siting issues, namely the location of the gas storage cylinders and proximity to housing at present, and the anticipated future storage location of hydrogen depending on whether or not plans were leaning towards developing a centralized or distributed storage system. The issue of risk relating to hydrogen appeared in both the survey and interviews, e.g. through free associations with hydrogen eliciting 'bomb' (9.2 per cent, $n=13$) and 'danger' connections, although danger in particular was mentioned by a very small proportion (1.4 per cent, $n=2$). For the interviewees, the risk posed by hydrogen was, however, considered minimal, due to the small scale of the project and levels of trust in PURE project staff:

> *'the only place you're going to get hydrogen is up at the PURE site and the way that everything's been thought out and the safety procedures that they have erm (–) you know are (–) very good, much better than I expected'* (Public interview).

In the context of energy generation, local production of energy was seen as a sensible option:

> *'there would be good reasons for it happening here first because this is probably the most expensive electricity that's generated anywhere in the country'* (Public interview).

Local fuel supplies were seen as advantageous, not only in the hope of bringing electricity prices down, but also in the broader sense of energy diversification and ensuring a secure energy flow in the face of dwindling fossil fuel supplies. Energy security and diversity were seen not only to be important in the provision of electricity but also in terms of community sustainability.

Community sustainability

The idea of wind–hydrogen energy embedded in the notion of the PURE project drew on two community sustainability issues; firstly, expectations of a secure energy supply and, secondly, anticipating community preservation through providing employment. The local generation of electricity was tightly linked with the economics of the community, self-sufficiency, and the context of Shetland more broadly:

> '*well we have for sale half a terawatt … we have a surplus here because of what we've done … now if you want that you can put the cable in and you can pay us at the going rate for this … in the meantime we can use this power for agriculture, we can use it to power vehicles, we can use it to run our lives completely, we can have satellite broadband for free for everybody, you know, it's the new oil industry*' (Public interview).

Anchoring wind–hydrogen energy to the oil industry illustrates the connection with Shetland's history where, through canny negotiation, Shetland benefited greatly from North Sea oil developments. Historical framings such as this were also seen in relation to other industries, e.g. fishing, where the 'boom and bust' era still resonated, influencing how new developments were seen as driving necessary change while integrating with existing ways of life to sustain the community.

Engagement with the project through its capacity to provide employment was therefore essential in this case. The recent history of Unst has seen people between the ages of 20 and 40 years leaving the island, leaving a noticeable gap in the population age distribution; therefore the opportunity to provide jobs matching people's abilities was seen as a real boon for the project:

> '*the fact that we have young graduates on the island already working … but the possibility it may be sustained and encourage others, local graduates, to see something that is challenging and innovative on the island that's worth their while to come back for*' (Public interview).

The perceived impacts of the project at the personal and island levels were evaluated by survey respondents. Personal impacts were seen as mostly neutral (36 per cent, $n=58$), with 28 per cent ($n=45$) giving a 'very positive' response. Impacts at the island level were regarded more positively, with 48.4 per cent ($n=78$) responding with 'very positive'. Across personal and island levels, the mean impact score was highest at the island level, which was interpreted as meaning that the strongest impacts of the project were expected to affect the island rather than the individual; a result which resonates with the emphasis placed on community sustainability and the potential for enhanced energy security and employment.

People and place

Nearly half the survey sample cited their origin as Unst (46.6 per cent, $n=75$), followed by residents originally from England (15.5 per cent, $n=25$) and other parts of Shetland (14.9 per cent, $n=24$); all were currently resident in Unst. In questions asking participants to rate various places in order of importance to them, the highest rating was for Unst (mean=4.84 from a 5-point rating scale) followed by Shetland mainland (mean=3.61). High scores for Unst were taken as suggesting that most respondents identified themselves predominantly with Unst, and Shetland in a wider geographical context. The importance of place, both generally and specifically relating to the project, was essential in understanding how the public engaged with the project.

Unst, being the most northerly place in Britain, is, amongst other things, a windy place. With hydrogen being objectified through the PURE project and electricity generated using renewable energy, wind was identified as an essential characteristic of the location, making it ideal for this type of energy generation. The weather on Unst, being very distinctive and familiar to all interview partici-pants, was seen as an effective local resource which the PURE project was able to use and which was expected to be developed in the future. The wind was seen very much as a part of the place, admired and respected by the inhabitants:

> '*there is an incredible incredible grandeur and magnificence about a fearful gale you know and the sea and everything, you'd just be about blown off your feet … er, you know, almost a feeling of being out of control, well it is, you can't do anything to control it so almost a sense of place within creation*' (Public interview).

Use of the wind as a local resource was objectified by two highly visible features of the PURE project, the wind turbines, and anchored in the historical use of windmills for energy generation:

> '*when I was a boy, 'bout '46, we produced electricity for our own home here with a windmill … the batteries were past their best with the result that you had a good light when it was a flying gale o' wind … it was before we got power at all*' (Public interview).

Historically, a degree of self-sufficiency was necessary, for energy and food, and in order to maintain the local economy. The characteristic independence of Shetlanders, as noted in the literature (Withrington, 1983), and by interviewees, 'we've got the "why not Unst" mentality you know, it's going to happen somewhere, well why not Unst?' (Public interview), reflected a widely held view that Unst was a place where anything can, and will, happen:

> '*what we've done is we've shown what can be done on a shoe-string … and so it's doable, it is clean and green, it does provide secure energy, and it does diversify the energy mix*' (Stakeholder interview).

This distinctive mentality was not only considered to be driving change, but also the source of great pride in the project itself and in those involved in its establishment.

The Wings Law Project

In contrast to the PURE project, Wings Law was developed and proposed by an Australian developer as a large-scale development (48 2MW wind turbines) in a local regional park. The hydrogen balancing facility was proposed for a site run by Scottish Enterprise in Glengarnock Industrial Estate, near Kilbirnie, approximately three miles from the wind turbines. The wind turbines and hydrogen facility were anticipated as being connected via the National Grid. The Wings Law proposal followed an initial proposal by the developer for 125 turbines (the Ladymoor project), which was rejected by the local authorities. Following rejection, the Wings Law proposal was submitted in July 2007, with the hydrogen proposal being submitted in July 2008. A well-organized opposition group exists to raise awareness of wind farm developments in the regional park and to petition against any proposals.

Local historical background

Clyde Muirshiel Regional Park (CMRP) covers an area of 108sq.miles and is located approximately 30 minutes west of Glasgow by train or car. The park was opened as a country park in 1970 and recognized as a regional park in 1990. The aims of the park are to conserve biodiversity, provide a site for leisure and recreation, and to 'promote and foster environmentally sustainable development for the social and economic well-being of the people and communities within the Clyde Muirshiel Park area' (Woodward, 2007, p6). A large area of the park has been designated a site of special scientific interest (SSSI) and is being considered as a special protection area (SPA) despite, at a larger scale, receiving no general special protection status in the same way that national parks do in Scotland. The park itself is widely used, not only by the residents of local communities but also by residents from the nearby city of Glasgow and tourists from elsewhere, with visitor numbers estimated at 1.5 million each year. Although the park authority is opposed to wind farm developments, turbines have been built at two separate sites: Haupland Moor, Ardrossan, where there are three turbines within the park boundary; and at Wardlaw Wood, where there are six turbines in the park. Despite ongoing rejection of wind farm proposals in CMRP by the park authority and the local councils, developers continue to submit proposals for the development of wind farms in the regional park.

Results from the Wings Law project

A total of 178 individuals took part in the research; 5 stakeholder interviews were conducted (developer, opposition group, local authority, regional park manager, community council (×2)), and focus groups with a total of 33 residents from Kilbirnie and Lochwinnoch. Interviews with project stakeholders for Wings Law were conducted between September 2008 and March 2009 ($n=6$), focus groups in September–October 2008 ($n=30$), and the survey between October 2008 and January 2009 ($n=142$). The total number of responses from the survey was 145

(44.8 per cent male, 51.7 per cent female). The nationalities of the survey sample were predominantly Scottish (83 per cent, *n*=112), with Kilbirnie being the place of permanent residence for 99.3 per cent (*n*=136), and 89.9 per cent (*n*=125) having lived there for over five years.

The most frequent associations with hydrogen were similar to the PURE project and most commonly related to 'science' (42.5 per cent, *n*=54), 'energy' (10.2 per cent, *n*=13), with associations including 'bomb' (8.7 per cent, *n*=11), 'dangerous' (7.9 per cent, *n*=10), and 'don't know' (7.9 per cent, *n*=10): 64.5 per cent (*n*=91) were either somewhat or extremely familiar with the project and, in contrast to the PURE project, 49.7 per cent (*n*=67) disagreed or strongly disagreed with the statement 'I support the Wings Law project'. Both focus group and survey participants supported renewable energy generally (51.2 per cent, *n*=62, agreed or strongly agreed with the statement that renewable energy had their full support) but nevertheless felt negatively towards the Wings Law project. Engagement with the project in this context was found to revolve around perceptions of the developer and the relationships between place, people and environment.

Developer expectations

The project developer, an Australian company, was not generally held in high esteem by the survey respondents, with 65.4 per cent (*n*=87) not trusting the developer at all, an opinion mirrored by focus group participants:

> *'I think you've got to have 100 per cent trust, and that's one of the reasons I put down, that what the company were saying was … they're being rather economical with the truth. To me, if you find out they're telling lies, you can't believe anything then'* (Kilbirnie focus group).

An information leaflet distributed by the developer prior to submitting a proposal may have influenced these perceptions, as it was found by the advertising standards authority to be misleading on several counts (ASA, 2008). Despite several public meetings and an amendment to the original proposition which saw a substantial decrease in the number of turbines being proposed, of those who were familiar with the project, 53.9 per cent (*n*=48) believed that the developer hadn't acted fairly in engaging with local people or listened to what local people had to say (65.5 per cent, *n*=57). A particular point of contention was the claim made by the developer that it would be able to provide work for local residents. Ordinarily, the prospect of work in an area with high levels of unemployment, such as in Kilbirnie, would be welcomed. However, recent history coloured thinking on this issue:

> *'It's as if they think that they come in here and it's as if the minute that they say, oh, we're going to give you local work, it's as if we should all stand and give them a round of applause, because they mention employ-ment, you know? And, I think the local population, we were just*

> *discussing the projects that have come and gone over the years in Kilbirnie, they come and take a subsidy, they disappear, unemployment doesn't go down, it's actually starting to wear a bit thin in the local population'* (Kilbirnie focus group).

Despite reducing the proposal to 24 turbines following consultation, the developer was not seen to be in a position of trust:

> M1: *'But certainly they've dropped down. I mean, to come from 125 down to …'*
>
> F1: *'Twenty-four, that's just to get started.'*
>
> F2: *'That's to get their foot in the door. That's like trying to sell something. You always ask for more and if somebody offers you less, you go, all right, fair enough; you walk away thinking you've got a bargain, you've not'* (Kilbirnie focus group).

'Getting a foot in the door' described how participants believed there to be an underlying agenda for wind farm development in the park, as the proposal was one of several currently under review. If every proposal was accepted, the cumulative effect would be a substantial area of the regional park populated with turbines (Figure 18.1). The following section explores the meaning of the park and its environment, and the implications of this for public engagement with, and subsequent rejection of, the Wings Law project.

Place and environment

The survey, carried out in Kilbirnie, a small town on the periphery of the regional park, showed levels of place attachment to be high, with 70.9 per cent (*n*=102) agreeing that they felt attached to Kilbirnie. Strong place attachment to both the locality and regional park area was also demonstrated in the focus groups, as the impacts of the project were considered detrimental to both. Furthermore, the negative impact of wind farms was discussed at different levels, for example, nationally, 'We want to keep it bonny Scotland' (Kilbirnie focus group); at the local, village level, 'They're going to destroy village life' (Lochwinnoch focus group); and at both regional and national levels:

> *'you look up, it was a beautiful night, it was silhouetted, the hills, and the sky was that greenish blue. I'm going – what if I looked at that and it was full of wind farms, wind turbines – horrifying. I mean they're actually destroying this country'* (Kilbirnie focus group).

Locally, the two villages of Kilbirnie and Lochwinnoch have contrasting characters. The former is a run-down town with a tight-knit community and a large number of take-aways; the latter is a picturesque conservation village attracting tourists. Both were considered good places to live, but participants expressed

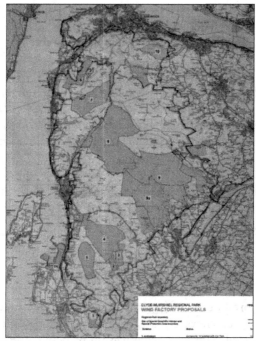

Figure 18.1 *Wind farm development proposals for Clyde Muirshiel Regional Park: shaded areas show affected areas*

Source: courtesy of Save Your Regional Park

concern that they would be negatively affected during any wind farm construction and, once the wind farm was built, for Lochwinnoch especially, visitor numbers would be adversely affected as the village became a less attractive place to visit.

The regional park itself, being visible and easy to access from both villages, was considered as a place for recreation, where the environment was – and needed to be – protected and, emphatically, not a place for 'industrial' development.

> *'I've roamed the hills for my whole life, it's beautiful, and then they're talking about putting roads up, no-go areas, that as well, you know, for operational purposes – I mean they can shut it off any time they want … you've got hen harriers, you've got black grouse and there's only two or three reportings of black grouse in the whole of Scotland, and one of them is in Muirshiel Park … and then they're just going to destroy their habitat as well as the enjoyment of the local people'* (Kilbirnie focus group).

With 66.9 per cent (*n*=89) of survey respondents considering the endangerment of local wildlife to be somewhat or extremely likely, further concerns over the visual impact of the turbines and disruption to the peat bog landscape contributed to the way that the project was understood as having a negative impact on local villages and as causing environmental damage to the regional park.

Despite relatively consensual levels of support from the sample for renewable energy and wind energy, a contradictory belief that the technology was inappropriate for the place and the lack of debate about renewable energy generally was also expressed:

> *'I don't think there's an agreed national strategy. I don't think we've had a really informed debate about the issues at all … no one's actually taken the bigger debate saying, well, you know, what are all the alternatives, what are the pluses and minuses for them and what's a sensible way forward?'* (Lochwinnoch focus group).

Strong place attachment, fear about damaging the park environment and concerns over the wider energy debate all contributed to negative public engagement with the Wings Law energy project.

Concluding Remarks

This research explored public engagement with wind–hydrogen technology in different contexts. Interviews, focus groups and surveys were used to reveal diverse and consensual aspects of what was, in principle, the same technology. An innovative aspect of this research was the application of social-psychological theory to the energy technology arena, moving beyond attitudes to looking at public understanding and acceptance of new technologies. The findings illustrated a range of concepts, some similar across cases, guiding the representation. For example, drawing on representations of place, each case identified why certain aspects of the locality were important to them and how this subsequently orientated their evaluation of the project. In the Wings Law case, the site of the proposed wind farm needed to be protected from industrialization; for the PURE project, the place was anticipated to benefit from the project through employment. In Unst, those directly involved with the project were trusted with its safe running, beneficial returns, and future prospects, whereas the developer in Wings Law did not benefit from such a positive appraisal. Developing technology which is seen to be congruous with a place can be seen as essential in the future development and deployment of wind–hydrogen energy. Going beyond the data, a corollary of the findings, which show that the smaller-scale, community-focused development had greater support, a more recent incongruous development has been demonstrated in Shetland. Here, a proposal for Europe's largest onshore wind farm (540MW) on Shetland mainland has met with widespread opposition, where residents have stated that they 'did not want to live on an offshore wind farm called "Shetland"' (Marter, 2009). It is interesting to consider whether or not a smaller, community-led project in Wings Law may have met with greater support, paying heed to the argument by Devine-Wright (2005) that a locally embedded approach to renewable energy developments may be beneficial.

Interestingly, the importance of understanding the energy generation process and each project's contribution to mitigating climate change was found to be of little importance in both cases, yet the government continues to promote the 20 per cent by 2050 idea, which has little resonance with residents experiencing local project development. More specifically, knowledge of hydrogen in this technology configuration was not found to be essential for engagement. The salience of hydrogen, in particular, varied between cases where greater engagement with hydrogen and the project was seen in Unst whereas, in contrast, hydrogen was secondary to the wind farm in Wings Law, and was communicated through the same language of scepticism and doubt over the truthfulness of claims made by the developer. In Wings Law, the same lens of interpretation concerning the wind farm and the developer was applied to engagement with the hydrogen technology. Greater familiarity with wind farm development influenced thinking about hydrogen and the project as a whole, preventing communication about any possible risk aspects of hydrogen coming to the fore. In essence, future successful development and deployment of renewable energy technology is likely to require place-specific engagement and a willingness to explore the extensive arenas of knowledge used by the public to engage with the technology in question.

Acknowledgements

We would like to thank the EPSRC for support via the FlexNet project (EP/EO4011X/1) and the ESRC for support through the Beyond Nimbyism project (RES-152-25-1008), enabling both data sets to be collected.

References

ASA (2008) *ASA Adjudications:Wind Hydrogen Ltd*, www.asa.org.uk/asa/adjudications/Public/TF_ADJ_44494.htm
Devine-Wright, P. (2008) 'Reconsidering public acceptance of renewable energy technologies: A critical review', in M. Grubb, T. Jamasb and M. Pollitt (eds) *Delivering a Low Carbon Electricity System: Technologies, Economics and Policy*, Cambridge University Press, Cambridge, pp443–461
Devine-Wright, P. (2005) 'Beyond NIMBYism: Towards an integrated framework for understanding public perceptions of wind energy.' *Wind Energy*, vol 8, no 2, pp125–139.
Devine-Wright, P. and Devine-Wright, H. (2006) 'Social representations of intermittency and the shaping of public support for wind energy in the UK', *International Journal of Global Energy Issues*, vol 25, no 3/4, pp243–256
DTI (2003) Energy White Paper. Our Energy Future – Creating a Low-carbon Economy, London
Joffe, H. and Washer, P. (2007) 'Public engagement with MRSA: Full research report', in *ESRC End of Award Report*, ESRC, Swindon, UK
Marter, H. J. (2009) 'A clear NO to Viking Energy', *Shetland News*, 29 September

Moscovici, S. (1976/2007) *La psychanalyse son image et son public (Psychoanalysis: Its Image and Its Public)*, Presses Universitaires de France, Paris/Polity Press, London

Ricci, M., Flynn, R. and Bellaby, P. (2007) 'Understanding the public acceptability of hydrogen energy: Key findings from focus groups in Teesside, SW Wales and London (October–November 2006)', UKSHEC Public Acceptability Work Package: social science working paper no 33

SINS (2004) *Shetland in Statistics*, Shetland Islands Council, Economic Development Unit, Lerwick, Shetland

Wagner, W., Kronberger, N. and Seifert, F. (2002) 'Collective symbolic coping with new technology: Knowledge, images and public discourse', *British Journal of Social Psychology*, vol 41, no 3, pp323–343

Withrington, D. J. (1983) *Shetland and the Outside World: 1469–1969*, Aberdeen University Study Series, Aberdeen

Woodward, C. (2007) *Clyde Muirshiel Park Authority: Park Strategy 2008–2011*, Clyde Muirshiel Park Authority

Chapter 19

Symbolic Interpretations of Wave Energy in the UK: Surfers' Perspectives

Carly McLachlan

Introduction

Under the Climate Change Act (2008), the UK has committed to reducing greenhouse gas emissions by at least 80 per cent by 2050, and CO_2 emissions by at least 26 per cent by 2020, based on a 1990 baseline. The deployment of renewable energy is seen as an integral part of achieving these targets. In July 2009, the Department for Energy and Climate Change published the UK Renewable Energy Strategy (RES), which proposes that over 30 per cent of electricity should come from renewable sources by 2020. Currently the figure is approximately 5.5 per cent, consisting mostly of biomass, hydro and wind. While wave energy is not expected to be a key contributor to these targets by 2020, it is seen as requiring strategic investment in order to develop its longer-term potential (DECC, 2009).

There are no commercial offshore wave energy developments yet operational in the UK. In 2008, three Pelamis devices were deployed near Aguçadoura in northern Portugal, and the development was billed as the 'world's first wave farm'. However, technical issues led to the devices being removed from the water, and although Pelamis Wave Power state that these problems have been resolved, there is currently no timetable for their redeployment (Blum, 2009).

This chapter considers the case of Wave Hub, Cornwall, UK. The focus is upon the response of surfers to the development and the various ways in which it was symbolically interpreted. However, the perspectives of other stakeholders are discussed in order to demonstrate areas of agreement and difference as well as the variety of symbolic meaning which can be associated with a renewable energy development. Surfers represent just one of the stakeholder groups in this case (for a fuller account of other stakeholders' symbolic interpretations, see McLachlan, 2009). While some actors portrayed the concerns of surfers as selfish or irrelevant, given the 'importance' of the project, they have been documented here for two reasons. Firstly, the interpretations did not relate only to surfing, and so may offer an early indication of the types of issues that could be raised as more marine energy developments are proposed and wider publics become engaged in discussions about their desirability. Secondly, as pointed out by Walker (1995), if the interests of certain groups are widely seen to be excluded in development decisions, then a sense of unfairness can lead to the issues being taken up by wider communities.

A number of studies of wind energy developments have identified that turbines can be seen to have a variety of meanings. For example, turbines have been seen to represent 'stewardship', 'ugly technology', 'responsible energy policy', 'destroying landscape', 'progress' and 'harking back to the past' (Thayer and Freeman, 1987; Thayer and Hansen, 1988; Lee et al, 1989; Gipe, 1993). Such studies identify that there can be a wide range of different symbolic meanings attributed to a development. However, the studies have tended to use surveys to gather symbolic interpretations. This approach may result in some of the symbolic meanings that people hold being overlooked, or indeed may prompt them to select a symbolic meaning that they had not considered before taking part in the survey. It has also been discovered that the location in which a development is proposed can be interpreted differently by stakeholders, even when a broad categorization such as 'rural' is agreed upon (Woods, 2003). Pasqualetti (2000) and Brittan (2001) discuss the importance of the interaction between interpretations of place and technology through discussion of whether turbines 'fit' in certain landscapes. However, such notions of fit have tended to lead to the provision of design 'rules' (e.g. size, colour, rest position) rather than further study of the reasoning behind assessments of congruence.

The Wave Hub case demonstrates that responses to renewable energy developments are, in part, related to interpretations of what both the technology and the location or 'place' are seen to represent or symbolize. The term 'symbolism' is used here to refer to the more abstract meanings that are associated with the physical or concrete characteristics of the developments or locations themselves. It refers to that which may not be observable, or agreed upon by all, but which has an effect on the responses that some stakeholders have towards the development. In particular, the interest here is in the multiple and potentially conflicting symbolic interpretations of both place and technology, and how these can explain differing assessments of why the development does or does not 'fit' in a particular location.

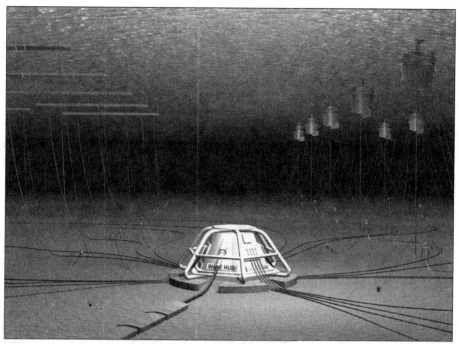

Figure 19.1 *Artist's impression of the Wave Hub*

Source: Industrial Art Studio: www.ind-art.co.uk

Wave Hub, Cornwall, UK

The Wave Hub project is funded by the South West Regional Development Agency (SWRDA), and is envisaged as a final pre-commercial facility. The UK is already home to the European Marine Energy Centre (EMEC) and the New and Renewable Energy Centre (NaREC), which can be used to test full-scale single wave devices and scale models, respectively. The Wave Hub would add to this testing capacity by allowing developers to operate arrays of full-scale devices in real sea conditions. The development is presented as a way of reducing risk and complexity for device developers, as consent, cabling and connection will already be in place. Up to four arrays of wave energy converters can then 'plug in' to the hub on the seabed, allowing the electricity that they produce to be brought onshore to an electricity substation connected to the National Grid. The project gained consent in September 2007, and is expected to be operational in 2011. Figure 19.1 shows an artist's impression of the Wave Hub.

Key Areas of Controversy and Sources

Whereas navigational and fishing stakeholders raised concerns about the siting of the development and the process of consultation (Joint Maritime Stakeholders,

2007), the objections of some surfers gained the most media attention. Perhaps the most high-profile coverage was an article in the *Sunday Times* entitled 'Get off our waves, surfers tell greens' (Booth, 2006). Concerns raised by surfers related to the impact on the height and quality of waves in the area. Although the developer sought representation of surfers through inviting Surfers Against Sewage and the British Surfing Association to take part in the stakeholder consultation process, many actors concerned about surfing accessed the debate through public channels (e.g. submitting written objections to the relevant planning bodies).

The notion of surfing as an important part of the Cornish economy was not contested by any of the actors, and the principle of there being a need to assess the potential impact on surfing was widely accepted. Three studies were conducted assessing the impact that the Wave Hub would have on local surf. Halcrow were commissioned by SWRDA to conduct a study as part of the Environmental Statement, academics at the University of Exeter undertook their own study and, following controversy over these two studies, SWRDA commissioned ASR Ltd to conduct an assessment of the previous studies which also included a new analysis of the impacts. The 'possible' impacts calculated in the studies ranged from a 0.31 per cent reduction in wave height to an 85 per cent reduction. The figures presented as 'likely' outcomes ranged from 0.31 per cent to 6 per cent. The 'potential' impacts discussed by surfers ranged across these reported levels. The findings of each of the studies were disputed among the project actors, with divergent assessments generally based on different views of: how best to represent a surfing wave; assumptions on how the devices would behave; the acceptability of making decisions based on modelled impacts rather than real data; and related concerns that the impacts of such an experimental facility were inherently 'unknowable'.

Support for the development came from local energy and environmental stakeholders, including Surfers Against Sewage. They were involved in the official stakeholder consultation process and aimed to give the developer-led impact assessment a 'surfers' perspective'. They argued that even the worst-case scenario impact of up to 13 per cent calculated in the study was acceptable given the climate change goals of the project and the 'more likely' impact of around 5 per cent. They stressed the potential impact of climate change on surfers, in particular increasing sewer overflows (Surfers Against Sewage, 2007a). They actively supported the development, organizing public relations activities (including a 'Mexican Wave of Support') and issuing supportive position statements. One, fairly novel, element of this case was the creation of internet discussion forums hosted on surfing websites which, at times, hosted direct discussions between supporters and objectors. One stakeholder, who runs a surf forecasting website, collected approximately 500 letters (emails) of objection and forwarded them to BERR (Department for Business, Enterprise and Regulatory Reform, which was disbanded in June 2009). Quotes from these emails are used throughout this chapter. The use of websites and forums to publicize concerns over the Wave Hub mobilized a wider 'community of interest' rather than communities of locality only (Walker et al, 2007). Objections to the proposal came from across the UK and those of surfers were reported internationally.

The case study was scoped using secondary sources such as the national press, internet forums, trade press, official stakeholder statements, the developer's website, planning documents and the collated emails mentioned above. These different sources were used to build up a picture of the development and to identify the key actors and areas of controversy. Semi-structured in-depth interviews with a range of key actors were then conducted. The quotes in this chapter come from across this range of sources. It should be noted that the interviewees were not at any time asked specifically about what the development 'symbolized'; instead, symbolic references were identified from analysis of general discussion of the development in transcripts and secondary data. Interviews were conducted in summer/autumn 2007.

Place

Place is defined by Cresswell (2004), as a location with *meaning*. Such meaning can be attributed at vastly different scales (from an armchair to the entire earth) and may be closely linked to notions of identity and sense of *belonging* (Tuan, 1977; Cresswell, 2004). It is unsurprising, therefore, that strong reactions may be encountered when something (e.g. a renewable energy development) is seen to threaten what that place means (Devine-Wright, 2009). Although wind farm controversy work has focused on landscape (with developments often being referred to by opponents as a 'blot' on a treasured landscape), Cresswell explains landscape as an intensely visual concept. He argues that *landscapes* are generally defined as something that the viewer is outside of; in contrast, *places* are something to be inside of and connected with.

The plurality of meanings given to a place affected by a development may be obscured at times by dominant or official assessments of what the 'place' is. However, these taken for granted or institutional assessments may in fact demonstrate a partial, selective use of certain aspects of place. By stressing certain aspects or histories of the location, respondents – both those who support and those who oppose the developments – can create particular images of the place (Hubbard et al, 2004). Drawing on historic images of a place can bolster the validity and credibility of claims to define the essence of that place. Activities that do not fit with this 'essence' are seen as being out of place and therefore unacceptable (Jess and Massey, 1995).

Jess and Massey (1995) also stress the importance of notions of 'ownership' of places. This 'ownership' may not be a legal definition but rather a legacy or moral ownership. A moral sense of common ownership, or indeed a moral sense that the place should not be privately owned, can be a strong factor in actors' sense of what the place *is* and how it should be used or protected. In addition, they call for a more fluid and porous approach to be taken, that sees place as being defined both by what is within it and its connections to the wider world, rather than an exclusionary approach of drawing impenetrable boundaries around places.

Technology Symbolism

Rather than thinking of the impacts that the technologies will have as being an exogenous, technical factor, following a 'science and technology studies' approach, the concern here is the multiple ways in which the technologies and their impacts are experienced and defined by respondents. These responses are born out of particular contexts rather than purely an abstract technology. Irwin (2001, p136) argues that, 'technologies are not simply "given" but are varyingly constructed, experienced, worried over and enjoyed'; it is these various experiences that this chapter explores.

In terms of renewable energy and other technologies justified through environmental protection, 'sustainability' is often presented as being an inherent property of the technology. Terms such as 'renewable', 'sustainable', 'clean' and 'green' may be used interchangeably. However, the 'environmental' status of renewable technologies may not be universally agreed upon, as controversy over the life cycle emissions of wind turbines, the construction costs and environmental impact of tidal energy, and the emissions and traffic movements required for biomass energy developments indicate. As scholars in the field of 'the social shaping of technology' have demonstrated, constellations of policies and institutional arrangements have facilitated the dominance or development of certain technologies, at certain times, in certain places (MacKenzie and Wajcman, 1999). Therefore, in responding to a particular development, stakeholders may be responding to the relationships that the development represents to them. Local opposition to developments may, therefore, be intertwined with concerns over much wider policies (e.g. renewable energy, climate change, urbanization of rural areas, commodification of nature etc.; Owens, 2002).

The concepts of place and technology symbolism are used here to consider the multiple interpretations, both positive and negative, of Wave Hub. By opening up the multiple interpretations of the location and the technology, a fuller understanding of the dimensions of 'fit' or congruency can be developed.

Interpretations of Place in the Wave Hub Case Study

Place is interpreted in numerous ways in the case study, and there is clear evidence of engagement beyond visual amenity. The differing ways in which the place is symbolically interpreted will now be discussed with exemplar quotations.

Boundaries of place

The scale of 'place' that surfers and other actors see as being relevant to assessments of the Wave Hub varies from the site boundary to the whole planet. The official studies of wave height impact were (unsurprisingly) limited to the impact of the Wave Hub development only. However, the studies of economic impact and potential impact on the renewable energy industry in the UK took the Wave Hub as a catalyst for further wave energy locally, nationally and globally (South West RDA, 2005). The development is presented as a way of putting Cornwall, the South West region, and the whole of the UK 'on the map' in terms of renewable energy development.

> *'The Wave Hub isn't about Cornwall and the South West, it is about the whole of the UK and maintaining the leading position the UK has already got'* (SWRDA interview).

Objecting surfers are concerned about the impact of such future developments and believe that this should be taken into account in deciding upon the appropriateness of this first catalytic development. This relates to issues of significance and precedent in the symbolic interpretations of technology which are discussed later.

Economic vulnerability and the importance of surfing

In both interviews and secondary data, Cornwall is generally described as being economically vulnerable. Both objectors and supporters of the project draw upon an image of economic deprivation to define what the place 'is'. In terms of objections, it is argued that the project will affect the surf and the image of surfing in the region, which will in turn affect tourism (seen as a major and vital industry in the area).

> *'Cornwall is already one of the most economically weak counties in the UK and relies on the surfing industry more than most realize. Anything that damages the regular swell would destroy this huge national and international income'* (Email objection, p3).

Alternatively the economic vulnerability of the area is used as a way of justifying what is presented as a small, insignificant or acceptable impact on the surf, to attract a much needed 'sustainable' industry to the area.

> *'[Cornwall has] the lowest wages in the country, high unemployment, very little sort of indigenous industries [...] SWRDA [are] taking a very [...] pragmatic approach and saying, "well this industry could actually employ, sustainably, a lot of people and also give us the renewable power that we want"'* (Device developer interview).

Some argue that it is any perception of impact rather than the 'actual' level that is important (as in the quote below). This links to a strong sense expressed by a range of actors that surfing is an integral part of Cornwall's identity; therefore, to affect the image of surfing in Cornwall is to affect what Cornwall is.

> *'To what extent this project will affect the quality of the surf is not the biggest issue. It is the perceived image of Cornwall as a prime surfing destination that worries us. Surfers will avoid the areas concerned and*

> *focus their travel/visits to areas not affected. It will surely push people to*
> *go elsewhere, even abroad'* (Email objection, p236).

Ownership

> *'The hub's pinching something up to 35 per cent of the waves' energy'*
> (Email objection, p23).

As identified by Jess and Massey (1995) the notion of ownership is invoked in symbolic and moral ways rather than a legal sense. Many of the objections raised relate to a sense of who owns the waves. There are many references to the oceans and waves being 'God-given' and that they are everyone's to enjoy. The developer is therefore often accused of 'stealing' the waves in the emails and letters from surfers (as in the quote above).

The development is seen by some supporters as locals 'doing their bit' for climate change or energy production. In contrast to the issues over the ownership of the waves and the sea, here a sense of ownership is used by some actors to attempt to mobilize support for the development – a sense of wanting to show what our place has achieved and stands for.

The place as a resource or as nature?

> *'The reality is that in future you are going to have to get as much as you*
> *can out of a sea area. If you have got one square mile you can't just spread*
> *out right across because of the competing interests'* (SWRDA interview).

Although the 'natural' or 'nature' status of the place is widely accepted, the interpretation of this differs. Some present it as a natural resource that should be used with maximum efficiency following a more instrumental understanding of value. For example, in the quote above, the developer explains that the sea is a congested resource that must be used efficiently. Alternatively, rather than seeing the sea as a 'natural resource', it is also presented as being in need of protection due to its intrinsic value and fragility to human intervention:

> *'The sea is a delicate world of its own, that has taken millions of years to*
> *get to the balance that it is in now, it should be respected and admired, not*
> *used to try to cover up what we've done on land'* (Email objection,
> p120).

The place in which the development will be deployed is interpreted in numerous ways, both within the surfing community and by other actors in the development. In line with the discussion of the concept of place, notions of moral ownership, different definitions of the boundaries of place, and the stressing of certain aspects (e.g. the already congested nature of the resource), all lead to different assessments of the desirability of the development in this particular context. In addition, the emotive links with place, while explaining some opposition to the development, also engender support due to a sense of wanting to show what 'our place' stands for.

Technology Symbolism in the Wave Hub Case Study

In addition to the multiple interpretations of place, wave energy technology was also interpreted in very different ways. It should be noted that the Wave Hub itself is not a wave energy device: although a range of wave energy devices will connect to it. Stakeholders talked about the Wave Hub in an operational sense, i.e. with the devices attached, rather than the hub on its own. While some respondents used certain devices as examples to make their points, particular wave energy devices are not identified as having particular symbolic interpretations; rather it is wave energy in general that is discussed.

Significance and precedent

For some supporters, a belief in the catalytic potential of Wave Hub that increases the sense of its overall significance makes localized impacts more acceptable. This is often justified through reference to the scale of the energy and climate change challenges that are now faced:

> *'Whatever the detrimental effects are, they are a very small price to pay for long-term climate stability'* (Surf magazine editor interview).

However, it is the scale of the energy and climate change challenge that makes some respondents more sceptical about the significance, and therefore desirability, of this particular project. For some stakeholders, the project will not produce enough electricity to justify the impacts. In particular, its 'experimental' status is seen to undermine the significance of electricity output (as in the quote below):

> *'The Wave Hub is likely to deplete wave height and therefore local revenue over a large stretch of coastline which relies heavily on the surf industry in exchange for only 3 per cent of the power requirement of Cornwall. It is not an equal pay-off. It is not enough to make an impact on global warming, or fossil fuel consumption'* (Email objection, p106b).

While some saw future developments as a reason to support this boundary-pushing development, it was exactly these potential future developments that concerned some surfers, as the quote below explains:

> *'If the hub works, great! But will this mean hub after hub being installed along the best surfing coastline in the UK? One may cause little effect, but what about one hundred in a line?'* (Email objection, p17a).

An interesting imbalance can be seen in relation to precedent. Whereas surfers' concerns about the impact of future developments were seen by the developer as being too uncertain to include, the developer's economic impact assessment was based on a specified additional amount of installed wave energy capacity in the region (South West RDA, 2005). Clearly such different conceptions of the scale and significance of the development relate to the different interpretations of the relevant boundaries of the affected place discussed earlier.

Commercial project or symbolic ownership

For some surfers, the project is seen very much as a local project for the people of Cornwall. References to the number of local households that could be supplied by the development, and claims that the development will show what Cornwall stands for, use attachment to place to develop a symbolic ownership of the project/technology itself. This can be seen in the quote below from Surfers Against Sewage. They are looking forward to using the waves they have been using for surfing to light their homes. This position makes no reference to the fact that local people will still be supplied by the same energy company and will be required to pay for the electricity that they use. By omitting this from the image of local natural resources being used for local energy generation, they increase the project's inclusivity and sense of symbolic local ownership:

> 'We look forward to using the same energy we've used to ride waves to light up our homes as well' (Surfers Against Sewage, 2007b).

Alternatively the development is seen as a purely commercial venture motivated solely by profit. The quote below demonstrates such sentiments:

> 'we're not stupid, and this is ultimately a commercial venture. Its set-up costs are reduced by its proposed location, but its output reduced – once this is built [the development partner has] made its dosh!' (Email objection, p34).

Although community ownership has been investigated as a possible way of improving local support for developments (Devine-Wright, 2005; Rogers et al, 2008), a more symbolic sense of ownership (rather than the direct purchasing of shares etc.) can also be important in developing support in such cases.

Experiment or pioneering

As noted in relation to significance, the technology is seen by many stakeholders as being 'experimental'. Again this 'experimental' status is interpreted both positively and negatively by different stakeholders. On the one hand, the project is seen being pioneering and pushing at the boundaries of solutions for climate change and energy security. Being at the forefront of innovation demonstrates the technical competence and potential commercial strength of the wave energy industry in the South West and the UK as a whole. Alternatively the 'experimental' status is seen as evidence that the impacts are unknown and/or unknowable. This results either in calls for more research to be done on the impacts, or for the project to be abandoned as the impacts are thought to be inherently unpredictable:

> 'The impact of large-scale installations, whether "green" or not, is significant and in this case nobody can say for certain what those impacts are' (Email objection, p42).

Benign or industrial?

For some supporters, the Wave Hub and the wave energy devices to be installed fit seamlessly with images of nature and stewardship. Using nature to solve an environmental problem has a certain 'fit', and the term 'benign' is often used in describing wave energy devices (e.g. Pelamis Wave Power, 2007). For Surfers Against Sewage, the development is seen to 'fit' with surfing, as the same waves are used to light 'our' homes and for surfing. There is no new intrusion in this analysis, just an extension of what is already, harmoniously, occurring. Alternatively, the development can be seen as an industrial installation. This symbolic image is created by drawing on industrial terms, such as pistons and pumps, or referring simply to the development as a power station. These terms work to strip the development of its 'green' credentials, associating it instead with a more traditional 'dirty' industrial power station image (as in the quote below):

> 'The proposed power station, to become operational in 2008, will involve anchoring 20 sets of turbines, pistons and pumps' (Booth, 2006).

These different symbolic interpretations indicate that the environmental credentials of a technology are rarely universally accepted. Understanding how respondents are assessing claims to 'greenness' and how trade-offs with other social and environmental goals are made is important in understanding how the desirability of this and other projects are assessed.

Discussion and Conclusions: Symbolic Logics

The multiple interpretations of place and technology offer a number of reasons for assessments of 'fit'. Figure 19.2 illustrates some of the potential logics of opposition and support. This is far from an exhaustive list of combinations and it is also possible that stakeholders' and publics' interpretations of place or technology may include a number of different symbolic elements.

From the analysis of the Wave Hub, it is clear that the symbolic interpretations of both place and technology are multiple and diverse, and give rise to various symbolic logics of opposition and support. The interpretations of place indicate

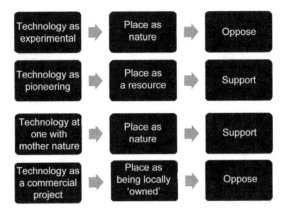

Figure 19.2 *Examples of symbolic logics of opposition and support*

that engagement with location is much broader than a purely visual notion of landscape. The changing nature of UK energy policy, with more decentralization and a focus on renewable energy (DECC, 2009), means that actors that previously had little interaction with energy beyond its delivery through a socket on the wall, may now find that energy is changing what a valued place means and how it is connected to other places. Specific places may now be connected to a much wider network of regional targets, national policies, global agreements and climate change impacts. This wider context is often discussed by respondents, and it is important to consider how these changes to what a place means can result in opposition and support positions being taken.

It is clear that any sense that marine energy will be an opposition-free alternative to wind energy, welcomed by all stakeholders, is misplaced. Wave energy has not in this case been viewed universally positively and, in a similar way to wind energy, green-on-green controversy has occurred, with different actors mobilizing different environmental arguments to bolster their position (Warren et al, 2005). Different wave energy devices were not identified as having particular symbolic interpretations; rather it was wave energy in general that was discussed by stakeholders. Clearly this may come to change as different devices are proposed and installed and their impacts are discussed, compared and monitored.

As more wave energy projects are proposed in the UK and in other countries, developers and planners may wish to engage with the diversity of symbolic meaning with which both the technology and the location can be imbued. Engaging with the range of symbolic interpretations could open up ways of reducing opposition and even developing support through building on positive symbolic associations. Interpretations of wave energy projects may vary significantly depending upon different cultural relationships with the sea and coast, and so should be carefully considered as this global industry develops.

Acknowledgement

This work was funded by the Tyndall Centre for Climate Change Research and the SUPERGEN Bioenergy Consortium.

References

Blum, P. (2009) 'A setback for wave power technology', *International Herald Tribune*, 15 April 2009

Booth, R. (2006) 'Get off our waves, surfers tell greens', *Sunday Times*, 2 July, www.timesonline.co.uk/article/0,,2087-2252557.html

Brittan, G. G. (2001) 'Wind, energy, landscape: Reconciling nature and technology', *Philosophy and Geography*, vol 4, no 2, pp169–184

Cresswell, T. (2004) *Place*, Blackwell Publishing, Oxford

DECC (2009) 'The Renewable Energy Strategy (RES)', Department of Energy and Climate Change, www.decc.gov.uk/en/content/cms/what_we_do/uk_supply/energy_mix/renewable/res/res.aspx

Devine-Wright, P. (2005) 'Local aspects of renewable energy development in the UK: Public beliefs and policy implications', *Local Environment*, vol 10, no 4, pp57–69

Devine-Wright, P. (2009) 'Rethinking NIMBYism: The role of place attachment and place identity in explaining place-protective action', *Journal of Community and Applied Social Psychology*, vol 19, no 6, pp426–441

Gipe, P. (1993) 'The wind industry's experience with aesthetic criticism', *Leonardo*, vol 26, no 3, pp243–248

Hubbard, P., Kitchin, R. and Valentine, G. (2004) *Key Thinkers on Space and Place*, Sage, London

Irwin, A. (2001) *Sociology and the Environment*, Polity Press, Cambridge

Jess, P. and Massey, D. (1995) 'The conceptualization of place', in D. Massey and P. Jess (eds) *A Place in the World? Places, Culture and Globalization*, Oxford University Press, New York, pp45–85

Joint Maritime Stakeholders (2007) Statement submitted to the 82nd session of the United Kingdom Safety of Navigation Committee, 22 November 2007

Lee, T., Wren, B. and Hickman, M. (1989) 'Public responses to the siting and operation of wind turbines', *Wind Engineering*, vol 13, no 4, p188

MacKenzie, D. and Wajcman, J. (1999) 'Introductory essay and general issues', in D. MacKenzie and J. Wajcman (eds) *The Social Shaping of Technology*, 2nd edn, Open University Press, Buckingham, UK, pp3–27

McLachlan, C. (2009) '"You don't do a chemistry experiment in your best china": Symbolic interpretations of place and technology in a wave energy case', *Energy Policy*, vol 37, no 12, pp5342–5350

Owens, S. (2002) '"A collision of adverse opinions?": Major projects, planning inquiries, and policy change', *Environment and Planning A*, vol 34, no 6, pp949–953

Pasqualetti, M. J. (2000) 'Morality, space and the power of wind-energy landscapes', *Geographical Review*, vol 90, no 3, pp381–394

Pelamis Wave Power (2007) 'Environmental impact', www.pelamiswave.com/content.php?id=154

Rogers, J. C., Simmons, E. A., Convery, I. and Weatherall, A. (2008) 'Public perceptions of opportunities for community-based renewable energy projects', *Energy Policy*, vol 36, no 11, pp4217–4226

South West RDA (2005) 'Wave Hub', South West Regional Development Agency, www.wavehub.co.uk/

Surfers Against Sewage (2007a) *Climate Change: A Surfers Perspective*, A Surfers Against Sewage report into the potential impacts of climate change on surfers in the UK, www.sas.org.uk/pr/2007/docs07/climate_change_report.pdf

Surfers Against Sewage (2007b) 'Surfers' NGO welcomes Wave Hub planning approval', www.sas.org.uk/pr/2007/wave_hub_2.php

Thayer, R. L. and Freeman, C. M. (1987) 'Altamont: Public perceptions of a wind energy landscape', *Landscape and Urban Planning*, vol 14, pp379–398

Thayer, R. L. and Hansen, H. (1988) 'Wind on the land', *Landscape Architecture*, vol 78, no 2, pp69–73

Tuan, Y. F. (1977) *Space and Place: The Perspective of Experience*, Minnesota Press, Minneapolis

Walker, G. (1995) 'Renewable energy and the public', *Land Use Policy*, vol 12, no 1, pp49–59

Walker, G., Devine-Wright, P. and Evans, B. (2007) *Community Energy Initiatives: Embedding Sustainable Technology at a Local Level*, ESRC End of Award Report, RES-338-25-0010-A

Warren, C., Lumsden, C., O'Dowd, S. and Birnie, R. (2005) '"Green on green": Public perceptions of wind power in Scotland and Ireland', *Journal of Environmental Planning and Management*, vol 48, no 6, pp853–875

Woods, M. (2003) 'Conflicting environmental visions of the rural: Windfarm development in mid Wales', *Sociologia Ruralis*, vol 43, no 3, pp271–288

Chapter 20

Heat and Light: Understanding Bioenergy Siting Controversy

Paul Upham

Introduction

This chapter draws together some of the insights from an interdisciplinary research programme that has investigated public and stakeholder attitudes to the cultivation and use of biomass for energy in the UK. The key empirical focus here is a bioenergy siting controversy involving a nationally significant advanced bioenergy gasifier, which serves to illustrate the very real tensions between national level energy targets and local expectations of democratic decision-making. While suggestions are made for mitigating these tensions, they are unlikely to be fully resolved, given the pressure of energy and climate change targets (BERR, 2008a). The chapter suggests that the politics and psychology of objection, particularly place attachment, are interconnected. Attitudes are in part contingent on their context: if national energy and climate targets are to be met, rural and coastal communities will need to be convinced that additional energy infrastructure is part of a serious national and international drive to mitigate climate change and that they are not being asked to unilaterally accept changes to the local environment without others also playing their part in emissions reduction.

A Bioenergy Siting Controversy

Research on attitudes to energy infrastructure repeatedly finds disjunctions between 'in principle' positive opinion of renewable energy options and opposition 'on the ground'. In the UK, national and regional public opinion surveys have found widespread support for renewable energy in general in Great Britain and Northern Ireland (e.g. Barker and Riddington, 2003a,b; MORI, 2003; TNS, 2003; GfK NOP Social Research, 2006; also repeat surveys by BERR, 2008b). However, specific developments often generate vociferous opposition, and government-commissioned and academic literature relating to bioenergy developments in England and Wales suggest that 'large' bioenergy developments need very careful siting in order to avoid significant local objections (Kahn, 2001; Sinclair and Löfstedt, 2001; Upham and Shackley, 2006a,b, 2007, 2006a,b; Upreti, 2004; Upreti and van der Horst, 2004).

The particular bioenergy siting controversy considered here was followed intermittently over a period of four years. The case concerns a nationally and regionally significant advanced gasifier that would have been – had it been successful – a flagship example of integrated gasification combined cycle technology coupled with a major regional expansion in an energy crop supply chain (specifically, the grass *Miscanthus*). The proposal involved building a 21.5MW(e) integrated combined cycle biomass gasifier (WINBEG – the Winkleigh biomass gasifier) on a disused airfield on the outskirts of the rural village of Winkleigh, Devon, England. This was granted £11 million support under the UK Bio-energy Capital Grant Scheme and was also financially supported by the regional development agency and by unnamed equity backers (the latter for £7 million). The relationships between the stakeholders are illustrated in Figure 20.1.

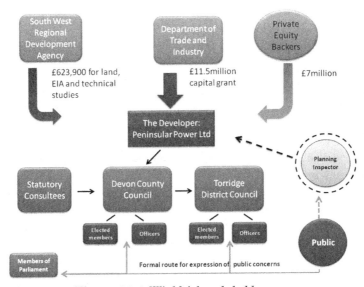

Figure 20.1 *Winkleigh stakeholder map*

In an attitudinal survey by the author in June 2004, 1200 questionnaires were distributed to all households in Winkleigh parish (two per household). These were returned by 573 people, representing 40 per cent of all adults in the parish. Opinion was overwhelmingly against the gasifier. The specific stated concerns of local people were varied, but the highest levels of shared concern were truck movements and associated pollution and nuisance, doubts about the developer's credibility, and gaseous emissions from the plant, including odour. In general, local people felt that they were being asked to accept an industrial-scale develop-ment that would lead to a major deterioration in their quality of life (Upham and Shackley, 2006a,b, 2007). In 2007, a follow-up survey was undertaken of the same population (questionnaires were returned by 290 people; about 20 per cent of the adult population) to determine how and whether local opinion had changed. Aspects of this opinion are considered and described selectively below, with a more explanatory and discursive consideration of the findings given in the subsequent section.

Attitudinal detail: the 2004 and 2007 surveys compared

The respondents were not identical in the two surveys, as a high level of sample control was not possible. Thus the 2007 respondents were older than the 2004 respondents, with people aged 65 years and older constituting 33 per cent of the 2004 group and 43 per cent of the 2007 group. Both sets of respondents were also older than the average of those in the locality, and there is also a greater number of older people in the locality than in the region as a whole and in the UK in general. Nonetheless, although age may well have been a factor in opposition to renewable energy infrastructure (Upham, 2009), statistical investigation showed that age, on its own, did not consistently correlate with attitudinal differences between the two surveys (Upham, 2009).

There were a number of statistically significant differences between the two surveys that provide some insights into the dynamics of the case. In terms of information sources, the percentage of people who said that they had been exposed to information on the gasifier distributed by the local opposition group 'DUST' and by means of the local newsletter had both increased. Increased exposure was not to information distributed by proponents of the development (i.e. the developer or the regional development agency that originally supported the gasifier financially). Rather, the increased exposure was to media and local campaign sources, which played a stronger dissemination and interpretation role than official and developer-provided information. In fact, this higher level of reliance on, and trust in, non-official information sources ran throughout the course of the controversy.

A variety of specific concerns also increased:

* concern about potential noise disturbance increased, from being expressed by 64 per cent of respondents in 2004 to 79 per cent in 2007;
* concern about landscape change from energy crops increased from being expressed by 69 per cent to 75 per cent of people;

- concern about other environmental impacts of energy crops increased from 60 per cent to 68 per cent of respondents.

Conversely, regarding benefits:

- expression of belief in the benefits of WINBEG for the incomes of Devonshire farmers fell, from being expressed by 16 per cent of respondents in 2004 to 9 per cent in 2007;
- belief in the environmental benefits of energy crops fell from 7 per cent to 3 per cent;
- belief that WINBEG will encourage tourism fell from 7 per cent to 3 per cent;
- belief that WINBEG will improve winter employment in agriculture fell from 15 per cent to 7 per cent;
- belief in the benefits of WINBEG diverting biomass from landfill fell from 11 per cent to 7 per cent.

At issue here is *why* there was so little trust in the official sources of information and so little belief in the potential benefits of the gasifier, as well as a hardening of negative opinion over time. At a surface level, the answer clearly lies in the perception that negative consequences, specifically deterioration of quality of life, would follow from the establishment of the gasifier. The anticipated amenity loss associated with frequent truck movements was important in this. Some 50 movements were expected daily by year 6, assuming trucks of 60m3 capacity (Scott Wilson Kirkpatrick & Co, 2004). Fifty movements equally distributed over a 12-hour day (0700–1900 hours) is about one every 15 minutes. This would be sustained for the plant's lifetime of some 25 years. Local people also expected municipal solid waste to be used as a fuel, with associated odour and effluent, were worried about the gaseous emissions, and were also worried that this would set a precedent for further, unwanted forms of development. Although the plant was proposed for a disused airfield on the outskirts of the village (a little over 1km from the village centre), the trucks would have used the nearby main road, and a retirement village of light buildings bordered the airfield site.

However, what is less amenable to a surface-level understanding is that few of those who responded to the questionnaires approved of other (hypothetically posed) renewable energy options that would provide approximately the same level of electrical output as WINBEG. Indeed a much higher percentage of respondents assigned a negative than positive rating for all but one of the renewable energy alternatives to WINBEG, with the exception being the option of 15 offshore turbines. With respect to the latter, nearly half (48 per cent) of the respondents were positive about the offshore wind alternative. Winkleigh is more than 30km from any coast, and so offshore turbines would not usually be seen by the villagers. The other options (including small bioenergy CHP plant and wind turbines) would have been onshore within the local region, such that objection to these does suggest that proximity was a key issue. In two focus group discussions with some 30 people in total, objectors told us that the local negativity that the questionnaire recorded, regarding a range of renewable energy options, arose due to a generalized anger at WINBEG. This, though, would appear to be only a partial explanation: also evident in the focus groups was scepticism about climate change, a perception of a mismatch of the potential of renewable energy output relative to energy demand and relative to fossil and nuclear alternatives, and a reluctance to make what people perceived to be a unilateral sacrifice, given a perception of energy wastage in towns and cities. Underlying all of these reasons, though, appeared to be a strong commitment and attachment to the positive aesthetics of the landscape: people valued this landscape and place highly and in many cases had moved to the locality specifically for its qualities. They did not want to see the intrusion of built infrastructure that was of no benefit to them.

A body of theory particularly relevant to this is that of place attachment and place identity. In this way of thinking, *place* describes not only the physical characteristics of a location, but also the meanings and emotions associated with that location by individuals or groups (e.g. Gieryn, 2000; Devine-Wright, 2005, 2009, 2010). The term *place attachment* has been applied both to the process of attaching oneself to a place and the outcome of this process (Giuliani, 2002). *Place identity* refers to the ways in which physical and symbolic attributes of particular locations contribute to an individual's sense of self or identity (Proshansky et al, 1983). Change to a location is sometimes termed a 'disruption' to place attachment (e.g. (Brown and Perkins, 1992) or a 'threat' to place identity (e.g. Bonaiuto et al, 1996)). Understanding the Winkleigh case and other siting controversies in these terms would appear to make considerable sense. It does, however, raise a number of issues relating to energy policy governance: most notably, how, if at all, to reflect such place attachment in local land use planning procedures.

Governance and engagement in the Winkleigh case

In addition to assessing perceptions of the planning and related governance system through direct interview questions and focus group discussion, we also used questions relating to perceptions of the level of communication by public bodies on the planning proposal. Between 2004 and 2007, the proportion of people approving of related communication by Torridge District Council and Winkleigh Parish Council rose from 5 to 22 per cent and from 34 to 67 per cent, respectively. Approval of communication by the Regional Development Agency (RDA) and Devon County Council (DCC), whose officers respectively promoted and supported the proposal, remained low, at 2 per cent of respondents in 2004 and 5 per cent in 2007 for the RDA, and at 2 per cent in 2004 and 9 per cent in 2007 for DCC.

In this case, the planning and governance context strongly compounded the community's frustration. Although a more consultative set of procedures would have mitigated this, it would certainly not have led to local approval of the planning application as it stood. What a more consultative set of procedures might have achieved, however, is an alternative and locally acceptable siting of the power plant in another part of southwestern England, or possibly a smaller version with fuel requirements that would be less likely to suppress smaller bioenergy plants regionally (a concern raised by the Planning Authority). In terms of the European Directive on Environmental Impact Assessment, point 3 of Article 5 of Directive 85/337/EEC as amended by Directive 97/11/EEC requires:

> '*an outline of the main alternatives studied by the developer and an indication of the main reasons for his choice, taking into account the environmental effects*'.

In the UK this is expressed through the Environmental Impact Assessment (EIA) Regulations 1999 (Schedule 4, Part 2, 2). Regarding alternative sites, the Environmental Statement (ES) for WINBEG states that five sites in Devon were examined by the developer during the evolution of the bioenergy project that became WINBEG. The ES emphasizes two criteria for choice of site: proximity to a suitable power line and to an adequate catchment area for fuel; and cites Winkleigh as being in a good position for both, compared with other sites (Scott Wilson Kirkpatrick & Co, 2004). However, the relative value of the site options may well have been different with a power plant of a much smaller capacity, or an otherwise different proposal. A much smaller proposal would also have increased the number of site options. Once a project of WINBEG's nature was determined upon (i.e. relatively large-scale electricity supply), the site options would have narrowed considerably.

The role of the RDA was important in this case, as the developer could not have proceeded with the proposal without the RDA's financial support in terms of land purchase and payment for the technical studies (including the EIA). As such, the RDA became a key focus for objection. Local people felt that neither the Regional Assembly nor the non-executive board of the RDA represented their interests. Although there were formal lines of accountability between RDA officials, its board, the regional government office, DTI and other government departments, complemented by a scrutiny role then performed by the Regional Assembly, local people still felt disempowered and excluded from the process. Indeed, our correspondence and discussion with the RDA revealed a distinct scepticism regarding the practicality of, and justification for, increased dialogue with local people on renewable energy planning, and an understandable preference for dealing with the smaller number of political representatives.

Use of Bioenergy for Local Heat and Combined Heat And Power (CHP)

The Winkleigh case study of a relatively large-scale, technologically advanced bio-electricity plant contrasted with our findings on public perceptions of 2030 bioenergy scenarios for the Yorkshire and Humber region of the UK. Use of the Yorkshire and Humber region's wood resource for small and medium-sized CHP and heat plants was found to be much more attractive than the use of the same resource for large or small electric power plants. Key reasons for this, mentioned by stakeholders and in two focus groups held with about 25 informed members of the public involved in considering energy options for their villages, included the higher energetic efficiency of CHP and heat relative to electricity, and perceptions of better performance in terms of local employment, local environmental impact and associated social benefits (Upham et al, 2007).

The focus groups with the public were held in March 2006, both involving local people who attended a monthly Energy Group. These groups were two of several funded and convened under the project dCARB-uk, a partnership project led by the Sustainable Development Commission, which worked with communities in Yorkshire towns and villages to develop long-term carbon reduction plans, as well as initiating specific carbon reduction projects. The focus groups were in villages not connected to a gas main, located within the North York Moors National Park. The stimulus materials used consisted of question prompts on bioenergy, graphical information on regional bioenergy scenarios and bioenergy crops and infrastructure, shown as photomontages in the locality (Upham and Shackley 2005; Upham et al, 2007).

Ownership and place attachment were again prominent themes: participants were primarily (though not solely) focused on supplying the energy requirements of their localities. Their main concern was not, therefore, the energy needs of the nation as a whole, or indeed of the Yorkshire and the Humber region, although most members of the groups did hold opinions regarding how best to meet the energy needs at these higher scales. Participants emphasized their preference for forms of bioenergy that would enhance their locality: they were concerned about biodiversity, landscape and visual impact, the local (rural) economy, and energy security, particularly in relation to their locality. There was disapproval of electrical transmission losses due to efficiency losses and a distrust of lengthy biomass transportation. Both groups were strongly in favour of biomass CHP in principle, but anticipated significant problems in practice (in particular the costs and other problems associated with installing pipelines in rural villages).

Despite the local focus of the groups, most participants also expressed a high degree of respect for national and global environmental integrity: climate change and other adverse environmental change were important to many participants. Generally, without further information, participants felt unable to commit themselves on the merits of displacing food crops for energy crops, but the carbon balance of bioenergy systems was both a familiar and important issue for many, and sometimes an issue of contention – that is, some participants expressed strong doubts that the full picture is captured by bioenergy life cycle analyses.

Moreover, the groups and their individual members were struggling to identify the best energy technologies for their individual and community situations. Despite a government subsidy, the capital investment required by individuals installing microgeneration technologies remains substantial relative to most UK household incomes and, in general, requires particular circumstances (e.g. boiler renewal or roof replacement) to be seen as financially justifiable. Similarly, individuals had to undertake considerable research in order to estimate payback periods for different technologies. The uncertainties were also high: for bioenergy, the logistics of securing a fuel supply can be complicated. More generally, some participants were also concerned that a change in government energy policy (e.g. heavily towards nuclear or stronger subsidies for renewables) could render their investment obsolete or unwarranted.

Making Connections: General Inferences

The case of the strongly opposed 21.5MW(e) bioenergy gasifier in Winkleigh, Devon, and the contrast with the public welcome for bioenergy for heat in the North York Moors National Park, Yorkshire, serve as a microcosm of much of the variety of public engagement issues relating to energy transitions in the UK. Social science research undertaken during phase 1 of the EPSRC Supergen Bioenergy and Biomass Consortium (for more detail, see www.supergen-bioenergy.net/) involved scanning many literatures in search of satisfactory explanatory accounts and policy-viable solutions.

In terms of the political dimensions, we argue elsewhere that enhanced local participation in renewable energy planning and enhanced accountability for regional development agencies could have led – in this case at least – to a more widely acceptable outcome consisting of relocating the gasifier to a point better served by transport links (Upham and Shackley, 2006a). Had this been achieved, it would have retained the investment in the region, helped to diversify the rural economy of the region, and have provided lower carbon electricity. Instead, a standoff between – on the one hand – the developer, the sponsoring government department and the regional development agency and – on the other hand – the local community, resulted in a lengthy, difficult and costly process of managing disagreement and dissent, and ultimately the loss of the project.

There are also demographic aspects to the case that may be more widely applicable: the age characteristics of the village, while not providing an explanation for opposition in themselves, do appear to have an indirect bearing through their association with a strong attachment to the rural qualities of the location and a scepticism about renewable energy (Upham, 2009). Relatedly, the social psychology of place attachment referred to above (Gieryn, 2000; Devine-Wright, 2005, 2009, Devine-Wright and Howes, 2010) has strong explanatory potential for this and other cases, given that residents saw the proposed development as a major threat to the locality (Upham, 2009).

Another literature providing relevant accounts is that of the psychology of climate change. This identifies a variety of features that we noted in qualitative work through the research programme: a general tendency to underestimate personal contributions to climate change and to identify causes of climate change with other people or other countries (Lorenzoni and Pidgeon, 2006; Whitmarsh, 2009) and with more 'distant' activities, particularly industry and deforestation (e.g. Nicholson-Cole, 2005; Whitmarsh et al, 2009; also see Upham et al, 2009). Perhaps most importantly of all, we found a conditionality to individual pro-environmental action: an unwillingness to make what are perceived as sacrifices without commensurate action by others, nationally and internationally (e.g. 60 per cent agree that 'If government did more to tackle climate change, I'd do more too' (DEFRA, 2007); see also Upham et al, 2009). Also informative are accounts of the role of symbolism in renewable energy siting controversies, as studied elsewhere in a bioenergy context (McLachlan, 2009). Here these were manifest as domestic and small-scale bioenergy being seen as having positive associations of community benefit – associations that were lacking for the larger-scale developments, particularly those for the supply of electric power to an anonymous National Grid.

Policy Implications: Context Matters

There are likely to be increased tensions between public opinion in rural and coastal areas in the UK and developers and advocates of new energy infrastructure, as climate and energy targets become more urgent, and as the UK's planning system becomes more centralized for major infrastructure projects under the 2008 Planning Act. If the UK seeks to decarbonize not only the power and heat sectors but also transport, with electric and hydrogen options for the latter gaining prominence (Palmer, 2009), then these conflicts will only intensify.

There will inevitably be 'winners' and 'losers' in this situation; the least that rural and coastal residents are owed is more explicit indication of the extent of new infrastructure that their locality may be required to support (Upham and Shackley, 2006a). While this may be as likely to provoke concern as to mitigate it, it would at least let people know where they stand. Acceptance of place disruption may also be mitigated through a clearer explanation of the limits to other potential components of a low carbon energy mix, notably demand reduction, fossil CCS (carbon capture and storage) and nuclear power (the latter referred to by objectors in the Winkleigh case as obviating the need for new renewable energy). However, there remain real differences in opinion regarding the relative roles of the different energy options. For example, a further theme raised in the Winkleigh focus groups was that of energy wastage through excess commercial lighting (i.e. shops and offices being lit throughout the night): people objected to being asked to bear what they regarded as significant disruption for the purpose of meeting excessive demand. Such contextual issues, including the specific issue of whether it is justifiable to use renewable energy supply to meet additional demand in societies that are already relatively affluent, are not incidental to energy siting controversy – but they have as yet received relatively little research attention. Value judgements run through this field: arguably the ethical case for requiring local acceptance of new energy infrastructure is weakened without concomitant, significant action on emissions reduction elsewhere in the economy.

Conclusions

Fully understanding local objections to renewable energy developments requires a relatively eclectic approach to the literatures, so as to address the different dimensions and levels of the problem. In the case discussed here, an understanding of siting controversy is aided by the application of literatures on place attachment, the influence of context on pro-environmental attitudes, as well as literatures on institutional trust. Of these, the contingent and contextual nature of attitudes is probably the least researched and merits closer attention.

The chapter also calls for a more locally explicit debate of the implications of national energy policy. Such calls inevitably seem somewhat idealistic and are readily open to challenge (Owens and Driffil, 2006). This critique is particularly understandable as we head towards breaching greenhouse gas concentration thresholds that are consistent with avoiding 'dangerous' climate change (Anderson and Bows, 2008). Moreover, planning policy trends are potentially moving away from local decision-making in the UK. As a reaction to planning delays in the UK (ironically, in some cases, to infrastructure that would increase GHG emissions, such as new airport capacity), under the new Planning Act (2008) an Infrastructure Planning Commission (IPC) will determine applications for 'significant infrastructure projects'.

Yet local debate need not, and should not, imply abandonment of national targets. Moreover, without wider and more coherent action to reduce greenhouse gas emissions nationally and internationally, objectors are likely to continue to perceive that they are being asked to accept a reduced quality of life unilaterally, while others continue their high rates of consumption and emission. It may be naive to call for policy integration from competing government departments, but if UK climate change policy is genuinely to move from statute to implementation, then significant action across all sectors is urgently needed. The role of local public participation in energy infrastructure siting will always be vexed, but the least that rural and coastal communities deserve, in return for hosting additional energy infrastructure, is the knowledge that other people and sectors are also playing their part in emissions reduction.

Acknowledgements

Thanks to the people of Winkleigh and to stakeholder interviewees. Thanks also to Dr Simon Shackley for commenting on this chapter. The content of this chapter and the interpretations therein are the author's responsibility only.

References

Anderson, K. and Bows, A. (2008) 'Reframing the climate change challenge in light of post-2000 emission trends', *Philosophical Transactions of the Royal Society A*, vol 366, no 1882, pp3863–3882, doi:10.1098/rsta.2008.0138

Barker, A. M. and Riddington, C. (2003a) *Attitudes to Renewable Energy*, MVA Project Number C32906, COI Communications, DTI, London, www.dti.gov.uk/renewables/renew_1.2.1.4a.htm

Barker, A. M. and Riddington, C. (2003b) *Attitudes to Renewable Energy: Northern Ireland*, MVA Project Number C33276, COI Communications, DTI, London, www.dti.gov.uk/renewables/renew_1.2.1.4a.htm

BERR (2008a) *UK Renewable Energy Strategy Consultation*, Department for Business, Enterprise and Regulatory Reform, HMSO, London

BERR (2008b) *Renewable Energy Awareness and Attitudes Research*, GfK NOP Social Research, Department for Business, Enterprise and Regulatory Reform, London.

Bonaiuto, M., Breakwell, G. M. and Cano, I. (1996) 'Identity processes and environmental threat: The effects of nationalism and local identity upon perception of beach pollution', *Journal of Community and Applied Social Psychology*, vol 6, no 3, pp157–175

Brown, B. and Perkins, D. D. (1992) 'Disruptions in place attachment', in I. Altman and S. Low (eds) *Place Attachment*, Plenum Press, New York, pp279–304

DEFRA (2007) *Survey of Public Attitudes and Behaviours Toward the Environment: 2007*, Department for Environment, Food and Rural Affairs, London

Devine-Wright, P. (2005) 'Beyond NIMBYism: Towards an integrated framework for understanding public perceptions of wind energy', *Wind Energy*, vol 8, no 2, pp125–139

Devine-Wright, P. (2009) 'Rethinking NIMBYism: The role of place attachment and place identity in explaining place-protective action', *Journal of Community and Applied Social Psychology*, vol 19, no 6, pp426–441

Devine-Wright, P. and Howes, Y. (2010) 'Disruption to place attachment and the protection of restorative environments: A wind energy case study', *Journal of Environmental Psychology*, vol 30, no 3, pp271–280

GfK NOP Social Research (2006) *Renewable Energy Awareness and Attitudes Research*, Management Summary, DTI, London, www.berr.gov.uk/files/file29360.pdf

Gieryn, T. F. (2000) 'A space for place in sociology', *Annual Review of Sociology*, vol 26, pp463–496

Giuliani, M. V. (2002) 'Theory of attachment and place attachment', in M. Bonnes, T. Lee and M. Bonaiuto (eds) *Psychological Theories for Environmental Issues*, Ashgate, Aldershot, UK, pp137–170

Kahn, J. (2001) 'Siting conflicts in renewable energy projects in Sweden: Experiences from the siting of a Biogas plant', Presented at New Perspectives on Siting Controversy Conference, Glumslov, Sweden

MORI (2003) *Public Attitudes Towards Renewable Energy in the South West*, Research study conducted for Regen SW, MORI Social Research Institute, London, www.regensw.co.uk/documents.asp

Lorenzoni, I. and Pidgeon, N. (2006) 'Public views on climate change: European and USA perspectives', *Climatic Change*, vol 77, no 1/2, pp73–95

McLachlan, C. (2009) 'Technologies in place: Symbolic interpretations of renewable energy', in R. Carter and N. Charles (eds) *Sociological Review Monograph: Society and Nature*, Wiley-Blackwell, UK

Nicholson-Cole, S. A. (2005) 'Representing climate change futures: A critique on the use of images for visual communication', *Computers, Environment and Urban Systems*, vol 29, no 3, pp255–273

Owens, S. and Driffil, L. (2006) 'How to change attitudes and behaviours in the context of energy', *Energy Policy*, vol 36, no 12, pp4412–4418

Palmer, J. (2009) 'Ministry push for low-carbon cars', http://news.bbc.co.uk/1/hi/technology/8248143.stm

Proshansky, H. M., Fabian, A. K. and Kaminoff, R. (1983) 'Place-identity: Physical world socialization of the self', *Journal of Environmental Psychology*, vol 3, no 1, pp57–83

Scott Wilson Kirkpatrick & Co (2004) *Winkleigh Biomass Electricity Generator: Environmental Statement, Volume 2, Main Report*, Scott Wilson Kirkpatrick & Co, London

Sinclair, P. and Löfstedt, R. (2001) 'The influence of trust in a biomass plant application: The case study of Sutton, UK', *Biomass and Bioenergy*, vol 21, no 3, pp177–184

TNS (2003) *Attitudes and Knowledge of Renewable Energy Amongst the General Public*, Report of Findings prepared for Central Office of Information on behalf of Department of Trade and Industry, Scottish Executive, National Assembly for Wales, Department of Enterprise, Trade and Investment, JN9419 and JN9385, Taylor Nelson Sofres, London, www.berr.gov.uk/files/file15478.pdf

Upham, P. (2009a) 'Applying environmental-behaviour concepts to renewable energy siting controversy: Reflections on a longitudinal bioenergy case study,' *Energy Policy*, vol 37, no 11, pp4273–4283

Upham, P. and Shackley, S. (2006a) 'The case of a proposed 21.5 MWe biomass gasifier in Winkleigh, Devon: Implications for governance of renewable energy planning', *Energy Policy*, vol 34, no 15, pp2161–2172

Upham, P. and Shackley, S. (2006b) 'Stakeholder opinion on a proposed 21.5 MWe biomass Gasifier in Winkleigh, Devon: Implications for bioenergy planning and policy', *Journal of Environmental Policy and Planning*, vol 8, no 1, pp45–66

Upham, P. and Shackley, S. (2007) 'Public opinion of a proposed 21.5MW(e) biomass gasifier in Devon: Questionnaire survey results', *Biomass and Bioenergy*, vol 31, no 6, pp433–441

Upham, P. and Shackley, S. (2005) *Indicative 2030 Bioenergy Scenarios for Yorkshire and Humber*, Tyndall Centre / Manchester Business School, The University of Manchester, www.supergen-bioenergy.net

Upham, P., Shackley, S. and Waterman, H. (2007) 'Public and stakeholder perceptions of 2030 bioenergy scenarios for the Yorkshire and Humber region', *Energy Policy*, vol 35, no 9, pp4403–4412

Upham, P., Whitmarsh, L., Poortinga, W., Purdam, K., Darnton, A., McLachlan, C. and Devine-Wright, P. (2009) *Public Attitudes to Environmental Change: A Selective Review of Theory and Practice*, LWEC, www.lwec.org.uk/news-archive/2009/30102009-report-published-public-attitudes-environmental-change

Upreti, B. R. (2004) 'Conflict over biomass energy development in the United Kingdom: Some observations and lessons from England and Wales', *Energy Policy*, vol 32, no 6, pp785–800

Upreti, B. R. and van der Horst, D. (2004) 'National renewable energy policy and local opposition in the UK: The failed development of a biomass electricity plant', *Biomass and Bioenergy*, vol 26, no 1, pp61–69

Whitmarsh, L. (2009) 'What's in a name? Commonalities and differences in public understanding of "climate change" and "global warming"', *Public Understanding of Science*, vol 18, pp401–420

Whitmarsh, L., O'Neill, S. J., Seyfang, G. and Lorenzoni, I. (2009) 'Carbon capability: What does it mean, how prevalent is it, and how can we promote it?', Tyndall Working Paper, no 132, www.tyndall.ac.uk

Chapter 21

From the Material to the Imagined: Public Engagement with Low Carbon Technologies in a Nuclear Community

Catherine Butler, Karen Parkhill and Nick Pidgeon

Introduction

In debates around low carbon energy technologies, renewable forms of generation are often the focus. In contrast, nuclear power, while being a low carbon form of electricity generation, does not invoke quite the same synonymy with the concept of low carbon energy. In this chapter we examine public engagement with these differing forms of low carbon technology – nuclear *and* renewable – focusing on tidal and onshore wind power as renewable technologies.

Both renewable forms of electricity production and nuclear power have been the source of vociferous public contestation. Renewable forms of energy, while having widespread support at the national level, have frequently met with local opposition; this is particularly true of onshore wind developments (Bell et al, 2005). In this context of widespread public approval for renewable forms of technology, such local objections have often been characterized as NIMBYism ('Not in my back yard'). This particular interpretation of local public opposition has been heavily critiqued for failing to adequately address complexities associated with opposition, power dimensions of local siting, and the significance of place attachments in these controversies (Wolsink, 2000; Devine-Wright, 2005, 2009).

Nuclear power shares some of the difficulties associated with newer forms of energy production but is also distinct in many senses. Nuclear power has long been associated with high levels of controversy and public opposition at both local and national levels. Indeed, recent efforts in the UK to develop new nuclear power stations have met with some strong opposition from non-governmental organizations such as Greenpeace. However, due to increasing political concern over climate change (and indeed issues of energy security), the low carbon credentials of nuclear power are being extolled, making the development of new nuclear power increasingly likely in the UK (Department for Business, Enterprise and Regulatory Reform, 2008). While nuclear power does not represent a new energy sector in itself, it does present an interesting case for examining transitions to a low carbon electricity sector.

In this chapter, using the case site of Hinkley Point in the west of England, we examine the local public(s) engagement with different forms of low carbon energy development either existing or proposed in the locality (i.e. nuclear power, tidal power and onshore wind energy). We trace the ways in which our participants relate to and contrast these three differing energy technologies; from their materially rooted and situated conceptions of nuclear power to their imaginings of the new energy infrastructures proposed in their locality.

Setting the Scene

A significant number of prior empirical studies have examined the perspectives of citizens in localities that host major infrastructure developments. The focus of such work has of course varied, but encompassed within this body of empirical research are works that have examined sites for energy developments, with nuclear energy and wind power receiving particular attention. The public acceptability of differing energy developments has often formed the focus of such studies, with issues of risk and anxiety frequently featuring as components of the analysis. Less work has questioned the significance of 'low carbon' discourses for local citizens in their conceptions of the particular energy infrastructures to which their areas play host. Drawing on our in-depth qualitative research described below, we examine the extent to which discourses of 'low carbon' form a component of the ways in which our participants attached meaning to these developments and formed views on the acceptability of different energy technologies operating in their locality. Moreover, we elucidate the varying ways that local members of the public engaged with each of the energy technologies either proposed or existing in their area. First, we briefly discuss the literatures and previous empirical findings pertinent to our analysis.

While, historically, nuclear power has been associated with high levels of public opposition and controversy (Wynne, 1992; van der Pligt, 1992; Rosa and Freudenberg, 1993), in more recent years, research on nuclear power has depicted increased levels of public acceptability. Pidgeon et al (2008) reported that despite finding that, on balance, a majority of people remained opposed to nuclear power, the levels of public disapproval were far below those found in the 1980s. Contextualized in relation to renewable forms of energy, however, they found that 'very few would actively prefer [nuclear] as an option over renewable sources or energy efficiency if given the choice' (Pidgeon et al, 2008, p81).

In relation to studies of local populations around existing nuclear power stations, lower levels of concern or greater degrees of acceptability have often been reported amongst those groups than within the wider population (Melber et al, 1977; Eiser et al, 1995; Greenberg, 2009). Such findings, however, are not straightforward, with studies indicating that even where acceptability or support is overtly expressed, this is often highly qualified, with some suggesting that a degree of underlying unease is always present in the discourses of local people (Zonabend, 1993). Other research relating to large socio-technical developments has suggested that a person may be unwilling to express concern or anxieties, as perceived negative views of the development and stigma from outside the area are seen as a greater threat than the technological infrastructures themselves (Baxter and Lee, 2004). The economic connections between local communities and facilities have also been posited as significant, either as the focus of the trade-offs that citizens make between negative and positive impacts of a facility, or as a dependency relation wherein local economic prosperity is tied to the facility, resulting in a tendency to downplay their concerns (Baxter and Lee, 2004).

More recently, in-depth qualitative work has examined discourses of local acceptance around nuclear power stations in terms of familiarity, normalization and extraordinariness; concluding that, while ordinariness represented the predominant framing adopted by those living close to such sites, anxiety and concerns also featured powerfully in local people's discursive constructions of nuclear power, leading the power station to be periodically reframed as a risk and threat issue (Parkhill et al, 2010). Thus the 'tolerability' (Simmons and Walker, 1999) of nuclear risk was found to be fragile, representing conditional support at best (Parkhill et al, 2010; see also Venables et al, 2009).

Within the wider socio-political discourse around nuclear energy, climate change and concerns about securing future energy supplies have featured prominently, with a notable shift towards greater favourability for nuclear power in the UK political milieu (Department for Business, Enterprise and Regulatory Reform, 2008). The extent to which these discourses have come to play a role in local public discourse is, however, less well understood.

In contrast to findings in nuclear communities, wind power has been found at times to invoke strong opposition and concern at local levels while achieving widespread public approval from general populations. Past explanations have characterized such findings as NIMBYism, wherein people are characterized as rejecting facilities for reasons of ignorance and irrationality, because of pure self-interest and selfishness, or a combination of these (Freudenberg and Pastor, 1992). This explanation for local opposition to developments has now been challenged, with issues relating to feelings of distrust and powerlessness, inequities in decision-making, and the significance of place attachments becoming more visible in later studies (Wynne, 1992; Burningham, 2000; Devine-Wright, 2009).

Although in the UK, at least, offshore wind developments have been viewed more favourably by citizens, again studies have found cases of local opposition (Kempton et al, 2005). Research has also found, however, that support for wind projects increases *after* development (Walker, 1995; Krohn and Damborg, 1999).

As an energy technology with few operating examples worldwide (La Rance in Brittany being a notable exception), tidal power has received significantly less attention in the literature, with limited research into public perceptions and acceptability (Walker, 1995). Research that has been conducted in this area tends to be found within grey literatures and remains broadly descriptive, with limited academic enquiry having taken place. A recent example of such work can be found in a report produced by the UK Sustainable Development Commission (SDC). Public engagement exercises were conducted in cities close to the UK Severn estuary, where proposed tidal schemes are currently under consideration (Sustainable Development Commission, 2007). This research found that:

- there was reasonable awareness of climate change but with varying degrees of opinion on its importance as an issue;
- there was less awareness of energy security, but concern once it was directly pointed out as an issue;
- only 55 per cent of people had heard of tidal power, and discursive analysis demonstrated some confusion between tidal and wave power;
- there was general strong support for tidal power, although when this was explored in more detail, participants were found to be more negative overall about a *barrage* in the Severn estuary (Sustainable Development Commission, 2007).

As Devine-Wright points out, in general, 'most of the literature [examining renewable energy] is empirical in nature, using quantitative survey tools, and "barrier oriented" in seeking to identify specific reasons for negative public attitudes to local development' (Devine-Wright, 2005, p126). As such, our qualitative discursive analytic approach offers a different take on public engagement with both renewable and nuclear energy forms, investigating how they are discursively constructed and negotiated. While previous research has been conducted from a realist perspective, maintaining that there is a distinction between objectively observable phenomena and subjective perceptions, we build from a position which emphasizes the significance of interpretive understanding. Moreover, although environmental concern has figured as an analytical category in previous studies, a specific focus on the construction of energy facilities such as low carbon has not been a prominent feature. In addition, to our knowledge, there are no comparative studies which have examined the way in which members of the public in local contexts formulate views on *different* forms of low carbon energy development in relation to one another. Previous research has tended to focus on a single form of energy technology (see, for example, Cowell, 2007) and has not been fully contextualized in relation to more contemporary policy frames or the complexity of trade-offs when negotiated by public(s) in areas where different low carbon options have particular salience (Kempton et al, 2005, being a notable exception). The specific features of our case study allow an examination of public conceptions of low carbon energies in a more holistic sense.

In the following section, we briefly describe in more detail the study that forms the basis for analysis. We then open up for explication the sophisticated ways in which members of the public engage with different low carbon forms of energy production either existing or proposed in their locality.

The Study

The research materials on which this analysis is based are drawn from a larger qualitative study which involved meeting with 53 interviewees (some interviews involved more than one person) on two occasions (total interviews, $n=82$) as well as visual methodologies within two case study sites (Aberthaw in South Wales and Hinkley Point in southwest England); for the purposes of this chapter we focus solely on the first interviews for one site: Hinkley Point.

Hinkley Point currently hosts two nuclear power stations (Hinkley 'A', which began operating in 1965 but is currently decommissioning, and 'B', which began generating in 1976 and has an estimated decommissioning date of 2016). It is also currently being investigated for the feasibility of hosting new nuclear power. In addition, the Severn estuary (the site for tidal energy proposals currently under consideration by the UK Government), and a wind farm (proposed in 2006 and later withdrawn) are in the case study area. These differing forms of energy production, their meaning for members of the public living in adjacent localities, contemporary policy issues of climate change and energy security, energy futures or transitions, and energy consumption formed the focus of in-depth, semi-structured qualitative interviews (participants, $n=26$) with the local public in the surrounding villages and towns during the summer of 2009.

Each interview lasted between one and two hours. Participants were recruited utilizing a previous questionnaire sample as a basis for contact, followed by a letter inviting them to participate. Interviewees were selected using a range of criteria (including gender, age, household tenure, length of residence, and whether or not they or a member of their family work or have ever worked at the power station – which we termed 'power station affiliation') to ensure diversity in social characteristics.

Analytically, we adopted an approach broadly derived from the interpretive tradition, developing themes from the interview material through an iterative process moving between the transcripts, literatures and writing processes to build the analysis laid out here (Pidgeon and Henwood, 2004).

Engaging with 'Low Carbon' Technologies: From the Material to the Imagined

In line with previous studies of populations living locally to nuclear power stations, many of our participants were positive about nuclear generation in general, and about the prospects for new nuclear power in their area in particular. Across the varying, but on the whole positive, conceptions of nuclear power, discourses of low carbon featured prominently:

> *'I wouldn't like to say [nuclear power] is carbon neutral, but it's got a lower carbon footprint than quite a lot of other energy production methods and it's not usually noisy, and it's reliable, generally. I think there's not the diurnal variation that you are going to get with wind and wave power either. So the National Grid can have a base load from it'* (Valerie).

As might be expected, our participants' views were not formed in a vacuum and they often drew comparisons in their reasoning about differing low carbon energy technologies, situating their perspectives in a wider frame of UK energy provision, climate change, historical development and socio-technical discourses. For some, nuclear power formed a straightforward preference for meeting challenges in energy provision and climate change:

> *'This is why I like nuclear ... allegedly there are no CO_2 emissions out of nuclear power stations ... I suppose there's a finite amount of coal and the like in the world, so eventually that will go, so they will become redundant. So we've got to look at alternatives; nuclear is my alternative'* (Bob).

For many, however, positive perspectives on nuclear power were not without reservation and were contrasted with a general preference for renewable forms of energy (see also Pidgeon et al, 2008). This preference was, however, tempered by the extent to which renewable forms of energy were seen as feasible, given their levels of development:

> *'I don't want to be pro-nuclear, but at the minute, because the money hasn't been pumped in the same way into the renewable industry as it was into the nuclear industry over the years, we are way behind where we need to be'* (Fred).

> *'It's clean energy. I mean they've got to do something ... With nuclear the technology is there to be used and it's safe, it has got a very good track record, but then my opinion might have changed if they were further down the road with wave power or tidal power ... you've got that tide coming in and out, you've got the second highest tidal reach in the world on the Severn, and why not harness it?'* (Peter).

As the above extracts indicate, positive views on nuclear power in their locality were linked to wider issues, such as the lack of adequate investment in renewable forms of energy. This was connected with a general sense of frustration at the limited development of renewable power, and particularly tidal power, in the UK. In some sense, then, we might characterize these discourses around nuclear power as a kind of resigned acceptance in a context of limited options, rather than a strongly 'pro' stance (for related findings, see Bickerstaff et al, 2008). For others, renewable forms of energy represented a *clear* preference in terms of low carbon technologies, with possibilities for new energy sectors increasing prior reservations about nuclear power:

> *'I've more reservations [about nuclear] since they've decided to bring this barrage forward, because I think I would like to see other forms of energy. I'd rather have something like that than nuclear. You know, in terms of green energy or non-carbon energy, wind and wave and all that, I'd probably prefer that but I don't really know enough about it'* (Pat).

While development of new nuclear power and existing nuclear power in the area was on the whole regarded positively, or at least acceptable to some degree even if tempered by a preference for renewable energy forms, this was not the case for all participants, with some finding real difficulty in grappling with the notion of nuclear power as part of the means to avert climate change:

> Interviewer: *'What do you think about the argument that we need nuclear power to help mitigate climate change?'*
>
> Participant: *'I don't buy into it. I can't buy into it ... It just seems to me, on all sorts of levels, it is a short-term fix'* (Ruth).

This perspective was linked to a view that changing energy infrastructure did not address wider sustainability issues at their core, but instead facilitated ongoing development and continuation of a way of life which, for some, was seen as fundamentally unsustainable.

Amidst the generally favourable perspectives on renewable forms of energy, wind turbines, in particular, were often characterized as least acceptable by participants. As has been found in other studies (see, e.g., Kempton et al, 2005), the significance of the local environment and the perceived loss of aesthetic pleasure derived from landscape played an important role in the ways in which our participants contrasted the differing technologies. Wind was conceptualized as producing small amounts of energy and thus being of little benefit for the wider social good in terms of energy provision, but at the same time causing significant loss to the local environment. This was contrasted with nuclear power (including nuclear waste), which was conceived as contained and confined to particular areas, as opposed to depictions of wind farms as sprawling industrial developments:

> '*In the right location in an industrial area I don't think [wind generators] really create a problem, but then if you visualized the skyline across the Mendip Hills or the Quantock Hills ... I wouldn't accept them because they are not creating sufficient energy to justify losing something that we really all ought to be enjoying and that is the heritage of the landscape*' (Charlie).

For this participant, wind power was only acceptable in particular places where losses to landscape were perceived as minimal or where electricity was otherwise difficult to obtain (such as islands). The focus of engagement, in this sense, was around whether the particular development was representative of, or synergistic with, the values, meanings and working practices of place; that it was 'in place' (see Cresswell, 1996; Parkhill, 2007).

It should be noted that, in contrast to the more negative conceptions of wind power, some participants expressed 'despair at the human race' (Hilda) that the proposed wind farm at Hinkley Point had met with local opposition, while others depicted such reactions as short-sighted, and even invoked the notion of NIMBYism.

Our participants frequently drew on negative wider social discourses around wind power (e.g. alleged poor generating capacity, visual and environmental impacts) to inform their views. Other social and media discourses were also drawn upon to reinforce such positions, e.g. notions that wind power developments were frequently rejected in other areas. This contrasted with nuclear power, where more negative social discourses (about, for example, safety, visual impacts or health) were countered through direct experience, localized social trust (in the safety of the power station at least), experiential knowledge, and familiarity with Hinkley Point in particular (see also Parkhill et al, 2010):

> Interviewer: '*Did you have any thoughts about the wind farm proposed at West Hinkley?*'
>
> Participant: '*Only that I think it would be better not to do that if you've got nuclear power ... you keep hearing about the wind farms on Scottish islands and whatever and out there they seemed to be turned down, nobody ever goes ahead with it because the residents complain and they think "okay we'll go somewhere else then" so ...*' (Matthew).
>
> Interviewer: '*What did you think about that proposal for a wind farm at West Hinkley?*'
>
> Participant: '*It's a bit complicated here, because I think that would have spoilt the coastline. Somebody could come back and say, you've got two great big blocks of concrete there anyway. That's something I've grown up with, so I've tended to accept that as a skyline*' (Bob).

In this sense, the familiarity and direct material experience of nuclear power served to temper wider negative social discourses about this form of power generation, whereas for wind, such negative discourses and perception of public dislike served as the main point of engagement for our participants. While wind power was viewed with greater scepticism regarding its capacities in energy generation, as well as its aesthetic and environmental impact, tidal power was on the whole regarded more positively:

> *'if you could generate a similar amount of power [to nuclear] from tidal then I suppose anyone with any sense would say "go for that one then"... because ultimately it would have less impact on the environment'* (Dave).

In the case of tidal power, very limited experience led participants to draw on general notions of the dependability of the tide, high generating capacity, associations with naturalness, and it being environmentally better than other forms of generation. Such wider social discourses and ideals were drawn upon in the absence of any material experience on which to base views:

> *'I don't think people know too much about tidal power because it's not there that you can see, it's not as if it's over in the field around the corner'* (Mel, Bridgewater).

Negative conceptions of tidal power tended only to come after greater thought (in the second interviews) or were expressed in terms of uncertainty about unintended consequences, or were again drawn from media or social discourse. Concerns tended to be focused around technological, engineering and environmental issues, e.g. that the turbines would be ineffectual or inefficient because of high levels of silt in the estuary, questions about the effect that a barrage would have on bird life. Such issues were discussed vaguely and reported as derived from media coverage but they did not feature as strongly as positive impressions.

The wider social discourses that surrounded both tidal and wind were of significant importance in contrast to those which surrounded nuclear power, as our participants' material and socio-historical familiarity with and experience of nuclear detracted from or tempered reliance on such discourses.

The way that our participants talked about these differing energy infrastructures in the context of their local area reveals a great deal about the way in which our participants were engaging with and thinking about these kinds of low carbon energy developments in quite *informal* ways. Their perspectives on *formal* structures for engagement with the development of such energy infrastructure add a further facet to our understanding.

(Dis)empowering and (dis)engaging public(s)

In debates around public acceptance of energy infrastructure, formal processes for engagement have been positioned as integral to siting and planning (Haggett, 2009). In attempting to provide understanding of public engagement with low carbon technologies in local contexts, then, how such processes are conceived can be seen as being of high significance. Our participants perceived formal engagement in relation to these local developments in a number of differing ways. While many of our participants professed that they did not get involved in meetings or consultation processes, this should not be taken to mean they are disengaged. Instead a number of factors, partly relating to their views on engagement processes, influenced our participants' decisions to become involved or not.

For some the practicalities of daily living (including child care, work and other such commitments) meant they felt unable to dedicate the time to such consultation and engagement processes: 'I feel quite tied up in my family responsibilities and it makes it very difficult to engage' (Ruth).

'Free' time held a high value and decisions to become involved in engagement processes were situated against a wide range of other activities on which that time could be spent. In this context, some were happy to rely on others, who they knew would become involved in engagement processes, for information or to represent their views. For most of our participants, engagement was seen only as a means to get information. Although for some this was unproblematic, for many this expectation was linked to the feeling that they *could not* influence decisions even if they would like to:

> *'If I thought it would make any difference then yes I suppose it would be quite nice to [engage], but to be honest I think these decisions are made for reasons and the public tend to be the last people that are consulted and certainly the last people it seems that are listened to'* (Douglas).

Such feelings were based on past experience or experience in other facets of life, and represented a frustration which led some to feel there was little point becoming involved in consultation and engagement processes.

The positive perspectives on nuclear power discussed in the previous section should be understood in this context of such views on engagement. Situated against these discourses, it is possible to see a more resigned acceptance of the likely development of new nuclear power in the area:

> *'Well they say that the consultations and the exhibitions are not very well supported, but I think that's because people, they accept it already, so they don't feel that they need to go on … I think there's also a feeling, a fairly general feeling, that what's going to be is going to be. The Government's probably already made up its mind what it's going to do or at least the Civil Service would have done I expect and that probably won't change with the Government of today either'* (Henry).

In contrast, participants expressed a clearer sense of empowerment with regard to capacities to influence things that were situated more as 'local' issues, e.g. the use of alternative road infrastructure to ease traffic density in or through the villages, housing of workers during the building phase, or routes for bringing in material for the build. These more locally situated aspects of development were viewed as negotiable and within the bounds of public influence.

Despite all this, even the more limited forms of consultation discussed (e.g. opportunities to ask questions or to voice their views even if they would not impact decisions) were valued by participants. Moreover, there were conflicting perspectives on public consultation, with some feeling that decisions needed to be taken strategically without the influence of local objections. This view was expressed in tandem with concern about the relative powerlessness participants felt they had in decisions but was connected to particular local events. For some, the rejection of the wind farm proposal after local opposition represented a frustration, while for others the most recent public inquiry for a Hinkley 'C' in the 1980s and the subsequent decision *not* to build at the time, despite planning approval, served as a concern, particularly in light of the recent decisions to proceed with nuclear new build.

Overall, our participants' reflections produced a complex picture of the way that members of the public view engagement around energy technologies. Such conceptions of engagement provide insight into the way that the public view formal processes in particular local contexts, but also might be taken as indicative of a sense of disillusionment with notions of engagement more generally. We leave it an open question the extent to which such perceptions of engagement may impact on the way that people formulated their views about the acceptability of these energy technologies, and open up for further scrutiny the notion that 'acceptability' may be associated with a kind of resignation or disillusionment in the processes of decision-making.

Concluding Discussion

For this chapter we have provided an overview of how the public can engage with low carbon energy technologies that goes beyond attitudinal surveying. We have shown that, while there was significant heterogeneity within the discourses of our participants, there were two key themes discernable amongst the complexity of perspectives. The first centred on the ways in which participants connected to low carbon technologies through material experience or wider social discourse. The second was focused upon the public's disillusionment with formal processes of engagement, and the implications of this for notions of acceptability. In this final section, we delineate our participants' engagement with low carbon technologies around these two broad themes.

Our study was located in an area where low carbon energy has particular local salience, with the rationale that this would make these often abstract entities more tangible. Against this original expectation, the historical development of nuclear power in the area did appear to imbue our participants' views on the prospect of new nuclear with specificities derived from material experience. In contrast, perspectives on renewable energy appeared to be less influenced by the local salience of such developments, with wider social and media discourse playing a greater role. While, in this sense, renewable energies were viewed as generically 'good' in broad conceptual terms, perceptions of wind power as widely undesirable as an imagined material manifestation and, more importantly, as having been rejected in multiple places, formed important aspects of the local public discourse about wind. Contrary to this, negative discourses around nuclear were broadly discarded or at least did not form the primary basis for participants' views, with lived experience being of greater importance. The significance of material experience extended not just to familiarity with a particular technology but to familiarity with, for instance, contained, centralized energy systems. For example, tidal power represented an appealing option because it was generally perceived as a relatively contained structure that could generate sufficiently high levels of electricity to meet the high levels of demand associated with contemporary living. In contrast, wind power was viewed as sprawling and as requiring impossible quantities of land to generate (correspondingly to nuclear power) high levels of electricity. Related to this were the connections participants made between development of wind and notions of significant societal change needed to facilitate reduced energy consumption. Trends toward increased energy demand led participants to feel that while reduced dependency on energy might be desirable it was unfeasible or unlikely. Ultimately then, there was a persistent notion that wind could not deliver the amount of energy current and future ways of living may necessitate, or it would require unacceptable levels of land use, when compared with other energy generating technologies. It remains questionable, however, whether more negative conceptions of wind were connected to a historical legacy of opposition between wind power and nuclear power, meaning that local salience potentially played a role in this respect. It remains questionable, however, whether more negative conceptions of wind were connected to an historical legacy of opposition between wind power and nuclear power, meaning that local salience potentially played a role in this respect.

Clearer from this analysis is that it would be wholly inadequate to characterize our participants' engagement with low carbon technologies proposed and existing in their localities in terms of NIMBYism, particularly in contexts where it is utilized to imply selfishness. Indeed, the wider societal benefits of differing energy technologies formed an important part of the discussions through which our participants gave meaning to energy developments, suggesting that notions of selfishness are inadequate as explanations of our participants' views (see also Wolsink, 2000). The low carbon nature of developments was important to participants, and beyond this the generating capacity, traded off against their local environmental and aesthetic impact, served as a focal point for comparisons between technologies and the formation of preferences. These wider social considerations featured strongly in the discourses through which our participants reasoned their acceptance or preferences. It is worth noting, however, that – in terms of local salience – our participants' engagement with the *low carbon* nature of energy developments may have been influenced by their position as a nuclear community; as climate change represents a key discourse within nuclear industry public engagement.

Our participants' views on differing low carbon options were situated alongside a conception of formal engagement as having little impact and a widespread sense that public views were ignored. In terms of local acceptability, then, these findings should be tempered by the sense of disillusionment in processes of societal decision-making and the relative sense of powerlessness that participants discussed. At the time of the research, some formal consultation processes around nuclear new build had taken place and previously there had been some local meetings about the wind farm proposals. Many of our participants were aware of such consultation processes, and a minority had been directly involved, but it was unclear the extent to which these experiences played a role in the formation of their views; discussion tended to be general, without reference to specific engagement processes. The forms of engagement discussed and perceived by participants entailed a focus on questions of impact and consequences of development, with local citizens' capacity to influence decisions felt to be limited to issues characterized as local concerns (e.g. traffic). It is worth noting that such characterizations of engagement stand at odds with contemporary calls for upstream engagement processes and efforts to engage citizens in two-way exchanges (Wynne, 2002; Wilsdon and Willis, 2004). While questions of siting and planning are not traditionally conceived in terms of upstream engagement (conventionally applied to notions of public engagement in science research questions and framing *before* technological development and implementation; Rogers-Hayden and Pidgeon, 2007), these decisions do raise fundamental value questions about, for example, the directions we move in as societies, the futures we are implicated in creating, and so forth. It was these questions that formed an important point of engagement for our participants. Linked to such questions were concerns connected to notions of 'false promise' to which perceived failings of previous technological endeavours had given form. While the 'ideal' of renewable forms of energy held promise for many, this was undermined by a sense that they might produce the kinds of negative impacts associated with other technologies in the future (e.g. nuclear power and the issue of nuclear waste). In this sense, the motives for development of renewable technologies were important for many, with profit motives, in particular, representing a concern. In this context, social (dis)trust in decision-making was of high importance.

Such public sentiment raises questions about the extent to which engagement in these areas has moved forward in discernable ways, and points to the possibility that engagement with wider value-based concerns about the purposes of development and the future societal directions created by decisions is of considerable importance for new energy developments, particularly in a contemporary context where trust in progress has been eroded. The extent to which such conceptions of public engagement will impact on efforts to develop new energy sectors remains an important open question.

Acknowledgements

This research was supported by Cardiff University and a major grant awarded by the Leverhulme Trust (F/00 407/AG). Thanks go also to all of the interviewees who gave up their time to take part in the research.

References

Baxter, J. and Lee, D. (2004) 'Explaining the maintenance of low concern near a hazardous waste treatment facility', *Journal of Risk Research*, vol 7/8, pp705–729

Bell, D., Gray, T. and Haggett, C. (2005) 'The social gap in wind farm siting decisions: Explanations and policy responses', *Environmental Politics*, vol 14, no 4, pp460–477

Bickerstaff, K., Simmons, P. and Pidgeon, N. (2008) 'Constructing responsibilities for risk: Negotiating citizen–state relationships', *Environment and Planning A*, vol 40 pp1312–1330

Burningham, K. (2000) 'Using the language of NIMBY: A topic for research not an activity for researchers', *Local Environment*, vol 5, no 1, pp55–67

Cowell, R. (2007) 'Wind power and the planning problem: The experience of Wales', *European Environment*, vol 17 no 5 pp291–306

Cresswell, T. (1996) *In Place out of Place: Geography, Ideology and Transgression*, University of Minnesota Press, Minneapolis, MN

Department for Business, Enterprise and Regulatory Reform (2008) *Meeting the Energy Challenge: A White Paper on Nuclear Power*, The Stationery Office, London

Devine-Wright, P. (2005) 'Beyond NIMBYism: Towards an integrated framework for understanding public perceptions of wind energy', *Wind Energy*, vol 1 pp125–139

Devine-Wright, P. (2009) 'Rethinking Nimbyism: The role of place attachment and place identity in explaining place-protective action', *Journal of Community and Applied Social Psychology*, vol 19, no 6, pp426–441

Eiser, J. D. van der Pligt, J. and Spears, R. (1995) *Nuclear Neighbourhoods: Community Responses to Reactor Siting*, University of Exeter Press, Exeter, UK

Freudenberg, W. and Pastor, S. (1992) 'NIMBYs and LULUs: Stalking the syndromes', *Journal of Social Issues*, vol 48, no 4, pp39–61

Greenberg, M. R. (2009) 'Energy sources, public policy and public preferences: Analysis of US national and site-specific data', *Energy Policy*, vol 37 no 8, pp3242–3249

Haggett, C. (2009) 'Public engagement in planning for renewable energy', in S. Davoudi, J. Crawford and A. Mehmood (eds) *Planning for Climate Change: Strategies for Mitigation and Adaptation for Spatial Planners*, Earthscan, London, pp297–307

Kempton, W., Firestone, J., Lilley, J., Rouleau, T. and Whitaker, P. (2005) 'The offshore wind power debate: Views from Cape Cod', *Coastal Management*, vol 33, pp119–149

Krohn, S. and Damborg, S. (1999) 'On public attitudes towards wind power', *Renewable Energy*, vol 16, pp954–960

Melber, B., Nealey, S., Hammersla, J. and Rankin, W. (1977) *Nuclear Power and the Public: Analysis of Collected Survey Research*, Human Affairs Research Center, Seattle, WA

Parkhill, K.A. (2007) 'Tensions between Scottish national policies for onshore wind energy and local dissatisfaction: Insights from regulation theory', *European Environment*, vol 17, no 5, pp307–320

Parkhill, K. A., Pidgeon, N. F., Henwood, K. L., Simmons, P. and Venables, D. (2010) 'From the familiar to the extraordinary: Local residents' perceptions of risk when living with nuclear power in the UK', *Transactions of the Institute of British Geographers*, vol 35, no 1, 39–58

Pidgeon, N. and Henwood, K. (2004) 'Grounded theory' in M. Hardy and A. Bryman (eds) *Handbook of Data Analysis*, Sage, London, pp625–648

Pidgeon, N., Lorenzoni, I. and Poortinga, W. (2008) 'Climate change or nuclear power – no thanks! A quantitative study of public perceptions of risk framing in Britain', *Global Environmental Change*, vol 18 pp69–85

Rogers-Hayden, T. and Pidgeon, N. F. (2007) 'Moving engagement "upstream"? Nanotechnologies and the Royal Society and Royal Academy of Engineering inquiry', *Public Understanding of Science*, vol 16, 346–364

Rosa, E. A. and Freudenberg, W. R. (1993) 'The historical development of public reactions to nuclear power: Implications for nuclear waste policy', in R. E. Dunlap, M. E. Kraft and E. A. Rosa (eds) *Public Reactions to Nuclear Waste: Citizens' Views of Repository Siting*, Duke University Press, Durham, NC, pp32–63

Simmons, P. and Walker, G. (1999) 'Tolerating risk: Policy principles and public perceptions', *Risk, Decision and Policy*, vol 4, no 3, pp179–190

Sustainable Development Commission (2007) *Turning the Tide: Tidal Power in the UK*, SD Commission, London

van der Pligt, J. (1992) *Nuclear Energy and the Public*, Blackwell, Oxford

Venables, D., Pidgeon, N., Simmons, P., Henwood, K. and Parkhill, K. (2009) 'Living with nuclear power: A Q-method study of local community perceptions', *Risk Analysis*, vol 29, no 8, pp1089–1104

Walker, G. (1995) 'Renewable energy and the public', *Land Use Policy*, vol 12, no 1, pp49–59

Wilsdon, J. and Willis, R. (2004) *See-through Science: Why Public Engagement Needs to Move Upstream*, Demos, London

Wolsink, M. (2000) 'Wind power and the NIMBY myth: Institutional capacity and the limited significance of public support', *Renewable Energy*, vol 21 pp49–64

Wynne, B. (1992) 'Misunderstood misunderstandings: Social identities and the public uptake of science', *Public Understanding of Science*, vol 1 pp281–304

Wynne, B. (2002) 'Risk and environment as legitimatory discourses of technology: Reflexivity inside out?' *Current Sociology*, vol 50, pp459–477

Zonabend, F. (1993) *The Nuclear Peninsula*, Cambridge University Press, Cambridge

Conclusions

Patrick Devine-Wright

Renewable energy is a vital element of national strategies to respond to the threat of climate change, as well as to address concerns over energy security. Social science has a vitally important contribution to make in the transition towards increased use of renewable energy, with two clear ways of informing policies and practices of engagement, both of which are evidenced by the chapters in this volume.

Two Roles Played by Social Science

Firstly, social scientists can systematically monitor and evaluate engagement activities, including participatory or deliberative mechanisms; seeking to identify whether objectives were met and goals realized, and making recommendations for future practice (see, for example, the chapters in this volume by Ashworth, Upham, Pasqualetti and Improta). Robust, independent evaluative research is beneficial for three reasons: (1) it can lead to a more coherent and cumulative evidence base, (2) it can provide evidence to challenge those who are sceptical about the value of citizen involvement, and (3) it can enable policy-makers and industrial organizations to better understand the dynamics of their own engagement activities in different political, social and economic contexts, and how these are perceived by diverse groups, in order to learn from past experience and to design more effective procedures for future practice. Such research should build upon a rapidly expanding literature on participatory research and practice (e.g. Renn, 2008) and can suggest contexts where participation is especially challenging, notably upstream engagement with highly innovative energy technologies (see Flynn and colleagues, this volume).

Secondly, social scientists can act as critics, maintaining distance from organizations undertaking engagement to lay bare those assumptions often left implicit about the value and timing of public engagement, and challenging existing representations and practices. Several chapters in this book, particularly the conceptual contributions in Section I, critique an array of inappropriate and misleading ways of thinking about technology siting and public engagement with renewable energy technologies, notably the 'NIMBY' concept with its deficit model of public knowledge or expertise and impoverished view of the backyard, and moves to streamline spatial planning procedures. As the chapters by Haggett, Barry and Ellis, and Cotton and Devine-Wright argue, streamlining planning procedures may prove counterproductive, only serving to fuel social conflict in contexts where citizens react negatively to attempts to restrict their input into decision-making processes. Indeed Ellis goes further, challenging the very notion that conflict should be avoided or minimized; instead arguing that conflict offers the possibility of engaging different parties about diverse energy futures in a transformative manner, and that seeking consensus overlooks a vital opportunity that can be taken to engender not just technical but socio-cultural change. This body of critical inquiry can offer a highly valuable body of impartial advice to policy-makers and industry, provoking reflection about the ways in which engagement is conceived, and suggesting innovative and creative responses to current dilemmas.

Towards a Broader Framing of Social Science Research

Above all, this volume suggests the limitations of a narrow framing of social science research into public engagement with renewable energy. A literature that to date has been rather dominated by research into residents' acceptance or resistance to developer-led, large-scale onshore wind farms (Devine-Wright, 2005) is revealed in this book to be much broader in scope.

Firstly, as Walker and colleagues make clear in Chapter 1 of this volume, public engagement encompasses both the different ways that technology promoters seek to communicate and consult with members of the public, and how individuals and groups perceive and respond to such initiatives. That is why different empirical contributions to this volume reflect both the representations of public engagement with renewable energy held by stakeholders (Section II, Part 1) as well as those held by members of the public (Section II, Part 2). As Walker and colleagues argue, these representations are interdependent. Stakeholder engagement activities are founded upon expectations and presumptions about public responses, and public responses are in turn founded upon expectations and presumptions about technologies and the organizations promoting them. Both operate within a wider context of media reporting of engagement initiatives, with journalists seemingly eager to propagate stereotypical concepts such as NIMBYism to describe, explain and denounce objection (see Chapter 8 by Hannah Devine-Wright). The dynamic interactivity at the heart of this conceptual framework indicates the need to adopt ways of thinking, and methodologies of research that can capture emergence and change, not just static representations of conceptions or practices. Research also needs to follow the example of Hodson and Marvin in this volume, who investigate the role of novel intermediary organizations that can occupy spaces in between conventional stakeholders and members of the public, transforming contexts of governance.

Secondly, the chapters in Section II highlight the range of technologies involved in public engagement with renewable energy, encompassing not just onshore wind turbines, but wind farms offshore, wave energy devices, solar photovoltaics at diverse scales of deployment, bioenergy projects, and wind–hydrogen schemes for generating and storing electricity. The varying scales and levels of maturity of these technologies have implications for the kinds of engagement that members of the public can undertake, from 'upstream' engagement with less familiar forms of energy such as hydrogen (see chapters by Flynn and Sherry-Brennan) and wave energy (see chapter by McLachlan) to 'downstream' engagement with more mature technologies such as wind turbines and bioenergy plants (see chapters by Firestone and Upham). The scale of deployment of these technologies is also important in shaping the forms of engagement open to members of the public, from the adoption of microgeneration as financial investors (see chapter by Roy and Caird), to the diverse responses to larger-scale power stations including project supporter and objector, and participant in community-scale energy projects (see chapter by Sherry-Brennan and colleagues). Research can also look across different low carbon technologies, including both nuclear and renewable energy, with a comparative approach (see chapter by Butler and colleagues).

Thirdly, there are numerous roles that members of the public can play in relation to renewable energy. Walker and Cass (see Chapter 4) identify ten such roles, encompassing the well-known role of project objector, but also including less-appreciated roles such as financial investors, active consumers, passive consumers, service users, local beneficiaries, project participants, project supporters, technology hosts and energy producers. Whilst several of these roles are investigated in this book (notably in chapters by Roy, Abi-Ghanem and Schweizer-Ries), there remains an imbalance in the research literature towards analysis of project objection, which needs to be countered by future research acknowledging alternative roles and how these may interconnect and mutually influence each other.

Fourthly, the diversity of public role and technology type make clear that public engagement is not merely timed to coincide with the 'siting' of large-scale energy technologies (for a critique of ways of thinking about project locations, see Devine-Wright, Chapter 5). As Ashworth and colleagues reveal in Chapter 10, social science can investigate and evaluate public input into deliberative engagement that aims to devise alternative energy scenarios at the national level, contributing public values into decision-making that could lead to radical reshapings of technology policies and trajectories, in response to the necessity to reduce fossil fuel use and increase the use of low carbon energy sources.

Finally, contextuality is an important feature of renewable energy initiatives, as argued by several chapters in this volume. As I have argued (see Chapter 5), conceiving the locations of energy projects as 'places' reflects the view that each locality is imbued with a unique set of meanings, emotions and values by local residents and visitors. To a degree, therefore, regardless of the apparent similarity of technology or development organization involved, every wind farm or bioenergy project will differ in important ways, involving a different set of actors with different histories and capacities, in locations with differing psychological associations and topographies. Unfortunately, this is commonly overlooked in the course of technology projects, where 'sites' and 'backyards' are the common frames of reference for stakeholders, leading to missed opportunities to devise technology emplacement strategies that enhance rather than threaten places and avoid disruption to place attachments.

This issue becomes critically important as the contexts of public engagement with renewable energy technologies become ever more diverse, and as technologies become increasingly widely deployed in developing country contexts, where comparatively little social research has investigated public engagement to date. The chapter by Improta and Pinheiro, detailing public engagement with Brazil's first large-scale wind farm, indicates both familiar (e.g. the lack of involvement of local residents in the project) and unfamiliar (e.g. the contrast between close proximity of advanced electricity-generating technologies and power-less local residents) aspects of this research. As the use of renewable energy grows around the world, the necessity to enable the capacity of social scientists in developing countries to research issues of public engagement will increase, requiring the networking of experts across national boundaries as part of wider efforts to increase research capacity amongst scholars in developing countries.

Conclusions

As an ever-increasing number of countries worldwide agree to adopt challenging targets to reduce carbon emissions and increase renewable energy use, policymakers may be tempted to devise more streamlined planning procedures that reduce opportunities by members of the public to participate in environmental decision-making (as has been happening in the UK: see Barry and Ellis, Chapter 3), with the aim of hastening planning consents and increasing the rates of technology deployment. But such a strategy is likely to prove counterproductive. It may unwittingly increase current levels of public scepticism, mistrust and outright opposition, with the result that an increased number of project proposals could be delayed or even abandoned. Rather than providing a mandate for reducing public input into procedures of technology development and policymaking, the chapters in this volume provide a pragmatic rationale for increasing the use of well-planned and implemented mechanisms of public participation, particularly those dubbed analytic-deliberative methods (see chapters by Ashworth and Flynn), which can increase the quality and legitimacy of decision-making, and enhance trust and understanding (National Resource Council, 2008).

This is not to say that participatory approaches will inevitably lead to increased trust or social acceptance, or that they are suited to all contexts of public engagement. This is why social science research has such a vital role to play, by revealing the consequences of certain engagement approaches and providing nuanced analyses of both the benefits and limitations of certain mechanisms. As Flynn and colleagues make clear (see Chapter 17), there are limits to the value of deliberation in contexts of upstream engagement with unfamiliar technologies. And as Sherry-Brennan's comparative analysis of wind–hydrogen projects shows (see Chapter 18), the same technology can be differently accepted largely as a function of the opportunities for participation provided to local residents. NIMBYism may be an easy to use and beguilingly simple way of thinking about objections to technology proposals, but social science reveals how inadequate it is as a means of capturing the dynamic interplay between the multiple actors involved in renewable energy deployment. The solution is not to caricature, undermine and exclude public responses, but to work towards better ways of integrating public beliefs into decision-making, preserving social consent towards the increased use of renewable energy.

Systematic, robust social science research has a vital role to play in moving beyond NIMBY-type conceptions of public engagement. To that extent, the diversity of contributions to this volume evidence an exciting field of scholarly activity that has burgeoned in recent years. Future research into public engagement with renewable energy must seek greater coherence and cumulative endeavour, encompassing both conceptual and empirical contributions and the use of different perspectives and methodologies. No single methodology, conceptual or disciplinary perspective is likely to prove sufficient to address the subject of public engagement. And there are welcome shifts in the literature away from a narrow use of opinion poll methods and case study designs, a willingness to adopt concepts from diverse academic disciplines including political science, geography, environmental psychology, sociology and planning, and the growing number of research studies operating across disciplinary boundaries, integrating scholars from diverse fields. To ensure that it continues, funding agencies, professional bodies and industrial organizations should continue to fund social science research activity and invest in capacity-building across national boundaries, so that well-designed evaluations of participatory activities become routine undertakings and so that critical commentary can continue to inform our understanding of public engagement with renewable energy.

References

Devine-Wright, P. (2005) Beyond NIMBYism: Towards an integrated framework for understanding public perceptions of wind energy, *Wind Energy*, vol 8, no 2, pp125–139
National Research Council (2008) *Public Participation in Environmental Assessment and Decision-Making*, The National Academies Press, Washington, DC
Renn, O. (2008) *Risk Governance: Coping with Uncertainty in a Complex World*, Earthscan, London

Index

Printed in the United States
by Baker & Taylor Publisher Services